THE
PUEBLO
SURRENDER

THE PUEBLO SURRENDER

A COVERT ACTION BY THE NATIONAL SECURITY AGENCY

ROBERT A. LISTON

M Evans
Lanham • New York • Boulder • Toronto • Plymouth, UK

M. Evans
An imprint of The Rowman & Littlefield Publishing Group, Inc.
4501 Forbes Boulevard, Suite 200, Lanham, Maryland 20706
http://www.rlpgtrade.com

10 Thornbury Road, Plymouth PL6 7PP, United Kingdom

Distributed by National Book Network

British Library Cataloguing in Publication Information Available

Library of Congress Cataloging-in-Publication Data Available

ISBN 13: 978-1-59077-326-0 (pbk: alk. paper)

♾™ The paper used in this publication meets the minimum requirements of American National Standard for Information Sciences—Permanence of Paper for Printed Library Materials, ANSI/NISO Z39.48-1992.

Printed in the United States of America

For Jean
who long ago in the moonlight
believed . . .

CONTENTS

ACKNOWLEDGMENTS

It has been nearly seven years from inception to publication of this book. A great many people offered information, advice, and encouragement.

Two persons were especially helpful. Fairly early in my research I was stymied. I knew I was missing some key point, but I couldn't figure out what it was. I asked recent college grad James A. Peeples of Shelby, Ohio, where most of the book was written, to see if he could find my error. A couple of days later he returned and asked a single question. It doesn't matter what it was now, but it opened up my thinking. From that point on I began to discover "what could never be known" about the *Pueblo* surrender. A little later my good friend Robert J. Doyle, professor of biology at the University of Windsor in Windsor, Canada, read an early version of the book. After muttering, "I've never read a book like this," he ultimately said, "This is a detective story; you must explain that to the reader up front."

Valuable research and helpful criticism was provided by three friends: Mrs. Eleanor R. Seagraves of Washington, D.C.; Mr. David O. Strickland, then of New York City; and Lt. Comdr. (Ret.) Ralph Eaton of Shelby. I would also like to thank Lt. Col. David Cotton of the Ohio Air National Guard; Ms. Maureen Farrell of the map section of the Cleveland, Ohio, Public Library; Ms. Ann Wood and the staff of the Marvin Memorial Library in Shelby; Ms. Dawn Puglisi, librarian of the Ohio State University, Mansfield Branch; and the staffs of the Richland County Library in Mansfield and the Santa Barbara, California, Public Library.

I would like to thank Edwin Brandt and Trevor Armbrister, whose earlier *Pueblo* research made mine possible; authors David Kahn and James Bamford; Ron Simon and Gaylord Hake of the Mansfield, Ohio, *News-Journal*; Bernard Weinraub and Anthony Lewis of the New York *Times*. Special appreciation goes to G. William Clark and Roger Nelson, both of Shelby; Joel Cabot of Everett, Washington; and William Boucher III of Baltimore, Maryland.

My deepest appreciation goes to my wife, Jean, who suffered through my floor pacing, discussed my ideas with me, and worked on the manuscript. Her affection was undiminished even after she discovered "harrassment" has only one *r*—and changed it throughout the manuscript.

I will always be grateful to George de Kay, president of M. Evans, for understanding what I've tried to say and having the courage to publish. I would also like to thank Elizabeth Horton and Evan Stone for their careful work on the manuscript.

Finally, without a shred of facetiousness, I would like to thank those five literary agents who rejected this book quite unread and the thirty-five editors who refused it. Of that number only one read the entire manuscript. Their comments nonetheless helped shape the book.

R.A.L.
Santa Barbara, California

INTRODUCTION

In the hours following the seizure of the USS *Pueblo* by the North Koreans on January 23, 1968, Sen. Edward M. Kennedy of Massachusetts disagreed with his colleagues who urged war, saying he wanted to know more about the incident, such as what really happened during the more than two and a half hours between the time the *Pueblo* was approached and its surrender.

It was a reasonable desire then and twenty years later it still is. Many millions of words, including eight books, have been written about the *Pueblo* incident. Yet none of them offers a clear, simple, agreed-upon story of the seizure. Instead there are several stories, indeed as many stories as there are people to tell or write them. Even worse, the same persons told different stories at different times to different people.

The sundry *Pueblo* stories are so full of discrepancies, disputes, conflicts in fact, omissions, suppression of important information, "mistakes," "can't remembers," and impossibilities that none of them can be believed today.

The fact is that we were never told the truth about the *Pueblo* surrender; rather, there was a massive, official cover-up. The eighty-two survivors of *Pueblo*, from Comdr. Lloyd M. Bucher on down, were prevented from telling all they knew and in some cases required to alter facts and even fabricate them in defense of the cover story.

It is not difficult today to see why the truth about the *Pueblo* seizure has remained deeply hidden for all these years. The essential facts are these:

1. The mission, movements, and communications of *Pueblo* were controlled not by the U.S. Navy, but by the National Security Agency (NSA), a supersecret branch of U.S. intelligence.

2. *Pueblo* and its crew were sent on a covert intelligence operation off the shores of North Korea under orders which placed them at great risk of capture and made it unlikely they would escape.

3. When North Korean vessels surrounded *Pueblo* and a boarding party was formed, Commander Bucher got his ship under way to escape. The North Koreans fired upon *Pueblo* to stop it. At this point damage was minor, casualties incidental.

4. *Pueblo* was then boarded and seized, not by North Koreans, but by armed Red Chinese *soldiers* ferried out in a North Korean ship. The Chinese quickly got *Pueblo* under way toward Wonsan, North Korea, while they rounded up the American sailors (who had been deliberately disarmed under NSA orders), blindfolded them, and led them below decks. But before the blindfolds went on, the Americans saw "a large warship" that was "coming fast" toward them. They knew it was not an American ship coming to rescue them.

5. As some of the American sailors suspected, the warship belonged to the navy of the Soviet Union. To stop the Chinese from sailing *Pueblo* into Wonsan, the Soviet ship fired on the American vessel, killing one American sailor and seriously wounding three others.

This much of the *Pueblo* story was knowable in 1971, when the last *Pueblo* book was published. Discovery lies in painstaking reading, comparison, and analysis of the sundry *Pueblo* stories. The truth lies in the mouths and pens of *Pueblo* crewmen. They saw the large warship coming fast and knew it was not American. They described the soldiers who first seized *Pueblo* so that we know they were Red Chinese and not North Koreans. There is much more, all of it sworn under oath and copyrighted in published books. Indeed, having given over five years of my life to this task, I am convinced the men of *Pueblo* tried to tell us what really happened to them, but no one would listen.

We should. It is not too late. The men of *Pueblo* made a great sacrifice for their country, indeed for the whole world. It is way past time we found some appropriate way to honor them.

But there remains much about the *Pueblo* story that no crewman can tell us. Those ill-fated, courageous men will not know what really happened to them until they read this book. The *Pueblo* surrender was a covert intelligence operation by the National Security Agency, conducted under a process called Need to Know and thereby so deeply secret that less than a dozen people knew the operation was planned before the fact—or that it had occurred after the fact.

Persons highly knowledgeable about the National Security Agency and the *Pueblo* surrender have now come forward to profess that the following information is factual:

• To aid NSA decoders in breaking Soviet codes used by the North Vietnamese military, a rigged U.S. code machine was secretly placed aboard *Pueblo* with the idea of inducing the North Koreans, who used the same codes, to capture and use the rigged machine. Messages sent over the machine would permit the virtually instant breaking of the Soviet system of codes.

• This original purpose changed, however, when crewmen of *Pueblo*, during their penultimate voyage into the waters off Wonsan, unknowingly intercepted a Soviet message dealing with Soviet plans to attack or invade Red China. *Pueblo* returned to Japan, where the importance of the intercepted Soviet message was recognized by the NSA.

• *Pueblo* was sent back to Wonsan for its final voyage as an American ship. At the same time both Red China and the Soviet Union were provoked into believing NSA disinformation that the intercepted Soviet message was still aboard *Pueblo*.

• The Chinese seized the ship to obtain the message and the Soviet Navy fired on *Pueblo* to stop the Chinese from obtaining the message. When no message of any kind was found aboard *Pueblo*, the ship was turned over to the North Koreans, who used the rigged code machine to radio Vladivostok for instructions.

Informants state that the ramifications of the *Pueblo* surrender were immense. It helped prevent a U.S. defeat in the Tet Offensive in Vietnam. The Soviet Union abandoned its military adventure in China. Rapprochement between Red China and the United States began. The Soviet KGB "overreacted" to the breaking of its codes and began a major overhaul of its overseas intelligence operations. Since this process would take years, the Kremlin, perceiving itself in a position of weakness vis-à-vis American intelligence, launched its policy of détente with the West. For these reasons, among others, persons knowledgeable about the *Pueblo* surrender call it "the greatest intelligence coup of modern times."

In describing the *Pueblo* surrender in detail, informants reveal more about the methods used by NSA than has ever been known before. They describe Need to Know not as a static means of protecting classified information, but as a highly dynamic process by which the beliefs, thoughts, and actions of a person can be manipulated. Through its exclusive control of all encoded and highly classified messages, NSA is able to withhold vital information or spread disinformation to influence the thinking of a person so as to provoke him to acts he would never perform on his own.

No better example exists than the *Pueblo* surrender. Commander Bucher would never, never, never have surrendered his ship without a fight. If given a direct order to do so, he would have disobeyed the order, and properly so. But the process called Need to Know not only induced Bucher to do the one thing he would never do, it also kept him—and the entire U.S. Navy—from realizing that this was exactly what was supposed to happen.

In my view there has been no greater victim of official government actions in modern naval annals than Commander Bucher.

This book, however, is not so much about the *Pueblo* surrender as it is the National Security Agency. Consider that more than six hours elapsed before *Pueblo* reached Wonsan and its crew was thrown into captivity which lasted nearly a year. During those six hours the world teetered on the brink of Armageddon. It was a military confrontation among the superpowers. China had seized an American naval vessel and the Soviet Union had fired upon it, causing casualties. Both were extremely serious acts of war. It was a crisis more dangerous than the events in the Gulf of Tonkin, which led America to escalate its involvement in Vietnam, and more immediately threatening than the Cuban missile crisis.

Perhaps to prevent World War III, certainly to mask the activities and powers of the National Security Agency, an elaborate cover story was concocted to hide Chinese and Soviet involvement. Everything was blamed on the North Koreans, who really acted at the behest of their two powerful neighbors. It is not entirely unthinkable that the intelligence agencies of all four nations, having miscalculated and come so close to provoking war, acted in concert to perpetrate the cover-up.

The cover-up not only deluded the American people, but also Congress, the Pentagon, and the White House. Persons at the highest levels of government spoke and acted on the basis of erroneous information supplied by the National Security Agency. Our most visible elected and appointed leaders were not told of Chinese and Soviet participation in the seizure, nor of the extraordinary actions by the NSA that provoked that participation.

The *Pueblo* surrender enables us to understand, for the first time, I believe, how the National Security Agency, as the exclusive codemaking and codebreaking arm of the United States government, is able to control all encoded information and use it to manipulate the beliefs and actions of our civilian and military leaders—a process duplicated by the KGB in the Soviet Union. Our concern here is not the Soviet Union but the United States, where the NSA's power and activities are an alteration of our constitutional form of government of profound importance.

A few words about format. I faced two tasks: first, to unravel the *Pueblo* cover story, and second, to figure out what really happened. The first, though time-consuming, was relatively easy. It forms the bulk of this book. This new *Pueblo* story may be denied, but no one can now trot out the old *Pueblo* yarn and expect it to run again. The second task was more difficult. I believe the basic facts of the story to be apparent, even obvious, but there remain details of which I am uncertain. I try to identify these.

In style of argument, this book is the reverse of that usually employed. Rather than making a statement, then offering evidence to support it, I compile the evidence first, then seek meaning from it. I am asking the reader to join me in seeing what we can learn about the *Pueblo* surrender, then in searching for meaning in what has been learned.

This book resembles a classic mystery story. Think of Agatha Christie's *Murder on the Orient Express*. A crime is committed—in this case the loss of an American naval vessel and the capture of its crew. Who committed the crime? Many people were present, but they all provide different facts and tell different stories. Sometimes they change their story each time they tell it. As Hercule Poirot did, we listen to (in this case read) all of the conflicting stories, trying to discover who can be believed and what the most common and pertinent facts are, so that the true events of the "crime" can be re-created and we can learn who did seize *Pueblo* and who caused the casualties.

Another way to describe the format is to liken it to a trial in which readers are the jury. Like jurors, they listen to detailed "testimony" from those aboard *Pueblo* and from the persons who talked to them, noting the conflicts, omissions, and impossibilities in what they say. There will even be mystery witnesses. The jury has to pay attention to a lot of detailed testimony, decide who is telling the truth, then reach a verdict on the basis of perceived fact and circumstantial evidence.

What is proof? In journalism the standard of proof is a source of information who will make a statement, on or off the record, and provide documents to support it. In the *Pueblo* incident, persons of high authority and impeccable reputation made statements, sometimes under oath. The press had no choice but to report them. But what can be done when sources of information either don't know the truth or lie, and when there either are no documents or those proffered have been deliberately falsified? Is there no way to discover the truth? Are we to be forever manipulated by "sources" and "documents"?

There is another standard of proof. It relies not on someone in authority telling us what happened, but on careful, rational analysis of an event. It is perhaps more the job of historians than of journalists, but it does offer a way by which we can eventually discover the truth and what it means for us today.

The *Pueblo* surrender was not a footnote to history, but a major event which shaped the world in which we all live. It offers us an opportunity to understand other inexplicable events of our times, as well as to grasp the truly awesome grant of power we as a people and as a government have given to the National Security Agency to manipulate our knowledge, our thoughts, and our behavior as a nation.

Let us begin by recalling what supposedly happened to *Pueblo*, as reported by the press.

THE
PUEBLO
SURRENDER

1

QUESTIONS WITHOUT ANSWERS

On January 23, 1968, North Korean naval vessels opened fire on the USS *Pueblo*. Fireman Duane D. Hodges was killed, three others seriously wounded. The *Pueblo* captain, Comdr. Lloyd M. Bucher, having made no effort to defend the ship, surrendered. The vessel was taken into Wonsan harbor where the ship's complement of six officers, seventy-four crewmen, and two civilians, eighty-two in all, were clapped into North Korean prisons.

The North Koreans, according to the press, said they seized the ship at a point 7.6 miles from nearest land, well inside their twelve-mile limit claimed as territorial waters. They maintained the ship had made repeated intrusions into their waters to spy on their defense installations and that the United States had ignored their warnings that such acts would not be tolerated. Within thirty-six hours they broadcast a statement alleged to be from Commander Bucher in which he admitted his ship had been in North Korean waters on a spy mission for the Central Intelligence Agency (CIA).

The United States conceded *Pueblo* was an ELINT (for Electronic Intelligence) vessel, but said it operated beyond the twelve-mile limit. The seizure was denounced as an act of piracy on the high seas. Bucher's statement was labeled as obviously phony and forced. CIA involvement was denied.

Seizure of the ship was humiliating to Americans, traumatic for the U.S. Navy. *Pueblo* was first approached by North Korean vessels at noon, Korean time. The Pentagon said *Pueblo* was in North Korean hands by 1:45 P.M., but remained in radio contact until 2:32 P.M. The ship reached Wonsan about 8:30 P.M. During all that time no U.S. ships or planes attempted a rescue. Thus, the world's most powerful Navy was made impotent by one of the puniest. Worse for Navy pride, *Pueblo* was the first U.S. Navy ship to surrender without a fight since 1807.

The initial response of the U.S. government was warlike. The nuclear carrier USS *Enterprise,* pride of the fleet, and a destroyer escort were ordered to steam for Korea. One destroyer was alerted to be prepared to enter Wonsan harbor and either sail or tow *Pueblo* out. An official order for such action was never given, however. President Lyndon B. Johnson ordered 14,878 Air Force and Navy reservists to active duty. Leading members of Congress, including some "doves" greatly opposed to the war in Vietnam, termed the seizure an act of war and urged military retaliation.

Any attempts to recover the ship and crew by armed conflict were quickly discarded in favor of diplomatic efforts. These proved to be most difficult, however. When asked by the United States to help gain release of the crew, the Soviet Union replied with a "chilly" negative. The North Koreans, believing they had us between a rock and a hard place, demanded the United States admit the spying mission and apologize for it. We were unwilling to do this, at least for a long time.

Negotiations dragged on at Panmunjom, where the armistice ending the Korean War was signed in 1953. The North Koreans endeavored to milk as much propaganda value as possible from the stalemate. Numerous "confessions" were obtained from the officers and crew of *Pueblo.* The men were paraded before cameras to indicate how well they were being treated, leading to a celebrated group photo in which crewmen gave "the finger." They were subsequently beaten in what they termed "Hell Week" when the North Koreans learned from reading *Time* what the gesture really meant.

The finger gesture was widely assumed to indicate the disdain of the Americans for their captors. Bucher gave another interpretation when he met the press immediately after his release. Bucher was asked what the gesture meant. He replied: "They were trying to tell you that we'd been had. We realized that if we were discovered, it was going to be 'Katie, bar the door,' but *we felt that it was important that we get that information out. So there would be absolutely no room for doubt in your minds, the American people's minds, that we'd been had* [Emphasis mine]."*

Release of the crew was gained through an action unprecedented in

---

*Quoted by Trevor Armbrister, page 344, in *A Matter of Accountability.* (See appendix). Several newspapers and news magazines also quoted portions of Bucher's statement, especially the words, "we'd been had."

world history. The United States admitted the spying mission and apologized, then promptly repudiated the confession, saying it was made only to gain release of the crew. Timing was precise. The United States repudiated the confession, then immediately signed it. Outraged, the North Koreans delayed the release of the crew another half hour. At last, at 11:30 A.M. on December 23, 1968 (Korean time), after eleven months of imprisonment, Commander Bucher led his crew and a casket containing the remains of Fireman Hodges across the Bridge of No Return to freedom. The men were haggard, suffering the effects of beatings and mistreatment, badly malnourished. One man's eyesight was permanently damaged because of the diet. Another had been castrated by North Korean physicians.

The *Pueblo* crewmen were put aboard buses. Armbrister reports (p. 343) that Bucher sat with Richard Fryklund, a deputy assistant secretary of defense. "He was extremely tense," Fryklund remembers. "The first thing he said was, 'Do you think we violated North Korean waters?' I told him I didn't, and he said, 'Well, that's right. *We doctored that evidence. You look at it carefully and you'll see how we doctored it* [emphasis mine].'"

Helicopters ferried the crew to the 121st U.S. Army evacuation hospital ten miles east of Seoul. Less than two hours after crossing the bridge, Bucher met reporters in the mess hall. He praised his crew as "simply tremendous." He said he had followed his orders "to the letter." *Pueblo* had "never once" intruded into North Korean waters. "We—I surrendered the ship," he said, "because it was nothing but a slaughter out there." He admitted that not all classified documents were destroyed, spoke of the brutality of his captors, and said he had signed confessions only "to save people from some fairly serious misfortunes."

Bucher again referred to the seizure (Armbrister, pp. 343–4): "And *I just couldn't. I couldn't fathom what was happening at the time, and to this day I'm not sure of everything that happened* [emphasis mine]."

Reporters at the scene felt he hadn't been "coached" in his replies, for there hadn't been time for that. Some newsmen burst into spontaneous applause for what they considered Bucher's impressive performance.

The crew was flown to San Diego. What happened then was strange. Having gone to extraordinary means to gain release of the crew, the United States then subjected them to what *Pueblo*'s executive officer, Lt. Edward R. Murphy, Jr., called "detention." The men of *Pueblo* were denied leave, although their families could visit them in San Diego. They

4 ■ THE PUEBLO SURRENDER

were forbidden to talk to the press or even discuss the *Pueblo* seizure with their loved ones. They were accompanied constantly by Navy or intelligence personnel. In an interview for this book, one crewman recalled that he was hospitalized for an injury suffered during captivity. He sneaked out of the hospital one night to go out on the town. The next day his every action was described to him, including whom he talked to and what he said. Then he was reprimanded and warned not to attempt it again.

An estimated one hundred "debriefers" from the National Security Agency, Naval Intelligence Command, the Naval Security Group, and the Marine Corps' Counter Intelligence Command interviewed the crewmen, taping every word they said. One was subjected to twenty-six separate interviews. Armbrister reports that 270 *miles* of tape were recorded from the crewmen. None of these words was ever released, at least publicly, not even in summary form. It was surely the best evidence of what really happened aboard *Pueblo,* but insofar as is known not one syllable of it was ever used in public investigations of the seizure.

The men of *Pueblo* were muzzled. Bucher's statements made upon his release were disavowed, the Navy saying he had spoken personally but not officially. For the next two weeks Bucher, said to be suffering "complete nervous exhaustion," was isolated from the crew and press. He was kept under guard in his hospital room, visited only by his wife, doctors, lawyer, and Navy personnel.

With Bucher held incommunicado, Murphy, the XO (executive officer), met with the press on two occasions. In his book, *Second in Command*, Murphy writes that "very strict limitations" were placed on what he could discuss. He was not to speak of any matter which "in any way touched on security." Murphy writes (p. 336), "I would not be allowed to discuss either the capture itself or the activities of the crew while in detention." He said this "muzzling" angered reporters. "I couldn't blame them. They wanted meat, and all I was able to give them was, literally, watery soup—the food we had been given was one of the few things I could discuss." At the insistence of reporters, two crewmen appeared at a press conference. One of those men, recalling the event, said they were surrounded by Navy officers who permitted them to speak, not about the seizure, but only about their captivity.

The reason given for silencing the crew was that statements from them might interfere with a formal Navy Court of Inquiry into the loss of *Pueblo.* This court convened on January 20, 1969—inauguration day for Richard Nixon—at the Naval Amphibious Base in Coronado, California, near San Diego. It was a full dress Navy affair held before five admirals, assisted by prosecutors, military and civilian attorneys, and various experts. Vice Adm. Harold G. Bowen, Jr., was president of the Court. With him were rear admirals Richard R. Pratt, Edward E. Grimm, Allen A. Bergner, and Marshall W. White. Counsel for the Court and chief interrogator was Capt. William R. Newsome, who later received the Legion of Merit for his work at the inquiry. (The only medals handed out to *Pueblo* crewmen were Purple Hearts, ten in all.) The Court was empowered to question witnesses under oath and summon any documents in an effort to find out who was responsible for the loss of a Navy ship and to erase forever this stain on the Navy's reputation for never giving up a ship without a fight.

At the outset the Court of Inquiry was denounced by members of Congress and other public officials as a case of the Navy investigating itself. James Reston of the New York *Times* wrote a column entitled "Who Will Investigate the Investigators?" When, on the second day of hearings, the admirals warned Bucher that he faced court-martial and that anything he said could be used against him, the Court of Inquiry was widely denounced as a witch-hunt designed to make Bucher a "scapegoat" for the Navy's own derelictions.

The Court convened in a 110-seat amphitheater which was heavily guarded. Significant testimony, especially about the intelligence functions of *Pueblo,* was taken in secret behind closed, guarded doors. The transcript of the *public* testimony before the nation's press and 110 spectators *was promptly classified and has not been released to this day.* How words spoken in public before the press can be a national secret has never been explained.

The Court raised questions that were never answered and heard conflicting testimony that was not resolved, as reporters were quick to point out at the time. Some items:

• The ship's position was given by Bucher as 15.8 miles from shore. Some crewmen admitted they might have been as close as 12 miles. Lieutenant Murphy, executive officer and navigator of *Pueblo,* testified that the ship's principal navigational instrument, called the loran, was sometimes off by as much as five miles, but that he was certain the ship was 15.8 miles from the nearest spit of North Korean land.

The five admirals never did, but they should have questioned this testimony. By 1968 navigation at sea had progressed far beyond shooting the stars and "dead reckoning," even beyond use of the loran. Navy ships picked up signals from navigational satellites which could pinpoint the vessel within three feet of its actual location on the planet. If *Pueblo* was not so equipped, that should have been pointed out as a matter of great importance. Moreover, the very functions of *Pueblo,* its reason for existing, depended on determining its precise location. It picked up radar, radio, and similar signals from shore installations. This information was recorded, then radioed at precise times to Japan and other shore installations over a directional antenna set to transmit in a two-degree arc. Of all ships, *Pueblo* had to know with great precision where it was at all times.

• The appearance of the North Korean vessels came as no surprise to those aboard *Pueblo.* Bucher wrote in his book, *Bucher: My Story,* that he knew his ship had been spotted by North Koreans on the previous day. The situation was worse than that. *Pueblo* officers told Armbrister that on January 21, *two* days before seizure, a North Korean SO-1 subchaser had approached within 300 yards of the ship. On the 22nd, North Korean fishing trawlers came within 30 yards of *Pueblo.* Crewmen had the impression they were followed during the night. They saw running lights and a flare. *Pueblo* knew it had been detected. Why didn't it leave?

• The North Korean subchaser was seen approaching *Pueblo* at high speed, men at battle stations, about noon on January 23. *Pueblo* was dead in the water, engines shut down. It still made no effort to get under way. Why?

• *Pueblo* displayed no national colors.* Crewmen were not in uniform. The two civilians, both oceanographers employed by the Pentagon, testified they had deployed Nansen bottles to take water samples as a "cover" for the ship's real ELINT operations. *Pueblo* remained dead in the water for a protracted interval; exactly how long is disputed by those aboard the ship. The North Korean subchaser asked *Pueblo* to identify itself. The United States flag was raised. The North Koreans signaled with international flags, HEAVE TO OR I WILL FIRE. Bucher testified that he then hoisted flags saying, I AM IN INTERNATIONAL WATERS. The signalman who hoisted the flags testified that he never raised any such signal. He testified that he didn't remember what he raised but it was "some kind of protest." Bucher reappeared before the Court to say the signalman was mistaken.

The Court of Inquiry never pursued this conflict in testimony, although it had the means to. At 1254, an hour after the North Korean vessels appeared, *Pueblo* transmitted a "Pinnacle" message, the first of two. According to this message, as reported by Armbrister, the subchaser

---

*In the movie based upon his book, Bucher (played by Hal Holbrook) explained the flag was not flown because it wore out in the wind.

asked for nationality, and *Pueblo* raised the national ensign, then a signal identifying itself as a hydrographer. On its third swing around *Pueblo*, according to the Pinnacle message, the subchaser raised its HEAVE TO OR I WILL FIRE signal. The message from *Pueblo* does not mention an I AM IN INTERNATIONAL WATERS signal. In view of Bucher's cryptic remark to Fryklund, the Pentagon official, immediately after his release that evidence had been "doctored," the question must be asked, was *Pueblo* in international waters and did it so signal?

• According to testimony, there was no alarm on board *Pueblo* at the appearance of North Korean warships. The crew considered it normal harassment. Even when *Pueblo* radioed its first Pinnacle message, naval officers in Japan deemed the harassment routine and to be expected. Not until the North Koreans began forming an armed boarding party did those aboard *Pueblo* become alarmed. Bucher testified that *Pueblo* finally got under way. Precisely when that happened is disputed, but the preponderance of evidence is that *Pueblo* remained under enemy guns for an hour and a quarter before moving. The North Korean ships then opened fire. *Pueblo* stopped. Exactly who ordered *Pueblo* to stop is hotly disputed among the officers on the bridge.

• Bucher said he ordered emergency destruction of classified gear and materials. This was denied in testimony by enlisted man James A. Kell, listed as a communications chief among the intelligence personnel. He said he never heard an order for emergency destruction from either Bucher or Lt. Stephen R. Harris, who commanded the ELINT operations aboard ship, but gave the order himself. At least two other men said they began emergency destruction on their own volition.

• Bucher testified and wrote in his book that *Pueblo* was raked by repeated salvos and it was "suicide" to go out on deck. He said his men had no chance to man the ship's guns or to go out on deck to incinerate documents. Ens. Timothy Harris told the Court of Inquiry, however, that he made seven or eight trips to the incinerator, remaining two or three minutes each time to burn papers. Although exposed to enemy guns, he was not fired upon. One crewman testified it was twenty to twenty-five minutes between the first and second enemy salvos. Another testified it was forty-five minutes to an hour between the second and third salvos.

• The North Korean subchaser ordered *Pueblo* to follow in its wake. Bucher said he obeyed to gain time to complete destruction of classified documents. He was surprised, he said, by the vast amount of classified materials. He had not signed for them at the beginning of the voyage. Fires were built on deck in a frantic effort to burn documents. Bucher said he constantly urged his men to build more fires and dump documents overboard. This was contradicted by several crewmen. Chief Kell and Senior Communications Chief Ralph D. Bouden told the court they were ordered to stop burning after "ten to fifteen minutes." They could not remember who gave the order.

• An expert told the Court there were over two tons of documents aboard *Pueblo,* an incredible amount. He later reduced his estimate to six hundred pounds, still an immense amount. No one ever questioned—or answered—what *Pueblo* was doing with so much "paper" aboard. An ELINT vessel, such as *Pueblo, records*—does not write down—electronic signals. Six hundred pounds of magnetic tape might be believable, but paper? And on its maiden voyage? How did all those documents get there? And for what purpose on a small, poorly armed ship snooping near an unfriendly nation?

• It was hardly an overwhelming force that boarded *Pueblo.* One or two officers carrying sidearms and six or eight soldiers bearing automatic weapons boarded the ship and took eighty-three unresisting American sailors prisoner. This occurred despite the fact there were ten Thompson submachine guns and numerous .45 caliber pistols, plus grenades, aboard. These were locked up and never broken out. The only reason given for this passive surrender was Bucher's statement that it was "suicide" to resist.

These and many other items of conflicting testimony—or lack of testimony—were noted by reporters covering the Court of Inquiry. But the press could not resolve the conflicts because the transcript was never released and the crewmen were not available for interviews.

Yet, acting on its own, the press dredged up information that raised still more questions about the loss of *Pueblo.* The New York *Times* uncovered a whole series of North Korean warnings about spy ships operating in their waters. On January 6, 1968, North Koreans said they would take "more determined countermeasures" against "provocative acts" that the United States was "incessantly committing" off their eastern coast. In a broadcast on January 11, North Korea warned against U.S. "spy boats disguised as fishing boats" off their coast. On January 20, three days before the seizure, the North Koreans registered a protest against "armed spy boats" infiltrating "into our coastal waters" and demanded such "criminal acts" be stopped. Gen. Pak Chung Kuk, the North Korean delegate to Panmunjom, where meetings with South Koreans were held, then said: "It is quite obvious that if one continued the provocative act of dispatching spy boats and espionage bandits to the coastal waters of the other side under the cover of naval craft, it will only result in disrupting the armistice and inducing another war. We have the due right to make a due response to your thoughtless play with fire. We will fully exercise our rights.''

The Defense and State departments at first denied the warning was issued. They were forced to admit it when the South Koreans released the transcript of the January 20 meeting at Panmunjom. The warning from North Korea, known to the United States, never reached *Pueblo*, which sailed on blithely believing it was on a "minimal risk mission."

The press also obtained statements from Defense Secretary Robert McNamara and Secretary of State Dean Rusk that neither had known of the *Pueblo* mission. Both said "their representatives" had known, however. They refused to identify their representatives.

Most damaging, and never explained, was the report in the New York *Times* and other papers that when another ELINT vessel, the USS *Banner*, undertook similar missions off the coasts of the Soviet Union, China, and North Korea, naval warships were nearby and military aircraft on "strip alert." No such precautions were taken for *Pueblo*. Indeed, when, seven months previously, Israeli aircraft had attacked another American intelligence ship, identified as the USS *Liberty*—killing thirty-four and wounding seventy-five—U.S. planes had scrambled to its aid. No such help came to *Pueblo*, although more than eight hours passed when it could have.

The work of the Court of Inquiry was sharply criticized at the time. It was pointed out that Bucher was called as the first witness. Those who came after were forced to follow his testimony. Crewmen were housed together, so all knew what questions would be asked, what others had said, and what answers were expected from them. All knew their naval careers hinged on fitness reports from superior officers. None of the men who performed the ELINT operations was questioned in public about the most vital functions of the ship.

As Bernard Weinraub of the New York *Times* pointed out, the five admirals did not call as a witness anyone from the Fifth Air Force in Japan to ask why they did not attempt to defend *Pueblo* from attack. Nor did the admirals call anyone from the naval yard that outfitted *Pueblo*, the Naval Ships Systems Command, which installed the electronic gear, the National Security Agency, the Defense Intelligence Agency, or the Office of the Joint Chiefs of Staff, all of whom played a role in the functions and mission of the ship.

The most serious oversight of all was the Court's failure to investigate, at least in public testimony, the transcript of radio messages between *Pueblo* and a ground base at Kamiseya, Japan. This transcript was edited, condensed, then declassified by the Navy and sent to the House Armed Forces Subcommittee, which inquired into the *Pueblo* incident. Even in its greatly attenuated form, the transcript raises serious questions about where *Pueblo* was, when it was boarded, and the events which occurred during seizure. The radio transcript remains to this day the only official document offering information about the seizure that is independent of the statements by participants—and it is in sharp conflict with many of those statements. Yet the five admirals never addressed themselves to the transcript. They ignored it. One is tempted to say they suppressed it.

(It defies belief, but the possibility exists that the admirals did not know about the transcript. During the hearings, the New York *Times* printed only the briefest excerpts from the transcript as a sidebar, excerpts which omitted the conflicts about time and place. Maybe that is the only portion of the transcript which the admirals possessed.)

The radio transcript will be examined in detail later on for what it tells about the last two hours and thirty-two minutes of *Pueblo*'s existence as an American ship. But at this preliminary point, two major questions raised by the radio transmissions must be addressed. At 1200 hours, Korean time, *Pueblo* radioed "COMPANY OUTSIDE." It stayed on the air, keeping the teletype circuit open with "chatter." The *Pueblo* operator radioed the first Pinnacle message at 1254 and a second Pinnacle message at 1321, an hour and twenty minutes into the seizure. This reported that three torpedo boats had joined the North Korean subchaser. Two MIGs circled overhead. A torpedo boat "IS BACKING TOWARD BOW WITH FENDERS RIGGED WITH AN ARMED LANDING PARTY." *Pueblo* had gone "ALL AHEAD ONE-THIRD. . . . INTENTIONS TO DEPART THE AREA."

Four or five minutes later, between 1326 and 1327, *Pueblo* radioed, "AND THEY PLAN TO OPEN FIRE ON US NOW, THEY PLAN TO OPEN FIRE ON US NOW, THEY PLAN TO OPEN FIRE ON US NOW."

At 1328, at the most two minutes later, *Pueblo* sent: "NORTH KOREAN WAR VESSELS PLAN TO OPEN FIRE, SHIP POSIT [position] 39-25.5N, 127-54.9E, SHIP POSIT 39-25.5N, 127-54.9E."

At 1330, two minutes later, *Pueblo* transmitted, five times, "WE ARE BEING BOARDED," followed by two repeats of the ship's position, and two repeats of "WE ARE BEING BOARDED." SOS was sent thirteen times, followed by two transmissions of a revised ship's position, 39-34N, 127-54E, eighteen more SOSs, and the new position once more.

At 1331, a minute later, *Pueblo* transmitted, "WE ARE HOLDING EMER-
GENCY DESTRUCTION. WE NEED HELP. WE ARE HOLDING EMERGENCY
DESTRUCTION. WE NEED SUPPORT. SOS SOS SOS. PLEASE SEND ASSISTANCE,
PLEASE SEND ASSISTANCE, PLEASE SEND ASSISTANCE, PLEASE SEND ASSIST-
ANCE. SOS SOS SOS. WE ARE BEING BOARDED. HOLDING EMERGENCY
DESTRUCTION."

At 1337, six minutes later, *Pueblo* radioed, "WE ARE LAYING TO AT
PRESENT POSITION. AS OF YET WE NO LONGER HAVE GOPI [Western Pacific
Operational Intelligence broadcast]. THIS CIRCUIT ONLY CIRCUIT ACTIVE
ON NIP [ship]. PLEASE SEND ASSISTANCE. WE ARE BEING BOARDED."

At 1345, eight minutes later, *Pueblo* radioed, "WE ARE BEING ESCORTED
INTO PROB [probably] WONSON REPEAT WONSON. WE ARE BEING ESCORTED
INTO PROB WONSON, REPEAT WONSON." (This is the spelling of Wonsan
used in the transcript.)

Thereafter *Pueblo* remained on the air until 1432, when it ended its
transmissions with, "HAVE BEEN DIRECTED TO COME TO ALL STOP AND
BEING BOARDED AT THIS TIME. BEING BOARDED AT THIS TIME. FOUR MEN
INJURED AND ONE CRITICALLY AND GOING OFF THE AIR NOW AND DESTROY-
ING THIS GEAR." It was the last message from *Pueblo*.

The most obvious question, to which the Court of Inquiry never
addressed itself, was this: Was *Pueblo* boarded at 1330 or 1432?

In its initial statement on the seizure, the Pentagon said *Pueblo* was
boarded at approximately 1345 Korean time and went off the air at 1432.
How could the tiny, 177-foot-long ship be boarded and still remain on the
air? In an effort to explain, unnamed Pentagon sources told Hedrick
Smith of the New York *Times* that Bucher and crewmen had locked themselves inside the "research spaces" (a euphemism for intelligence operation) for forty-five minutes to an hour, destroying gear and documents
after the North Koreans boarded the ship.

In his testimony and in his book, Bucher gave a different account. He
said he followed the North Korean subchaser at one-third speed to gain
time to destroy that mass of papers. He even came to a full stop. The
North Koreans opened fire again, forcing him to resume speed. They then
ordered him to stop. He did and the North Koreans boarded. It was 1432.

Bucher did not address himself to the 1330 portion of the radio transcript either in testimony or in his book. It is as though it never existed.
Others, notably Lieutenant Murphy and Trevor Armbrister, attempted to
explain the 1330 transmission. They said the *Pueblo* radio operator, identified as CT (communications technician) First Class Don E. Bailey, was
"mistaken." He *thought Pueblo* was boarded, but he was *wrong*. He was

still wrong seven minutes later at 1337 when he again said *Pueblo* was boarded.

This is surely strange. How is it possible for an enlisted man in the United States Navy to sit there, on his own initiative, without command of officers, and send out—quite erroneously—numerous distress calls and pleas for assistance because his ship is being boarded and emergency destruction being held? One would think the five admirals would want to get to the bottom of this failure of command aboard one of their vessels. After all, it was a serious "mistake." If indeed U.S. planes and ships had wanted to aid *Pueblo,* the erroneous transmission could have prevented it. Air Force planes might not have scrambled because they thought *Pueblo* was already seized. If there actually was another hour before the ship was seized, then some kind of rescue might have been attempted. Surely the five admirals should have delved into all this. At least in public testimony, they never uttered a syllable about it.

The radio transcript raises another question. At 1328 *Pueblo* radioed its position, when it said the North Koreans planned to open fire, as 39 degrees, 25.5 minutes North latitude and 127 degrees, 54.9 minutes East longitude. It repeated it twice. At 1330—the "WE ARE BEING BOARDED" transmission—it repeated this position twice more, then sent a revised position of 39 degrees, 34 minutes North latitude, 127 degrees, 54 minutes East longitude.

The difference between the two positions is nine nautical miles. Is this another of Bailey's "mistakes"? If so, how in the world was it made? When the North Korean vessels approached about noon, Bucher, Murphy, and others checked and rechecked the ship's position to determine if they were in international waters. Yes, they were—15.8 miles from land. Bucher said he raised flags to declare his ship in international waters. Yet, at 1328 and 1330, the ship's radio operator, believing the ship was under attack and being boarded, sends SOS many times, appeals for help, and gives the *wrong* ship's position four times. When he "corrects" it, the ship is now nine miles farther to the northeast.

How could it happen? *Pueblo* was old, capable of twelve knots at full speed, and could not have sailed nine nautical miles in two minutes. That would indicate a speed of 270 miles an hour. More to the point, where was *Pueblo*? In its initial announcement, the Pentagon said *Pueblo* was seized at 39 degrees 25 minutes North latitude, 127 degrees 54.3 minutes East longitude. This was the location, give or take a mile or two, which was consistently reported in the press. The only time *Pueblo* was moved nine miles away was in the radio transcript, with the "revised" position given at 1330. Is this some of the "doctoring" of evidence which Bucher told the Pentagon official about?

Again, one would assume the five admirals on the Court of Inquiry would have wanted to clarify the ship's position. Surely heads ought to have rolled because such "errors" were made in giving the ship's position during "mistaken" distress calls. At least in press accounts of public testimony, the admirals never breathed a word about it.

Something is clearly wrong, either in the radio transcript released to Congress or in the testimony to the Court of Inquiry or in both. Where was *Pueblo* when seized? And at what time was it boarded? The only explanation given for the diverse times and places is in terms of "mistakes" which went officially unnoticed and uncorrected.

The Court of Inquiry adjourned on March 13, 1969, having conducted six weeks of hearings. On May 5, it recommended that Bucher be court-martialed on five charges: permitting his ship to be searched while he had power to resist; failing to take immediate and aggressive protective measures when his ship was attacked; complying with orders of North Koreans to follow them to port; negligently failing to complete destruction of classified material aboard *Pueblo* and permitting such material to fall into North Korean hands; and negligently failing to ensure before departure for sea that his officers and crew were properly organized, stationed, and trained in emergency destruction of classified material.

Lt. Stephen Harris, who commanded the "research detachment" (intelligence personnel) was charged with three counts: failing to inform his commanding officer of a "certain deficiency in the classified support capabilities of the research detachment"; failing to train and drill his men in emergency destruction procedures; and failing to take effective action to complete emergency destruction after Bucher ordered him to do so.

Lieutenant Murphy, the executive officer, was to receive a letter of admonition for failing to organize and lead the crew on the day of seizure, especially in emergency destruction. Letters of reprimand were recommended against Rear Adm. Frank L. Johnson and Capt. Everett B. Gladding. Admiral Johnson, as commander of naval forces in Japan, had failed to plan properly for effective emergency support for *Pueblo*. Captain Gladding, then director of Naval Security Group, Pacific, had failed to develop procedures to ensure the readiness of *Pueblo*'s research detachment for its mission and to coordinate other services to provide intelligence support to *Pueblo* during its mission.

As soon as the Court's recommendations were made, Navy Secretary John H. Chafee issued a statement dropping all charges because the men had "suffered enough." Then Commander Bucher was paraded before TV cameras and the press one more time. Ill, unable to speak because of laryngitis, he had his civilian attorney, E. Miles Harvey, read a statement in which Bucher accepted the findings of the Court without animosity. Pressed for some statement, Bucher replied in a raspy voice that he was looking forward to a "return to normalcy" in the Bucher family.

In his book, written later, Bucher gives his true reaction to the charges. He writes, "I couldn't believe my ears. I could not recall there was a single word of testimony to support the charges, except for the loss of classified materials to which I had already admitted in Court." It was elsewhere reported that Bucher wanted to demand a court-martial, but he was told not to by attorney Harvey, a former member of naval intelligence. "If you do," Harvey reportedly told Bucher, "it is sayonara. This is where I get off."

Lieutenant Harris said he was "very, very happy" over the outcome of the inquiry. It may have had nothing to do with it, but Harris was soon promoted to Lieutenant Commander.

Murphy was outraged. He wanted a court-martial but could not request it because only a letter of admonition was recommended for him. In his book, Murphy writes: "I was deeply disappointed in the verdict. I was not about to say: Thank you, Mr. Secretary, for pardoning me for a crime I didn't commit." He quickly resigned his commission.

As will be shown in pages to come, all the charges against Bucher, Steve Harris, Murphy, Admiral Johnson, and Captain Gladding were utterly lacking in validity, which a court-martial would have shown. Even at this late date the charges should be expunged from the records of these men and a formal apology made.

During the couple of years following the Inquiry, eight books on the *Pueblo* incident were published. They were Trevor Armbrister's *A Matter of Accountability*, Ed Brandt's *The Last Voyage of the USS Pueblo*, Lloyd Bucher's *Bucher: My Story*, Don Crawford's *Pueblo Intrigue*, Daniel V. Gallery's *The Pueblo Incident*, Stephen R. Harris's *My Anchor Held*, Edward R. Murphy, Jr.'s *Second in Command*, and Carl F. Schumacher, Jr.'s and George C. Wilson's *Bridge of No Return* (see appendix). A movie was made, based on Bucher's book. None of these made much of a ripple in the national consciousness, although the books, when compared, contain myriad conflicting statements. *Pueblo* had left a bad taste in the national mouth. It was dead as a news story. Everyone wanted to forget it. Forget it we did.

Yet the questions remain. Where was the ship when seized? When was

Pueblo boarded? Why did the crew make no effort to defend the ship? Why did it remain dead in the water so long after the North Korean vessels appeared? Why didn't U.S. ships and planes come to *Pueblo*'s aid? Why was the crew silenced upon their return home? Why did the Court of Inquiry take so much testimony in secret and refuse to release a transcript even of public testimony? Who was responsible for sending the ship on its mission? What intelligence agency supervised the main functions of the ship? What were all those documents doing on board? If the ship was seized on the high seas in an act of piracy, why isn't there *one* clear story of what happened instead of so many varied ones? The questions go on and on.

Doubts and queries still haunt the minds of *Pueblo* crewmen. There can be no doubt of this. In July 1988, forty-five of the *Pueblo* crewmen met in San Diego for their annual reunion. The Associated Press in its coverage quoted Chief CT James A. Kell as saying: "It [the seizure] made 82 people become very close . . . but I know some are still bitter about it." Crewman Stuart Russell said, "Almost invariably the stories you hear are about funny and stupid things that happened. The real heavyweight stuff isn't talked about much. It's still been kind of intense, but really good therapy." The Associated Press said: "The lingering emotional and physical wounds inflicted 20 years ago still haunt many of the crewmen." Then AP quoted Marine Sgt. Robert J. Chicca, organizer of the reunion: "The principal emphasis of it is the moral support. It's a real healthy therapy form, and we all leave here feeling better than when we came." Veterans Administration readjustment counseling therapist Jack Jones addressed the group about the "post-traumatic stress many still experience." He added: "They talk about a lot of the good times, but they avoid a lot of the pain . . . instead of letting it out." Jones said three crewmen remain patients of his after twenty years.

In an interview for this book, Radioman Lee Roy Hayes said, "I always thought we were set up. I never knew why, but I always believed we were." He was asked what led him to conclude that *Pueblo* was "set up." His reply: "Oh, there were lots of things. It may not have meant anything but it seemed strange to a lot of us that the eighty-three men on board represented thirty-four states. Then the crew was awfully green. There were lots of last-minute replacements and men new at their jobs or called back into the Navy. There were just too many men who didn't know what they were doing. I had been out of the Navy for two years, then I reenlisted. I'd only been back in four months, then I was ordered aboard *Pueblo* in Japan. I was the last man to come aboard, less than an hour before we sailed. I did my job, but I had a hard time because I was unfamiliar with my equipment.

"A lot of us thought it strange that the crew was disarmed. My job called for me to keep a .45 pistol in my desk. It was taken away. Then there were no explosives aboard. We had no ability to sink ourselves. I smashed my equipment with an axe.

"But I really became convinced we were set up when I returned. We were denied leave, although my folks came out to San Diego. There were Navy or intelligence guys with us every second." Hayes then told about sneaking out of the hospital one night. "We were ordered not to discuss *Pueblo*. Shortly before the Court of Inquiry began the whole crew was addressed by Bucher and some other officers on what not to say. We were not to say *Pueblo* had secret orders to remain in the area to see how much harassment the North Koreans would give us. We were not to talk about that. I think they goofed. I'd been on the bridge and that was the first I'd heard about any such orders." (In the interview I asked Hayes what else they were told not to talk about. He hesitated. I had the impression he wanted to say something more but felt he couldn't or shouldn't. Pressed, he finally said they were told not to mention how pleased the North Koreans were with the utterances of then Ohio Sen. Stephen Young.)

Hayes continued: "Then I learned there were warnings from the North Koreans which were never taken into account. The messages upgrading our mission from 'minimal risk' were mysteriously lost. There were no planes on strip alert during our mission—and there had been for *Banner*. A destroyer was just beyond the horizon just in case *Banner* was attacked. We had none of that.

"I guess the biggest thing was that help never came. It seemed to take forever to reach Wonsan. I still had my watch. It was after eight in the evening when we got there. Every minute of the time we kept expecting American planes to bomb the Koreans and rescue us. They never came. None of us could believe it. All that time and no one tried to help us! Later, I talked to two Air Force F-105 pilots. They had been on strip alert at Osan, South Korea, ten minutes flying time from *Pueblo*. They were on alert for something else, but when they heard our distress calls they scrambled to their planes, intending to take off and help us. They taxied out to the runway, then they were recalled before they could take off.

"I used to give speeches saying a lot of this. Then I was called to Washington and told to keep my mouth shut, particularly about secret orders to remain in the area when the North Koreans approached."(I interviewed Hayes rather early in my research, before I had discovered what really had happened during the seizure. Hayes provided some insights and I quote him, but later research showed him to have been less than forthcoming with me. He was guarded in what he said and continued to stonewall the cover story. I concluded that finding and interviewing the *Pueblo* crewmen after all these years would not lead to the truth any more than it did when they were interviewed originally.)

Clearly, after twenty years, Hayes is trying to tell us something, just as his shipmates did when, as Bucher revealed, they gave the finger not to their North Korean captors but to their fellow Americans by whom they had been "had," just as they did at the Court of Inquiry when they disputed the testimony of their officers. But the five admirals wouldn't listen. No one would.

We all should have. Precisely how and why these men were "had" was known or easily knowable twenty years ago. No secret sources of information, no classified documents are needed to discover it even today. The *Pueblo* story is where it has always been, in the library waiting for someone to read it. The men of *Pueblo* made a great sacrifice for us all, yet it went unrecognized by the Navy, Congress, press, and public. Instead, we were given a massively implausible cover story. That it was accepted at the time, let alone since, defies belief.

In arriving at what really did happen to *Pueblo,* no national secrets are revealed—at least none that aren't in the library. Rather, there is a story of great courage and devotion to duty. It's time we knew this bit of American history.

Before beginning the story, we need to examine the sources of information. A mass of material was written about the *Pueblo* incident, surely hundreds of millions of words, for it remained a news event for over fifteen months, from January 23, 1968, to May 5, 1969. Most of what was written is duplication, the same story filed by news services or slightly different stories written by reporters attending the same press conference, briefing, or event. Most of the press coverage dealt with the diplomatic efforts to gain release of the crew. After they returned home, attention focused on how cruel the captivity was and how glad the crew was to be home. Prevented from gaining information about the seizure, reporters had to write about whether crewmen violated the Military Code of Conduct while in captivity.

In all those millions of words, surprisingly little was ever written about the seizure itself—and that is the focus of this book. No clear, step-by-step account of the seizure was given at the time—and that, I'm now sure, was no accident. The only information about the seizure came from the Naval Court of Inquiry. And that was Bucher's story. The others were forced to follow it. Oh, testimony from crewmen showed discrepancies in the seizure tale, and reporters were quick to point them out. But they were in no position to follow up. They could only ask questions which had no answers. The five admirals on the Court certainly weren't going to give any.

Congress kept threatening to investigate and did empower a House Armed Forces Subcommittee, chaired by Rep. Otis G. Pike of New York (which became known as the "Pike Committee"). It questioned high-ranking Navy, Pentagon, intelligence, and State Department officials, seeking to assess responsibility for the loss of *Pueblo,* but the committee never did go into the seizure itself.

Thus, except for press accounts of the Court of Inquiry, about the only real knowledge we have about the seizure lies in eight books written subsequently to the investigation. Four are by *Pueblo* officers in collaboration with newsmen or writers—Bucher, Murphy, Steve Harris, and Schumacher. Bucher and Murphy present detailed though highly contradictory accounts of the seizure. Schumacher's book was written with George C. Wilson, distinguished military correspondent for the Washington *Post.* Wilson's byline is of equal size with Schumacher's, and he obviously contributed information that Schumacher could not possibly have known. Steve Harris, who was in charge of the ELINT operations, the heart of the ship, offers only the briefest story of the seizure—three pages! His book deals with the captivity and how his religious faith helped him endure.

These four books by *Pueblo* officers are all in one way or another self-serving, designed to put Bucher, Murphy, Schumacher, and Harris in the most favorable light. All four were censored. The authors were all naval officers and all had some security clearance. I don't know how much censorship was imposed and by whom, but there can be no doubt there was some. In my opinion, there was a great deal, including major deletions and extensive rewrites.

The fifth book is by Rear Adm. (Ret.) Daniel V. Gallery. His is a short, punchy book seeking to assess blame for the loss of the ship, which he places both on *Pueblo* and the Navy. But his account of the seizure is based largely on Bucher's and adds little information.

There are three books written by independent persons. Of these the one by Don Crawford is a paperback, written for the religious press. It deals mostly with Steve Harris's religious experiences and adds little to the knowledge of the seizure.

Thus, there are only two truly independent studies of the *Pueblo* seizure. By far the best is *A Matter of Accountability* by Trevor Armbrister, then a reporter for the old *Saturday Evening Post* and now with the *Reader's Digest* in its Washington bureau. He single-handedly conducted a far better investigation of *Pueblo* than the Court of Inquiry, interviewing more than three hundred persons, including most of the *Pueblo* crewmen, and offering a highly detailed account of the seizure, not just aboard ship, but in military and government offices. He named names. He sought to provide a complete story of the *Pueblo,* even acquiring documents no one else had published. It would be impossible to duplicate his work today.

The other valuable book is Ed Brandt's *The Last Voyage of the USS Pueblo.* Quite frankly, it was the "sleeper" in my research. The book is obscure, difficult to obtain, and was the last one I read. Ed Brandt, at the time a Norfolk, Virginia, newsman and now special projects editor for the Baltimore *Sun,* interviewed fifteen *Pueblo* crewmen, including some truly key persons aboard. The crewmen Brandt interviewed are Tim Harris, Charlie Law, Stuart Russell, Chuck Ayling, Don McClarren, Vic Escamilla, Mike O'Bannon, Don Bailey, Jimmy Layton, Angelo Strano, Jimmy Shepard, Larry Mack, Frank Ginther, Steve Woelk, and Robert Hammond. What makes Brandt's book so valuable is that *his was the first book published.* His book came out in 1969. Indeed, his preface, usually the last thing written, is dated in July of that year, only two months after the Court of Inquiry terminated its work. Thus, Brandt got to some extremely important crewmen very early—in my opinion before their stories were changed to fit the cover story.

To clarify the timing of the interviews, I spoke to both Brandt and Armbrister by phone. Brandt said that on May 5, 1969, when the recommendations of the Court of Inquiry were made and the navy secretary said the men of *Pueblo* had "suffered enough," he was in a Norfolk motel room conducting his second day of interviews with Ens. Tim Harris. Thereafter, he interviewed fourteen crewmen, several at a time, in San Diego and on the east coast. Brandt described the mood of the men he interviewed as "angry," because they hadn't been given a chance to tell their stories to the Court of Inquiry. His interviewing was completed by the "third week in May" and he wrote his book during the next five weeks. Armbrister said he attended the Court of Inquiry as a reporter. Some interviewing was done as early as January 1969—he referred to Schumacher specifically—but then he made a trip to the Far East and the bulk of his interviews were conducted after July 1969. He began writing his book in the fall of 1969. His cutoff date for interviews was March 1970.

Both books are invaluable. Of the two, Armbrister's is the most thorough. Brandt's book is more limited in scope, largely confined to what the fifteen crewmen told him in interviews. Both Armbrister and Brandt report a great deal of information which is not in the other's book. The same crewmen frequently told conflicting information to Armbrister and Brandt in interviews or, more significantly, neglected to report information to Armbrister they had already told Brandt. It is of the utmost significance that Bucher, Murphy, Schumacher, and Harris all told Armbrister something quite different from what they related to the Court of Inquiry or penned in their own books. Armbrister himself is now cognizant that at least one person he interviewed was less than candid with him. In a phone conversation with me (on August 9, 1984), Armbrister said: "Just the other day I was talking to one of the persons I interviewed for my book. He used to be involved with the Agency but is now retired. He said, 'If I had told you the truth about *Pueblo* I would have been killed.'"

These eight books create an unusual situation for a researcher. Because of the ineptness of the Court of Inquiry and because it suppressed the radio transcript and its own public testimony, these eight books are not secondary, but *primary* sources. Just about all the public can learn about the seizure of *Pueblo* lies in these stories written by four officers or told to Armbrister and Brandt, who interviewed the participants. In my view, the words spoken and written by Bucher, Murphy, et al. are not just primary evidence by eyewitnesses and participants, but in large measure the *only* evidence.

Of all the accounts of the seizure, Bucher's is paramount—and why not? After all, he was captain of the ship, supposedly in command of all things aboard *Pueblo*. It is to be assumed his book had the largest sales. He was best known of anyone aboard, spokesman for the whole crew, something of a celebrity for a while, and certainly an intriguing figure. (In his book Murphy writes that Bucher's advance from Doubleday was $375,000. I have no knowledge whether that is correct.)

Bucher wrote in detail. If a person reads only Bucher's book, uncritically, it is perhaps believable. But difficulties arise when a person reads a second book and a third or an eighth, then studies the New York *Times* on microfilm, peruses the magazine stacks in the library, and visits with a crewman. Every account of the seizure differs from the others, sometimes in highly significant ways. The crewmen didn't see the same thing. Events happened in a different order. With great frequency, what one person said happened another denies or ignores completely. Even if all due regard is given to faulty memories at a moment of trauma, a person is left to conclude that all these differing accounts cannot possibly be true. And none of them explains the transcript of last radio messages from *Pueblo* which the Navy released to the Pike Committee.

A researcher coming along twenty years later and trying to find out what really happened during the *Pueblo* boarding and capture—when? where? how? by whom? and above all, why?—faces a most difficult task. Commander Bucher and lieutenants Murphy, Harris, and Schumacher have all cemented their stories in print, *although Murphy admitted the whole story of* Pueblo *had yet to be told and Bucher hinted at it.* They are unlikely to change their stories now. All of them, as well as most crewmen, were interviewed by Armbrister and Brandt. Indeed, a common reaction is surprise that I'm doing a book on *Pueblo.* What else is there to report about it?

The problem is worse than that. Hunting up and interviewing crewmen is extremely difficult today. A great many have moved from their hometowns. A surprising number have unlisted phone numbers. Even when contacted, they or members of their families refuse to talk or deny they were aboard *Pueblo.* Beyond that, interviewing the *Pueblo* crewmen— even if they were to change their stories and bleed out their guts in the absolute truth as they know it—still won't reveal what happened during the seizure. *Most don't know.* All but four were blindfolded and only two of those were in a position to see what happened. One of those, Helmsman Ronald Berens, has said very little for twenty years, the other . . . I assume the conditions which compelled Commander Bucher to remain silent about certain events and to relate a cover story still exist. If he now wishes to change his story, he is free to do so. I refuse to interrogate him or anyone else. My purpose is not to challenge anyone's veracity, but rather to discover what really happened to the men of *Pueblo.*

Great effort went into preparation of the cover story. It began during captivity in North Korea. Murphy writes (pp. 260–3): "By now it was apparent that there were greatly differing recollections as to exactly what happened on January 23, 1968. This was not at all surprising, memory being what it is and the events themselves so emotion-charged. There was also the fact that, due to our varying duties, none of us was participant in every bit of the action. I remembered things one way, Skip [Schumacher] another, Gene [Lacy] still another, and so on.

"But Bucher wouldn't accept this. When the Court of Inquiry convened there had to be a 'single consistent account' of the events. Otherwise,

Bucher claimed, the Navy would drop anchor on all of us. To get this story, he ordered all of the officers and the key enlisted men to write down their recollections, these then to be compared by him and melded into one account." Murphy writes that he opposed this. The men were forbidden to make "unauthorized writings" and North Koreans had beaten men for it. Too, if the written recollections fell into North Korean hands, they would contradict "confessions" already made, creating great difficulties. Murphy also felt getting the true facts was the business of the Court of Inquiry, not Bucher. But Bucher went ahead, obtaining his written statements.

Murphy: "Once Bucher had the different accounts, he set out to disprove any recollections which contradicted his own. 'Don't you mean . . .''What you mean to say is . . . ' and 'Isn't this the way it happened?' became his favorite expressions. He had a whole bag full of tricks, and he used them all. He would give in on the small points, but hold fast on the large. If one officer refused to agree with him, he would try to get the support of another. When all the officers disagreed with his version, he would seek concurrence among the enlisted men. Often he found it, some of the men agreeing to statements they had no knowledge of, apparently simply because they were flattered that Bucher wanted them to settle a dispute among the officers. This didn't always happen. Many of the men, such as [Quartermaster Charles] Law, had the integrity to make exceptions and hold fast to them, but when it did happen, Bucher would come back to us and say, 'Five men disagree with you. Are you saying that you're right and all five of them are wrong?' Nor was he above reminding us that when we returned to the United States he was the man who would be writing our fitness reports. . . .

"It was a mock trial, a Court of Inquiry, and a quest for absolution, all in one. Bucher was obsessed with proving himself blameless. In the process, he simply wore us down. We had twenty minutes for each meal, about an hour and a half to two hours additional each day for exercises and recreation. These were the only times we had together, the only times we were not isolated in our individual cells. And Bucher was dominating every minute of them with his endless rehearsals. Occasionally we gave in on a point just in hopes that he would shut up.

"There was also a psychological process at work. The more frequently we heard Bucher's version, the more familiar it became. After a while, we began to remember certain things not because we actually saw them but because someone else had described them so vividly and often. All this took its toll. The chronology of the twenty-third became terribly confused in the minds of everyone. It was only with great effort that the individual could keep his own story straight. Inevitably, doubts began to creep in. Maybe I *am* the only one out of step, you found yourself thinking. Maybe I'm remembering it all wrong.

"One by one, we caved in, not necessarily agreeing to Bucher's version, but no longer wanting to take the trouble, or weather the consequences, of contradicting him. It was difficult enough trying to resist the North Koreans, without having to fight the captain too.

"Only on one point did Bucher remain indecisive.

"Some days he would maintain that the KORCOMs [North Korean communists] had seized the ship by force, that no formal surrender had taken place, apparently forgetting he had ordered three men to help the boarding party up onto the deck.

"Yet on other days he would admit that he had surrendered the ship. The reason, he now claimed, was the same one he had used to justify his confession: he did it to save the crew. His first duty, he embellished, was safeguarding the lives of the young men who had been placed in his charge.

"It was apparent that he was trying out both accounts, to see which best fit.

"He also began modifying each, touching them up a little here and there, polishing and refining. The one SO-1 subchaser became two SO-1 subchasers. Another P-4 [torpedo boat] appeared over the horizon, bringing the total of them to four. The jets, instead of just buzzing the *Pueblo,* dropped several torpedoes, all of which fortunately missed the ship. The number of shells fired at us increased tenfold. That none of us had seen these things bothered Bucher not a bit. Through repetition he was sure to pick up a few true believers who would support him. Hopelessly outgunned and outmaneuvered, the lives of the entire crew in jeopardy, he had no choice but to surrender the ship.

"Thus a single account emerged, one which blended the best parts of both arguments. He tried it out on us as one would practice a speech in front of the family, before delivering it in public. And as he rehearsed it, over and over, we could see that he had begun to believe it himself."

Murphy, once an officer in the United States Navy, second in command of a ship, has written this. No one who wasn't there can challenge his veracity. I can only point out that, as we will see, there existed a deep animosity between Bucher and Murphy. The two officers spare no quarter in "having at" each other. Their antipathy colors many of the events of the *Pueblo* story.

Whether or not Murphy's version of these events is correct, there can be no doubt some effort went into preparation of the cover story while in North Korea. Bucher himself describes it this way (pp. 324–6):

"During our first month in the new prison, Gene [Lacy] had fallen into a deep, brooding depression which began wasting him away more than the starvation diet we were being fed. The cause of this was his realization and bitter remorse over his conduct on *Pueblo*'s bridge during the confrontation and seizure.

"I had tried to review the events of those fateful few hours, principally to discover whether I had blacked out sometime between being fired upon and wounded, and the boarding of *Pueblo*. No hour of January 23, 1968, escaped my examination. Nor were my sleeping hours free of flashbacks that were real nightmares. To try and clear my mind, I asked during our mealtime gatherings that all officers give me their individual recollections of the action, scribbling them down on smuggled notes, or passing them on to me verbally when they could. Everybody eagerly complied, including Gene Lacy, but I was struck by him omitting any mention of his having rung up ALL STOP without my orders, then disobeying them completely when I was checking things in the SOD-Hut by speeding up the ship in compliance to KORCOM signals as they escorted us toward Wonsan. When I questioned him about this, he flatly denied having done any such thing. He had a look of chagrined horror on his face. I knew Gene well enough that I knew he was not deliberately lying. Whose memory had blanked out, his or mine? I had to know.

"It happened that my memory of the events was confirmed by some of my other officers, and also by Quartermaster Law, whom I met in the latrine, and was able briefly to question on the subject. These people also were able to make Gene realize he must have done something terribly wrong at a time of which he had no recollection. He became so crushed and despondent that I began regretting ever having brought up the matter. My anger with him had long since passed. At the time, all of us had been overcome by a sudden, shattering development which we had not been trained to cope with, or indeed, assured that it *would not happen* [Bucher's emphasis]. I had no intention of shifting the blame to Gene. I was the captain and therefore ultimately responsible. In any case, even if Gene had not blacked out and acted irrationally, I doubt that the outcome would have been different. My problem became, under very difficult circumstances, to convince Gene of this, and to let him know that I still considered him a good friend and reliable officer."

As he continues, Bucher finds others to join Gene Lacy on a guilt trip.

Bucher: "It took several weeks to snap Gene Lacy out of his private misery and rejoin us in our communal one. Each of us had to live with his own devils of doubt, guilt, and self-recrimination which became particularly cruel and persistent during those lonely hours of tossing on our verminous bunks at night, half awake with worry, half asleep with bad dreams. Gene had a particular hell trying to penetrate the blank spot of his mind that hid actions which he only knew from the account of others. Steve Harris agonized over his inability to completely destroy the classified material in his SOD-Hut. Ed Murphy worried over an accumulation of failures. Sergeants Hammond and Chicca suffered because they had been unable to interpret the KORCOMs intentions while there was still time, and brooded over having given useless warning to the officer who assigned them to *Pueblo* of their limitations in the Korean language. Corpsman [Herman] Baldridge suffered over Duane Hodges' death and because he had been prevented from succoring the other wounded men. Radioman Hayes suffered from the curse of the fate which had sent him to my ship as a last-minute replacement of a miscreant, just as she was pulling out on an ill-fated mission. And I suffered for all of them. Yet we all sensed the necessity of mutual support in order to survive our ordeal. The officers and men of *Pueblo* were never more united in purpose than they were during their darkest days together."

Clearly, as both Bucher and Murphy tell us, considerable effort was made, even in captivity, to prepare a cover story, an effort using guilt and mind-bending psychological processes as a means of persuasion.

As this cover story is related in ensuing pages, we will discover both its fallaciousness and what really happened during the *Pueblo* surrender.

2

DUAL COMMAND

The USS *Pueblo* was a most unlikely vessel to play such a historic role. It was a very small ship, 176 feet, six inches long, 32 feet in beam. Its draft was 9.3 feet. And it was slow. Its speed was given in *American Fighting Ships*, published by the Navy, as 12 knots, but those aboard said it had a top or "flank" speed of 12.6 knots. One person even upgraded it to 13.1 knots.

Pueblo was built for the Army Transportation Command and designated FP-344, a general supply vessel. It entered the water on April 16, 1944, at the yards of the Kewaunee Shipbuilding and Engineering Corp. of Kewaunee, Wisconsin, sponsored by Mrs. C. L. Duvall. The ship was later redesignated FS-344, serving in the Philippines as an Army harbor craft. Taken out of service in 1954, it was mothballed first at Clatskamie, Oregon, then at Rio Vista, California.

The vessel was transferred to the Navy on April 12, 1966, renamed *Pueblo* (AKL-44), after the city and county in Colorado, on June 18 of that year, and converted to an environmental research vessel at Puget Sound Naval Shipyard. It was redesignated AGER-2 (for Auxiliary General Environmental Research) on May 2, 1967.

The size of *Pueblo* was the first thing everyone noticed. Murphy describes his first impression this way (p. 4): "Then I saw her: 'Boy, she's a long one,' I thought. Not until I was closer did I discover that what I had seen was not one ship, but two—the USS *Pueblo* and her sister ship, the USS *Palm Beach*, both of which were to be commissioned at the same time. The *Pueblo* was not only smaller than I had anticipated; I could see, even in the dim light, that she was far from new. And, unlike most Navy ships, it was necessary to climb down from the pier, rather than up, to get on board.''

Murphy refers to the fact that *Pueblo*'s stern was only a few feet above water. This would ultimately become a great aid to those who boarded and seized it.

Pueblo was old. It had frequent breakdowns of its engines and electrical generators. Its steering mechanism was cranky, as anyone who ever sailed it attested. The ship had eight antennae and radar masts and thus was top-heavy, especially when ice accumulated during rough weather in frigid waters. Danger of flounder was ever-present and Bucher often set his men to chipping and steaming away ice. *Pueblo* was also greatly overcrowded. Designed for a crew of forty, the vessel had eighty-three men aboard when captured. Berthing spaces were jammed. Mess was held in three shifts.

But it was not being small, slow, old, and overcrowded that made *Pueblo* unusual. It was its command structure. *Pueblo* was a Navy ship all right, but it was not the run-of-the-mill destroyer or aircraft carrier. In performing its main functions—monitoring and intercepting foreign radar, radio, and similar communications—*Pueblo* took orders from a U.S. intelligence agency.

How this came to be was explained by James Bamford in his provocative and important book *The Puzzle Palace* (see appendix). On page 229 he relates that when a U.S. intelligence agency began laying plans for civilian ELINT vessels, "The Navy quickly fired off a salvo of protests and insisted that all future SIGINT [Signals Intelligence, which Bamford uses rather than the more common ELINT] ships be traditional naval vessels manned by naval crews." But as a result "now the Navy had become little more than seagoing chauffeurs and hired hands" for an intelligence agency.*

The intelligence-gathering activities aboard *Pueblo* were classified. Those who performed this work—even their name suggests their separateness from the rest of the crew—were called the Special Operations

---

*Bamford adds that the Navy began using destroyers and destroyer escorts for its own surveillance activities. "The destroyers and escorts were also very provocative. Where few nations would notice an old, converted supply ship slowly cruising up and down a shoreline, they would have ample reason to be alarmed if it was an American warship. The destroyers *Maddox* and *Turner Joy* were cruising on just such missions, known as 'DeSoto patrols,' in the Gulf of Tonkin in 1964 when they were allegedly attacked by enemy torpedo boats, an incident that led to the first U.S. bombing of North Vietnam."

Detachment and sequestered within the SOD-Hut at midships. Access to the SOD-Hut was denied to all but authorized personnel.

Just how secret the SOD-Hut was is described by Schumacher, the operations and communications officer of *Pueblo*, in his book *Bridge of No Return*. On page 48 he writes: "The gray aluminum door to the SOD Hut had that name written on it, in dark-blue letters. But I could not go through that door the whole time we were in San Diego training for our deployment. It had three separate locks: a key lock in the aluminum door handle, a combination lock, and five black buttons mounted on a brass plate just above the combination dial, which had to be punched in a certain sequence." He said Bucher did not bother with all that and simply pounded on the door to get in. "I could not do the same thing because I did not have the Special Intelligence clearance required."

Schumacher writes that he told Steve Harris "at every opportunity" that it was "patently ridiculous" for the officer in charge of operations and communications to be "locked out of the ship's main center of operations and communications." Harris agreed, but said it would take time for Schumacher's clearance to come through. Schumacher said he was handicapped even in ordering supplies for the ship. He didn't know what *Pueblo* did, so how could he know what it needed?

Schumacher (p. 49): "The same bureaucratic situation had our training in irons. We were under the operational control of the Naval Training Command while in San Diego. The command was supposed to establish drills to test our readiness for our mission. But the command's officers were not cleared to know what we were getting ready for. It was just luck that they had an officer formerly attached to our sister ship, the *Banner*. He came through with some meaningful training exercises.

"After receiving the training, we came under the control of Commander Service Group One—also located in San Diego. The command was supposed to inspect the *Pueblo* and make sure she was ready in all respects for her mission. Again, however, the command was not cleared to know our mission. The inspecting team who came aboard found that many questions on their list did not apply or could not be answered by *Pueblo* officers for security reasons. Frustrated, they gave up and declared us ready—for something."

The SOD-Hut was surely secure. It was a box made of armor plating (resistant to all but armor-piercing shells from large guns) which was welded on to *Pueblo* at midships. There were no portholes or windows. No one could see in or out. And there were no means of communications between the inside of the SOD-Hut and other parts of the ship. *Pueblo*'s loudspeaker (called the 1MC) could not be heard inside the SOD-Hut. The only link between the pilothouse and the SOD-Hut was a telephone outside the door. If it rang from the pilothouse, a sentry or someone inside would open the door, answer the phone, and relay the message. As a practical matter most communications were by messenger, who would pound on the triple-locked door until it opened. All of these difficulties in communications between the pilothouse and the SOD-Hut would play a crucial role during the seizure.

What was inside the SOD-Hut that required all this secrecy? Little was known in 1968 and not much more today. Literature about *Pueblo* refers to various pieces of equipment, such as gear to detect radar, radio, and other signals, tape decks (said to be valued at $60,000 each) on which to record intercepted signals, teletypes, and code machines. The code machine is perhaps the best-guarded and most secret device in the world. When set by inserting a cryptocard (a keypunch card something like a U.S. Treasury check) it can be used by anyone to send or receive messages. The presence of an operating code machine alone would compel the extreme secrecy about the SOD-Hut.

The best indication of what went on in *Pueblo*'s SOD-Hut came in September 1983 in an article in the Denver *Post*, which was reprinted in other newspapers. Its authors were T. Edward Eskelson and Tom Bernard, described as former "communications intelligence specialists." They were in the Air Force, not the Navy, and were describing the capabilities of the RC-135 planes that flew over the Sea of Japan at all times during the shooting down of KAL-007, the South Korean airliner. The RC-135 has a "super-advanced, ultra-secure communications system which is linked to the most sophisticated communications network in the world." The specialists aboard the plane can transmit messages over an extremely broad range of radio frequencies, including those used by other civilian and military aircraft, ships, ground stations, and air controllers, according to Eskelson and Bernard. During the Vietnam War such planes warned U.S. pilots when missiles were being fired at them. There is equipment on the plane to jam and "confuse" communications between pilots and ground stations or radar-controlled anti-aircraft systems. And much more.

The point made by Eskelson and Bernard was that the RC-135 flying over the Sea of Japan had ample capacity to warn the South Korean pilot of Flight 007 that he was off course or to jam communications between the Soviet fighter pilots and their ground stations so as to have prevented the loss of 269 lives. They asked why this wasn't done.

The SOD-Hut aboard *Pueblo* surely contained similar, highly advanced equipment capable of intercepting, recording, and transmitting in secure codes a wide range of electronic signals in the area in which it operated.

Who operated all this equipment? Who had access to the SOD-Hut? It was under the command of Lt. Stephen R. Harris. Under him were twenty-nine men. They consisted of two Marine sergeants, brought on at the last minute as interpreters of the Korean language, and twenty-seven specialists, usually referred to as Communications Technicians, or CTs, but the correct terminology is Communications Technical Technicians, or CTTs.

All of these men, although in the Navy or Marines, were trained and supervised by the National Security Agency, headquartered at Fort George G. Meade in Maryland, near Washington. So were Eskelson and Bernard, quoted above, although they were in the Air Force. As they write in their Denver *Post* article: "The RC-135 is a Strategic Air Command (SAC) long-range reconnaissance aircraft that carries an electronic and communications intercept platform. It is flown by a SAC crew, but the intercept platform is manned by some 30 U.S. Air Force Security Service personnel. In addition, several electronic warfare officers are assigned to the platform. All the personnel aboard the RC-135 are under the operational authority of the National Security Agency (NSA)." The similarities between the *Pueblo*'s SOD-Hut and the RC-135 are obvious.

The role of the National Security Agency in the *Pueblo* surrender will be discussed in pages to come. At this preliminary stage it need only be said that in 1968, as today, the NSA was the most supersecret agency in the U.S. government. Little was known about it in 1968. Indeed, most people had never heard of it. The NSA was created in 1952 by Executive Order of President Truman, an order which has remained highly classified to this day. It is the superior organization to the CIA and receives the lion's share of intelligence funds, an amount which is never made public. Appropriations are hidden throughout the federal budget and are unknown to most members of Congress.

All that NSA does is not known, but thanks to Bamford's book it is known that NSA is massively equipped to intercept virtually every electronic signal passing through the atmosphere, space, under the oceans, and even a great many wired ones. Through satellites, planes, ships, and powerful ground stations it communicates those messages and other information throughout the world. The NSA maintains the world's largest computer complex—Bamford writes that the computers are measured in "acres," not in numbers—for the purpose of breaking codes used by other nations. The NSA is also in charge of developing codes used by itself and other military and civilian agencies of the U.S. government. The codes are, it is hoped, unbreakable.

The crew of *Pueblo* was divided into two groups: thirty men who had access to the SOD-Hut, performed the ELINT operations, and took orders from the NSA, and fifty-one regular crewmen who ran the ship. (There were two civilians aboard.) There was friction between the two units, for the highly trained and very skilled CTs often considered themselves superior to the "swab jockeys" on the regular crew.

Thus, there was dual command aboard *Pueblo*. We think of a ship captain as lord and master, commanding all things aboard his vessel. But aboard *Pueblo* (and all other intelligence ships) the ship captain had no authority over the CTs as they ran the intelligence-gathering operations. This point is beyond dispute. Bucher admitted it and all other writers refer to it. But Bucher didn't like the dual command and in his book describes running quarrels with Steve Harris over who gave orders to CTs. Radioman Hayes said these quarrels occurred even in the presence of embarrassed enlisted men. Murphy lamented that he was in the middle. Bucher said he could not even inspect the SOD-Hut and was denied access to files.

The situation was worse than that. As captain, Bucher could not even receive his own radio messages. All incoming messages came to the SOD-Hut. In his book Bucher says he railed at Harris over delays in receiving even routine messages intended for him. Radioman Hayes stated in his interview that he could transmit, but not receive. He was restricted, furthermore, to sending weather reports and such.

As captain, Bucher was in a position analogous to that of a taxi driver—an analogy used by Murphy and others aboard *Pueblo*. Bucher took his ship and its highly skilled passengers in the SOD-Hut to where they wished to go and "parked" until they told him to go somewhere else. The ship had virtually no other function than its ELINT operations. For members of the regular crew, most of whom had never set foot inside the SOD-Hut and had only the vaguest idea of what went on there, sailing *Pueblo* was extremely dull duty.

The five admirals on the Court of Inquiry surely knew of the distinctive command structure aboard *Pueblo*. Even in retirement, Rear Adm. Daniel V. Gallery knew of the dual command and both described and decried it in his book, *The Pueblo Incident*. The Court of Inquiry visited *Pueblo*'s sister ship *Palm Beach* and thus surely acquainted itself with the difficulties in communication between the bridge and the SOD-Hut and in control of radio traffic.

Yet, in their findings, the five admirals recommended that Bucher be court-martialed for failing to organize the CTs and complete emergency destruction. Murphy was admonished for failing to lead the CTs. How they could be held responsible for the actions of a special detachment they did not control or give orders to is difficult to understand. On the surface, at least, the admirals were on safer terrain in recommending charges against Harris, who supposedly commanded the CTs. But in so doing, the admirals were acknowledging the separateness of command aboard *Pueblo*.

Who commanded the SOD-Hut? There is considerable evidence that Lieutenant Harris was only nominally in command and that true authority was invested in senior petty officers among the enlisted CTs. James A. Kell, identified as a communications chief, told the Court of Inquiry he gave the order to "commence emergency destruction in the research spaces." He said he never heard Bucher or Harris give such an order and did it on his own volition. Ralph D. Bouden, described as senior chief CT, testified (along with Kell and others) that he was ordered to stop burning documents after ten or fifteen minutes but didn't remember who gave the order. He testified that he was the last man to leave the SOD-Hut. Keys he carried were taken from him by North Koreans. A third man, CT First Class James D. Layton, identified as a shift supervisor, testified that he "told his men to start [destroying] the top secret material and work down." He also said he received no orders from Harris, nor did Harris participate in the destruction of materials. Others said Harris was not even present during the crucial period of emergency destruction. As this story unfolds, we will see that the role of Stephen Harris aboard *Pueblo* was surely strange. (Persons familiar with ELINT ship operations, who asked not to be identified, told me that command of the SOD-Hut is always invested in an enlisted man. He may actually be an officer, but he masquerades as an enlisted man. This is done precisely, I was told, so that the person in charge, the man who controls the vital code machine, cannot be easily identified in the event of capture. I was told the same technique is used by the Soviet Union aboard its "fishing trawlers." The real commander is an enlisted man and extremely difficult to pick out.)

Thus it may be seen that *Pueblo* was an old, slow, overcrowded ship with a highly unusual dual command structure. Bucher commanded the ship and fifty regular crewmen, but had no authority over the thirty CTs as they ran the SOD-Hut. Indeed, insofar as where the ship went and how long it remained, he took orders from someone in the SOD-Hut who acted on orders from the National Security Agency. Whether this person in the

SOD-Hut was Harris or some enlisted man is open to question.

Yet the dominant personality aboard *Pueblo* was Bucher, then thirty-eight. At this writing, I have never met Comdr. Lloyd M. "Pete" Bucher, nor have I talked with him by phone or corresponded with him. I have not even made an effort to contact him, although I would naturally like to chat with him some day. (While I was offered an opportunity to meet with Commander Bucher, I could not be alone with him and I was to be restricted in what questions I could ask. I declined the offer.)

For the record, and I mean this with utmost sincerity, I consider Commander Bucher to be a person of immense personal courage, an officer in the finest traditions of the United States Navy. One of my motives for writing this book is to finally, at long last, after twenty years, redeem the reputation, courage, and integrity of a man who has suffered inordinately in the service of his country. All he did was follow orders—"to the letter," as he repeatedly said—orders the significance of which he could not possibly understand. He tried to save his ship and his men, doing his best to protect them even during eleven months of captivity.

For doing so, he was charged with court-martial offenses and driven from the service he loved and wanted more than anything in his life. He endured personal calumny and the whispered word "coward." Most unsavory of all, he was compelled in the name of national security to conceal all he knew and to mouth and write a cover story which was foolishly implausible. Because Commander Bucher was up front, in the spotlight, telling the cover story, it may appear that in attacking the cover story I am attacking Bucher. I am not. Bucher, a good officer, did what he was told to do in the name of national security and the Navy's honor, risking his own veracity. He is to me a supremely fascinating and tragic individual. I trust his fellow Navy officers who denigrated him will now show a little of the courage he had and express their regrets for their treatment of him. It could have been any one of them. (Perhaps not. I was told one reason Bucher was chosen to command the ship to be surrendered is that he was a Naval Reserve officer. The NSA didn't want to ruin the career of an Annapolis man.)

At the time of the *Pueblo* seizure, Bucher was the stuff of heroes. Orphaned, adopted, losing that home, he ended up at Boys Town in Nebraska, excelling in both academics and athletics. From humble beginnings he carved out a naval career in diesel submarines, rising to executive officer. *Pueblo* was his first command. Even those who denigrated him admitted that he was an excellent navigator and ship handler, a fine mentor for young officers, and a superior handler of men.

The most credible and certainly flattering portrait of Bucher was drawn by Schumacher, the young lieutenant and operations officer, in his book. He describes a Renaissance-type individual, a blend of the physical and the introspective. Schumacher refers to Bucher as muscular with thick brown hair and bulging black eyes, a man "constantly in motion"—a portrait far removed from the haunted, wasted man released from North Korean prisons. "The captain projected power, lots of power," Schumacher wrote (p. 46). "His words conveyed the same kind of self-assurance and power as did his barrel chest, boxer's neck and muscled arms."

Bucher was a man of stunning contrasts. He enjoyed classical music while declaring Johnny Cash his favorite musician. In his cabin he kept both a collection of *Playboy* magazines and a complete set of Shakespeare's plays, reading both. His reading was wide-ranging and catholic, a few pages here, a chapter there on various subjects, much of which he apparently retained. He was a superior conversationalist—one is tempted to say enthralling, for he could blend information, ideas, even some degree of erudition with the ribald. Bucher was a raconteur.

His crew adored him. He was a by-the-book man, a stickler for having a job done right, and the right way was his way. A physical man, possessed of a generous rage, he was apparently an ass-chewer of note. But the crew loved him, if only because his origins made him one of "them." He had made it into the officers' ranks, offering them hope to do the same. And, when work was done, Bucher played hard. He was a two-fisted drinker when occasion permitted, quite capable of dressing up in costumes, being the life of the party, appreciating a well-turned thigh, and, it must be imagined, wearing a lampshade if that brought a laugh. Yet, as Schumacher points out (p. 53), "He had depth as well as spirit; he was no belly-up-to-the-bar seadog who could talk only about sex and promotions."

The crew's adoration of Bucher came principally from his unstinting defense of them. While at Bremerton, Washington, during the outfitting of *Pueblo*, Bucher had himself been caught in a gambling raid—and reprimanded. When his crew got in trouble, he rushed to their aid. One night the Shore Patrol picked up *Pueblo* crewmen for being out of uniform. Bucher got out of bed and went to the brig, chewing out the Shore Patrol as "chickenshit," even calling them "Nazis." By any standards, Bucher was a fascinating man, charismatic, a born leader, disciplined officer yet party-goer, physical and well read. As Vice Adm. Harold G. Bowen, president of the Court of Inquiry, would tell Trevor Armbrister, "That

man could have been the greatest hero in the history of the U.S. Navy."
Rear Adm. Marshall W. White, also on the Court, added, "If only he had
fired one shot. . . ."

Second in command as executive officer and navigator was Lt. Edward
R. Murphy, Jr. He was slender, slight of build, wore glasses. More shy,
introspective, his feelings more internalized, Murphy was a devout Christian Scientist and just about everything Bucher was not. Murphy was not
popular with the crew, perhaps because, as XO, his job was to carry out
the captain's orders—that is to say, do his dirty work.

Bucher and Murphy began by not getting along, never did find a way
to work together, and ultimately came to loathe each other. In their books
these two officers have at each other in the most unseemly, unsavory, and
truly embarrassing fashion. Murphy seeks to portray his captain as a
drunkard, womanizer, and nit-picking martinet who tried to run *Pueblo*
as though it were a submarine. He twice openly compares *Pueblo* to Herman Wouk's fictional *Caine* and Bucher to his "Captain Queeg." For his
part, Bucher portrays Murphy as disloyal, a sniveling coward, and
grossly incompetent. I personally want no part of this, except to say: so
much for the myth of brother officers in the service of our country.

The third key officer aboard was Lt. Stephen R. Harris, who supposedly commanded the "research detachment" in the SOD-Hut. The same
sort of opportunity for friction that existed between Bucher and Murphy
was also there between the captain and Harris. He came from a more privileged background, had graduated from Harvard, spoke four languages
including Russian, and had esoteric technical knowledge which was
Greek to Bucher. Moreover, Harris was quiet, scholarly, anything but a
lampshade-wearer, devoted to his recent bride, and deeply religious. He
was Protestant lay leader aboard the ship and conducted a worship service
attended by two other individuals.

Somehow Bucher and Steve Harris managed to find some accommodation so they could work together, despite the fact they quarreled regularly
and often about the dual command aboard the ship. The basis of the quarrel was that Bucher was determined to command all things aboard the
ship, as he felt a captain properly should, and "make sailors" out of the
CTs. Harris fought him at every turn, insisting his was a *detachment*, not
a department of the ship, separate from the regular crew and under his
command. He even obtained a letter from higher headquarters certifying
that, a letter which Bucher swore he would have countermanded when he
returned to base. Yet, to keep peace, Harris allowed his CTs to be used
for shipboard duties—at least until the ship arrived off North Korea. Then

he became all business and told Bucher to stuff it. Murphy (p. 113): "The change in Steve Harris was pronounced, too. He had a job to do; he wanted to do it, without interruptions. From here on in, his manner made clear, he wasn't about to take any of Bucher's gaff. He couldn't care less about the details of shipboard routine. Bucher was placed in a position somewhat analogous to that of a taxi driver, his passengers telling him where they wanted to stop and how long they wanted to stay at each place."

One of the oddities in Bucher's book is that while he admits the dual command aboard *Pueblo* and expresses at length his frustration over it, he also tries to maintain that he commanded all things aboard, including where the ship went and what type of intercept was performed. On page 168, Bucher reports this fascinating piece of dialogue between himself and Steve Harris:

"About 1000 hours, Steve came to my cabin where I was examining records.

"'Well, Captain, we are finally getting some interesting signals and recording them.'

"'That's great, Steve. I'm delighted that you've finally hit some pay dirt.'

"'I've got my best people in there now,' Steve said.

"'Is there anything I can do to position the ship more advantageously?' I asked.

"'Not that I'm aware of, sir, but I'll keep you cut in.'

"'Notify the OOD [Officer of the Deck] to the extent that he's cleared,' I ordered.

"'Will do, Captain.' Steve hastily departed with real purpose in his stride for the first time since we commenced Ichthyic 1 [the code name for the *Pueblo* operation]."

To me, Bucher's efforts to shoulder responsibility for a detachment he did not command are admirable. It is also pathetic that the Navy forced him into a position to have to do it. No matter how much evidence there was to the contrary, the Navy was simply never going to admit any of its ship captains were in anything less than *total* command. In a word, the hell with Bucher's good name, reputation, and career.

There were three other officers aboard *Pueblo*. Lt. (jg) F. Carl Schumacher, Jr., twenty-four and unmarried, had served aboard a refrigerated cargo ship in the Western Pacific. Although listed as operations and communications officer, he was greatly inexperienced and by his own description had virtually nothing to do with the ship's communications or its ELINT operations, which were run from the SOD-Hut. When he came aboard he didn't even have a security clearance to know the ship's purpose.

Ensign Timothy Harris was twenty-one and recently married. He had dropped out of Navy flight training and was on his first assignment. He had little knowledge of ships and was in a learning experience. His primary job was supply officer.

The most experienced and capable person on *Pueblo*, certainly in terms of surface ships, was Chief Warrant Officer Gene Howard Lacy, the engineering officer. He was thirty-six, erect, dignified, and, in Schumacher's words, "often mistaken for the ship's captain." A veteran looking forward to retirement, thoroughly professional, he would bear stoically both captivity and, upon release, some extremely distasteful remarks by his best friend aboard ship, Commander Bucher.

3

WHERE WAS PUEBLO?

Where was *Pueblo* when seized?

Surely that question, in an age of navigation by satellite, ought to be known, but it isn't. I have accumulated a significant list of locations where *Pueblo* was said to have been when seized.

Geography first. Korea, both North and South, is a peninsula sticking out like an attenuated thumb on the land mass of Manchuria in China. The thumb is pinched at about the 39th parallel to form Choson Bay along the east coast. Wonsan, North Korea's major east coast seaport and a steelmaking center, sits at the base of the bay. A natural, deep-water port, Wonsan is further shielded by Yonghung Bay. This is formed by the Hado Peninsula on the north, the end of which is marked by a lighthouse. Another smaller peninsula, called Kalma, just to the east of Wonsan, sticks into the bay from the south. The area in between, dotted by islands, forms the entrance to Wonsan harbor. It is guarded by submarine nets. Farther out is Yo Island, about ten miles from Wonsan, lying just east and a few miles south of the lighthouse. Yo Island is a rocky crag containing a small settlement. To the north and slightly to the east is the flatter Ung Island, claimed by North Korea.

Thus, the twelve-mile territorial waters claimed by North Korea extend twelve miles from Ung Island—a good twenty-five miles from Wonsan.

Bucher writes in his book—and Murphy and others agree—that when the North Korean subchaser approached at about noon on January 23, *Pueblo*'s position was checked and double-checked to make certain the ship was in international waters. It was, comfortably so. Bucher

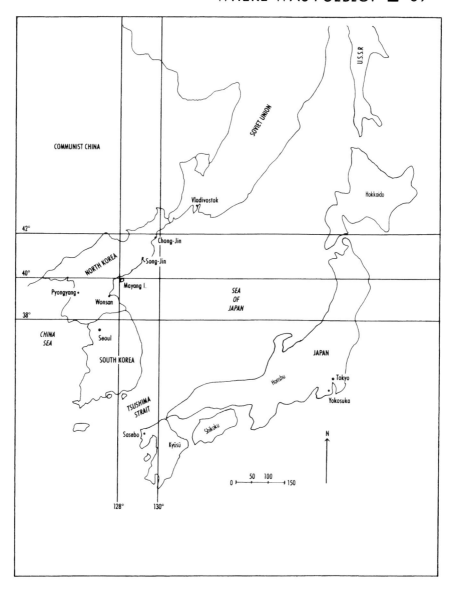

COMMUNIST CHINA

SOVIET UNION

U.S.S.R

Hokkaido

Vladivostok

42°

Chong-Jin

NORTH KOREA

Song-Jin

40°

Mayang I.

Pyongyang

SEA
OF
JAPAN

Wonsan

38°

CHINA
SEA

Seoul

SOUTH KOREA

JAPAN

Honshu

Tokyo

Yokosuka

TSUSHIMA
STRAIT

Shikoku

N

Sasebo

Kyūsū

0   50   100   150

128°

130°

writes that he personally went to the chart room to verify the ship's position, plotted by Quartermaster Charles B. Law and confirmed by *Pueblo*'s radar. Bucher (p. 178): "*Pueblo* was now a tenth less than sixteen miles off the island of Hung Do."*

As navigation officer, Murphy is more precise in his book: "39 degrees 25.2 minutes North, 127 degrees 55.0 minutes East, 15.8 miles off Ung Do." This was the position Murphy arrived at when "we reached our operating area about 1000 [10 A.M. on the morning of January 23] and lay-to dead in the water while the CTs got to work." Murphy adds: "Although some low-lying haze to the west obscured our visual observations, our position was easily verifiable by radar, which showed the distinct outlines of the peninsula of Hado Pando and the two off-shore islands, Yo Do and Ung Do, the latter being closest to us, the other farther south."

At 1145 hours Murphy took the noon position and reported it to Bucher in the wardroom where he went to lunch. Shortly thereafter Quartermaster Law reported the first sighting of the subchaser. Murphy: "Spooning another helping of food onto his plate, Bucher told Law to call back if the ship came within three miles. He also ordered him to light off [turn on] the radar and verify the position I had given him just fifteen minutes earlier. Law called back less than five minutes later. My position was exact, and the [North Korean] ship was now less than three miles away and closing fast."

Ed Brandt, who interviewed Law for his book, reports something different (p. 36): "Law lit off the radar to confirm the *Pueblo*'s position, then went to the pilot house to look at the charts. He came back to the bridge and reported to Bucher that the *Pueblo* was 15.2 [emphasis mine] miles from Ung Do. Bucher said, 'Very well' . . . ."

The precision with which Bucher and Murphy located *Pueblo* is also undermined by other writers. In particular Armbrister describes great navigational difficulties aboard *Pueblo*. He refers to Bucher, the old submariner, as "excellent," Murphy as "capable," and says Law "consid-

*Korean place names reach English in a variety of spellings. What Bucher calls Hung Do is usually spelled Ung Do. Since the word *do* in Korean means "island," its use is superfluous in English. Therefore (except in quotes) this book will speak of Ung Island. This also applies to Yo Do. In English we would say Yo Island. In Korean, the word *man* means "bay," so the Korean name is Yonghung-man. We will speak of Yonghung Bay and the larger Choson Bay. The Korean word for peninsula is *pando.* We will speak of Hado (also written as Hodo and Nodo) Peninsula. Most library atlases, based upon the Chinese and Japanese who controlled Korea for so long, have different names for all these places. For example, Hado Peninsula is frequently called Taegant. To simplify the Korean language further, this book also omits the diacritical marks which alter the Korean pronunciation.

ered himself, perhaps justifiably, as one of the better navigators in the Pacific Fleet.'' But there were difficulties nevertheless. Bucher and Murphy had other duties and Law ''—who was averaging eighteen hours a day on the bridge—desperately needed relief.''

The reason Law needed relief stemmed from a royal foul-up and a large flap aboard *Pueblo*, reported at length by Armbrister. To enter the chart room, a person had to have a Secret clearance. This is true of all Navy ships. Bucher, Murphy, and Law were all cleared for Secret, but Quartermaster Third Class Alvin H. Plucker and other men on the navigation team were not. Way back in June 1967, Bucher had told Murphy to request clearances for these men. Murphy told Yeoman First Class Armando M. Canales to take care of it. Apparently overworked and underpaid, Canales neglected to do so. Bucher found this out on a visit to the ship's office in January. The clearance requests had been typed but never mailed. Bucher chewed Murphy's ass ''something awful,'' a crewman told Armbrister. (This incident apparently was the last straw in relations between the two men, and they thereafter remained in a state of antipathy.)

Bucher made a second visit to Canales' office. He told Armbrister that he said to Canales, ''I'm gonna inspect this office, so open up all your drawers and let me check what you got down there.'' He did. As Bucher told Armbrister, ''I found mail from back in June that hadn't been distributed yet. And this was January. There had never been an officer control data report (OCDR) submitted, and this was something that had to be done every month. Well, none had ever left that ship. I was so goddamn mad. . . . I spent a whole night sleeping on it, then had Canales in for a Captain's Mast [a nonjudicial disciplinary proceeding] and busted him. Ed [Murphy] deserved to be busted, too. Well, I really had his ass.'' (In the crewlist of his book, Bucher says Canales is a Yeoman First Class. Bucher either never busted him or gave him back his stripes.)

With the trained navigators lacking clearances to enter the chart room, Bucher pressed untrained men, who did have clearances for Secret, into navigation duties. They were Photographer Larry Mack, Signalman Wendell Leach, and Electronics Technician Clifford C. Nolte. A cameraman, a flag raiser, and a repairman of electronic gear ''had to become instant navigators,'' as Armbrister put it. They had problems. Mack told Armbrister he had difficulty operating the loran. ''If I got two good fixes in a four-hour watch, I was doing pretty good.''

(The loran is a navigational device in which pulsed signals sent out by two pairs of radio stations are used to determine the position of a ship or plane. By 1968, the loran had been supplemented or superseded by "keying a bird," or picking up a signal from a satellite. It was easier and far more accurate than loran. No mention of satellite navigation is made in any *Pueblo* stories.)

Armbrister (pp. 25-6): "What puzzled Mack even more was that he was supposed to enter all his fixes—the bad as well as the good—in the quartermaster's log. He couldn't erase the obvious mistakes. He and [Signalman] Leach talked about this, and one night Leach mentioned it to Murphy. 'Sir, are you sure you want us to log these erroneous fixes?'

"Naval regulations were very specific about this. 'Yes,' Murphy said."

What happened to the log and charts? Murphy writes (p. 138) that he told Quartermaster Law "to destroy everything but our logs, charts, loran books, and other navigational records. By firing on us while we were in international waters the North Koreans had violated every accepted law of the sea; it seemed to me that in some way they would have to justify their actions. Thus it was extremely important that all our navigational records be preserved, as they constituted evidence that at no point had we intruded into claimed territorial waters."

Quartermaster Law told Ed Brandt the exact opposite of what Murphy reports. Brandt (pp. 50-51): "Law, meanwhile, had left the pilot house and gone to Lieutenant Murphy's stateroom. He wanted to be sure the charts of the track of the *Pueblo* since it left Sasebo would be destroyed. He found them on Murphy's desk and handed them out to some CTs who were burning material in the passageway." Obviously, both Murphy and Law cannot be correct, one wanting to preserve the logs, the other wanting "to be sure" they were destroyed. (As we will see, there is grave doubt anyone aboard *Pueblo* burned anything of significance. The North Koreans recovered the logs and charts of the ship and used them in an effort to show *Pueblo* was in their territorial waters. Law and ultimately Bucher are endeavoring to indicate the North Korean claims are false by saying the logs and charts were destroyed. Too bad they didn't get their stories straight.)

The certainty with which Murphy and Bucher place *Pueblo* 15.8 miles from Ung Island is challenged by some contrary visual evidence. In an interview, Radioman Hayes, who was on the bridge, said he thought *Pueblo* was in international waters. He could see an island but it "seemed a long ways away." The night before the seizure the lights of Wonsan were "very bright." That same night, Murphy writes, he "could see the lights of Wonsan" off to his left.

These observations do not suggest a ship 15.8 miles from Ung. Sailors use a rule of thumb in estimating distance: if a six-foot person stands at sea level on a clear day, the horizon he sees is twelve miles away. Again, *Pueblo* was a small ship. If located 15.8 miles from Ung, it was over 25 miles from Wonsan. It is extremely unlikely that the lights of that city (screened behind Kalma Peninsula) would have been "very bright" at that distance—or even visible at all. Even in daylight—particularly if there was a haze to the west, as Murphy reports—the rather flat Ung, or even the craggy Yo Island, were unlikely to be visible from 15.8 miles away.

One more item of argumentation. Bucher always said he followed his orders "to the letter." But these orders, in so far as they are declassified and known, contain an innate conflict. *Pueblo*'s orders were called "Ichthyic One Sailing Order," Ichthyic being the code name for the operation, and came from the commander in chief, Pacific Fleet. As discussed by Schumacher* in his book, one part of those orders instructed *Pueblo* to remain at least thirteen miles from the coast of North Korea. But an earlier part of the order, number 003120.24A, authorized a *three* mile limit. Schumacher did not print the order, which was classified, but had the following to say: "C. Commander in Chief Pacific Fleet Instructions 003120.24A (These classified instructions—which the North Koreans captured—detailed, country by country, how close to Communist shores American ships could go. One part states that 'patrols to the three mile limit off North Korea are authorized.' The North Koreans later used the phrase 'three mile limit' to prove that the *Pueblo* had been ordered to violate their territorial waters, ignoring the specific orders to stay at least thirteen miles from North Korean land. . . .)"

The fleet orders were surely ambiguous. Don't go closer to North Korea than thirteen miles, yet "patrols to the three mile limit off North Korea are authorized." Whether or not he did, Bucher could have sailed as close as three miles to land and still followed his orders "to the letter."

Again, where was *Pueblo* when seized?

Murphy, the navigation officer, was specific (p. 122 of his book). *Pueblo* was 15.8 miles off Ung Island, lying dead in the water, when the North Korean subchaser approached. This was verified by radar. Bucher,

---

*Schumacher's book has the most complete text of *Pueblo*'s sailing order. The excerpts in the appendix of Bucher's book are greatly attenuated.

The word *ichthyic*, uncommon in English, is surely worthy of a spelling bee. The best-known form of the word is *ichthyology*, which is the study of fish. The code name ichthyic could best be translated into everyday English as "fishy."

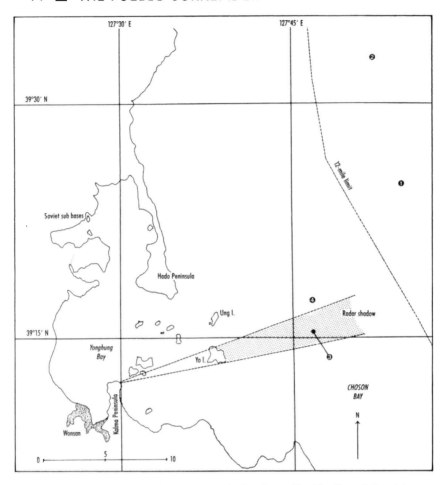

In this scale map of the Wonsan area (1) is where *Pueblo* first claimed it was when seized, 39°25.5′ North, 127°54.9′ East, 15.8 miles from Ung Island; (2) is the "revised" position given in its distress call, 39°34′ North, 127°54′ East, about nine miles farther north; (3) is the location arrived at by subtracting 10 minutes of a degree from position 1, placing *Pueblo* in the radar shadow of Yo Island about 15.8 miles from Wonsan, not Ung Island; and (4) is the place where the North Koreans say they captured *Pueblo*, 39°17.4′ North, 127°46.9′ East, 7.6 miles from Ung Island. These are but four of numerous locations given for *Pueblo*, leading to the question: Where was *Pueblo* when seized? All the positions must be labeled as "claims." There is no "proof" for any of them. It may also be seen from this map that when writers place *Pueblo* "twenty miles north and east of Wonsan" or "twenty-five miles southeast of Wonsan," they are locating the ship well within the territorial waters of North Korea.

whom everyone describes as a superior navigator, agreed, although he gave the distance as 15.9 miles. When Bucher sent the first Pinnacle message that *Pueblo* was under harassment, he gave the ship's position as that above. This first Pinnacle message was sent by *Pueblo* to Kamiseya, Japan, at 1254 hours, nearly an hour after the North Korean subchaser appeared.

At 1328, now an hour and a half into the incident, *Pueblo* teletyped Kamiseya that "NORTH KOREAN WAR VESSELS PLAN TO OPEN FIRE" and gave the ship's position as 39 degrees, 25.5 minutes North, 127 degrees, 54.9 minutes East.

The difference in these numbers may seem slight, but in these waters a minute of a degree is about one nautical mile on the earth's surface. Thus, from its original position, *Pueblo* moved three-tenths of a mile to the north and one-tenth of a mile to the west. This cannot be accounted for by drift since the current runs southeast.

Two minutes later, at 1330, *Pueblo* radioed "WE ARE BEING BOARDED" and gave a "revised ship's position." *Pueblo* was now at 39 degrees, 34 minutes North, 127 degrees, 54 minutes East.

The difference in position is surely cardinal. *Pueblo* is now approximately eight and a half miles farther north and almost a mile to the west, closer to North Korea. As observed earlier, this is an impossible distance for *Pueblo* or any other ship to travel in so short a time. Something has to be wrong somewhere.

In its original announcement of the *Pueblo* seizure, the Pentagon gave the ship's position as 39 degrees, 25 minutes North and 127 degrees, 54.3 minutes East, saying it was about twenty-five miles off the Korean coast.

This position places *Pueblo* three-tenths of a mile to the south and seven-tenths of a mile west of where Murphy reckoned, a half-mile south and six-tenths of a mile west of *Pueblo*'s first distress position, and nine miles south and three-tenths of a mile west of the revised distress position.

For their part, the North Koreans claimed they seized *Pueblo* at 39 degrees, 17.4 minutes North and 127 degrees, 46.9 minutes East. This is approximately eight miles to the south and eight miles to the west of the position calculated by Murphy. It is almost seventeen miles to the south and over seven miles to the west of *Pueblo*'s second radioed position in its distress call—as well as deep inside territorial waters claimed by North Korea.

Where was *Pueblo?* I am merely suggesting that the five admirals on the Court of Inquiry should have picked up on the various positions given by *Pueblo* and the Pentagon, as well as on the navigational problems aboard the ship, and investigated to determine precisely where *Pueblo* was when seized. In an era of navigation by satellite, precise location within three feet is easily determined. I attach significance to the fact neither the Court of Inquiry—nor anyone else—ever located the ship.

I also attach significance to Commander Bucher's first words uttered upon his release. Recall his statement to a Pentagon official: "Do you think we violated North Korean waters?" The official told Bucher he didn't. Bucher replied, "Well, that's right. We doctored that evidence. You look at it carefully and you'll see how we doctored it."

"That evidence" was never released to the public, so it is impossible to know with certainty how it was "doctored." But it is possible to theorize.

One theory was offered by an Air Force pilot-navigator. He knew nothing about the *Pueblo* incident and was simply helping me pinpoint the various published coordinates on the accompanying map. I mentioned my efforts to try to figure out the "doctoring." Without hesitation, the pilot replied, "Simply subtract ten minutes of a degree from the reported position and see what you get." Instead of being at 39 degrees 25.2 minutes N and 127 degrees 55.0 minutes E, as Murphy calculated, suppose *Pueblo* was at 39 degrees 15.2 minutes N and 127 degrees 45.0 minutes E. This places *Pueblo* about ten miles closer to Wonsan, less than three miles from where the North Koreans say they captured it. It also coincides with some—though not all—of the maneuvers Bucher claims he made.

This theory of "doctoring" also does something else. It places *Pueblo* in an advantageous position for electronic snooping. About seven miles to the west is Yo Island, a rocky crag (unlike the flat Ung Island) which could screen *Pueblo* from the North Korean radar station on the tip of Kalma Peninsula. Thus, *Pueblo* could lie undetected within the radar "shadow" of Yo Island.

I do not claim this theory is correct. In pages to come, when *Pueblo*'s last desperate maneuvers are reported, we will examine the theory again. In my view it doesn't matter a whole lot to the *Pueblo* story whether the ship was in North Korean or international waters. But the issue is part of the *Pueblo* story and must be considered.

4

COVER STORY: A MAIDEN VOYAGE

Pueblo **left San Diego** November 6, 1967, entered Pearl Harbor November 14, left there November 18, arrived Yokosuka (pronounced YoSOOka), Japan, December 1, departed there January 6, 1968, for Sasebo, left Sasebo at 0600 hours January 11, 1968, bound for a mission off the coast of North Korea. It was her *first* and *only* mission.

Every word uttered or written about *Pueblo* gives these dates for the movement of the ship. These dates are supported by written orders from the Navy.

Nonetheless, a great deal of evidence suggests that *Pueblo* was *not* on its maiden voyage and that it had operated in the Sea of Japan prior to January 1968. This matter of whether *Pueblo* was on its maiden voyage is of some importance, so we must pursue it.

According to the cover story, *Pueblo* was a newly outfitted ship with all new equipment in the SOD-Hut, the latest in electronic snooping gear. A greener crew is hard to imagine. Bucher was on his first captaincy, even his first surface vessel in thirteen years. He came from submarines. Murphy was acting as exec officer for the first time and had been on shore duty. Harris was new to his job and had gone back to Washington for some schooling. Communications Chief Kell told the Court of Inquiry he had been aboard only twenty days prior to the capture. Senior Chief CT Bouden told the five admirals he was on his first shipboard duty. Radioman Hayes said he came aboard ten minutes before sailing from Yokosuka. Only one CT had ever served on an ELINT ship before, according to Murphy. Indeed, only four members of the entire complement had ever been to sea before. One seaman was placed aboard *Pueblo* after only eleven days of boot camp!

Nine men are reported to have come aboard *Pueblo* just for its last voyage. This is more than 10 percent of the crew, making it look as though one crew sailed it across the Pacific and another took it to North Korea.

The nine men are significant and need to be listed. One was Radioman Hayes, the last man to come aboard.

In Japan, the two civilian oceanographers, Donnie Tuck and Harry Iredale III, came aboard with their equipment. They figure prominently, of which more later. Also making a date with history were Marine Sergeants Hammond and Chicca, both Robert J. They came aboard as Korean interpreters, but it had been two years since language school and they were rusty. They couldn't read the language without a dictionary and they couldn't understand spoken Korean. It was too fast and gibberish. They are also important members of the cast of the *Pueblo* story.

Finally, four absolutely key CTs came aboard in Japan to work in the SOD-Hut (technically six, with Chicca and Hammond). One was Communications Chief James Kell, who ordered emergency destruction to begin and heard someone order it to end ten to fifteen minutes later. Second was CT First Class David Ritter. He would testify to the Court of Inquiry that he never saw Harris in the SOD-Hut and that no one was supervising emergency destruction during the seizure. Third was CT First Class Don E. Bailey. He was the man on the teletype to Kamiseya, the author of *Pueblo*'s half of the radio transcript, the man who made all those "mistakes" about when *Pueblo* was boarded. The fourth was Ralph McClintock. In the crewlist initially released by the Navy to the press, he was listed as a "communications chief." Thereafter, every other list demoted him to CT Third Class, the lowest rank reserved for men just out of CT school in Pensacola.

Ed Brandt, who is the only person to report these last-minute personnel changes, says Bailey came aboard to straighten out the communications difficulties aboard *Pueblo*, McClintock "volunteered" to replace a man who had appendicitis, and Kell "volunteered" to replace a chief petty officer "who was due to be transferred and whose replacement had not yet arrived." Brandt gives no explanation for Ritter's arrival.

My point is this: if *Pueblo* was just over from the States, why are men "due to be transferred" already? Why so many replacements just for this one voyage? Why such an inexperienced crew?

Persons familiar with ELINT operations say it is patently ridiculous to believe the NSA would send out such a ship and crew to eavesdrop off unfriendly shores. The equipment on such a ship is highly esoteric and specialized. New equipment must be tested and carefully calibrated, and it invariably has "bugs" and "gremlins" which must be identified by receiving stations and corrected. The CTs who operate it must be carefully trained on the specific gear they operate. The capabilities of the ship, including the type of intercept it performs, are highly classified. The ship is transmitting in the most secure and sensitive U.S. codes. The NSA would simply never jeopardize its most precious codes and intercept capabilities by sending out a green, untrained crew on a ship making its maiden voyage. One example was given. Every nation on earth protects its radio signals by using a directional antenna. This sends a very narrow signal over a two-degree arc. For the signal to get through, the antenna must be precisely aligned with the receiving station. And if the antenna is not properly set, it will send out a wide signal to the rear and each side. The message can be picked up over a wide area and its security is lost.

These persons familiar with ELINT ship operations state emphatically that a vessel such as *Pueblo* would have gone through a long period, many weeks or months, during which its equipment was checked, repaired, and refined and the crew trained and the accuracy of its intercept verified.

Every written account of *Pueblo* contains references to events aboard the ship which are surely curious for a vessel just over from the States and on its maiden voyage.

Pueblo had gross difficulties in reaching the ground station at Kamiseya, Japan, via teletype. Most of a night was spent in efforts to establish radio contact with Kamiseya. Brandt reports that radio communications with Japan were so bad that Bailey was put aboard *Pueblo* just before its last voyage to straighten out the difficulties. Bailey was from Kamiseya and an expert on shipboard communications. If *Pueblo* was on its maiden voyage, just over from San Diego, how did anyone know it had all these communications difficulties?

Lieutenant Schumacher says he replaced David Behr, an officer of the same rank, at Bremerton, Washington. Officers were being replaced so quickly? Bucher says he was due for replacement shortly after *Pueblo* returned from its North Korean missions. He had supposedly just taken command. How could his tour of duty be up so quickly? Murphy and Bucher refer to a rendezvous with a tanker. *Pueblo* didn't carry enough fuel to make it from Hawaii to Japan?

In his book (pp. 153–4), Bucher describes in detail *Pueblo*'s last voyage from Yokosuka to Sasebo and on up to Korea. "Our destination was the northernmost of our intelligence-gathering area, code-named Pluto and lying close to the North Korean–Soviet Russian line near Vladivostok. It was nearly six hundred miles of steaming across the widest portion of the Sea of Japan; under optimum conditions which could hardly be expected this time of year, it would take some sixty hours at our eleven knot cruising speed. . . . Toward afternoon, *we changed course to angle up the middle of the Sea of Japan* [emphasis mine] and by early evening found ourselves out of sight of land with lowering skies and freshening winds laced with snow flurries.''

Bucher then describes a violent storm. ''While trying to make as much progress as possible toward Mars it became a matter of holding our own and not actually losing ground. For hours we tacked from one course to the other like an old sailing ship beating her way to windward. Some of our tacks were very frightening when huge waves caught us abeam and thrust *Pueblo* over in a 50-degree roll. As usual, seasickness was rampant. . . .''

Murphy, the executive officer of *Pueblo*, also describes the voyage (pp. 109-10): ''On Bucher's instructions, I charted a course that would keep us close to the Japanese coast the first day (after leaving Sasebo). . . . The second day, January 12, *we made a run for it across the Sea of Japan toward Korea* [emphasis mine]. But there was no outrunning the storm. As *we headed northward, parallel to the Korean coastline* [emphasis mine], its icy blasts remained a constant companion.''

Clearly the ship captain and his second in command are not describing the same voyage. Bucher says he sailed up the middle of the Sea of Japan. Murphy says they crossed the narrow Tsushima Strait and sailed up the coast of Korea. If *Pueblo* was on its maiden and only voyage to North Korean waters, how can the accounts vary so much? Surely it would have been cemented in the memory of both officers.

In his version of the voyage, Murphy writes (p. 110): ''As we moved north, the weather grew colder, and shipboard activities settled into a routine—watches, meals, afternoon and evening movies on the mess decks or in the officers' wardroom. It could have been any routine voyage. But it wasn't, and though not everyone knew our sail order, there was a different feeling aboard ship—not apprehension exactly, rather a kind of waiting.

''In the crew's quarters the poker game rarely stopped, one man dropping out to be replaced by another.

''Boredom began to set in.'' (Schumacher writes [p. 44], ''For some reason, Monopoly was the *Pueblo*'s game—not poker or acey-ducey or chess.'')

This is astounding. Here is the *Pueblo* crew, fresh over from the States, most of them never to sea before and on their maiden voyage, highly *bored*. They play poker around the clock. The voyage, according to Murphy, was "routine" with a "different feeling" aboard ship. Different from what? Clearly, Murphy is describing the actions and attitudes of a crew, not on its maiden voyage, but which has been on many boring voyages.

There is more. Bucher described to Trevor Armbrister his gross upset when he discovered mail and other reports in the desk of Yeoman Canales. Some of it dated back seven months to June 1967. At that time *Pueblo* was supposedly in Bremerton, Washington, being outfitted. Yeoman Canales was incredibly inefficient if he did not mail letters in Bremerton, San Diego, Honolulu, or Japan and carried them to North Korea. It is simply easier to believe that in June 1967 *Pueblo* was somewhere on the high seas where the letters couldn't be mailed, and were then stuck in a drawer and forgotten.

Among the items in the drawer were the requests for security clearances of Quartermaster Third Class Plucker and others on his navigational team. This caused gross difficulties on *Pueblo*. Untrained men had to be pressed into navigational duties. This is curious. Surely Bucher must have discovered his lack of cleared navigators on the voyage from San Diego to Japan. It would have been a simple matter to ask naval headquarters in Japan about the delay in granting clearances or to request their replacement by men who had been cleared. After all, Radioman Hayes came aboard at the last minute to replace a radioman whom Bucher had busted. This whole incident suggests that either the officers and crew of *Pueblo* were extremely incompetent or that the ship was long at sea and not on its maiden voyage.

One final piece of evidence. In printing the declassified portions of *Pueblo*'s Sailing Orders called Ichthyic One, as well as commenting on them, Schumacher writes (p. 67): "1. Ichthyic One formerly Pinkroot One. (These were the present and former code names of the *Pueblo*'s eavesdropping operations . . . .)" The use of the word *former* to refer to Pinkroot One clearly suggests that *Pueblo* was *not* on its first mission in January, but had been on previous missions codenamed Pinkroot. Still another "former" code name—Clickbeetle—is given by Armbrister (p. 65).

A large question must be asked: Why claim *Pueblo* was on its one and only voyage into North Korean waters if it wasn't? Why go to all the trouble of creating orders to "prove" *Pueblo* was in one place when it was in another?

Answers are not hard to find. Because of the Israeli attack on USS *Liberty* in June 1967 and many other protests about our electronic snooping—the Red Chinese had made so many the United States had virtually ceased reporting them—the United States wanted to minimize the extent of our ELINT operations. Toward this end, *Pueblo* was portrayed as old, unseaworthy, on its maiden voyage, manned by a green crew. It never accomplished anything of value. After its capture by the North Koreans, the whole "experiment" in ELINT ships was mothballed.

The desire to minimize our ELINT operations—and perhaps protect our ships from the fates of *Liberty* and *Pueblo*—the cover story became rather elaborate. Supposedly, prior to 1967, the entire U.S. ELINT fleet consisted of one vessel, USS *Banner* (AGER-1), which went into service in 1965. Two ships, *Pueblo* and *Palm Beach*, were outfitted together at Bremerton. *Pueblo* was to sail to the Pacific to replace *Banner*. *Palm Beach* headed for the Atlantic (from San Diego) where, Bucher reports in his book, it suffered "total breakdown" and never went beyond Norfolk, Virginia. (Somehow, *Palm Beach* made it back to San Diego, where the five admirals on the Court of Inquiry inspected it in person.) After the loss of *Pueblo, Banner* was decommissioned in 1970. The whole ELINT experiment was abandoned as useless and a waste of money. Bucher writes that he disagreed with this decision.

There is compelling evidence that the U.S. ELINT fleet consisted of more than *Banner, Pueblo*, and the useless *Palm Beach*. At least three other, larger, intelligence-gathering ships are mentioned by Bamford in *The Puzzle Palace: Liberty, Jamestown*, and *Georgetown*. In its cover article on the *Pueblo* seizure, *Time* referred to eighty ELINT ships in our "ferret fleet." When Bucher told the Court of Inquiry that his ship contained no automatic destruct mechanisms and CTs had to use axes and sledgehammers to destroy their top secret equipment, the Navy promptly announced it was installing destruct devices on *fifteen* similar ships.

That ELINT ships still operate today, although perhaps in altered form, is suggested by more recent events. In November 1984, the USS *Nimitz*, a nuclear-powered aircraft carrier, was ordered to steam for Cuban waters. It did so on an emergency basis, leaving a thousand crew members behind on shore leave in the Virgin Islands. The *Nimitz*, along with the guided missile cruiser USS *Arkansas*, was dispatched to rescue a civilian "oceanographic survey boat," the 105-foot *Seaward Explorer*, and its five-man civilian crew. It had drifted into Cuban waters. A Cuban patrol boat was attempting to tow it into port when it got into difficulties itself. A U.S. Coast Guard vessel sped into Cuban waters and brought out the

Seaward Explorer. There was a mysterious, never explained fire aboard the rescued vessel. Reporters, understandably perplexed as to why our mightiest ship was dispatched to rescue such a minuscule civilian vessel, recalled the incident in September when the Soviet Union seized the *Frieda K.*, a "supply vessel" with five Alaskans aboard, which strayed into their waters in the Bering Sea. The ship and crew were held for a week.

The similarities between the *Seaward Explorer* and *Pueblo* are apparent, especially that mysterious fire. Certain it is the Navy did not send any ship, let alone an aircraft carrier, to rescue *Pueblo*.

It is understandable that the Navy and the NSA wanted to minimize the extent of our ELINT operations and that they would refrain from identifying any more of the eavesdropping ships than they had to, but to insist that our *entire* fleet consisted of *Banner* prior to 1968 is hard to believe. We were, after all, fighting a major war in Vietnam and using every means at our disposal to intercept enemy radio, radar, and other communications.

The USS *Banner* sails through the *Pueblo* story as a gray ghost. It, too, was built in World War II as an Army supply ship and converted into an ELINT vessel. It was almost identical in size and appearance to *Pueblo*. It is said to have made eighteen missions off the Soviet Union and China.

The activities of *Banner* influenced all that happened aboard *Pueblo*, its replacement. In *The Last Voyage of the USS Pueblo*, Ed Brandt, who interviewed fifteen crewmen, wrote (p. 24): "The *Pueblo* crew, growing daily more savvy about the ship's mission, heard other things from the *Banner* [which was docked next to *Pueblo* at Yokosuka in early January 1968], which had been on several intelligence missions in the general area in preceding months.

"The *Banner* had undergone considerable harassment from Soviet ships, and on one occasion had been signaled: HEAVE TO, OR I WILL FIRE ON YOU. The *Pueblo* crew learned that the *Banner* had been lightly brushed by a Russian destroyer on one occasion, and that once it had been surrounded by Chinese fishing boats, their guns trained on the American ship. The story went that the captain of the *Banner*, Comdr. Charles R. Clark, got out of that predicament by pointing his ship at the nearest boat and ordering full speed ahead. If the stories worried the men of the *Pueblo*, they didn't let on, although there was some joking about the North Koreans throwing a line on the ship and towing it into Wonsan Harbor."

This story told to Ed Brandt is important because it reveals that the men of *Pueblo* knew, prior to their own voyage, that *Banner* had had several narrow scrapes with Russian and Chinese forces and that *Pueblo* could expect the same thing. In other words, the men of *Pueblo* anticipated "harassment" from Communist ships. More importantly, the part of the story about Captain Clark of the *Banner* pointing his ship at the nearest Chinese boat and ordering full speed ahead to escape harassment indicates what Bucher may have done with *Pueblo*. This story appears only in Brandt's book. Neither Bucher nor any other *Pueblo* officers mention it. I believe this to be an example of the crewmen of *Pueblo* trying to tell us what happened during the seizure.

Bucher was also well acquainted with the history of *Banner*. In his book Bucher describes how Commander Clark had briefed him on *Banner*'s missions. Clark carried a tape recorder into which he described his encounters with opposing ships. Bucher listened to those tapes and wrote (p. 130):

"One occasion which specially impressed me occurred in the China Sea, with hostile ships circling her, when *both* engines broke down, leaving her drifting helplessly while the engineers sweated blood to regain propulsion. A Seventh Fleet destroyer some four hundred miles away was started toward her assistance and Fifth Air Force fighter-bombers were on strip alert to provide air cover in case the CHICOMs [Chinese communists] made a serious attack. The support was comforting, but too far away for immediate effectiveness, one hour for the aircraft and nearly twenty for the destroyer to reach her position. The tension was agonizing until her engineers got her old 'rock-crushers' going again and she was able to pull out of a very tight situation.

"Chuck [Clark] confirmed the fact that on the one occasion he had passed along it, he had encountered no hostile reactions at all off the North Korean coast. Near the Soviet and Red China territorial waters (he *never* intruded) they invariably sent out shadowing units, either armed auxiliaries or destroyers, which did not hesitate to intimidate him with maneuvers which threatened collision and signals which included HEAVE TO OR I WILL FIRE backed up by guns manned and ready to shoot. In each case his only defense had been to stick as closely as possible to the rules of the road as they apply to International Waters and *proceed on his course* [emphasis mine] and business according to his orders: in each case, the hostile forces had stopped their harassment just short of outright attack. It was nerve-wracking, but I decided that with the detailed experience he was passing on to me, I could steel myself to play the same game of Chicken."

This story is also important in understanding the *Pueblo* surrender. Bucher is telling us that during its missions *Banner* was watched over by ships and planes, something which did not occur during the seizure of *Pueblo*. He is also suggesting that the Soviets and Red Chinese sent out "shadowing units" to harass *Banner*, but that the North Koreans did not. This story also indicates that Bucher was familiar with the signal HEAVE TO OR I WILL FIRE. During the seizure he will claim to not understand it and be confused by it.

The hand of the censor may be detected here. Bucher says *Banner* passed along North Korea on "one occasion." Perhaps, but if *Banner* operated in the Sea of Japan, it is possible but unlikely that it would go all the way north to Vladivostok without surveilling the North Korean coastline. Also, Admiral Johnson, commander of naval forces in Japan, told the Court of Inquiry that *two* missions to North Korea had been made without incident prior to *Pueblo*'s. Finally, the parenthetical statement "he *never* intruded" was surely added by the censor. Bucher had already written that *Banner* was "near" Soviet and Red Chinese waters. The "he *never* intruded" is not only unnecessary but is ungrammatical. This form of censorship will be encountered again in Bucher's books.

Most important in this story are the words "proceed on his course," which I emphasized. This is a cardinal difference between *Banner* and *Pueblo*. Except when his engines broke down, Clark had his ship under way to escape harassment. Even in that instance he got under way as soon as he could. *Pueblo* did not, but remained dead in the water for over an hour—a fact Bucher tries to ignore and deny, but which is reported by every other source of information. This failure to move became a major issue between Bucher and his second in command, Murphy. The executive officer expected Bucher to "disengage" and move away. But "according to our orders" Bucher did not, and Murphy could not understand why he didn't.

5

COVER STORY: A DO-NOTHING SHIP

The supposedly first and only and most assuredly the last voyage of the USS *Pueblo* began January 11, 1968, when the ship left Sasebo, the then-large U.S. Navy base on the southwest coast of Japan.

By whatever route, along the Korean coast or across the Sea of Japan, *Pueblo* arrived at the northern station called Pluto, which covered the area between the 42nd and 41st parallels. Chongjin was the major North Korean city along the coast. Then *Pueblo* headed south to operating area Venus, said to lie between the 41st and 40th parallels. Songjin was the important coastal city. Finally *Pueblo* sailed south to area Mars, between the 40th and 39th parallels. The important coastal city was Wonsan.

What was accomplished during this trip off the North Korean coast? If Bucher, Murphy, and Schumacher are to be believed, very little—almost nothing. Murphy writes (pp. 114-5): "Our first stop [Chongjin in area Pluto] was a disappointment. We spotted very little shipping, freighters and fishing boats mostly. As for Steve's [Harris] equipment, it worked well enough, but he just wasn't getting the raw data he expected."

Bucher writes (p. 164): "After we had been surveying Chong-Jin for several hours of the next day, I called Steve to my cabin and asked him if he'd got any positive results. 'If anyone actually lives in the area, Captain, we sure have no sign of it. We are confirming many of the known KORCOM radar sites but otherwise there is nothing new.'

"'O.K., Steve, that's all I wanted to know,' I told him. 'We will pull out to about 25 miles this evening and then head down to our next target, Song-Jin.'"

Then Bucher writes, "Song-Jin turned out to be the same disappointment that Chong-Jin had been. The CTs were bored to death." He was disappointed. "A day and a half passed," he writes, "and our only significant contributions were the readings and the oceanographic samples that Friar Tuck and Harry Iredale [the civilian oceanographers] were recording and bottling. . . . My mood was one of futility and frustration."

Schumacher writes that "this whole trip had been pretty unproductive." In twelve days of monitoring, *Pueblo* had "picked up nothing new or interesting for the intelligence boys back in Japan and Honolulu." Schumacher writes that he had to agree with what Bucher wrote in the daily narrative reports in the space reserved for "Commanding Officer's Comments." Schumacher continues (p. 72): "He [Bucher] stated categorically that the mission had been a worthless exercise. He referred to it, in Navy language, as 'unproductive' and a 'poor utilization of the platform,' which could be translated as 'stupid' and a 'waste of the taxpayers' money.' I wondered how the staffs who had put together this mission would like reading that. One thing about the Skipper, though, was that if he had a place on a Navy form to put down his opinion, he put it down straight. 'Well, they asked me, damn it, didn't they?' he would say."

Schumacher, who was keeping the "narrative report" of the voyage, had little to write. He said the report, "like everything else about this mission, was dull." The intercept in the SOD-Hut was already known to the Navy. "We just had fancier equipment and worked with radar antennas and radio direction finders instead of the peloruses or trusty thumbs weekend sailors used." Schumacher writes that Bucher told the civilian oceanographers, "for lack of anything better to do," to perform as much research as time permitted. Schumacher goes on: "Friar [Tuck] and Harry [Iredale] had mapped out some forty different locations along our route where they would like to take water samples. They also wanted to record water temperatures by dragging a fancy thermometer behind the ship. However, these oceanographic stations, our briefers had informed us, did not have to be covered by the *Pueblo*. They were to be included only if we had time. As things were turning out, we had time, plenty of time."

This repeated portrayal of a useless voyage that was a waste of tax money simply cannot be believed. Bucher, Murphy, and Schumacher, by their own admission, had only extremely limited access to the SOD-Hut. And even if they had been standing at the shoulders of CTs as they worked, they would not have understood what was going on. By their own admission, they lacked technical training and had only the vaguest notion of the operations of the SOD-Hut. Knowing little or nothing about the real activity of the ship, operating a ship that lies dead in the water for long periods was "dull" duty, of course.

When *Pueblo* operated in area Pluto off Chongjin, it was just south of the Soviet coastline and Vladivostok, Russia's foremost Pacific seaport and military base. The area around Vladivostok contains naval bases, sub bases, airfields. Red Army commands and major defense installations are there. It is to be assumed the whole area is bustling with shipping and aircraft, much of it military. Given the nature of the area, it has to be assumed the atmosphere was filled with electronic signals. For a ship equipped as was *Pueblo,* this area south of Vladivostok had rich pickings to offer in signal intercept. That *Pueblo* achieved nothing simply taxes belief.

(I first found it hard to believe that *Pueblo* restricted itself to the North Korean coast and did not operate off Vladivostok, as *Banner* had, but I could find no evidence that it did on this voyage. Later, when the actual events of the seizure became apparent, it was obvious that surveillance off the Soviet coast was the last thing *Pueblo* would have been permitted to do.)

And there is strong evidence that it accomplished a lot. Armbrister reports that at dusk on January 18 (five days before the seizure) *Pueblo* steamed south toward Songjin. He writes (p. 24): "As *Pueblo* passed Orang-dan, Tuck thought he saw smoke rising from shore. Later that evening, near Musu-dan, one of the young CTs told Harris that he had just intercepted a powerful electronic signal.

"By nine o'clock next morning [the 19th] *Pueblo* lay dead in the water 15 miles east of Songjin. The sky was overcast. The ice up forward had diminished to a point where Tuck was able to remove the tarp from his winch and lower a Nansen cast with no trouble. In the research spaces the CT's were beginning to log the first of thirty different radar signals they would intercept that day. From all indications one of them was a new 'CROSS-SLOT,' or early air warning radar. They couldn't be sure; the ship's direction-finding antennae hadn't locked onto it long enough to pinpoint its type or exact location."

A powerful electronic signal, thirty different radar signals in a day, and Cross-Slot radar belies the portrayal by Bucher, Murphy, and Schumacher that their voyage was useless. It is also evidence that *Pueblo* operated closer to shore than twelve miles. *Pueblo* was a small ship, low in the water, and its antennae were not high enough to pick up powerful electronic signals, particularly Cross-Slot radar, unless *Pueblo* was close to the transmitter. But above all the reference to Cross-Slot radar is one of the most important clues to what *Pueblo* was doing in the area and why it was seized.

What is Cross-Slot radar? This was new in 1968—state of the art in radar—and deployed in very few places. It is still used today, although greatly refined. As it was then, Cross-Slot sent out two beams, one vertical, one horizontal, to locate incoming aircraft or other aerial targets. This information was fed to another form of radar which locked onto the target, while the Cross-Slot continued its scan of the heavens for more targets. In 1968, Cross-Slot radar was a new system by which anti-aircraft missiles could be guided. Prior to Cross-Slot, missiles such as the Soviet SAMs were heat-seeking, and rather easily evaded by pilots. Cross-Slot radar enabled missiles to be guided to their targets by radar and made them much deadlier weapons.

When *Pueblo* picked up Cross-Slot radar, it meant the Soviets had installed their latest wrinkle in anti-aircraft defenses in North Korea. More importantly, since *Pueblo* picked up the signal, it meant *the radar was aimed toward the Sea of Japan.* That could only mean the Soviets were worried about U.S. air attacks from Japan, Okinawa, or carriers at sea. Since the United States, deeply involved in Vietnam, was hardly making aggressive moves toward the Soviet Union or North Korea—the area had been quiet for a long time—the question must be asked, as surely the NSA did: why would the Soviet Union install its newest, rarest, and best anti-aircraft defense system along the North Korean coast aimed out to the Sea of Japan? They had to be guarding against U.S. air strikes. But why? What was going on that might bring U.S. air strikes? The answer had to be obvious to the NSA. We will come to it in due course. Suffice it to say at this point that the discovery of Cross-Slot radar is an important piece of the *Pueblo* puzzle.

Clearly, the image of a do-nothing *Pueblo* wasting tax dollars is not correct. *Pueblo* was accomplishing a lot. Picking up Cross-Slot radar alone was a tremendous accomplishment. Again, the men of *Pueblo* were trying to tell us something, but no one listened.

Then there were the activities of Tuck and Iredale. The image given by every writer is that the two civilian oceanographers were aboard as a "cover" for *Pueblo* to make it look like a hydrographic ship. They took water samples in Nansen bottles and cast a "fancy thermometer" into the sea.

This yarn should have been questioned at the time. Tuck and Iredale testified before the Court of Inquiry and were interviewed by Armbrister.

An obvious question—perhaps it was asked, but no answer is recorded—is what were civilians doing aboard a Navy ship? That they were casting Nansen bottles into the sea to make *Pueblo* look like a hydrographer is an unacceptable answer. It is to be assumed the Navy had hundreds of oceanographers within its ranks. Why bring aboard higher-paid civilians? And if all they were doing was making Nansen casts as a "cover," then a couple of common seamen could have done that.

What were Tuck and Iredale really doing on board *Pueblo*? They had been aboard *Banner* (as Armbrister and others report) and were transferred to *Pueblo* shortly before it left Yokosuka in January. Obviously, they were to continue the work they were doing aboard *Banner*. The nature of that work was classified in 1968, so perhaps no one aboard *Pueblo* knew what they were really doing. But it is known today.

In those days both the United States and the Soviet Union (and other countries, it is to be assumed) were testing a then-new means of underwater communication. Using high-power, low-frequency radio waves, messages could be sent a long distance underwater—on the order of from Honolulu to the West Coast. The waves rode the thermal layers in the ocean. In 1968, this system of communication—obviously highly useful in submarine warfare—was being tested by both the United States and the USSR. The state of the art was that a message would be sent underwater, then it would be checked via atmospheric communication to determine if it had been received correctly.

Tuck and Iredale were busy men, performing important research. Their "fancy thermometer" was recording the thermal layers in the waters off the Soviet Union and North Korea, where the Russians maintained major sub bases.

Since this new means of underwater communication was highly classified in those days, it is to be assumed that the Soviets were not too happy to have U.S. vessels snooping off their sub bases, trailing thermometers and other gear to determine their progress with this means of communication, and perhaps even picking up their underwater messages. Indeed, one of the reasons for seizing *Pueblo* may well have been to find out what Tuck and Iredale had learned. As Armbrister describes it, before the seizure the two civilians went to great pains to destroy their records, tearing them into tiny pieces. If they were only operating an innocent "cover," why would they have done that?

A larger question: Why go to all the trouble of portraying *Pueblo* as on a useless voyage when clearly it wasn't? One answer is that NSA, wanting to minimize the extent of U.S. ELINT operations, sought to suggest we had only a couple of ships which never accomplished anything of value, so the whole scheme was dropped. But there is something else. What if *Pueblo* had picked up truly important messages in addition to Cross-Slot radar? This would provide a reason for seizing the ship—not a justifiable reason, perhaps, but still a reason. Since the United States wanted to portray *Pueblo* as the innocent victim of an act of piracy, it was necessary to try to convince the world that *Pueblo* never accomplished anything of value.

The *Pueblo* cover story told to Americans and the world contains another important element. Much was made during the Pike Committee hearings of the fact that the Navy and other federal agencies had failed to alert *Pueblo* of North Korean warnings, even threats, against American spy ships. Even the NSA warned the Navy that *Pueblo* might not be on a "minimal risk mission." Mysteriously, none of these warnings ever reached *Pueblo*. Nor was it informed of a North Korean raid on the South Korean presidential palace, the Blue House, on the evening of January 21.

Nonetheless, *Pueblo* had ample knowledge that it faced difficulties from the North Koreans. Bucher, Murphy, and every other writer attach great importance to the need for *Pueblo* to go undetected. The ship raised no national ensign. Its guns were covered. The crew wore a variety of mufti. It tried to avoid other shipping and observed EMCON—emission control. This means *Pueblo* did not use its radio or radar. It was sending out no signals.

All this seems strange on several counts. If *Pueblo* was operating in international waters, what was there to hide? The United States operated ELINT ships all over the world. *Banner* had made trips to these waters. That the United States had ELINT ships and snooped along these coasts could hardly be a secret to the Soviets and, as their warnings made clear, it certainly wasn't to the North Koreans.

And trying to stay undetected was a hopeless exercise. The Sea of Japan is hardly Antarctica. It is one of the busier bodies of water on earth, named for one of the world's major maritime nations. The waters off North Korea are a major area for international fishing, used by the Russians, Koreans, Japanese, Chinese, and other nationalities. Even U.S. fishing boats go there. At that time of year herring was running and fishing fleets were out. One more suggestion of shipping activity comes from Armbrister (p.28). On January 19 the captain of a Japanese freighter returned home from a voyage to Wonsan to report he had never seen so much *naval* activity at that time of year. Clearly, for *Pueblo* to go undetected, especially in an age of radar, was a bit like hiding a goldfish in a sake cup.

Furthermore, there is strong evidence that the Navy *wanted Pueblo* to be detected. The Ichthyic One Sailing Order, as printed by Schumacher (whose comments are in brackets), includes these items: "4C. Intercept and conduct surveillance of Soviet naval units operating Tsushima Straits. [This was a leaf out of the Soviet book. The Russians had been monitoring American fleet movements for years with their fishing 'trawlers.']"

Under Order 6, "Special instructions," is the following, as quoted by Schumacher: "D. Operate at least five hundred yards [from Soviet units] as necessary for visual/photo coverage. [This is close quarters on the open ocean. My guess is that the United States wanted the Russians to get a good look at the *Pueblo* before her mission was over and conclude that the Americans were serious about surveying the Soviet fleet. The Soviets, of course, would take their own pictures of the *Pueblo,* as they had of the *Banner.* The Kremlin would know the United States had at least two ferret ships in the western Pacific; that the *Banner* was not one of a kind. The concept of 'parity'—each side capable of doing the same thing as the other—would thus be established firmly by the *Pueblo.*]

"E. Do not interfere with Soviet exercises but maintain a position on the periphery for observation purposes. [The *Pueblo* would thus help to write the book of etiquette for seagoing snoopers. The Navy hoped the Russians would learn from it and do likewise, discontinuing the game of chicken they had been playing too often for either nation's safety. Who wanted to go to war over scraped fenders?]

"F. If unable to establish or gain contact with Soviet units within twenty-four hours arrival Tsushima Straits area, advise originator immediate precedence. [This was another expression of eagerness to have the Soviets spot the *Pueblo.*]"

It seems impossible to me that Bucher had not seen and read these orders, especially since he insisted he followed them "to the letter."

In addition to a wide variety of shipping, the area had to include aircraft. Yet the only time any of the published *Pueblo* stories mentions aircraft is when the two North Korean MIGs buzzed the vessel during seizure. *Pueblo* was operating in waters off sub bases used by both the Soviets and the North Koreans. It was equipped with sonar and presumably other detection devices, yet no foreign submarine ever viewed the American ship. We are supposed to believe—somehow—that *Pueblo* operated for days off the North Korean coast, stopping frequently for long periods, yet remained undetected and unidentified until the day before the seizure.

In an age of radar this is ridiculous. Bucher makes no mention of his ship being picked up by North Korean radar until very late in his account, just before the seizure. He insists on giving the impression that *Pueblo* went undetected prior to January 22, the day before the seizure.

Murphy belies this. He writes (pp. 114-5): "One thing he [Steve Harris] did learn [off Chongjin], however. The North Koreans had picked us up on their radar. We discussed this at some length, in the pilothouse, then later in the wardroom. The consensus was that the North Koreans had just picked us up on a sweep and had no idea what they had."

This, too, is ridiculous. *Pueblo* sprouted eight antennae. Its configuration indicated it was an ELINT vessel and nothing else. Murphy himself had admitted this six pages earlier: "On Bucher's instructions, I charted a course that would keep us close to the Japanese coast the first day [out of Sasebo], hoping the weather would be better here, hoping too that among the fishing boats and other ships we would be less conspicuous. The latter was wishful thinking at best. With all her rounded domes, multiple antennae, direction finders, and other protuberances, the *Pueblo* was about as inconspicuous as a billowy maternity dress. From even a good distance you could see that she was pregnant with electronic gear."

Having pointed out the distinctiveness of *Pueblo*—and it was painted battleship gray with GER-2 prominently on the bow—Murphy tells of seeing "two large merchantmen" which were "guessed" to be from one of the Balkan countries. Then he writes: "Had they spotted us? We were inclined to doubt it."

What provokes incredulity about the repeated claims by Bucher and Murphy that they doubted *Pueblo* had been identified is that their books were published in 1970 and 1971, respectively. It had been firmly established as early as January 1969 (during the Court of Inquiry) that the North Koreans had spotted the ship and issued numerous protests and warnings. These came on January 6, 11, and 20 of 1968, even as *Pueblo* steamed southward toward Wonsan and capture. It is conceivable, however unlikely, that Bucher and Murphy may have thought their ship undetected at the time, but as they were writing a year later, a person expects them to mention that their presence was, of course, well known to the North Koreans.

On January 19, four days before the seizure, *Pueblo* left Songjin for Mayang Island, which was in the operating area Mars. Mayang is an island just off the coast and rests squarely on the 40th parallel at the northern rim of Choson Bay. From there the coastline turns sharply southwest toward Wonsan. Korea is a small peninsula and the distances are not very great. As the crow flies, it is only about forty miles from Songjin to Mayang Island, and another seventy-five miles or so down to Wonsan. Thus, *Pueblo,* a twelve-knot ship, spent about four days traveling a little over a hundred miles. This indicates the leisurely, stop-and-go nature of the voyage. It also makes it hard to believe *Pueblo* went undetected and explains North Korean annoyance with the ship and their warnings to do something about it.

Bucher writes (p. 165) that his "primary interest" off Mayang was to "sight and photograph KORCOM submarines of Russian origin suspected of operating in these waters." This, he said, "would pay for the whole operation." Being an old submariner, his eagerness is surely understandable. He never does say whether he saw the subs, but Armbrister, Murphy, and others say he did not.

Bucher's eagerness to "sight and photograph" the North Korean subs illuminates his limited role aboard *Pueblo* and the boundaries of his knowledge about the activities of his ship. A photograph of a World War II–type Soviet sub now used by the North Koreans would doubtlessly have some usefulness, but hardly a whole lot. It is to be assumed the Navy and U.S. intelligence had dozens of photos of Soviet subs. But photography was about the only part of *Pueblo*'s surveillance activities which Bucher could control. He could tell Mack what to photograph and when. Obviously, if the North Korean subs were underwater, there would be nothing to photograph. But the CTs, using sonar, might well have obtained a great deal of information which Bucher knew nothing about. At least he makes no reference to such knowledge.

One other thing happened off Mayang Island. Armbrister writes: "As the ship steamed south [from Mayang], Murphy expressed his forebodings to Photographer Mack. 'Most of the crew doesn't know this, so don't say anything," he warned, 'but they've had fire control radar locked on us for days.'" He was referring to radar which controls gunfire.

Murphy writes, on the same subject: "Steve [Harris] had confided to me, 'They've got fire-control radar locked on us now.'

"We had anticipated this might happen, at some point. And since we were well out to sea, this did not mean we were in any danger, nor did it even mean we had been identified. We may well have been just another blip on their scope, possibly one of a number. Yet, realizing that they were watching us was disconcerting.

"For just a moment I was able to put myself in the place of the North Koreans."

In his version, Bucher makes no mention of fire-control radar. Rather, he goes directly (in the next paragraph after he mentions his desire to photograph subs) to an event which other writers place a day or two later. A North Korean SO-1 subchaser approached *Pueblo*. Bucher says it was "quite well into the evening twilight and he [the subchaser] was almost clothed completely in silhouette." Bucher calculated the "friend" would pass "at the closest point of about 1500 yards, over a half mile."

Bucher is very sure the sighting was off Mayang Island and figured the subchaser was involved in some training exercises with the North Korean subs based there. He had Mack take photographs, but the light was bad. He could make out a two-digit number on the hull, the last numeral being a 6. The SO-1 was modified to carry rockets. "Mack made several exposures while the ship approached and as it passed its closest point before drawing away. None of us ever saw a single person aboard; not even a deck watch was present."

Bucher charted that the subchaser was heading for Wonsan. Steve Harris questioned his CTs, but no radar signal had been picked up from the North Korean vessel. Bucher: "After a quick conference with my officers we all agreed that we were still undetected within the meaning of our orders." *Pueblo* proceeded to the Wonsan area that night, arriving the next morning, Bucher says.

Murphy writes about the same incident (pp. 116-7): "It was just at dusk, on January 21 [which is at least one and perhaps two days later than in Bucher's account], that we spotted the ship, steaming southward at about twice our speed. Calling Photographer's Mate Mack to the bridge, we had him take pictures of her. It was too dark, however, to get clear shots. But as she passed, about five hundred yards off our port bow, we could see a single man on deck, and Steve was able to make a positive identification of the ship. She was North Korean, a modified SO-1 subchaser. After passing us, she proceeded toward Wonsan.

"This was the first military craft we had encountered since arriving on station. Again there was a discussion on the bridge. Had we been spotted? She had passed close. Still, it was almost dark, and she had shown no apparent interest. Lacy was sure she had seen us. Schumacher, Steve Harris and I were unsure, but were inclined toward agreement with Bucher, who was positive she had not."

Armbrister (p. 30): "At 5:20 on the afternoon of January 21 Lacy summoned Bucher to the bridge. In the gathering dusk, about 1,000 yards away, he could make out a North Korean subchaser, a modified SO1, churning southward at better than 25 knots. *Pueblo* was laying to; her ensign was down, as it had been throughout the patrol, and the only hint of her nationality was the 'GER-2' on the bow. The subchaser slowed as she approached: 500 yards, 400. Bucher ordered Larry Mack to photograph her. Mack saw only one man on her bridge. The subchaser passed 300 yards off *Pueblo*'s port bow, then turned toward Wonsan. Lacy read the beads on her hull—number 26—and felt it was 'impossible for us not to have been detected.' Mack agreed. On the flying bridge Bucher, Murphy, Steve Harris, and Schumacher talked about this. The subchaser had evidenced no *real* [Armbrister's emphasis] interest. Bucher decided the North Korean was probably asleep at the switch. *Pueblo* had not been detected. 'It was a call on our part,' Schumacher remembers. 'In hindsight, a bad call.' Hours later, Bucher set a course for Wonsan. If he still had no success by the night of the twenty-third, he'd leave Wonsan, steam north toward Songjin, and cruise back down again."

This incident, surely significant, depicts Alice tiptoeing through Wonderland. Somehow the whole story demeans officers in the United States Navy. Armbrister has Lacy calling Bucher to the bridge. Bucher says Schumacher called him and makes no mention of Lacy even being present. Murphy says "we spotted," suggesting he was there and responsible. Bucher and Murphy have *Pueblo* under way (Murphy refers to "twice our speed"). Armbrister was told *Pueblo* was "laying to; her ensign down." Bucher sees the subchaser as 1,500 yards away. Armbrister is told 1,000 yards. Murphy says 500 yards, Armbrister has it closing to 300—and has the ship slowing as it approaches. Bucher never sees anyone on deck. Everyone else sees at least one person. Bucher can hardly make out the 6 on the ship's number. Armbrister quotes Lacy as clearly seeing the number 26 on the ship's hull.

Lacy felt it was impossible for them not to have been detected. Bucher writes that after a conference with "my officers, we all agreed" that *Pueblo* was undetected. Armbrister says that after the night of the twenty-third, Bucher planned to sail north to Songjin and return. Bucher writes that *Pueblo* sailed that night to Wonsan, arriving the next morning: "It was January 22 and I planned to spend just one more day after this one and then depart area Mars and head for what at least had some promise of productive activity if we could locate the Soviet ships in the Tsushima Strait." This separates Japan and *South* Korea.

It just seems to me that officers, describing what was supposedly a single voyage of historic importance, writing at leisure with ample time to ponder, confer with one another to refresh memories, and correct their words, should not set to paper stories with such discrepancies. Incidentally, Schumacher, who was on the bridge and a party to the sighting and conference among officers, does not mention the incident. Brandt reports the sighting briefly as "another little alarm bell."

A larger question: Why was it so important for *Pueblo* to be undetected? Surely it was impossible, and the preponderance of evidence from all these accounts is that the ship was seen, both visually and by radar. Why is going undetected so important to Bucher and the others, especially when the sail order as reported by Schumacher requires *Pueblo* to observe and photograph "Soviet naval units" at close range?

An answer becomes apparent if a person believes, as I do, that *Pueblo* was not on her first and only voyage to North Korean waters but had made many previous voyages. The sail order was the general order governing all such missions. On these previous trips, *Pueblo* was seen regularly, even routinely, by the North Koreans. Indeed, *Pueblo wanted* to be seen by Soviet bloc countries, as Schumacher informs us in his discussion of the sail order.

But for what became the *last* voyage, Bucher received new orders instructing him to remain undetected and notify headquarters when he was. Why have *Pueblo* try to remain undetected for this particular voyage? I hope it is not getting too far ahead in the story to suggest two reasons: (1) the NSA hoped the Soviet Union would not realize *Pueblo* had returned to Japan and was now on a new voyage; and (2) the NSA hoped for *Pueblo* to avoid any contact with the Soviet, Red Chinese, or North Korean navies until its own disinformation was in place and the stage set for the *Pueblo* surrender.

I believe that in discussing their efforts to remain unobserved, Bucher, Murphy, et al. are trying to show that on this voyage they had orders different from previous missions. Bucher's main defense is that he followed his orders "to the letter." But those orders, as we will see, were "his eyes only" orders, to be read and destroyed. No other person aboard *Pueblo* saw those orders, including Murphy, who quite unjustly condemns his captain for actions he knows nothing about.

When Bucher was first released from captivity he told reporters he followed his orders to the letter. At that point, I am sure, Bucher expected to be exonerated, even become a hero, for he assumed his orders came from the Navy and his superiors knew of his orders. When he discovered they did not know and no such orders as he had followed existed, he must have been personally devastated. No wonder he suffered "complete nervous exhaustion."

6

COVER STORY: THE DAY BEFORE SEIZURE

The next day, the twenty-second, one before the seizure, there could be no doubt *Pueblo* had been detected by North Korean vessels.

Murphy first: "It was warmer now, and ice was no longer a major problem. We were due east of Wonsan when, at 12:25 on the afternoon of January 22, the watch reported what appeared to be two fishing boats approaching.

"I was navigating in the charthouse. Going to the Big Eyes (22-inch binoculars), I was able to make out the names on their gray sides. These were later translated as 'Rice Paddy 1' and 'Rice Paddy 2.' Their configuration was familiar. I was sure I had seen it in one of the identification pubs I had been studying. Thumbing through it, I determined they were Soviet-type trawlers, but with slight modifications, indicating they were probably North Korean-built.

"An order was sent over the loudspeaker for all hands to lay below decks. We didn't want the visitors to count the crewmen, and wonder why so many.

"One of the trawlers steamed directly toward us, then swerved aside, passing less than one hundred yards off the starboard bow, close enough for us to see fishing nets and some half-dozen men on deck. They weren't wearing uniforms, and there was no sign of armament.

"Skip [Schumacher], as operations officer, was drafting a SITREP (situation report). I carefully pinpointed our position for him. We were twenty miles from the nearest land. I had no doubts about this. Our dead reckoning . . . fixes tallied perfectly with the readings I got from the loran, radar and fathometer.

"The two trawlers disappeared to the northwest.

"At this time we were flying the international signal for hydrographer, but not the national ensign. Would they accept that as identification? I doubted it.

"Curious to see if Steve [Harris] had been able to intercept any of their radio messages, I went below to the sod hut [Murphy's spelling]. He had picked them up all right, but the North Koreans had spoken too quickly for our two Marine interpreters, Chicca and Hammond, to make out the words.

"I was still in the sod hut when the two ships reappeared sometime later. Returning to the bridge I again confirmed our position: we were well outside any claimed territorial waters. This time when they passed, the number of personnel on deck had increased significantly. Several of the men were pointing cameras at us. Mack snapped his shutter right back at them. Obviously, after our first contact they had been ordered to return and photograph us. But still no sign of guns, and still no attempt at harassment. After passing us, they headed straight for Wonsan.

"This time there was no need for debate. We had been spotted."

Now Bucher (p. 168): "Just after our noon meal, Gene [Lacy] called me from the bridge and reported two trawlers in the distance who were heading our way." Bucher went immediately to the flying bridge, where Lacy was using the Big Eyes. Bucher checked them himself and declared, "Those are Russian-built, Lentra Class, trawlers." Lacy replied, "Yes sir, I can see that now."

Bucher gave a verbal order for Mack and Schumacher to come to the bridge and for the SOD-Hut to be alerted "so they can be prepared to look for this type of ship." This makes no sense: alerted to be prepared to look. Is Bucher suggesting the CTs in the SOD-Hut sat around waiting for Bucher to give an order which galvanized them to action? Since their equipment was in continuous operation, it is difficult to understand how the CTs could be alerted to be prepared to look.

Bucher continues: "As the fishermen drew closer, I began to suspect they might not be exactly what they appeared. They were painted a uniform gray color and outfitted with exactly the same superstructure and fishing rig. Could it be then that they were coming out to shadow our operation?"

Bucher says the two trawlers circled *Pueblo* slowly at a range of about five hundred yards. Where Murphy had one ship a hundred yards away approach with a half dozen men on deck, Bucher has both ships five hundred yards away. "What must have been their entire crew appeared on deck in typical fishing clothing. They were pointing at us and jabbering among themselves excitedly." He says several of his own crew came out on deck. He became concerned that some of his men might get "carried away with the excitement and shout or gesture some obscenity" at the KORCOMs. He also didn't want to give "any clue as to the actual number of people" aboard *Pueblo*, so he ordered the weather decks cleared of all personnel not actually on watch.

"After the two ships had completed their circle of *Pueblo*," Bucher writes, they steamed away at a speed of ten knots to a distance of about two and three-quarters miles—they didn't "disappear," as Murphy has it—then "drew close together and lay to while apparently discussing what they had just seen." Bucher goes on: "I immediately prepared my first situation report (SITREP) to be filed as soon as all information necessary could be included." In addition to this sighting, Bucher included in this initial message "all the worthwhile information that I'd collected thus far on our mission. This included such items as the number and type and where possible the position of coastal radars, also the number of visual contacts we'd made and the percentage of fuel and lube oil remaining in our tanks." Bucher cannot have it both ways. He cannot say *Pueblo* picked up no ELINT, much to his "frustration," and now refer to the number and type of coastal radars picked up. In this message (below) he refers to nineteen ship "sightings," yet doubts *Pueblo* was detected.

In the next sentence he writes, "Therefore this first message took considerable pain and preparation but Skip Schumacher was quite equal to the task and had all the necessary information compiled very quickly."

While this was being done, the two fishing vessels headed back toward *Pueblo*. Bucher writes: "As we were lying to I feared an intentional ramming from one or both, so I passed the word to the engineroom to light off the main engines and stand by to answer bells [signals from the bridge].

"The senior watch captain in the engineroom, [Rushel J.] Blansett, quickly reported: 'Ready to answer all bells.'"

Bucher saw smoke from the stacks and that its color looked good. The North Korean ships approached at a speed of three knots, circled *Pueblo* at a distance of "only about 25 yards with all hands out on their decks and gazing intently at what they were seeing." Bucher noted they were unarmed. He had Mack photograph them. Bucher kept notes and a running account on a casette recorder slung over his shoulder.

At this point Bucher can make out the Korean lettering on the bows of the ships and summons Steve Harris to the bridge along with one of the Marine interpreters, Sergeant Chicca.

Bucher says: "'Chicca, do you see the Kongi Marks on the bows of each ship?'

"'Yes, sir, I can see them clearly.'

"'O.K., what do they mean?'

"'I'll get my Korean dictionary and find out right away.' A few minutes passed and the ships were still with us when Chicca returned and gazed intently at them. 'One of them is *Rice Paddy* and the other is *Rice Paddy, 1,* Captain,' he announced.

"'Thanks, Chicca, you may return to your other duties.'"

After that the fishing boats left "toward the north again and soon became small vanishing specks dissolving into nothingness."

On the basis of his interviews, Armbrister gives a slightly different account. The ships bore numbers 1065 and 1062. One ship approached within a hundred yards on the first pass. Bucher counted nineteen men aboard. On the second pass, the two ships circled *Pueblo* within thirty yards before sailing off to the northeast.

Armbrister (p. 34): "The moment those trawlers reached port, he [Bucher] knew, their captains would report *Pueblo*'s presence. Now was the time to break radio silence; he prepared a situation report: ' . . . these are the first craft to display any interest of 19 sighted since we departed Tsushima Straits . . . at 220325 Zulu Jan/68 two North Korean ships . . . have made 26 BT drops [the thermometer] and 10 Nansen casts at present posit . . . Intentions: remain in present area. . . . ' He gave the message to Radioman Hayes and told him to send it out immediately." Armbrister does not identify where he obtained these fragments of the message—nor does he have to. He is a good reporter and his book is the only one containing specific contents of various messages from *Pueblo*.

Brandt's account of the encounter is brief, but contains one illuminating sentence (p. 32): "As the vessels approached off the port bow, Bucher, Schumacher, Lieutenant Harris, Chicca, and Hammond discussed the vessels and agreed that the subchaser they had seen the evening before had probably detected the *Pueblo* and that the visit by the Korean fishing vessels was the result." If this is the case, then Bucher's certainty about being undetected the day before was short-lived—contrary to what he writes in his book.

There is a serious discrepancy in all these versions of the same incident which lends an unreal quality to it. Murphy says they were "due east" of

Wonsan, twenty miles from nearest land. Armbrister says the ship "lay dead in the water twenty miles north and east of Wonsan"—a position that would place *Pueblo* well within North Korean territorial waters. Bucher, Schumacher, and Brandt don't say where *Pueblo* was. Where did the trawlers go when they left *Pueblo*? Murphy says they headed "straight for Wonsan." Bucher says they went north and Armbrister says they went northeast. While neither Bucher nor Armbrister specifically says they went to Wonsan, Armbrister states that Bucher knew *Pueblo*'s presence would be reported as soon as the trawlers reached port—suggesting Wonsan. Indeed, Armbrister quotes Schumacher as saying to Bucher, "You know, Captain, I'll bet those guys are sitting in Wonsan right now looking at pictures of us."

The trouble is, if *Pueblo* was due east or north and east of Wonsan, and the trawlers were traveling north, as Bucher has it, or northeast, as Armbrister reports, that would take the trawlers *away* from Wonsan. From the locations of due east or north by east, the heading for Wonsan was either due west or southwest. There is absolutely no possibility of any ship going north or northeast to Wonsan—except by overland portage. Something has to be wrong. The choices are (1) one or more of the writers simply made an error in direction; (2) the trawlers didn't go to Wonsan but to some other port to report what they had seen; (3) *Pueblo* was in some other location; or (4) Murphy is the only one who is correct. My argument, one more time, is that the *Pueblo* seizure was a single, historic event of short duration. There ought to be one clear-cut story of what happened, not greatly differing stories from each teller, some of which make no sense. At least the directions ought to be right. Unfortunately, this sort of conflict only worsens on the day of seizure.

After describing the encounter with the fishing boats, Armbrister writes (p. 35): "At dusk *Pueblo* withdrew from the coast and lay to at a point 25 miles southeast of Wonsan." It remained there overnight. Armbrister is the only writer to refer to a deliberate movement by *Pueblo* on the twenty-second, the night before the seizure. In so doing, Armbrister creates a serious challenge to U.S. claims that *Pueblo* was in international waters. He reports that *Pueblo* was "20 miles north and east of Wonsan" and that it "withdrew from the coast." He does not give map coordinates, but being twenty miles north and east of Wonsan would place *Pueblo* along the coast of Hado Peninsula, well within Korean waters. To have *Pueblo* withdraw to a "point 25 miles southeast of Wonsan" would place the ship a few miles from the North Korean coastline, well within a twelve-mile limit.

When the fishing trawlers left, one of the most peculiar events of the entire *Pueblo* voyage occurred. Having decided to break radio silence to report that *Pueblo* had now definitely been sighted by North Korean vessels, *Pueblo* could not reach Kamiseya! Murphy treats the incident briefly (p. 119):

"By about 1700 hours (5:00 P.M.) [on the twenty-second] the SITREP was ready. Handing it to Radioman Lee Roy Hayes, Bucher told him to break EMCON [emission control or radio silence] and radio Japan we had been detected.

"It took our radioman fourteen hours to make contact with Japan and relay the message.

"By this time it was the morning of Tuesday, January 23, 1968."

Bucher's account is a little lengthier. After getting the names of the North Korean ships, dismissing Chicca, and seeing the "vanishing specks dissolving into nothingness" to the north, Bucher writes: "I returned to my cabin and smoothed up the first SITREP I had filed. I called the OOD to get Hayes to light off the transmitter and to key it to the dummy antennae. This permits the radioman to set up his transmitters without emitting external signals. Steve [Harris] was writing up his own technical message which would go to different addresses than mine. His message was written in a language all its own, which could only be clearly understood by another intelligence specialist. It annoyed me that he was reporting to a different commander and that he had the authority to release messages that might wittingly or unwittingly reflect adversely on *Pueblo*. . . .

"The messages were both released at about 1645 [4:45 P.M.]. Radioman Hayes had the transmitter set on the proper frequency of the day, I know this because I personally checked it out. Then began a long disturbing frustrating night and early morning while the best communication talent aboard were unable to get a response to our signals to Kamiseya.

"The night dragged on and I plagued the responsible CTs every hour and sometimes more often. *I even took three to four more looks at the transmitter and told Hayes to try the spare one, because maybe the output meter on the transmitter we were using was in error. But it performed no better than the first one* [emphasis mine].

"'Keep on trying, Hayes,' I admonished him. Then [I] told Steve Harris, 'I want you to stay on top of establishing communications. Let me know the minute we have a solid signal.'

"There was no feeling of apprehension aboard, nor even tension among those of us who were directly concerned with what was going on—rather a feeling of irritation over the very unsatisfactory communications with headquarters when we finally needed them.''

Armbrister devotes several pages to the breakdown in communications (p. 35): "Inside the radio shack Lee Hayes was still attempting to reach Japan. He used Morse code to establish initial contact and asked the Naval Communications Station at Yokosuka to activate the 100-words-per-minute Orestes circuit to Kamiseya. If he could 'terminate' with Yokosuka on circuit 32, technicians there could patch him into Kamiseya on circuit 21. Now he could hear Japan, but Japan couldn't hear him. 'Change frequencies, change frequencies,' Japan advised.''

In other words, Hayes could reach the *Navy* facility at Yokosuka, but when transferred over a special, secure channel to the *NSA* facility at Kamiseya, he was told to "change frequencies." Hayes's transmitter was working fine to the Navy base, but not to the NSA facility. This is vital to understanding this whole incident.

Armbrister continues: "In the tiny crypto room adjacent to the research spaces, a lean, mournful-eyed communications technician first class named Donald E. Bailey had already cut and scanned the tape that he would send through a machine called the KW-7. It would emerge as a random stream of marks and spaces. This encoded stream would then modulate the ship's transmitter. Bailey was ready to send Bucher's situation report. But he couldn't begin to transmit until Lee Hayes established a link. And Hayes was having no luck.''

Lee Hayes and Don Bailey, then, are the major participants in this minidrama the night before *Pueblo* was captured. Hayes was young, slender, red-haired, the last man to come aboard before *Pueblo* departed Yokosuka. He had been aboard USS *Mars* and wasn't very happy about the last-minute transfer. Neither was Bucher. He wanted a radioman first class to replace a man who had been transferred off. None was available. He settled for Hayes, a second class, because he knew Morse. There was another distinctive feature about Hayes. He was rusty. He had been out of the service for two years and had come back only four months before. He was unfamiliar with his radio equipment and having a hard time with it.

The exact opposite in expertise was Bailey. He was thirty-six, two years younger than Bucher, and a CT first class, one grade below chief. Bailey was also one of the last to come aboard *Pueblo*. According to Brandt, he was a specialist in ship-to-shore communications and he was based at Kamiseya. In fact, he had been on the receiving end of communications from *Pueblo*—surely indicating *Pueblo* operated in the Sea of

Japan prior to its "maiden" voyage in January—and had figured out what the trouble was. He went to his superiors at Kamiseya and suggested someone go aboard *Pueblo* and straighten out the problem. He was sent. Thus, in Brandt's words, "Bailey, a veteran and a highly knowledgeable communications specialist, found himself on the *Pueblo* because he was too conscientious." He was scheduled to be on board for only this one voyage.

Armbrister lists the difficulties Hayes was having. "Ionospheric disturbances at night played crazy games with communications," he writes, and Kamiseya lay behind a mountain range. (True, but the antennae were on top of the mountains.) In addition, "sheer congestion" on frequencies made contact difficult. Many ships waited until this time of night to transmit, and most of them had more powerful transmitters than *Pueblo*. (This is not germane, for as Armbrister himself reports, *Pueblo* had a special circuit for its exclusive use. The problem was not reaching the Navy at Yokosuka, but the NSA at Kamiseya.) Armbrister writes (p. 36): "And then, in order for a coded message to get though, both operators—Bailey in the spaces below and the CT at the other end—had to synchronize perfectly. If *Pueblo*'s signal faltered for even half a second, that synchronization would collapse. Hayes would have to start the process all over again."

At 8 P.M., after three hours of futility, Armbrister writes that Hayes "walked down to the research spaces and asked Steve Harris if he could send out the situation report in Morse code; that way he knew he could get it through. Harris said no. The message was classified; it had to reach Japan on a secure circuit. Anyone could intercept Morse code. To be sure, the sandy-haired radioman could use an old code, transfer it to Morse, and send it out in that manner. Harris thought that would be too tedious. 'Keep trying,' he said. Hayes walked back to the radio shack."

All this is odd. In his interview with me, Hayes said he never set foot in the SOD-Hut. "The closest I came was to look in the door once." Since Armbrister says Hayes walked *to* the SOD-Hut, perhaps he knocked on the door and Harris came outside to speak to him. Hayes asked permission from Harris—not Bucher—to send the situation report in Morse. Harris thought it "too tedious" to encode the report by hand and send it out in Morse. Considering the three hours Hayes had already spent fiddling with his transmitter, tediousness seems a thin concern.

Hayes worked all night. He tried a dozen frequencies and none worked. By 4 A.M., he was "getting kinda nervous," he told Armbrister. "I was afraid the captain and the other officers—they might think it was all my fault."

Bailey was also waiting for Hayes to establish contact with Kamiseya. Armbrister (p. 37): "He told Communications Technician Second Class Donald R. McClarren to wake him if anything happened. Then he left the crypto room, climbed into his bunk, and within two minutes was sound asleep."

Armbrister (p. 38): "Lee Hayes was beginning to worry about his number two transmitter. It had always been temperamental, and now, at 9 A.M., it was overheating—its output varying between 300 and 500 watts. He decided to switch over to transmitter number one and telephoned Steve Harris in the research spaces to tell him about it. The lieutenant was unhappy. 'Number one isn't that good,' he said. But half an hour later Harris called back. 'We have them five-bye [a perfect signal], he cried. 'Don't touch that transmitter. Don't breathe on it.'"

I have no doubt this information was imparted to Armbrister in interviews, but it must be questioned on several grounds. Bucher has already told us that Hayes tried the spare transmitter and it didn't work any better than the other one. Then there is the matter of time. Armbrister is told the circuit was established about nine-thirty on the morning of the twenty-third. But the radio transcript released by the Navy says, "The circuit was established at 1054 Korean local time on January 23, 1968." This is about an hour before the seizure began. If the circuit was established at 0930 or thereabouts, no one was in a hurry to use it. Then there is the matter of Hayes "telephoning" Harris and having the quoted conversation. Again, there is no communication between the inside of the SOD-Hut and any insecure place. In a moment we will come to an even more compelling reason to doubt this story told to Armbrister.

Ed Brandt, who interviewed Bailey and McClarren, but not Hayes, gives a radically different account of the "breakdown" in communications (pp. 33-4): "Commander Bucher didn't consider the visit [from the fishing ships] any more than routine [surely a far different image than Bucher and others present], but his orders were to inform ComNav 4, Japan, as soon as he was certain that *Pueblo* had been detected, so he asked Lieutenant Harris to prepare a message for transmission to Kamiseya. About 4:30 Lieutenant Harris came into the crypto center and told Don Bailey to get the circuit operable." This version of events is considerably different from that given by Bucher or Armbrister. Harris, not Schumacher, prepares the message. Harris tells Bailey to send it, rather than Bucher telling Hayes.

Brandt continues: "Under ordinary circumstances it would take about ten minutes to make contact with a big Navy *relay* station. Bailey called Yokosuka first, telling the station there to call Kamiseya and activate the special secure channel to the *Pueblo*. Several minutes later, Bailey got an acknowledging message from Kamiseya and tried to reply. But Kamiseya couldn't pick up the signal clearly. Bailey continued to punch out his call letters every thirty seconds, trying to make clear contact. . . .

"Bailey thought there were two reasons [for the failure]. The *Pueblo*'s signal was relatively weak and had trouble squeezing through the stronger signals pouring into Kamiseya. There was also atmospheric interference. Bailey stayed at the job the entire night, frustrated because he could read Kamiseya clearly but couldn't get the *Pueblo*'s signal through. The operator at Kamiseya, a friend of Bailey's, stayed right with him. *Bailey could have gotten through by transmitting in the clear on another frequency but he had orders not to do so unless there was an emergency* [emphasis mine]. About 8 A.M. Bailey, who had been up for twenty-four hours, went below to rest and turned the sending apparatus over to McClarren, who continued to try to reach Kamiseya."

The difference in this version told to Brandt is surely cardinal and so obvious as to need no enumeration here. Bailey clearly told different stories to Armbrister and Brandt. I leave it to the reader to guess which of these stories is correct. I certainly cannot. But I can point out that Bailey was a transmission specialist based at Kamiseya, the NSA facility in Japan. He had detected the cause of *Pueblo*'s communications problem and was sent aboard to straighten it out. It is hard to believe that such an expert would stay up all night "to punch out his call letters every thirty seconds to make clear contact." And, if what he told Armbrister is correct, he didn't. He went to bed.

Bailey's statements to Ed Brandt are important for two reasons. First, they confirm that the problem was not in reaching the Navy base at Yokosuka, but the NSA facility at Kamiseya. Second, Bailey admitted that he "could have gotten through by transmitting in the clear on another frequency but had had orders not to do so unless there was an emergency." *There were alternate means of communication!* But Bailey had "orders" not to use them.

Schumacher adds some informative details (pp. 79-80): "When we had a message to transmit, we would first call Japan on an insecure—or open—CW (continuous wave, or Morse code) frequency and ask them to 'open circuit 21P.' The Navy radioman in Japan would know, by this unique signal, that it was the *Pueblo* calling. He would radio us on one of the circuits to which we were listening that he was ready to receive and would suggest a frequency. We could then transmit by teletypewriter, which was much faster and, through an electronic coding system, absolutely secure."

The next morning Schumacher had a crack at establishing communications himself (p. 82): "I walked toward the SOD Hut. I punched the panel of black buttons on the door to gain entrance. CT2 Donald R. McClarren was on watch inside, up to his neck in work. I riffled through the messages we had received during the night from Japan while we attempted to establish communications. Then I sat down in front of one of the receivers and listened. The only frequency that sounded clear was 9881 kilocycles. All the others were still blocked with static.

"I phoned to Hayes up in the radio shack and told him to signal Japan by Morse code that we would be sending on 9881. This was not in line with the established procedures. But we had tried some six or seven frequencies over the past twelve hours or so with no success, which was not exactly the instant communication we should have had. The plan worked out on shore was not getting us through at sea. I figured: What the hell! Here's a good frequency. Let them sweat tuning it in.

"'Open channel 21P on 9881,' Hayes tapped out like a nineteenth century railroad man on this ship pregnant with twentieth-century communications equipment. He called me back on the phone linked to the crypto room, where I was sitting by a teletype. 'They rogered for it, sir,' he reported, 'and told me to stand by.'

"I punched out the *Pueblo*'s call sign, NGVE, on the teletype paper tape, along with a few other requests in a communications shorthand: how were they reading us, signal strength, et cetera. I fed the tape into the machine and waited for a response to type itself out in front of me on the teletype machine. Nothing came. I tried a few more times. Still nothing. It was nearing 0900, and I had other work to do. I turned the teletype machine back over to the radioman and told him to keep trying. My big chance to be a supercommunicator had gone."

Persons familiar with ELINT ship operations disbelieve Schumacher's story. They point out that security in the SOD-Hut of an ELINT ship is such—recall Schumacher's earlier statement that he could not even enter it until he obtained a security clearance—that he would have been shot had he entered, "riffled" through messages, and attempted to use a code machine. And if by chance it did happen, the CTs who permitted it to happen would have been severely disciplined. My sources also reiterate that there is absolutely no communication between a SOD-Hut (most definitely not a cryptoroom!) and an insecure place.

Be that as it may, Schumacher does reveal that *Pueblo* was *receiving* messages during the night, and that the procedures for reaching Kamiseya were worked out "on shore." When Schumacher violated these procedures and tried to teletype Kamiseya on a channel they had "rogered for," he received no reply—nothing.

In an interview for this book, Radioman Hayes said, "I had the only transmitters on board and I destroyed them at the time of boarding. It was my last act even as they were boarding." When Hayes admitted he had never set foot inside the SOD-Hut, I asked him if there could be other transmitters in there which he didn't know about. He replied, "There could have been, I suppose. But I *thought* I had the only transmitters aboard *Pueblo.*"

Asked how the process worked, Hayes said, "The SOD-Hut would patch in through my transmitters, telling me what frequency they wanted. I didn't receive any messages personally. They went through my equipment right to the SOD-Hut. It was the same in sending messages. I could not transmit without permission from the SOD-Hut. I mostly sent weather reports and such."

By his own admission, Hayes never set foot in the SOD-Hut and had little idea what went on there. Persons familiar with ELINT ship operations explain that ships like *Pueblo* were in the business of communications, indeed had no other purpose, and the SOD-Hut possessed several R-90 transceivers (which could both transmit and receive messages) as well as other means of sending messages. Hayes may have thought he had the only transmitters on *Pueblo,* they state, but it simply was not so. I was further told that the CTs in the SOD-Hut might well have wanted to send the situation report through the ship's transmitters because they considered it routine and unimportant. *Pueblo* was in a beehive of electronic activity. Wanting to make maximum use of their own circuits, they would use the ship's transmitter to send a low priority message.

These persons acquainted with ELINT operations further state that of all Navy ships, an ELINT vessel has the most precise communications. Its location is known at all times and its lines of communication are always open. *Pueblo* would have been capable of transmitting via satellite if need be. The very idea that *Pueblo* failed to raise Kamiseya for seventeen hours the night before the seizure is to them absurd. In this light, recall Bailey's statement to Brandt that he could have reached Kamiseya on another channel but was under orders not to do so. Whose orders?

This seventeen-hour "breakdown" in communications the night before the seizure is surely strange on a ship, top-heavy with antennae and other communications gear, which contained several R-90 transceivers, teletypes, and code machines. There is even a man, Bailey, placed on board at the last moment as an expert in transmission difficulties for the precise purpose of straightening out "problems" so *Pueblo* will always be in touch with Kamiseya.

But what makes this "failure" in communications truly unbelievable is the events reported by Bucher in his book. One of the first acts of the boarders, he tells us, was to disconnect Hayes's transmitter, which was still running. *Hayes hadn't destroyed it!* About twenty or thirty minutes later, Bucher is forced to conduct the North Koreans on a tour of *Pueblo*. Inside the SOD-Hut, Bucher tells us, *the teletype to Kamiseya is still running,* and the North Koreans also disconnect that. If that is correct, then *Bailey's teletype wasn't operating through Hayes's transmitter.*

If the teletype link to Kamiseya wasn't established through the ship's transmitters operated by Hayes, then why tell all these elaborate stories about a "breakdown" in communications which ended only shortly before the seizure began? Even the Navy cited the breakdown in its radio transcript released to Congress.

It is a puzzle—an important one we need to pursue. One possibility is that there never was a "breakdown" and that all the stories told about it are made up and untrue. This I find hard to believe. A more likely possibility is that Bucher, Murphy, Schumacher, and all the crewmen who talked to Armbrister and Brandt *thought* there was a breakdown when, in actuality, the communications link could have been established at any desired time (as Bailey told Brandt)—and was indeed established over some channel which did not go through Hayes's transmitters! Recall that *Pueblo* could hear Kamiseya clearly saying, "Change frequencies, change frequencies." Hayes did, a dozen times. It went on all night. Finally, at mid-morning on seizure day, the same equipment produced a "five bye" signal. But it didn't. As Bucher informs us, the teletype was still running *after* Hayes's transmitter was shut down. Clearly another transmitter was in use in the SOD-Hut.

Why wasn't it used the night before? There are only two possibilities. One is that the SOD-Hut was busy and the CTs didn't want to tie up their transmitters sending routine messages they considered of little importance. If that was the case, why not simply say to Hayes, especially after he couldn't get through, that the SOD-Hut would send the situation report when it got around to it? Why keep Hayes up all night fiddling with his transmitters, worrying Bucher and himself about the failure in communications?

The second possibility is that the NSA-employed CTs at Kamiseya deliberately refused to accept the signal from *Pueblo,* at least the one Hayes was sending, and kept saying, "Change frequencies, change frequencies." Even when Schumacher violated procedures and was "rogered" through to Kamiseya, no reply was forthcoming.

Why on earth would the NSA-employed personnel at Kamiseya refuse to accept a message from *Pueblo* for seventeen hours? One reason comes to mind. If Bucher's situation report that he had been sighted by North Koreans didn't get through until an hour before the seizure began, then *no U.S. ships and planes would be on alert to come to Pueblo's aid during the seizure.*

As we will see shortly, Hayes's troubles were not the only failure of communications aboard *Pueblo.* At the most crucial moment in the seizure, when *Pueblo* is being fired upon and is in dire straits, the words are heard again, "Change frequencies, change frequencies."

If a person starts with the premise, as I do, that the United States Navy would do all it possibly could to protect its men in ships that are in a high-risk situation and under enemy attack, then an extremely large question must be asked: Did the NSA, which controlled *Pueblo* and communications with it, prevent the Navy from learning that their ship had been spotted and was at risk so they couldn't do anything about it until it was too late?

The night before the seizure was not uneventful in another way. Brandt writes (p. 34): "The night of January 22 was mildly interesting to Charlie Law. He had the eight-to-midnight watch. About nine o'clock Law saw a string of lights moving out from Wonsan.

"As the lights came closer, Law determined that he was seeing a fishing fleet moving out. By counting the lights he figured there were thirty to thirty-five boats in the fleet. About 10:30, Law saw a large merchantman coming toward the *Pueblo* from the direction of Wonsan. It passed within three thousand yards of the ship. There was sufficient light for Law to determine with a pair of binoculars that it carried Russian-made radar."

Murphy writes (p. 120): "During the night the CTs had logged eighteen contacts, the closest about three thousand yards. At 0145 (1:45 A.M.) someone had sent up an orange flare. It had illuminated the sky for about thirty seconds, but was too far away to reveal either the *Pueblo* or any other ship."

Murphy does not mention an event of that night which Armbrister reports (p. 36): "Gene Lacy felt uneasy. He saw occasional lights flicking on and off and sensed the ship was 'being followed.' Or was it only his imagination? The watch changed at midnight. The dead-reckoning track placed her 20-odd miles from shore. But loran indicated that she was inside the 13-mile line.* Damn that loran anyway; always malfunctioning. He mentioned his problem to Ensign Tim Harris, the officer of the deck. Reluctantly, Harris called Murphy to the bridge.

"The navigator was exhausted and in a grouchy mood. 'Some people think I'm made of iron,' he grumbled.

"'Well, sir,' Mack replied, 'I'm not sure of our position, and it would be most unfortunate if we got into that red area and they came out and threw us a line and said, "You're our prisoner."'

"'I wouldn't worry about that,' Murphy said. 'We'll pull off and tell them to go suck egg.'

"Murphy lit off the radar. No reason to worry anymore. The ship was well outside the red line.

"Off to the left Murphy could see the lights of Wonsan. Directly ahead about 2 miles some fishing boats were laying nets. At 1:45 that morning a bright orange flare shot up over the fishing boats. It hung in the stillness for ten or fifteen seconds."

Bucher never writes a word about any of this. Nor does Schumacher, but he does report the following conversation with Lacy, who came to relieve him in the pilothouse at 0715 on the twenty-third, a half hour early (p. 81).** "Briefly I filled him in on what had happened during my watch—in a word, nothing. I told him about the communications difficulties and then went over the chart with him.

"'You're not sure where you are, are you?' Gene said good-humoredly.

"'Of course, dummy,' I answered. 'In the Sea of Japan. Anyway, don't sweat it. We've been drifting in the right direction, and Law's on his way up to take the morning posit.'"

---

*Recall that Armbrister earlier reported that *Pueblo* spent the night twenty-five miles southeast of Wonsan. This would put the ship well inside the twelve-mile limit.

**Something is wrong here. Law told Brandt he had the 2000 to 2400 watch the night before. Lacy's comment to Armbrister indicates he had the watch then and was relieved at midnight by Tim Harris. Schumacher had the 0400 to 0800 watch and says he was relieved by Lacy. It is this sort of mix-up in details which makes re-creation of events difficult.

7

COVER STORY:
THE ENEMY
APPEARS

January 23, 1968.

Murphy arose before dawn, intending to shoot the stars for navigational purposes, but it was overcast. He learned that radio contact with Kamiseya still had not been established, despite Hayes's efforts. He also learned about the eighteen sightings and the orange flare. He writes (p. 120): "Were the North Koreans looking for us? If so, there was no sign of them now."

Bucher writes (p. 173) that he arose shortly before 0700 hours, "feeling stiff and unrested" after staying up most of the night waiting for the elusive radio contact to be made. After coffee, he went to the bridge, noted a "comparatively mild" twenty-degree temperature, a four-knot wind, a sea with "gentle swells," and a high thin overcast. The "rugged" Korean coastline was not visible in the pre-dawn darkness, but he could see "a few faint lights" on the higher ridges. "They were just clear enough," he writes, "to establish our position and confirm it as 25 miles offshore by checking the bottom contour with our depthsounder." He ordered Lacy, who was OOD, to close that distance to fifteen miles so *Pueblo* could monitor electronic traffic in the Wonsan area.

Murphy remembers these events differently (p. 120). "A little after seven, Commander Bucher came topside. By taking radar cuts on the island of Nan Do, we verified the position I had earlier logged [25 miles from shore, 16 from Nan Do].* After being briefed on the night's activ-

---

*Detailed 1:250,000 military maps of the Wonsan area show no Nan Island, nor is such a place listed in the *Korean Gazeteer*. I'm not saying there is no Nan Do, only that I can't find it and would like to know where it is.

ities, Bucher asked for a course that would take us fifteen to sixteen miles from the island of Ung Do. *This was not too far from where we had been the previous day* [emphasis mine], and it would place us in a good spot to monitor coastal traffic and observe ships leaving the port of Wonsan. I recommended a course of 300.'' (Recall that the night before, according to Brandt, Law saw fishing boats and a freighter with Russian-made radar leaving Wonsan. *Pueblo* returned to where the fishing boat had sighted it the day before!)

Armbrister gives essentially the same account, but is more specific. During the night *Pueblo* drifted five miles to the southeast, which is out to sea. Armbrister (p. 30): "At eight o'clock Bucher ordered full speed ahead, north by northwest, on a course of 300 degrees."

This is a sentence of utmost significance in trying to locate *Pueblo*. Armbrister reports that at dusk on the twenty-second, *Pueblo* withdrew from the coast to a point twenty-five miles southeast of Wonsan, then drifted five miles further southeast during the night. If the next morning *Pueblo* sailed north by northwest on a course of 300 degrees, this would take *Pueblo* to a point in the radar shadow of Yo Island near where the North Koreans say they captured it.

My point is this: Trevor Armbrister was not aboard *Pueblo*. A skilled journalist, he simply reported what people said to him. When crewmen during interviews told Armbrister that *Pueblo* was twenty-five miles southeast of Wonsan, they did one of two things. They either made a slip of the tongue that destroys the cover story that *Pueblo* was in international waters, or they deliberately left a clue to their true location. We will shortly encounter other, similar slips of the tongue or pen.

In their versions, Bucher and Murphy place *Pueblo* twenty-five miles from "nearest land." That location would make *Pueblo* a good forty miles from Wonsan, making it highly unlikely that Murphy had seen the lights of Wonsan the night before. Wherever *Pueblo* was, it now got under way. Murphy writes that *Pueblo* arrived on station at 1000 hours. Why it took two hours at full twelve-knot speed to go ten nautical miles was not explained by anyone.

Schumacher provides another, quite startling version (p. 81). "I had just sat down [in the wardroom for breakfast] when the Captain, dressed in a T shirt, khaki trousers, and shower slippers, shuffled in, poured himself a cup of coffee, yelled for the steward, and mumbled a good morning. He ordered eggs and chipped beef. I filled him in on the night's inactivities. *Rice Paddy* and *Rice Paddy I* had not returned. No one seemed much interested in us. [Note that Schumacher, who was relieved at 0715 hours, encounters the casually dressed Bucher in the wardroom—while Bucher and Murphy place the captain on the bridge shortly after 0700.]

"The Captain thought my report over while chewing on a piece of toast. 'Draft up a message, Skip, saying we consider the incident closed and that we're returning to EMCON [Emission Control]. Also, while you're at it, check on the communications. Christ, I can't figure out what the hell the trouble is, but I don't trust those goddamn electronic machines. Tell 'em to go off-line if they can't get through in an hour.' This meant to encrypt the messages separately and send them by CW [Morse]." Hayes had already asked to do that, but Steve Harris told him it was too tedious.

Schumacher: "Just before I left the wardroom, word came down from the bridge that we had drifted a good twenty-five miles from the nearest land, somewhere south of Wonsan.

"'Jesus Christ, how the hell did we manage to get so far out?' the Captain asked the wardroom at large. Then, in one of those quick decisions that can change the course of history, he told the bridge, over the wardroom phone, 'Let's get back in there!'"

If I had to select one utterance which suggests that *Pueblo* was much closer to Wonsan when seized than anyone admits, this would be it. Bucher writes they were twenty-five miles from land and orders the ship to go to fifteen. Armbrister says *Pueblo* had drifted five miles to the southeast and lay sixteen miles from the island of Nan, wherever that is. Murphy says *Pueblo* had "drifted slightly" to the southeast but was twenty-five miles from shore, sixteen from Nan. Schumacher says they are "somewhere south of Wonsan"—an utter impossibility unless *Pueblo* was on land. Schumacher hears Bucher ask, "Jesus Christ, how the hell did we manage to get so far out?" then say, "Let's get back in there!" Technically, going from twenty-five to fifteen miles qualifies as going "in," but Bucher's dismayed reaction to being so far out and his abrupt order to "get back in there" suggest, to me at least, that "in" is more in than fifteen miles.

Lee Hayes made radio contact with Kamiseya at about 0930 and Bailey, bending over the teletype, sent his situation report, drafted the previous afternoon, at about 1045, according to Armbrister and the radio transcript.

Bucher writes (p. 175): "There was absolutely nothing to suggest we were some fifteen miles off the entrance to North Korea's principal east-coast commercial and naval port; not a single patrol craft, coastwise tramp, nor even a lowly fishboat." Has Bucher slipped up here? His claim has been that they were 15.8 miles from Ung Island, 25 miles from Wonsan. When he writes of being some 15 miles from the "entrance" to

Wonsan, he is placing the ship in the radar shadow of Yo Island, approximately where the North Koreans say it was. It all depends, of course, on what he means by "entrance." A study of maps suggests the entrance to Wonsan is the area between the Hado and Kalma peninsulas. That is where the submarine nets are. It also suggests another simple way Bucher could have "doctored" evidence of the ship's position, as he admitted doing. Being 15.8 miles from *shore of the mainland* puts *Pueblo* well within North Korea's 12-mile limit.

Bucher continues: I was in a way disappointed, deciding that yesterday's flurry of excitement had been a passing thing. They had come out to let us know they knew of our presence, and having decided we were irritating but harmless capitalists conducting oceanographic research in the Sea of Japan, were now ignoring us and had withdrawn into their hermetic Communist isolation. It moved me to make up another SITREP to supplement the one we had been trying to send all night, the meat of this message being:

' . . . No significant ELINT . . . No longer under surveillance . . .

Intentions remain in area . . . This is last SITREP this incident.

UNODIR reverting to EMCON.'

"This was meant to convey to higher commands in Japan that the situation had cooled off since my last message, I was peacefully proceeding with our mission, and reverting to our status of radio silence. Radioman Hayes, red-eyed and weary from his efforts to establish a workable frequency with headquarters throughout the night, roused himself with equal dedication to overcome the difficulties in finding a suitable frequency for this less critical, but necessary, reassuring signal of the morning." Every other account has Bailey, not Hayes, sending this message. Indeed, Hayes has no authority to send messages.

Armbrister writes (p. 38): "In the crypto room below, Don Bailey stepped back to his teletype machine. He had slept less than three hours. He finished transmitting Bucher's initial situation report, then turned to the captain's second report. The circuit to Kamiseya was solid at last; he wouldn't need fourteen hours to send this one.

" ' . . . 68% fuel,' the message began; 'weather: wind, 280; four knots, sea state 0; barometer 30.25, falling . . . had 18 different contacts during the night. No identification made due to darkness. Closest was 3,000 yds. At 221645 Zulu* one contact ignited a large orange flare which glowed

*Zulu (frequently just Z) is U.S. Navy terminology for Greenwich Mean Time, used all over the world. By using Greenwich or Zulu time a person can calculate the time in whatever zone he is in. The number 221645 means it was 1645 (4:45 P.M.) on January 22 in London.

for about 30 secs. Meaning purpose unclear. No escorts during the night or early morning. No attempt made at surveillance/harassment. No significant ELINT; water depth 36 fathoms; intentions: remain in area. No longer under surveillance. This is last sitrep this incident. UNODIR reverting to EMCON.''

Bucher's reference to no significant ELINT comes despite the fact he says Harris told him that North Korean radar had picked them up and that "for an interesting change," according to Bucher, "there was some 'chatter' on nearby Korean voice communication frequencies."

In his book, Bucher mentions not one syllable about eighteen sightings and an orange flare—nor does Schumacher, who actually drafted the message, although Bucher approved it. Bucher and Schumacher would have us believe the sightings and flare never happened. Yet Murphy says he was told. Armbrister quotes Bucher's second situation report in which he mentions it. Why does Bucher ignore these events in his book? I don't know and it is up to him to say. Perhaps it was an oversight. Perhaps mentioning the nocturnal sightings would have destroyed the mood he is creating in his book. For pages he gives great detail of a ship in routine operation—watches changing, ice being chipped, plans made to air the ship's linen, enginemen "sprucing up . . . their inert diesels." He digresses with a discussion of how good the ship's food was, praises the cook, and gives the lunch menu: meatloaf, succotash, potatoes, and gravy. Everyone had second helpings. He quotes his lunchtime conversation with Lacy, Schumacher, and Steve Harris about Newfoundland's Grand Banks. All this sets the stage for the dramatic arrival of the North Korean subchaser. Perhaps mentioning ships and flares during the night—and the fact that *Pueblo* returned to where it had been spotted the day before—would have made it difficult to portray *Pueblo* as in an utterly routine situation with no foreboding of danger.

One other conclusion may be reached from Bucher's omission of the previous night's surveillance. He is bending over backward to indicate he had no inkling *Pueblo* was at risk. When the subchaser came near *Pueblo* south of Mayang Island, Bucher writes that all his officers agreed the vessel had not detected them, failing to mention Lacy, who felt it was "impossible" for them not to have been seen. In the episode with the fishing vessels, Bucher knows they have been spotted and identified, but the vessels leave and thereafter show no interest, "having decided we were irritating but harmless capitalists conducting oceanographic research," in his words. If Bucher had mentioned eighteen nocturnal sightings and an orange flare, he would have had to answer a large question: Why was

Pueblo, having been subjected to so much North Korean interest, remaining in an area where it had been spotted?

At 1145 hours, Lacy was replaced as OOD by Quartermaster Law, the only enlisted man aboard authorized to serve in that capacity. Murphy describes Law as "a good man, blustery, cocksure, but dependable, well liked by both officers and crew, and already an excellent navigator." Murphy takes his noon position, which is the same as at 1000, and goes to the wardroom for lunch. While Bucher ate meatloaf, succotash, and potatoes, seconds all around, Murphy had turkey with cranberry sauce, peas, and mashed potatoes and gravy. He, too, praises Harry Lewis, the cook, for managing to serve eighty-three men from the "minuscule galley," declaring it a "miracle of the highest order." Steve Harris also writes that he had turkey for lunch.

Not only was Murphy's menu different at the last meal any one of them would eat aboard *Pueblo,* so was the conversation. Murphy writes (p. 123): "As we ate, we discussed our encounter with the trawlers the previous day. At the time, there had been some disagreement over my identification of the ships. However, after Mack developed his pictures in one of the heads that doubled as a makeshift darkroom, the photos had been compared with those in the identification pubs. Everyone agreed that I had called them right. No one attached any great importance to the incident or the fact that we had been spotted. If anything, we were all a little bored and perhaps just a trifle disappointed that thus far the voyage had been so uneventful."

Whatever the topic of conversation, Bucher's lunch was interrupted by a call from Law that a vessel had been sighted "about eight miles to the south" and was approaching. Bucher told him to let him know when the ship was within five miles. (Murphy says three miles.) "Eating and conversation resumed. The sighting was routine and worried nobody," he writes. Such élan is at least a little remarkable considering the great efforts of a day or two before to keep *Pueblo* from being detected.

Bucher says he had "just started my second portion of meatloaf" when Law buzzed back to report the ship was now five miles away and "rapidly closing." Bucher writes: "It had covered three miles in four minutes, indicating a speed of better than 40 knots. It was no longer a routine sighting." Bucher headed for the bridge, hearing Lacy "make a last casual crack" that "maybe this won't be another dull day after all!"

Bucher trained the "big eyes" on the ship and made a tentative identification—a submarine chaser flying the North Korean ensign and bearing down at flank speed. He was "not alarmed, only slightly annoyed that he would show up at lunchtime." He summoned Steve Harris, Schumacher, and Photographer Mack to the bridge. He decided to "make sure" *Pueblo* looked like an oceanographic research vessel, and ordered international flags raised identifying the ship as a hydrographer and ordered Tuck and Iredale to "put on an extra Nansen cast for the benefit of our visitors." Then he checked the ship's position in the pilothouse. *Pueblo* was "a tenth less than sixteen miles" off Ung Island.

Harris came to the bridge. After having spotted a North Korean subchaser two afternoons before, Harris now "flipped through his identification book," Bucher writes, and announced: "She's a Russian-built, modified SO-1 class submarine chaser. One hundred-thirty feet overall by twenty-one feet beam. Speeds up to forty-eight knots through sea-state two. Normally armed with depth charges and automatic cannons, but other configurations, including missiles, may be encountered. Normal complement is three officers and sixteen crewmen." (To compare the two ships, recall that *Pueblo* was 176 feet long, 32 feet in beam. The subchaser was roughly two-thirds the size of *Pueblo,* much more heavily armed, and had four times the speed. *Pueblo,* however, carried eighty-three crewmen, as against nineteen on the North Korean vessel.)

Bucher said that was what he made her out to be also, then ordered Harris to the SOD-Hut to "find out if your CTs can eavesdrop on any talk with her base. It might be fun to know her impressions of us."

Harris replied, according to Bucher, "We'll do our best, Captain. Our circuits are still open to report her presence."

And Bucher said, "Okay, but don't get everybody in an uproar. Remember that another one like her just peacefully steamed past us the other evening."

And Lieutenant Harris replied, "Yes sir, I'll keep you informed."

With Steve Harris now off to carry out his orders in the SOD-Hut, Bucher ordered all crewmen below deck and out of sight except the oceanographic people on the foredeck and those assigned to the bridge. All wore "conglomerate non-regulation cold weather clothing that I permitted on this distant independent mission. I was myself wearing a heavy leather flight jacket and woolen ski-cap crowned by a fuzzy red tassel." The purpose of this order was to aid *Pueblo*'s masquerade as a hydrographer, which would normally carry a crew of only thirty.

Bucher looked back at the subchaser through his binoculars. At a thousand yards he could see that "her twin automatic cannon was fully manned and aimed at us. She was charging us in a state of General Quarters—Battle Stations!" This did not signify imminent battle to

Bucher, "only the same kind of harassment that *Banner* had endured many times and that I had been briefed to expect for my own ship." Not wanting an enlisted man as OOD, he replaced Law with Lacy. Then he ordered the engineroom "to start up our diesels and be ready to answer bells."

Murphy's recollections are considerably different (p. 124). He begins by reporting, "In the crypto room, outboard of the sod hut, Radioman Don E. Bailey interrupted the message he was transmitting to Kamiseya, Japan, to quickly tap: COMPANY OUTSIDE." (I don't know what Murphy means by "outboard." The crypto room was *inside* the SOD-Hut. Non-CTs also make the mistake of calling any place a code message is sent the "crypto room." Among CTs, that term is reserved for the separate, highly secure room where the code machine is housed. I cannot determine if Bailey was in the crypto room or another part of the SOD-Hut. Murphy's use of the word "tapping" suggests Bailey was sending in Morse. He was not. At least Murphy acknowledges Bailey's activity—and the transcript of *Pueblo* radio messages which resulted—something Bucher does not do for quite a long time. It should be noted, however, that at the time, Murphy, in the pilothouse, could not possibly have known what Bailey was sending or that he was sending any message at all.)

Murphy says Bucher looked through the "big eyes," "at the same time yelling down the voice tube to the pilothouse that he wanted Steve Harris to report to him immediately with his identification manuals. Because there was no telephone link between the signal bridge and the SOD-Hut, each order had to be repeated by whoever was manning the phones in the pilothouse, a waste of precious time and potentially a source of confusion." What Murphy doesn't explain is that there was no communication between the pilothouse and *inside* the SOD-Hut, either.

Murphy (p.124) says Harris came, exclaiming "excitedly" on climbing the ladder to the bridge: "You should hear things buzzing down there! . . . They must have every fire-control radar in the country locked on us. If they wanted to, they could blast us right out of the water!" This is surely a different Harris and a different conversation than Bucher described.

According to Murphy, by the time Harris reached the bridge, the subchaser had "closed to less than a mile," which is roughly two thousand yards. "Taking the glasses, Steve immediately identified her as a Soviet-type SO-1 subchaser." Murphy says "we" could see "men on deck at battle stations. She was a warship, primed and ready for action, and she was headed straight for the *Pueblo* at close to flank speed."

Murphy writes that "Bucher had a choice to make, and it had to be made quickly." Murphy recalled "our sail order" referring to "Soviet ships in the Tsushima Straits region." *Pueblo* was to operate "at least five hundred yards" away and "not interfere with Soviet exercises but maintain a position on the periphery for observation purposes." Murphy said *Pueblo* also had the "experience of *Banner*" to draw on, which was "observe; don't get involved; when threatened *disengage* [Murphy's emphasis]." He adds, "It was also the procedure we had followed thus far on this voyage." He does not explain this statement. *Pueblo* had observed and tried not to get involved, but when was it threatened? And when did it disengage? On the 21st and on both the afternoon and night of the 22nd, *Pueblo* remained dead in the water, making no effort to leave, as North Korean vessels approached. Were there other voyages when *Pueblo* did disengage and sail away?

Murphy continues (p. 125): "But to disengage in our present position would mean to light off [start up] the engines and make a run for the open sea.

"Whether because he felt to do so would look as if he were running from a fight, or whether because, a gambler at heart, he was sure he could buck the odds, Bucher decided to bluff. *He gave no engine orders* [emphasis mine]. The *Pueblo* remained dead in the water. As with most of his decisions, he did not ask any of his officers for concurrence or advice."

The captain of *Pueblo* says he ordered the engineroom "to start up our diesels and be ready to answer bells," while his executive officer, second in command, writes that "he gave no engine orders."

Armbrister, using his many sources aboard *Pueblo,* reported this about the engine orders (pp. 41–2): "The number one engine had been down for the past few minutes. A fuel injector had burned out, and Engineman Third Class Darrell D. Wright was trying to change it. Norman Spear was there to help him. They slipped the new injector into place, and Wright decided to test it. He called the pilot house and asked Murphy for permission to light off the engines. Murphy said no. There was some activity up on the surface. It wouldn't be wise to create any unnecessary disturbance.

"Almost immediately, Bucher countermanded that order. To be sure, the captain thought, this would turn out to be nothing more than routine harassment. The SO1 might keep him company for the next day or two, in much the same way that Soviet ships had shadowed USS *Banner.* Still, he might have to engage in some tricky maneuvers. Better to light off both engines now. Wright received his instructions and reported back within seconds: 'Ready to answer all bells.'"

It should be observed that while this quote appears to substantiate Bucher's claim that he started his engines when the subchaser appeared, it really does not. In the first paragraph, Armbrister quotes enginemen who say they were told not to test the engines. The second paragraph is based, obviously, upon Bucher's statement to Armbrister. Moreover, Armbrister later provides the contents of the first Pinnacle message, sent nearly an hour into the seizure. The message says *Pueblo* was "dead in the water." This message was prepared by Schumacher, who writes in his book that the engines were started well into the seizure, when *Pueblo* tried to escape North Korean boarders. Brandt, writing of events fifteen minutes into the seizure (p. 37), says: "The *Pueblo* was dead in the water with no engines running, as it had been all along." The Naval Court of Inquiry also was told *Pueblo* was dead in the water.

Thus, Bucher is all alone in his statement that he ordered the engines started when the seizure began. When the engines were lit is of importance. It will come up again, as the story progresses.

The matter of Nansen casts is also important. Murphy (p. 125): "There is some disagreement over whether Bucher or Tuck then suggested as a 'cover' the oceanographers should take a Nansen cast. Both, however, agreed it was a good idea, and Tuck hurried toward the well deck to drop the bottles. At the same time Bucher ordered Signalman Leach to hoist flags identifying us as a hydrographer."

Armbrister adds details. "Bucher turned to Leach, the sallow-faced signalman, and told him to raise the international signal for conducting hydrographic operations.

"Harry Iredale had stepped into the chief petty officers' quarters to get his foul-weather jacket, cap, and gloves, and now he was waiting for Tuck to come by. Tuck didn't appear. That was odd—they always went forward together. Iredale glanced at his watch. Maybe Tuck had gone forward by himself. He decided to look.

"Tuck was having trouble removing the tarp over the oceanographic winch. It was covered with ice; the ropes around the bottom were stiff, and it took him about five minutes to pull it clear. Then Iredale arrived. They lowered the cable slowly, attaching the heavy brass bottles at standard intervals."

This description is fine, except Bucher has reported Tuck and Iredale made Nansen casts that morning and already had one line out, writing, "I called my oceanographers from their meal to put on an *extra* Nansen cast.'' Whether there were one or two casts will also become important.

The SO-1 "began cutting a wide but tightening circle" around *Pueblo*, Bucher writes. Armbrister reports that on her second circle the ship was five hundred yards from *Pueblo*. The SO-1 hoisted international signal flags which Leach read as, "What nationality?"

Bucher ordered, "Raise the ensign." Armbrister gives a precise time for this—1214 hours, roughly fifteen minutes into the seizure. Murphy says the flag *Pueblo* raised was "the biggest American ensign we had aboard." Bucher saw the flag cause a "flurry of activity" on the North Korean ship, seeing through his lens a "silent pantomime picture of surprise and momentary confusion." Bucher adds that by this time Skip Schumacher and Ensign Tim Harris had come to the bridge, "looking over the situation with an eager, youthful curiosity which neither could hide beneath attempts at acting unperturbed." He set Schumacher to drafting a Pinnacle message on the situation and said to Harris, "Make yourself at home in my bridge chair and start keeping a running narrative log on whatever show they decide to put on."

Bucher continues: "At this moment, Gene Lacy suddenly sang out: 'Three high-speed torpedo boats, bearing 160, range short ten-thousand yards with zero angle on the bow!'

"Grateful that he had had the foresight to keep a sharp lookout beyond the diversion within our immediate vicinity, I aimed my binoculars toward the sighting which was in the general direction of Wonsan, confirmed it, and called after Skip: 'Add that to the JOPREP PINNACLE! Ask them to keep the circuits open for more.'

"I meant by that a full-fledged harassment operation appeared to be imminent, as opposed to the surveillance by a single unit of the North Korean navy I had initially anticipated."

Apparently, even though the subchaser was at battle stations and circling his ship, it still constituted surveillance to Bucher. He recalled that on "several occasions" *Banner* had been "surrounded by several intimidating Red Chinese or Russian vessels." Apparently he was in for the same. He adds: "It flashed through my mind that here was the unexpected opportunity to really test, *according to our orders* [emphasis mine], their reaction to our presence near their territorial waters. *Near* [Bucher's emphasis]—not inside them."

I have emphasized words in this paragraph because they leave no doubt that Bucher had orders—unlike Clark on *Banner*—to remain where he was and "test" North Korean reactions to *Pueblo*'s presence. In other words, what would the North Koreans do if *Pueblo* didn't leave?

Bucher then writes: "The SO-1 was making its second circle around us and had closed to within five hundred yards so we could clearly see her crew wearing their peculiar foot-soldier uniforms. They now raised a second hoist of signals which read: HEAVE TO OR I WILL FIRE!"

What is important is the order of events. Bucher has Lacy sighting the three torpedo boats, *then* the subchaser signaling HEAVE TO OR I WILL FIRE. Every other writer has the subchaser so signaling as soon as the U.S. flag is raised. The sighting of torpedo boats comes much later.

All accounts report Bucher was dumbfounded by the signal. He quotes himself as saying, "What the hell does he mean by that? We are already lying dead in the water!" Dead in the water means shut down and floating. This statement belies Bucher's earlier claim that he ordered his engines started. He can't have it both ways.

There followed then some confusion about the meaning of "heave to." Bucher yelled to Murphy, "What the hell's the precise meaning of 'heave to'?" Murphy says he was sure Bucher knew as well as he did, but he consulted Harris in the SOD-Hut. Some of the CTs, green to the sea, thought it meant to get under way. Harris consulted a dictionary of nautical terms. "There's only one meaning," Harris told Murphy. "To bring a vessel to a standstill." Murphy (p. 127) says he wrote the definition on a piece of paper and ran all the way from the SOD-Hut to the flying bridge to give it to Bucher. He could not resist a jibe, writing, "There was at least one advantage to Bucher's asinine decision to conn [control] the ship from the signal bridge, I decided. It was a damned good way to lose weight." (Observe that Murphy went to and from the SOD-Hut. He didn't phone.)

Murphy writes: "I handed the sheet to Bucher. His puzzled look matched my own. How could we come to a standstill if we were already dead in the water? *We could only guess the North Koreans meant for us to stay exactly where we were* [emphasis mine]." In his account (p. 42) Armbrister takes a moment to say what was going on in the mind of Steve Harris: "There was no porthole in the research spaces, and Harris—who had just returned there—wondered what was happening outside. Initially, there hadn't been any reason for concern. The presence of an enemy ship—*this was what he and his men had been hoping for* [emphasis mine]. He knew that *Pueblo* still lay dead in the water [another vote!], and, surprisingly, he felt a 'sudden urge to get out of there.'" Why was that surprising? For a virtually unarmed ship to flee from a vessel at battle stations would be a normal desire of most people.

The emphasis in the paragraph is mine. Why would Harris and the CTs hope for the presence of an enemy ship, especially after all the supposed efforts to avoid detection? Could it be that their orders were to remain on station until harassed, then stick around to monitor messages? Every author, save Bucher, says the SOD-Hut controlled the ship, telling Bucher where to take it as a "taxi driver." If Harris, officer in charge of the research detachment, had an urge to leave, why didn't he exercise his authority and tell Bucher to get *Pueblo* under way?

I don't know, maybe the confusion over HEAVE TO—and Bucher, Murphy, Schumacher, and Armbrister all describe it in a similar fashion—is meant for comic relief, for it is enough to make a weekend sailor, let alone an admiral, cringe with embarrassment. A U.S. Navy ship captain asking for the meaning of "heave to"! Bucher, who had undergone extensive briefings with Commander Clark of *Banner,* had to know the North Koreans were using a standard flag signal. Even crewmen aboard *Pueblo* knew this, as reported earlier from Brandt.

What did Bucher reply to the HEAVE TO signal? The question ought to have an easy answer, but it doesn't.

Bucher: "I . . . ordered my signalmen to make the International flag-hoist: I AM IN INTERNATIONAL WATERS."

Murphy: "Returning to the signal bridge, Bucher had Leach hoist a new set of flags: I AM IN INTERNATIONAL WATERS.

"But he couldn't leave it at that. He had to add the Bucher touch, a nose-thumbing gesture of defiance: INTEND TO REMAIN IN THE AREA UNTIL TOMORROW."

Armbrister: "Back on the flying bridge again, he [Bucher] told Leach to hoist a reply: 'I am in international waters.' And then, 'I intend to remain in present location until tomorrow. . . .'"

Schumacher: "The Captain signaled the North Koreans that he was in international waters."

Steve Harris: "At 1,000 yards the SO-1 signaled, HEAVE TO OR I'LL FIRE, then FOLLOW IN MY WAKE. I HAVE A PILOT ABOARD. The captain ordered our signalman to signal back, I AM IN INTERNATIONAL WATERS."

Brandt: "Then he ordered Leach to raise a signal flag meaning, 'I am hydrographic.'"

Leach told the Court of Inquiry that he never raised the I AM IN INTERNATIONAL WATERS signal. He raised "some kind of protest," but couldn't remember what it was. Bucher made a reappearance before the Court to say Leach was mistaken.

Poor Leach. Everyone is against him except Brandt. Even Hayes, in an interview with me, said, "I heard Bucher order that signal. Leach was unfamiliar with the signals and having a hard time." (If Bucher and Leach were on the signal bridge and Hayes was in the radio shack, it is difficult to understand how Hayes came to possess this knowledge.) Even Brandt's support for Leach is diluted. He writes (p. 41) that much later when *Pueblo,* faced with imminent boarding, was under way to escape, "Bucher ordered Leach to send a signal by *semaphore:* 'Am in international waters. Am leaving area.' He told Law to watch through binoculars for a reply." The emphasis is mine. Waving semaphore is not hoisting flags.

Leach may take comfort from the first Pinnacle message sent to Kamiseya from *Pueblo.* As reported by Armbrister (p. 43), it reads:

AGER-2/JOPREP/PINNACLE 3/100: USS *Pueblo* encountered one SO1 North Korean patrol craft at 0300Z posit 39.25.2N/127-55.0E; dead in the water. . . . SO1 pennant number 35 approached from 180, speed 15 and circled the ship once, on second trip around hoisted code Juliet Oscar Bravo translated as nationality. *Pueblo* hoisted US ensign, then ran up Hotel Juliet Delta, code translated hydrographer. On third swing no. 35 code Oscar Lima translated, "heave to or I will fire on you." . . . Ship continued to circle *Pueblo*; intentions: to remain in area if considered feasible otherwise to withdraw slowly to the northeast. . . .

There is not one syllable here about an I AM IN INTERNATIONAL WATERS signal. Nor does it show up in the second Pinnacle message from *Pueblo.*

The first Pinnacle message was drafted by Schumacher on Bucher's orders. There had been so much harassment of ELINT ships that the Navy had prepared a standard form for reporting incidents. Schumacher went to the radio shack and began to fill one out.

Armbrister reports the message "would go out to the high-level officers in Address Indicating Group (AIG) 7623 as a Joint Operational Report (JOPREP), an umbrella the Navy uses to cover anything from harassment at sea to a measles epidemic. The 'Pinnacle' designator would merit special attention and the precedence—'flash'—would hurry it along."

Bucher writes that Schumacher, showing him the message, "urgently asked me" if the message priority should be upgraded from "Flash" to "Critic." This was, as Bucher describes it, a "new priority that had been devised to flag important messages that were to go through immediately to all echelons of higher command including the White House." As this was a new system, never used by anyone to Bucher's knowledge, he asked Schumacher for a quick review of the purpose of the Critic message. After listening, Bucher authorized the Critic priority.

Schumacher, who wrote the Pinnacle message and ought to know, gives a strikingly different account (pp. 86–7): "I took the [Pinnacle] message down to the SOD Hut at 12:50 P.M. and watched the CT on duty there, McClarren, quickly pound it out on the teletype. It took him two minutes to punch a paper tape and feed it into the teletype machine for mechanical transmission to Japan. So it was 12:52 when the machine started transmitting. Two minutes after that, Japan rogered for it. Our commanders on shore knew from that moment on that we were in a tight situation. [We will see that they knew no such thing.]

"This first message was called Pinnacle I/JOPREP (Joint Operational Report) 3. 'Pinnacle' identifies a dispatch as one of special interest to the Joint Chiefs of Staff, the National Military Command Center at the Pentagon, and the White House. [This differs from the description of a Pinnacle given by Bucher and Armbrister.] We assigned a message transmission priority of Flash to this first harassment report. 'Flash' meant that the message should be transmitted by the worldwide Navy communications system ahead of any other message. There was only one designation higher than Flash. Steve Harris reminded me of it in the SOD Hut. 'We have a Critic tape already cut, Skip, if the Captain wants to wake up the President.'

"'All right, Steve, I'll tell him about it.'

"The 'Critic' designation is supposed to assure speedier handling by opening a clear channel direct to the White House, the National Security Agency, and the Pentagon. It is a designation reserved for the most urgent crises."

The difference in these versions is that Bucher, upon approving the first Pinnacle message, learns about the new Critic designation from Schumacher and authorizes its use. Schumacher says he went to the SOD-Hut with the message designated as Pinnacle, saw it sent, then was reminded of the Critic priority by Harris. Schumacher says he will tell Bucher about it. Somebody's wrong. As it turns out, when the second Pinnacle message was prepared, according to Schumacher, and he returned to the SOD-Hut at 1314 to have it sent, Steve Harris said to him, "We've got good communications with Japan. And we've prepared a Critic message. It's all ready to send." Schumacher says he replied, "Okay, Steve. I'll keep you informed." He still hadn't talked to Bucher about the Critic priority! He refers later to Harris having sent his prepared

Critic message on his own. No reference to a Critic message shows up in the transcript of *Pueblo* messages released by the Navy.

It is possible to clear up this confusion about Critic messages. Armbrister, who is the only person to interview personnel in Japan, reports that the two Pinnacle messages from *Pueblo* were upgraded to Critic *in Japan* when it was realized a U.S. Navy ship was under attack. Clearly, Bucher, Schumacher, and Steve Harris, all learning later that a Critic message was sent, tried in separate ways to account for it. All three simply made up something which seemed plausible—only it wasn't correct. No Critic message ever left *Pueblo*. These after-the-fact "explanations" occur frequently in the books by Bucher, Murphy, and Schumacher—damaging their credibility.

What was happening topside? Bucher (p. 182): "As the four torpedo boats closed in, broke their loose formation, and deployed themselves to cover us from all sides, near enough for me to see with the naked eye that they had fully manned machine-gun mounts aimed at us, I became aware of how rapidly things were happening. It had only been a little over twenty minutes since the SO-1 was first sighted."

Murphy, second in command, is in the pilothouse, present, and events are not the same to him. He writes (p. 128): "Bucher probably felt he had good reason to be cocky." Murphy refers to Bucher's hoist of the INTEND TO REMAIN IN THE AREA UNTIL TOMORROW signal. "Thus far his bluff appeared to have worked. Nearly *forty minutes* [emphasis mine] had passed since the subchaser was first sighted." What took twenty minutes to Bucher took twice as long to Murphy.

Murphy continues: "Although the SO-1's circles grew ever tighter—she had by now closed to not more than a hundred yards—there was no indication this was other than the standard harassment the *Banner* had experienced. Even the 'Heave to or I will fire' threat wasn't novel. But there were two differences. The *Banner* had been moving when the Soviets hoisted their signal; Clark had ignored it and continued to disengage. And we were not dealing with the Russians or the Red Chinese, but with a new and unpredictable adversary.

"With five words from Gene Lacy, who was at the Big Eyes, the whole picture changed: 'Three more contacts, bearing 160!'"

For the non-nautical, which includes me, compass directions are based on a circle of 360 degrees. Zero and 360 degrees are due north. Due east is 090, due south 180, due west 270. The first Pinnacle message, as quoted by Armbrister, says the subchaser came on a heading of 180, which is due south. This is difficult to understand. If *Pueblo* was where it was said to be, twenty-five miles north and east of Wonsan, due south is open water for a long distance. To reach *Pueblo* from Wonsan, the subchaser would have had to go easterly for perhaps twenty miles, then turn sharply to the north. A more direct route would have taken it from the southwest, a bearing (to *Pueblo*) of about 250. When Bucher and Murphy say the torpedo boats came from 160 that is even worse. That has them arriving from somewhere in the Sea of Japan. And when Bucher says that the sighting of the torpedo boats "was in the general direction of Wonsan" he refers to an utter impossibility. Wonsan is to his *southwest,* not southeast.

Even if *Pueblo* was where the North Koreans say they boarded it (or close by in the radar shadow of Yo Island) these compass directions still make no sense. The most direct route for the subchaser from Wonsan would have brought it from the southwest, not due south.

There is one way the 180 bearing does make sense. If *Pueblo* was indeed hiding in the radar shadow of Yo, the North Koreans wouldn't have been certain where it was or even that it was there. The subchaser may have been sent out to search for it, thus approaching from the south.

This does not account for the 160 heading of the PT boats. Later, as we discover what really did happen to *Pueblo,* an explanation for this 160 heading will be offered.

Murphy has the three torpedo boats sighted *after* the subchaser has circled *Pueblo,* raised its HEAVE TO signal, and gotten a response of I AM IN INTERNATIONAL WATERS and INTEND TO REMAIN IN THE AREA UNTIL TOMORROW. Bucher sees the torpedo boats* after raising the U.S. flag and *prior to* the HEAVE TO signal from the subchaser. They cannot both be correct, and the timing of these events is hardly academic.

Murphy (p. 128): "They [the torpedo boats] were closing, and fast, from the general direction of Wonsan [which again cannot possibly be a heading of 160 degrees]. In what seemed an amazingly short time, the white wakes changed to sharp configurations. After thumbing through the pubs, Steve [Harris, who supposedly is back in the SOD-Hut, not on the bridge or in the pilothouse] identified them as North Korean P-4 motor

---

*I'm sure it is just a typo, but on page 182 of his book Bucher sees four torpedo boats. On page 183, there are three, as quoted above.

torpedo boats, length 63 feet, maximum speed fifty knots, or four times faster than the *Pueblo.*

"Bucher apparently questioned Steve's identification, arguing with him several minutes before accepting it.

"He then barked several orders: Tim Harris, who was already on the signal bridge, was to keep a running narrative of everything that transpired; Schumacher was to prepare a new Pinnacle, apprising COMNAVORJAPAN and CINCPACFLT [naval commands in Japan and Hawaii] of our worsening situation, this message, on Schumacher's suggestion, to be upgraded from Flash to Critic [another attempted after-the-fact explanation]; . . . and I was to set up a team to chart the movements of the four ships.

"But still no engine order. And no order to man the machine guns."

Murphy's order of events, then, is that forty minutes elapsed while the SO-1 closed its circles on *Pueblo.* Then the three torpedo boats were sighted. He says Bucher argued "several minutes" about their identity, then barked orders, one of which was to prepare the second Pinnacle message.

Bucher's order of events is different. After sighting the subchaser, he ordered the ship's engines started, ordered the extra Nansen cast, raised the U.S. flag, saw the torpedo boats coming, ordered the first Pinnacle message prepared, saw the subchaser's HEAVE TO signal, replied I AM IN INTERNATIONAL WATERS, and saw the torpedo boats surround his ship—all within twenty minutes.

To Bucher the torpedo boats were circling "within fifty yards with their machine guns aimed" and "their decks filled with what looked like soldiers or marines armed with Russian-type automatic carbines." He also saw the subchaser still flying its HEAVE TO OR I WILL FIRE flags. At this point, he writes, he hoisted his INTEND TO REMAIN IN THE AREA signal—which Murphy and Armbrister say he raised at the time of the I AM IN INTERNATIONAL WATERS signal. Bucher adds: "Noticing that my signalman was little shaky as he tied in the flag-hoist, possibly as much from the intense cold as from the mounting tension, I breezily exclaimed for the benefit of all the personnel on the flying bridge:

"'We're not going to let these sons-o'-bitches bullshit us!'"

He then hears and sees a pair of Russian-built MIGs flashing on a low pass over the ship. "Then I spotted a fourth torpedo boat appearing out of nowhere and bearing down on us from a distance of less than a mile." He also sees the white wake of a second subchaser "coming out to join in the fun." At this point Schumacher returns to the bridge after taking the first Pinnacle message to the SOD-Hut for transmission. Bucher asks him if he got it off. Schumacher nods. Bucher says: "Okay! Then get set to plug in number two!" He "started rattling off the bare facts of the developments over the past ten minutes to supplement our first report."

Twenty minutes and another ten make a half hour. It should now be about 1230 hours, half an hour since the whole incident began, according to Bucher's calculation.

Bucher's timing is way off. Schumacher was precise (and correct) that the first Pinnacle message went off at 1252 and was acknowledged at 1254. After that he returned to the bridge and "found the situation worse. Three torpedo boats were speeding toward us from Wonsan. We could see their rooster tails and then their profiles. We decided from the pub that they were Soviet-designed P-4's, which were eighty-two feet long [not Murphy's sixty-three] and had a top speed of over fifty knots. The *Pueblo*'s pitiful top speed was 13.1 knots.

"The subchaser kept circling as the PT boats closed in. The PT's trained forty-millimeter [!] machine guns on us. They also had loaded torpedo tubes and carried helmeted troops armed with AK-47 automatic rifles.

"Two MIG fighters screamed overhead, banking into wide circles off our starboard bow. One of them, the Captain told me, had fired a rocket way beyond us while I was below. A fourth torpedo boat came out from Wonsan to join the others. We could just make out a second subchaser on the horizon. . . .

"We sat tight. The torpedo boats surrounded us as we lay dead in the water, swinging as close as fifty yards, like sharks getting ready to rip. . . . The Captain weighed his narrowing options. His orders said not to give way to Communist harassment. But he was responsible for the safety and security of his ship and crew, even if that might mean running away. He had to decide on his own when the Communist bluffing stopped and the real danger to his ship began.

"The Captain told Lacy to start the main engines and to have the word passed to prepare for emergency destruction. I drafted a follow-up harassment message. . . .

"The subchaser raised a new flag signal. 'Follow in my wake; I have pilot aboard.' The Captain did not respond."

Brandt reports an important event as occurring at this time. *Bucher left the bridge.* As Brandt reports (p. 40), "Bucher . . . had left the bridge and run down to the research space. He told Don Bailey he was concerned about the amount of tension building up and dictated a message to CT

Jerry Karnes, twenty-two, of Havana, Arkansas, for transmission by Bailey. Bailey assured Bucher that the circuit was working well, and then sent Bucher's message, which outlined briefly the general situation and said he would ignore the subchaser's signals and steam out to sea.''

No other account, including those of Bucher, Murphy, Schumacher and Armbrister, refers to Bucher leaving the bridge and dictating such a message. The words do not show up in the radio transcript. The closest is a message which Brandt says Bailey sent following Bucher's: "Then Bailey sent a message on his own hook, 'Sure looks like we could use some help out here,' he punched." Something similar to those words ("—AND SURE COULD USE SOME HELP NOW") shows up on the transcript at 1411—very late in the transcript.

I assume Brandt's reporting is accurate—although it is possible Bailey made another of his "mistakes" in what he told Brandt. There remains, however, a powerful reason to believe something like this did happen. Bucher is a "taxi driver," sailing his ship to a specific location and remaining until authorized to leave. Under orders, as he states, to "test" North Korean intentions, but seeing a rapidly deteriorating situation, he goes to the SOD-Hut to "outline briefly the general situation" and inform headquarters that he plans to "ignore the subchaser's signals and steam out to sea."

This excerpt from Brandt indicates Bucher's true authority aboard his ship, the nature of his orders which he was following "to the letter," and the difficulties he faced in trying to extricate his ship from the "general situation." It also indicates that NSA was warned shortly after 1300 hours, not an hour later, by Bailey that it "sure looks like we could use some help out here." They didn't get it. They never did.

What was happening when Bucher returned to the bridge from the SOD-Hut? Murphy tells us that it was after 1315 when the MIGs appeared. He continues (pp. 129–30):

"I was too preoccupied to do more than acknowledge their [the MIGs] presence. Watching through my binoculars from the pilothouse, I could see that the men on the decks of the SO-1 and the P-4 seemed to be conferring. Then I saw something that sent chills down my spine. Rubber tires and rope mattings had been slung over the side of the P-4, and some dozen men, wearing helmets and carrying automatic arms, had moved from the SO-1 onto the P-4's deck.

"They were forming a boarding party!

"Running back up the ladder to the signal bridge, I told the skipper what I had seen. But Bucher had just spotted it himself. I expected him to call repel-boarders Drill. But he didn't. He just stood there quivering with anger. They had called his bluff! Suddenly all his accumulated failures and frustrations came out in one loud bellow of rage: *'I wish I could dive this damn thing!'* [Murphy's emphasis] Bucher cried."

There is clearly great discrepancy in time. Bucher describes a quick, fast-moving series of events, taking a half hour from sighting to attempted boarding. Murphy and Schumacher describe a slower-moving seizure taking almost twice as long. Armbrister is in accord, reporting it was 1317 when "the P-4 was backing down toward *Pueblo*. . . . The P-4 continued backing down on *Pueblo*'s starboard quarter: 100 yards, 50, 30. Mike Alexander heard the soldiers cocking their rifles. He glanced at his friend, Communications Technician First Class Charles R. [Joe] Sterling. Sterling had heard them, too. For a moment neither man spoke.

"Bucher stared at the troops in the boarding party, stunned by their sheer gall. Those guys were *serious* [Armbrister's emphasis]."

Fortunately, there is a record of time and at least some semblance of order of events: the transcript of radio messages between *Pueblo* and Kamiseya. We look at this in the next chapter.

8

COVER STORY: THE FLIGHT

The edited, declassified transcript of *Pueblo*'s last radio transmissions was given to the Pike Committee on March 13, 1969—surely in plenty of time for the Naval Court of Inquiry to have seen it. It was sent to Frank Slatinshek, staff counsel for the House subcommittee, by Rear Adm. Leslie J. O'Brien, Jr., special assistant to the Chief of Naval Operations for *Pueblo* Matters.

The transcript reviews the communications difficulties of the night before the seizure. The "first record of contact" by *Pueblo* with a shore station was at 1820 on January 22. The Navy described ship-to-shore communications in the area as "sometimes difficult" and "not always satisfactory." Thirteen different frequencies were tried before two-way communication was established at 1054 hours on January 23. As we have seen, this is more than an hour later than other writers state. The circuit was described as a "100 word-per-minute simplex (one-way reversible), crypto-covered, high frequency radio teletype circuit." The circuit remained open from 1054 to 1432, "when *Pueblo* went off the air to destroy the crypto equipment." (As we will see, it was not destroyed.)

As released by the Navy, the radio transcript is in three columns (see appendix 1). To the left is the Korean local time. The second column is a record of the transmissions between *Pueblo* and Kamiseya. The third column describes the actions taken by the Navy on the basis of *Pueblo*'s messages.

Who were the operators of the teletype? Armbrister says Don Bailey was at the *Pueblo* end and a chief communications technician named Richard A. Haizlip was at Kamiseya, the NSA base in Japan. Apparently they were friends, co-workers until Bailey made this one trip to straighten out *Pueblo*'s communications difficulties. Murphy also says it was Bailey. So does Schumacher. Ed Brandt, who interviewed both Bailey and CT2 Donald R. McClarren, says the two took turns manning the teletype. The facts seem to be that Bailey manned it most of the time, McClarren relieving him occasionally.

At 1100 hours *Pueblo* completed transmission of the SITREP 1 message, which Bucher and Schumacher had drafted the previous afternoon after the fishing boats circled *Pueblo*. At Kamiseya the Navy's "Watch Officer Intelligence" read it and "filed [it] on interest board."

At 1135 *Pueblo* completed transmission of "Intel-Tech Rpt #1." This was Steve Harris's report on his activities and its precedence "was Routine and message was addressed to [related to] fifteen activities." The Navy concluded: "Routine patrol; *no action* required."

At 1140 *Pueblo* completed service (or routine) message, requesting missing broadcast numbers. The Navy said, "Routine action taken to rebroadcast missing numbers requested."

At 1150 *Pueblo* completed transmission of SITREP 2. This was the report Bucher and Schumacher compiled the morning of the twenty-third, reporting the night's surveillance and the flare—although Bucher says nothing about such events in his book. The transcript says, "This report had priority precedence and was addressed for action to CTF-96 and to the following for information." The "following" is an impressive list: Commanding General, Fifth Air Force; Commander in Chief, Pacific; Commander in Chief, Pacific Air Force; Commander in Chief, U.S. Pacific Fleet; Chief of Naval Operations; Commander, Fleet Air Wing Six; Commander Service Force, U.S. Pacific Fleet; Commander, Seventh Fleet; Director, Naval Security Group; Fleet Air Reconnaissance Squadron One; Headquarters, National Security Agency, Pacific; Joint Chiefs of Staff; Naval Field Operations Intelligence Office; Naval Security Group Activity (Kamiseya); and Oceanographer of the Navy.

The watch officers in intelligence at Kamiseya read the second situation report and , again, "filed" it on the "interest board."

At 1200 hours, the transcript reads, "*Pueblo* operator stated he had another message being prepared for transmission and that there was 'COMPANY OUTSIDE.'" By all accounts this refers to the arrival of the North Korean subchaser and the beginning of the seizure.

At 1210, *Pueblo* transmitted a second intelligence technical report on the SOD-Hut activities of January 22. "Precedence was Routine and message was addressed to several (15) intelligence activities. The watch officer at Kamiseya concluded: "Routine patrol; no action required as indicated."

For the period from 1210 to 1244, the transcript reads: "Exchange of transmissions between *Pueblo* and Kamiseya operators regarding garbled or misunderstood portions of four messages sent by *Pueblo;* reruns of parts of messages, checks of routing indicators assigned, etc. At approximately 1230, *Pueblo* operator advised, 'DON'T WANT TO GO DOWN YET. WE STILL GOT COMPANY OUTSIDE. WILL ADVISE ASAP [As soon as possible].'"

At 1244, the *Pueblo* operator sent: "WE ARE FINISHED FOR NOW BUT GOT COMPANY OUTSIDE AND MORE COMING SO WILL HAVE TO KEEP THIS UP FOR AWHILE. WILL ADVISE ASAP."

The reference to "more [company] coming" signals the approach of the three North Korean torpedo boats. The encounter with the North Koreans is forty-four minutes along when the torpedo boats appear. In his book, Murphy uses this to hammer Bucher for his statement that only twenty minutes had elapsed. (Actually, Bucher has the torpedo boats sighted much earlier in the twenty-minute period.)

Bucher simply could have erred. After all, elapsed time is difficult to judge in a crisis situation and certainly hard to recall. But Bucher had ample time to refresh his memory. His book was published a year after the radio transcript was made public. He could have referred to it and adjusted his times—as Murphy obviously did.

Bucher did not. Why would Bucher refer to twenty minutes of elapsed time when the transcript indicates it was more than twice that? In his book, Bucher ignores the radio transcript until much later, when he describes himself going to the SOD-Hut to dictate a message for Bailey to send to Kamiseya. Thus, he did know about the transcript, yet he otherwise ignores it. Again, why?

An answer is apparent. For whatever motive, Bucher is obviously determined to portray the seizure as a quick, sudden hit, coming without warning, catching him defenseless and overwhelmed. Toward this end he altered events on January 21 when the North Korean subchaser appeared, insisting "all my officers" agreed *Pueblo* was still undetected, ignoring Lacy's belief that it was "impossible" for them not to have been. When the two fishing boats appeared on the twenty-second, Bucher knew he had been detected, but decided the North Koreans really weren't interested. Harris had reported that *Pueblo* was picked up by fire-control radar for days, but Bucher does not mention this until the day of the seizure. He studiously avoids any mention of the eighteen sightings and the slow-burning flare at night.

Bucher may want to portray the seizure as sudden, quick, and overwhelming, but it simply won't wash. *Pueblo* was detected at least two days prior to the seizure. On the twenty-third, it returned to the spot where the fishing boats had encountered it. The SO-1 came at 1200 hours and made ever-narrowing circles around *Pueblo*. The subchaser was at battle stations. It raised a HEAVE TO OR I WILL FIRE signal. *Pueblo* remained dead in the water. There is a dispute whether it even started its engines, with Bucher the only one maintaining that he did. Forty-four minutes into the encounter, three torpedo boats come out to reinforce the subchaser. *Pueblo* still doesn't move.

The facts are clear. *Pueblo* could have moved, but didn't. *Pueblo* *wanted* the harassment. Bucher's own words—"here was the unexpected opportunity to really test, according to our orders, their reactions to our presence near their territorial waters"—admit this.

We now return to the transcript.

Between 1245 and 1249, *Pueblo* and Kamiseya operators exchanged "primarily personal chatter, such as, sea duty is rough, be glad to get back, see you about 7 FEB, etc." This sounds like Bailey and his buddy Haizlip "talking" by teletype—actually keeping the line open. At the end of the period (1249) Bailey sent: "I AM TRYING TO FIND OUT WHAT THE OIC [Officer in Charge, apparently Steve Harris] WANTS (Garble) NOW BUT EVERYONE IS TOPSIDE WORRYING (Garble) HAVE RIGHT NOW WILL ADVISE ASAP." This was followed shortly by, "CHANGE YOUR TAPE AND GOT A FLASH COMING FOR YOU NOW. AM GETTING IT READY NOW. STANDBY FOR FLASH."

Between 1250 and 1254, according to the transcript, *Pueblo* transmitted the first Pinnacle message twice and "Kamiseya receipted at 1254." Kamiseya advised, "FLASH GONE," indicating the message was being relayed.

Thus, the first Pinnacle message, which Bucher says was prepared within the first twenty minutes, actually was sent and receipted fifty-four minutes into the seizure. The situation is obviously considerably different from that portrayed by Bucher. Fifty-four minutes into the encounter, *Pueblo* still has not moved, although it is surrounded by a subchaser and at least three torpedo boats, all armed and at battle stations—and has been so for almost an hour.

The first Pinnacle message told of the SO-1 circling the ship, asking nationality, *Pueblo* hoisting the U.S. flag. The message said the subchaser hoisted its HEAVE TO flags and continued to circle *Pueblo*. Bucher says his intentions were "to remain in the area if considered feasible, otherwise to withdraw slowly to the northeast. . . ."

This message, sent fifty-four minutes into the seizure, indicates no particular alarm on *Pueblo's* part and was so taken at Kamiseya. The "actions taken" part of the transcript says the first Pinnacle message was received at Commander Naval Forces Japan at 1313 and "hand-delivered to Chief of Staff by Intelligence watch officer." It was also delivered to the Operations Control Center. Actions taken: "Harassment reported was no worse than expected nor as bad as previously experienced by *Banner*."

While the Navy in Japan is reaching this conclusion, the teletype is running between *Pueblo* and Kamiseya.

Between 1255 and 1315, a twenty-minute period, *Pueblo* advised, according to the transcript, "GOT SOME MORE COMING SOON SO WILL HAVE TO STAY UP. WILL ADVISE WHEN WE GET READY FOR YOU." This apparently refers to the second Pinnacle message. The transcript says Kamiseya acknowledged this message and requested a rerun of a line from the first Pinnacle. *Pueblo* complied. Kamiseya acknowledged and sent, "DO YOU HAVE ANYMORE TRAFFIC? HOW IT FEEL TO BE THREATENED?" *Pueblo* responded, "GOT SOME MORE COMING IN A MINUTE BUT DON'T HAVE IT IN COMM [Communications] YET. WILL PASS IT AS SOON AS I GET. IT IS WORSE OUT HERE NOW, GOT MORE COMPANY AND NOT DOING SO GOOD WITH THEM SO WILL HAVE TO KEEP THIS CIRCUIT UP, WILL ADVISE ASAP AND PLEASE STAY WITH ME ON CIRCUIT."

More company. The transcript doesn't say, but this more than likely refers to the MIGs which buzzed the ship, for between 1318 and 1321 *Pueblo* transmitted the second Pinnacle message. Armbrister reports its contents as follows:

. . . SO1 joined by 3 P-4 patrol craft number 601, 604 and 606. SO1 has sent international code translated "Follow in my wake; I have a pilot aboard." SO1 and P-4 604 lying to discussing situation 300 yards on starboard bow. 606 is just forward on starboard beam and 601 is on the starboard quarter. Two MIG's sighted on starboard bow circling; 604 is backing toward bow with fenders rigged with an armed landing party. . . . *Pueblo* all ahead one-third. . . . Intentions to depart the area.

This message left *Pueblo* by 1321—an hour and twenty minutes into the seizure—and was repeated until 1325. At Kamiseya the second Pinnacle was relayed to Commander Naval Forces Japan at 1322. The "intelligence watch officer hand-delivered [it] to Chief of Staff who ordered,

'RELAY INFO TO 5TH AF AND PUSH THE BUTTON FOR CONTINGENCY ACTION.'" The Navy was at last taking the situation seriously. No more filing on the "interest board."

What was happening topside on *Pueblo?*

Bucher had seen the MIGs, the fourth torpedo boat, and the second sub-chaser. Lacy asked him, "Should we think about going to General Quarters, Captain?"

Bucher writes (pp. 183–4): "While I am not known to back away from a fight when challenged, my instructions to not act provocatively, together with Admiral Johnson's parting admonition specifying that I was not out here to start a war, had to remain a primary influence on all my actions. 'I don't want to go to General Quarters,' I answered him, 'because that would give these bastards the impression we're here to conduct hostile operations. All they'd need to turn a harassment into a full-fledged international incident.'

"Gene accepted my decision without question, but with worry still clouding his handsome face."

Schumacher returns from sending the first Pinnacle message and Bucher tells him to "get set to plug in" the second. He started "rattling off the bare facts of the developments over the past ten minutes to supplement our first report."

But even as he did this, he writes, "things were happening too fast for me to keep up with the message content." What was happening was that one of the torpedo boats "drew close alongside their SO-1 flagship, communicating first by semaphore, then by megaphones which amplified their gibberish loudly enough for us to hear it echoing across the three hundred yards of slow swells. They drew close together, bumped for a moment, while a dozen armed, stocky figures jumped across from the larger vessel, then the smaller one started backing down toward us with the obvious intention of putting a reinforced boarding party aboard *Pueblo.*" (Again, Bucher cannot have it both ways. He has already reported the torpedo boats "within fifty yards," "their decks filled with what looked like soldiers or marines." Now he sees a "dozen armed, stocky figures" leave the subchaser for the PT boat, which a page or two before was already "filled" with such people.) Bucher continues: "I shouted at Skip [Schumacher] to include this unexpected action in the message, then swore:

"'I'll be Goddamned if they are going to get away with it!'"

Bucher's reaction to the boarding party was low-key. He mentions no rage or desire to "dive" the surface ship, as Murphy says. Rather, he writes: "The sight of this brazen attempt had me more furious than worried, but I instantly realized the time had come to remove ourselves from a harassment situation that went beyond my briefings and seemed on the brink of getting out of control. *Banner* had never experienced a serious threat of seizure on the high seas, but these KORCOMs seemed crazy enough to try it. I did not want to test them that far, and lost no time in calling down the voice tube: 'All ahead one-third! Navigator! Give the best course to open from land!'

"'Zero-eight-zero, sir!' came Murphy's reply, sounding a bit thin.

"'Steer zero-eight-zero,' I confirmed. 'Build up speed to two-thirds, then full. We are making a dignified withdrawal, not a run for it.' I happened to glance through the lucite windscreen down at the welldeck where poor Friar Tuck was looking quite perplexed while standing by his hydrographic winch that had some 30 fathoms of Nansen cast paid out over the side. 'Belay all oceanographic activity!' I shouted down at him. 'Haul in those damned bottles on the double!'"

Bucher describes "a series of catarrhic coughs" erupting out of the *Pueblo* stack as the "engineroom answered the bells by throwing the idling diesels into gear and advancing the throttles." He sees the torpedo boat with the rigged fenders "within a few yards" of *Pueblo* and that the "boarding party was braced to jump over our railings." But, he writes, *Pueblo* moved ahead, "leaving behind the torpedo boat with its boarding party looking somewhat foolish." Then he writes: "I still hoped to get clear, but I had to consider now the eventuality that I would not. I ordered the word passed over the ship's 1MC [loudspeaker] to prepare for destruction of all classified material, then had a long signal hoisted which I hoped would cause a stall while they broke it down: THANK YOU FOR YOUR CONSIDERATION—AM DEPARTING THE AREA."

Murphy's story of these events is this (pp. 131-2): "The P-4 began backing down on the *Pueblo*'s starboard bow, fenders rigged for boarding. Finally, one and a quarter hours after the high-noon maneuvers had begun, Bucher decided to leave the area. I had returned below [to the pilothouse] when he called for a course recommend that would take us to deep water in the quickest possible time.

"'Zero-eight-zero,' I advised.

"Bucher accepted the recommendation and passed an order to Chief Monroe Goldman in the engine room. There was a big puff of smoke. Although INTEND TO REMAIN IN THE AREA UNTIL TOMORROW was still flapping in the breeze, anyone within miles could see that we were lighting off the engines. Bucher had Leach haul down the flags and replace them with a new message. Again the temptation to get smart proved irresistible. Bucher had to save face, even if it meant the Orientals had to lose theirs. THANK YOU FOR YOUR CONSIDERATION, read the new flags. I AM DEPARTING THE AREA.

"To Helmsman Ronald Berens he shouted down through the voice tube: 'All ahead full.'

"Swinging around in a wide circle, the *Pueblo* started for the open sea.

"'Stop! For God's sake, stop!' The anguished cry came from 'Friar' Tuck. We had forgotten the Nansen cast; the *Pueblo* was still towing her 'cover'; the quick start had brought the bottles boiling up to the surface astern of us.

"Bucher ordered speed reduced to one-third. As the equipment was brought back aboard, several more precious minutes were wasted. But not wasted by the North Koreans, who used them to take up positions around the *Pueblo*. We were now surrounded by ships. The P-4 began backing down again. She came to within twenty feet. The men at the rail could look right into the unsmiling North Korean faces.

"With the bottles up, Bucher ordered speed increased to two-thirds, then full. But we'd lost the element of surprise, if ever we had it. The North Korean ships stayed right with us."

The difference in these two versions is astounding. And the differences are crucial to learning what really happened aboard *Pueblo*. To clarify, Bucher says his engines were on idle when he saw the torpedo boat with the boarding party backing toward *Pueblo*. He decided to get under way, ordered all ahead one-third speed, and accepted a course of 080. Then, glancing at the welldeck, he saw the Nansen casts and ordered Tuck and Iredale to haul in the bottles on the double. He says he saw the boarding party come within a few yards but *Pueblo* pulled away leaving the boarders "looking somewhat foolish." Finally he hoisted flags aimed to confuse the North Koreans.

Murphy has *Pueblo* dead in the water as the boarders approach. Bucher then starts the engines, raises the flags that Bucher describes, orders all ahead full, swings around in a wide circle, and heads on a course 080. Then, Murphy says, Tuck cried for the ship to stop. Bucher reduced speed to one-third while the Nansen bottles were retrieved, thus losing valuable time and enabling the North Korean ships to stay "right with us."

A study of third-party versions produces Brandt's version: "He [Bucher] didn't like the way the three torpedo boats had surrounded his ship, and he was deeply concerned when he saw armed soldiers transfer to one of the torpedo boats. About that time two MIG jets flew over at about four thousand feet and started circling. Bucher watched the jets, and when he looked down again he saw a torpedo boat backing down on the *Pueblo*'s starboard side, a man standing on the bow with a line to throw aboard the *Pueblo*. Law saw that the boarding party of about eight soldiers carried carbines with bayonets attached. He saw the soldiers working the actions of their guns, and thought it was time for the *Pueblo* to bug out of there.

"Bucher was furious. The PT boat was within twenty feet of *Pueblo* when he yelled into the voice tube: 'Those sons of bitches are trying to board us!' He ordered the ship ahead one-third; it started to move almost immediately.

"Bucher asked Law to give him the course to the open sea. Law suggested 090, or a right turn. Bucher set the course at 080 and told Leach to hoist another signal flag: 'Thank you for your consideration. I am departing the area.' As the *Pueblo* came right he ordered full ahead and the *Pueblo* began leaving the torpedo boat behind. Then a second PT boat pulled in front of the *Pueblo* and began zigzagging across its bow.

"Law turned to Bucher and said, 'It looks like we're out of it. Leach must have said his prayers right.' Bucher laughed and said he was saying his prayers, too."

Brandt is writing on the basis of interviews with Law. Although an enlisted man, Law was quartermaster, keeping the ship's log, serving as officer of the deck, and was considered a superior navigator. He indicated *Pueblo,* not moving, was facing north. To reach the "best course to open from land" which Bucher requested, Law recommended due east, 090, which necessitated a full right turn. Bucher chose 080, made the turn at one-third speed, and went to full speed when it was accomplished.

Some very big questions must be asked. If *Pueblo* was 15.8 miles from Ung Island, the nearest land, as claimed, *it was in open sea.* To escape imminent boarding, the ship could have gone in any compass direction, even due west. Why ask for the "best course to open from land?" Land was almost sixteen miles away and only an island at that, the real shore being twenty-five miles away. Wanting to escape boarders, why would Bucher negotiate a sharp, 80 degree turn to the right at one-third speed before going to full speed? Why not just sail away in any direction as fast as he could—if he was 15.8 miles from nearest land?

Brandt makes no mention of Tuck and his Nansen casts. When were *Pueblo*'s engines started? He does answer that (p. 39): "Things were getting hotter on the flying bridge. Bucher ordered the engines started, and the subchaser responded by hoisting a signal: 'Follow in my wake. I have pilot aboard.' Law, looking through binoculars, could see a man standing on top of the subchaser's pilot house waving red semaphore flags. He wasn't attempting to signal a message. He was waving the *Pueblo* toward shore. Bucher ordered another signal flag raised: 'I plan to remain in this area, depart tomorrow.' Again, the *Pueblo*'s signal had no visible effect, and the Korean on the pilot house kept waving the *Pueblo* toward land."

In this version *Pueblo*'s engine were started not at the start of the encounter, as Bucher has it, or at the moment of flight, as Murphy says, but sometime in between—either twenty or forty minutes into the operation, depending on whether Bucher or Murphy is believed. Note that Brandt, like Armbrister, Schumacher, and Steve Harris, mentions the FOLLOW IN MY WAKE—HAVE PILOT ABOARD signal from the subchaser as occurring early in the encounter—and that neither Bucher nor Murphy has reported it yet.

Schumacher's version adds illuminating information. After the MIGs, the fourth torpedo boat, and the second subchaser appeared—and Schumacher was back topside after sending off the first Pinnacle message—"the Captain told Lacy to start the main engines and to have the word passed to prepare for emergency destruction." Then the subchaser raised a new signal: FOLLOW IN MY WAKE; I HAVE PILOT ABOARD. Schumacher says Bucher did not respond.

Schumacher then saw the boarding party form on the P-4, which backed down toward "our stern." Bucher made his be-damned-if-they're-going-to-get-away-with-that statement and shouted, "All ahead one-third." He asked Murphy for the best course "to put maximum distance between the *Pueblo* and land" and sailed on 080, "only gradually" increasing speed to full. He ordered the flags, reported by others, to confuse the North Koreans.

Schumacher: "Flying that message was the only thing I would have done differently that day. I felt it was a bit flippant. I favored—but did not suggest—a more threatening signal, such as 'My government has been notified; help is on the way.' Maybe this would have given the North Koreans pause. *I did not know at that time that the subchaser had already chosen his course of action, and at 1306 had radioed his superiors, saying, ' . . . according to present instructions we will close down the radio, tie up the personnel, tow it and enter port at Wonsan. At present, we are on our way to boarding. We are coming in* [emphasis mine].'"

Schumacher says he added the boarding attempt to the second Pinnacle message, "scribbling while the Captain pounded me on the back and shouted, 'Get it going, get it going. Hurry up, goddamn it.'" Schumacher raced to SOD-Hut and the message went out, he says, at 1315. He is a few minutes off. It went out at 1321.

Armbrister begins by referring to the animosity between Bucher and Murphy. After telling Leach to hoist the long flag signal to confuse the North Koreans, Bucher spoke to the pilothouse and told Law to ask Murphy to suggest a "new [?] course—one which would enable him to open the coast, gain room for maneuvering [in the open sea?] and reach the 100-fathom curve as soon as possible." Armbrister continues (p. 46):

"Law called back, 'Zero-eight-zero.'

"Where was Murphy? Why wouldn't Murphy ever speak to him directly?

"'Is the navigator there?'

"'Yes sir,' Law replied. Murphy stepped to the voice tube.

"'Ed, is this a good course?'

"'Yes sir,' Murphy said."

(I have no doubt Bucher told Armbrister of this conversation during his interviews. But it does seem unlikely that Bucher, his ship *in extremis,* trying to escape boarders, would have given a lot of thought to his feud with Murphy and wonder why his XO didn't talk to him. Indeed, Bucher makes no reference to this in his own book. But I can't blame Armbrister for printing it. The degree of antipathy between Bucher and Murphy is certainly notable. Incidentally, both Bucher and Murphy denied before the Court of Inquiry that they had a "personality clash.")

Armbrister says Bucher gave the course to Helmsman Berens and ordered, "All ahead one-third." Armbrister also reports the difficulties with the Nansen bottles. "Slow down, slow down," Tuck yelled. Bucher bellowed back, "Friar, get that damn gear up here because I'm leavin'. Now."

There is no consensus in these various reports of the same events. Bucher says he got under way at one-third speed from idling engines. Murphy declares he started his engines, ordered full speed ahead, then slowed to one-third to bring in the Nansen cast. Brandt says the ship went at one-third while making a right turn, then to full speed. He doesn't mention Nansen bottles. Schumacher says the captain ordered one-third speed. He doesn't mention the Nansen cast either. Armbrister says one-third, and has Tuck yelling to Bucher to slow down.

All this is important, and it seems to me the five admirals on the Court of Inquiry ought to have pursued the matter. It is one thing for *Pueblo* to remain under harassment for thirty minutes, engines idling, as Bucher has it, and quite another for it to stay seventy-five minutes with engines down. If the Court had considered the matter, they might have noted that *Pueblo* had a speed of twelve knots. Its absolutely all-out "flank" speed is given as either 12.6 or 13.1 knots. At one-third speed, it would travel at about four knots. A comfortable walking speed is three miles an hour. A leisurely jog is four or five. So, it may be said that a competent swimmer could have kept up with *Pueblo* at one-third speed for at least a short distance.

Pueblo couldn't go much slower than four knots. Yet, according to Armbrister, Tuck yells, "Slow down, slow down," when Pueblo is at one-third speed. Why would Tuck yell at him to slow down when the ship was already going about as slow as it could? At that speed he could surely haul in his Nansen bottles—and remember, Bucher said there were at least two casts. Even Murphy, who claims Bucher ordered full speed, says the ship slowed to one-third to haul in the casts. Question: Why not just cut the lines? Who cares about a few Nansen bottles? Was there much more important gear on those lines which couldn't be lost?

There is another point to be considered. The entire purpose of getting under way was to avoid a boarding party on a torpedo boat which was backing toward *Pueblo,* fenders rigged. It was only a few yards away, so close the faces of the North Koreans are seen and it is observed they are braced to leap across to *Pueblo.* They are heard to cock their weapons. Bucher orders a speed of four knots, "leaving behind the torpedo boat with its boarding party looking somewhat foolish." Possible, even probable. *Pueblo* surely has its engines lit by now and is no longer dead in the water. The PT boat backs toward her. Just as the North Koreans are to jump across, *Pueblo* moves "in a wide turning circle toward the open sea," as Bucher writes. This could have conceivably moved *Pueblo* away from the torpedo boat, leaving its occupants "looking somewhat foolish."

But only momentarily. The speed and maneuverability of a torpedo boat is such that at four knots—or twelve knots—*Pueblo* could not long avoid anyone seriously determined to board it. The stern of the torpedo boat was level with the stern of *Pueblo.* It was just a short leap, perhaps even just a step, from the torpedo boat to *Pueblo.*

Yet, according to Bucher, this didn't happen. Despite its slow start, *Pueblo* got to its twelve-knot speed—a quarter that of the torpedo boat—and outdistanced the subchaser, with its speed of forty knots. It hauled down its HEAVE TO OR I WILL FIRE signal, Bucher writes, and "appeared to jog along indecisively in our wake, dropping behind more than two thousand yards"—roughly a mile. The four torpedo boats (apparently including the one left behind moments before) kept up with the speeding *Pueblo*. Bucher writes that two "stuck close to our stern," while the other two "porpoised around our bows, zigzagging as close as ten yards with the obvious purpose of blocking our withdrawal." Bucher says the second SO-1 subchaser "had caught up and was joining the fray, making *six* hostile vessels confronting us!" Murphy never did see a second subchaser; indeed, he saw only four vessels—and there is not one syllable anywhere that refers to what the second subchaser did after it arrived.

The importance of these events is indicated when the radio transcript is read. What was Bailey sending over the teleprinter to Kamiseya? Between 1318 and 1321, *Pueblo* sent the second Pinnacle message. This reported the arrival of three P-4 patrol craft, the subchaser raising the FOLLOW IN MY WAKE signal, two MIGs circling overhead, and the torpedo boat approaching with the landing party. *Pueblo* was "all ahead one-third" with intentions to depart the area. Kamiseya received the message at 1322, and *Pueblo* repeated the message from 1322 to 1325. Since *Pueblo* was under way when Schumacher drafted the second Pinnacle, it is to be assumed *Pueblo* got under way at roughly 1315 (a time given by others) and by 1325 had been moving for about ten minutes.

Between 1326 and 1327, *Pueblo* sent: "AND THEY PLAN TO OPEN FIRE ON US NOW, THEY PLAN TO OPEN FIRE ON US NOW, THEY PLAN TO OPEN FIRE ON US NOW."

The next transmissions have been reported earlier, but they bear repeating:

1328   *Pueblo* again commenced sending PINNACLE 2 but interrupted to send, "NORTH KOREAN WAR VESSELS PLAN TO OPEN FIRE, SHIP POSIT 39-25.5N, 127-54.9E, SHIP POSIT 39-25.5N, 127-54.9E." Kamiseya acknowledged this and asked, "HOW MANY FLASH HAVE YOU SENT US?" Kamiseya continued to acknowledge receipt of *Pueblo* posit info, and invited *Pueblo* to transmit.

1330   *Pueblo* transmitted, "WE ARE BEING BOARDED," five times followed by two repeats of previous ship's position, and two repeats of, "WE ARE BEING BOARDED." "SOS" was then sent thirteen times, followed by two transmissions of a revised ship's position, "39-34N, 127-54E," eighteen more SOSs and the new position once more. Kamiseya acknowledged receipt of all these transmissions and invited *Pueblo* to continue sending.

1331   *Pueblo* resumed transmitting a few minutes later with, "WE ARE HOLDING EMERGENCY DESTRUCTION. WE NEED HELP. WE ARE HOLDING EMERGENCY DESTRUCTION. WE NEED SUPPORT. SOS SOS SOS. PLEASE SEND ASSISTANCE (sent four times), SOS, SOS, SOS. WE ARE BEING BOARDED. HOLDING EMERGENCY DESTRUCTION." Kamiseya acknowledged and again invited *Pueblo* to continue sending.

1331–
1337   At about 1337, *Pueblo* advised, "WE ARE LAYING TO AT PRESENT POSITION. AS OF YET WE NO LONGER HAVE GOPI (WEST-PACOPINTEL broadcast). THIS CIRCUIT ONLY CIRCUIT ACTIVE ON NIP. PLEASE SEND ASSISTANCE. WE ARE BEING BOARDED."

1338   Kamiseya responded to last *Pueblo* transmission "QSL (roger) YOUR LAST AND PASSING ALL INFO." No other transmissions this period, except a call by Kamiseya for *Pueblo* to transmit.

1345   At 1345 *Pueblo* advised, "WE ARE BEING ESCORTED INTO PROB WONSON REPEAT WONSON. WE ARE BEING ESCORTED INTO PROB WONSON REPEAT WONSON."*

This transcript, as released by the Navy to Congress, describes in a fashion far more gripping than any writer could a ship about to be fired on, a ship in distress, a ship calling for help, a ship being boarded at 1330, a ship holding emergency destruction at 1331 as it was being boarded, a ship with only one radio circuit open, stopping at 1337, a ship staying out of radio contact for eight minutes before saying it was being escorted into probably Wonsan.

The transcript suggests sharp visual images, on the basis of what we know. It is not difficult to see the North Korean soldiers, wearing their quilted jackets, carrying AK-47 attack rifles, leaping from the torpedo boat across to the unarmed *Pueblo*, spreading over the ship. Nor is it difficult to see the CTs in the SOD-Hut destroying their top-secret gear. Emergency destruction begins at 1331. Six minutes later Bailey reports his is the "only circuit active" on the ship. The GOPI, which is identified as Western Pacific Operational Intelligence broadcast, is gone. *Pueblo* is no longer an ELINT ship. The teleprinter operated by Bailey is *Pueblo*'s only link with the outside world.

Within six minutes millions of dollars worth of equipment is destroyed and *Pueblo* has only a teleprinter running.

*Prob means "probably." This is the spelling of Wonsan given in the transcript.

Reading the transcript, I may see visual images of a ship boarded at 1330 and CTs quickly destroying their top-secret gear, codes, and papers, but I am apparently alone in that. Bucher never mentions the transcript or these radio transmissions. It is as though this document, released to Congress by the Navy, doesn't exist. If people read only Bucher's book, they will never learn about the transcript. Schumacher likewise does not mention the transcript. Steve Harris doesn't either, but he does quote *Pueblo*'s last message at 1432.

As discussed earlier, the Court of Inquiry never questioned anyone in public about the transcript and released only a greatly attenuated portion of it to the press. Brandt, writing shortly after the Court of Inquiry finished its deliberations, apparently never saw the transcript either. He does not refer to it, but he did interview Bailey and McClarren and thus adds significantly to our understanding of what happened.

Three writers knew about the transcript and tried to deal with its content. Admiral Gallery included the complete text of the transcript in the appendices of his book, yet he dismisses it as "chatter" between radio operators. Murphy quotes large sections of the transcript, but he omits certain important times and messages. For example, he quotes the 1326 "THEY PLAN TO OPEN FIRE" message, but omits the 1328 message giving the ship's position and the 1330 "WE ARE BEING BOARDED" message. He quotes the 1331 "HOLDING EMERGENCY DESTRUCTION" message but does not give the time. He next quotes the 1337 "WE ARE LAYING TO" message, then writes: "*Again* Bailey was wrong about the boarding. The SO-1 had now raised a new set of signal flags: FOLLOW ME I HAVE PILOT ABOARD."

The use of the word *again,* which I emphasized, is intriguing. Careful reading of Murphy does not indicate where he said Bailey was wrong the first time. My guess is that Murphy had included the omitted messages, declaring Bailey wrong, but that these were blue-penciled out. Also observe that Murphy finally mentions the FOLLOW ME signal—which every other writer, save Bucher, has occurring much earlier. Clearly, delaying mention of this signal until this time is intended to be some sort of "proof" that Bailey was mistaken.

Armbrister also interviewed Bailey and gives this account of what happened (p. 47): "Don Bailey sat at the teletype in the crypto room, his back to the men in the research area. An old leg injury was bothering him; he couldn't see what was going on, and nobody was telling him anything definite. Steve Harris had said he wanted to check every transmission—to make sure that every word that left the ship was accurate. But where was

Harris now? Bailey knew Schumacher had come into the spaces, and he thought he heard [CT] John Grant mention a boarding party. Someone else was asking about emergency destruction. Mistakenly, Bailey assumed the worst; he leaned forward over the machine."

Later, Armbrister describes Bailey sending another message (p. 53): "In the tiny crypto room Don Bailey was kneeling in front of the teletype. 'I figured it was time to get scared,' he says. 'There was so much smoke I couldn't see a foot and a half away. Layton told me (mistakenly, at that moment) that the ship was being boarded. Other guys were giving me stuff, sticking their heads in and hollering. I wouldn't even look up. In a situation like that, you don't wait to see who's telling you.'" (It should be pointed out that if the SOD-Hut was full of smoke, then emergency destruction was in progress. Bailey was not "mistaken" about that.)

Thus, Armbrister joins Murphy and Gallery in declaring Bailey mistaken in sending his messages. He even quotes Bailey explaining the situation in which he was transmitting, one of smoke and confusion.

Was Bailey mistaken? It is a vital question. Brandt, who interviewed Bailey, adds some details (p. 48): "After a slow start the destruction was well under way. The research space was full of smoke from four or five fires in the passageways set by crewmen to burn material. Bailey in the crypto center was giving Kamiseya a blow-by-blow account of events as relayed to him by Jimmy Layton, who was standing in the doorway of the research center, picking up information from anyone who happened past."

Bailey was interviewed by both Armbrister and Brandt. It should be noted that in neither case does Bailey himself say he was mistaken. Brandt, who apparently had not seen the transcript, doesn't suggest he is. Armbrister, on his own, based on information he possesses, says both Bailey and Layton, who was giving him information, were mistaken.

Were they? Bailey was no green kid. He was thirty-six, a veteran, a specialist in transmission problems at the NSA facility at Kamiseya, and, with the rank of CT First Class, a man possessed of a high security clearance. James D. Layton, twenty-six, was also a CT First Class. He told the Court of Inquiry that he, not Bucher or Steve Harris, ordered emergency destruction—as he properly should have, for Layton was watch captain on the first shift. This means Layton was actually second only to the chief CT while on duty. Make no mistake, Layton was an important individual in the SOD-Hut.

Layton may well have been mistaken, as Armbrister suggests, and so might Bailey, as both Murphy and Armbrister say, but I for one would hesitate to say so. Certainly the fact they were enlisted men would be no basis for assuming error on their part.

And if Bailey and Layton are mistaken, so is the whole Department of Defense. The initial Pentagon statement announcing the seizure said *Pueblo* was boarded at 11:45 P.M. Eastern Standard Time, which is 1345 Korean time. This statement said *Pueblo* remained in radio contact with Japan until 1432, but *the 1345 figure for time of boarding was given consistently until testimony before the Court of Inquiry established 1432 as the time of boarding.*

One of the most important questions to be asked about the entire loss of *Pueblo* is this: When was it boarded, 1330 or 1432?

The official Navy transcript clearly states the ship was boarded at 1330 and by 1345 was being escorted into Wonsan. The Navy and Pentagon apparently accepted those times, saying the ship was boarded by 1345, although it remained in radio contact for another forty-five minutes.

The 1330 boarding time is dismissed as a "mistake" by Bailey, a senior man, acting upon erroneous information given him by Layton, a shift supervisor.

Perhaps, but a far better case can be made for maintaining that *Pueblo* was boarded at 1330, or shortly thereafter, than can be made for "mistakes." Before doing so, however, we must continue with the narrative of the seizure as reported by participants and those who interviewed them.

9

COVER STORY: THE FIRING

Bucher says *Pueblo*'s getting under way surprised and perhaps confused the North Koreans aboard the subchaser and it fell behind—estimates are two thousand and even three thousand yards, well over a mile—although the four torpedo boats kept pace with *Pueblo*.

Why did the subchaser fall behind? It had a speed of forty knots and could easily keep pace with the U.S. vessel. No one suggests it, but the reason is not hard to figure out. The subchaser contacted someone, perhaps Wonsan, for instructions. The attempt to board has been thwarted. *Pueblo* is escaping out to sea. What do they do now? The instructions to the subchaser show up clearly on the radio transcript in Bailey's transmission of 1326: "AND THEY PLAN TO OPEN FIRE ON US NOW, THEY PLAN TO OPEN FIRE ON US NOW, THEY PLAN TO OPEN FIRE ON US NOW."

These words leave no doubt as to their meaning. "They *plan* to open fire." Clearly, CTs aboard *Pueblo* were monitoring the North Koreans' ship-to-shore radio if they learned of a *plan*. There can be no doubt *Pueblo* had the capacity to do this. Recall that Bucher spoke of listening to Korean radio "chatter." And, somehow, as Schumacher reports, *Pueblo* learned at 1306 that the North Koreans planned to board *Pueblo* and tow it to Wonsan.

But there is a problem, which provides a vital clue to what really happened to *Pueblo*. Much is made of the fact that Hammond and Chicca, the Marine sergeants who came aboard at Yokosuka, were inept interpreters of the Korean language. They had gone to school two years previously and forgotten most of what they learned. They couldn't understand the

Koreans—they spoke too fast—and had to tape their words and then laboriously use dictionaries to make a translation. Yet *Pueblo* did learn of the North Korean *plan* to open fire—their intentions.

How? There are really only four possibilities: (1) Chicca and Hammond were better interpreters than has been let on; (2) there was another person aboard *Pueblo* who understood Korean; (3) North Korean radio was being picked up somewhere else, translated, and *Pueblo* informed over another radio frequency; or (4) *some language other than Korean was being spoken*, a language easily interpreted by persons aboard *Pueblo*.

There can be no doubt that every transmission made at the scene was monitored by the United States. Murphy writes (p. 439): "Although we were unaware of it until after our return to the United States, American intelligence monitored the ship-to-shore communications of the SO-1 while the incident was taking place. Exactly how this was done has never been declassified. It is known, however, that the AGERs were only one part of the American intelligence network, that the United States also has spy satellites, EC-121s, and powerful land-based monitoring stations, the latter at various points in the Far East, presumably including South Korea. Whatever was responsible for the intercept, at 1210 hours, ten minutes after noon, on January 23, 1968, as the SO-1 first approached the *Pueblo*, she sent a message to shore which was translated as: 'The name of the target is GER 2. I judge it to be a reconnaissance ship. It is American guys. It does not appear that there are weapons and it is a hydrographic mapping ship.'"

(It is now known that aircraft, the RC-135 or its predecessor, were used to monitor signals. All of these intercept "platforms"—ships, planes, satellites, ground stations—were (and are) operated by the NSA. What Murphy is saying is of paramount importance to the thesis of this book. NSA was monitoring ship-to-shore communications while the incident was going on. It had knowledge very early of the seizure, indeed of plans for the seizure, yet the Navy was not informed immediately. The Pentagon, State Department, and White House would not learn until even later, as we will see.)

Murphy continues: "Although the Pentagon was against making this information public, arguing that to do so would compromise some of its secrets, President Johnson gave Ambassador [Arthur] Goldberg permission to include it in his speech to the UN because of the importance of another part of the same message, in which the SO-1 gave its position as 16.8 miles from shore, clearly placing it, and the *Pueblo*, well outside territorial waters. (As I have pointed out, however, the placement isn't clear at all. The coordinates were not given. Without them, the question must be asked: What shore? The shore of Ung Island or the shore of Wonsan? If the latter, the sighting was well within North Korean territorial waters, approximately where the North Koreans say *Pueblo* was. It should also be noted that throughout "shore" has meant the mainland, not Ung Island.)

Schumacher quotes the same North Korean transmission, saying knowledge of it came from "friendly forces"—apparently the same friends who quoted the North Korean message at 1306 that they were going in to board *Pueblo*. Incidentally, Bucher never refers to any of this in his book.

There can be no doubt that North Korean voice transmissions were being monitored. We knew what they were doing—and so did *Pueblo*. All this, of course, knocks into the proverbial cocked hat all the Navy assertions that there wasn't enough daylight left to send planes to aid *Pueblo*. The United States had independent knowledge at 1210 that the incident was under way and by 1306 knew the North Koreans intended to board the ship—leaving five hours of daylight in which to do something about it. The Navy had to know. Or did it? Could it be that the NSA, monitoring the North Korean signals, simply failed to inform the Navy and Air Force of the threat to *Pueblo*?

Returning to the seizure scene, the subchaser fell behind, received instructions to fire on *Pueblo* to stop its flight—which *Pueblo* knew—and quickly got under way. Bucher said the SO-1 "rapidly regained the distance she had lost during her brief hesitation." Bucher then writes that the subchaser, having lowered its HEAVE TO OR I WILL FIRE flags, now raised them again. This doesn't make a whole lot of sense. Why lower flags and then raise them?

The answer is that it isn't what happened. Bucher (Murphy, too) studiously avoids mentioning the subchaser's signal FOLLOW IN MY WAKE—HAVE PILOT ABOARD (sometimes translated FOLLOW ME—HAVE PILOT ABOARD). They mention it all right, but as we will see, not until later, *after Pueblo* has been fired upon and stopped. Except for Bucher's and Murphy's, every account has the signal raised earlier in the encounter. The subchaser raised HEAVE TO, lowered that, and sent up the FOLLOW ME signal. It was mentioned in the second Pinnacle message, which Bucher approved. This signal apparently flapped for an extended time. Brandt, among others, reports a North Korean aboard the subchaser's pilothouse with red flags waving *Pueblo* toward shore. It is a visual image of people trying in the worst way to get the American ship to Wonsan.

Why do Bucher and Murphy avoid mentioning the FOLLOW IN MY WAKE signal? Because if they had, it gives another whole cast to the seizure. Bucher is trying to portray a quick, vicious assault on his ship, an act of piracy. But by every other account, it didn't happen this way. The subchaser comes out, raises its HEAVE TO signal, then lowers it to hoist FOLLOW ME. *Pueblo* doesn't move. Maybe the signals aren't understood. A fellow is sent atop the pilothouse to wave *Pueblo* toward Wonsan. The torpedo boats come. They circle the ship, obviously trying to scare *Pueblo* into going to Wonsan. But the ship won't move. Finally, at 1306, after an hour of futile signaling, waving, and circling, orders are sent for the North Koreans to board *Pueblo* and take her to Wonsan. Obviously, they want the ship in Wonsan in the worst way—for reasons we will come to shortly. As the boarders approach the ship, *Pueblo* at last gets under way, but not toward Wonsan—out to sea.

This—and it fits the most often reported facts—is a radically different image of the seizure than Bucher reports. (I would include Murphy, except that he accurately describes the elapsed time and the arrival of the PT boats at 1244.) It was not a sudden, piratical seizure, but one in time-lapse, with *Pueblo* remaining on station for seventy-five minutes, ignoring a variety of signals to go to Wonsan. When Bucher sees the boarders, he decides to head out to sea to escape.

The SO-1 falls behind, awaiting orders. They come: Fire on *Pueblo* to stop her. The subchaser quickly catches up with the American ship, taking down its FOLLOW IN MY WAKE flags and hoisting the original HEAVE TO OR I WILL FIRE signal. There can be no doubt of its meaning now. *Pueblo* has received a clear warning.

Bucher saw the flags. He writes: "I ignored that [the flags] beyond an instinctive reaction to present as small a target as possible, just in case her intentions were serious, and shouted down the voice tube to our helmsman: 'Come right ten degrees!'"

That's not what happened. Even if the SOD-Hut had not informed him of its interception of the North Korean plans to open fire, Bucher soon had to discover the subchaser's intentions were serious. He doesn't mention it, but others do. The subchaser didn't just open fire. It couldn't, for fear of hitting its own torpedo boats. These moved away from the ship. The subchaser turned to bear its bow turret directly on *Pueblo*. Bucher had to see this and know the subchaser's intentions. He ordered ten degrees right rudder to present a smaller target, he says.

Bucher writes that the North Korean vessel "easily countered" this maneuver, "turning outside of me to give her gunners a broadside shot." Bucher ordered, "Come right ten more degrees!" The subchaser adjusted again.

The image is clear. Two ships are maneuvering, one for a good shot, the other to present a smaller target. Once more, Bucher's portrayal of a quick, warningless attack does not hold up.

Then Bucher writes, "I was considering that any more right rudder on our part would inevitably bring our heading back toward North Korea."

This is another petard, and U.S. claims that we were in international waters are crumbling before it. If *Pueblo* was at the coordinates claimed, 15.8 miles from Ung Island, if *Pueblo* got under way on a course of 080, if it adjusted ten degrees right rudder to 090 and another ten degrees to course 100, as Bucher writes, then the nearest landfall was across the Sea of Japan on Honshu Island! To head back toward North Korea, he would have had to order right rudder until he was sailing west—or at least southwest—from his alleged position. Even if he ordered right rudder until his heading was 180, due south, he had to sail the width of Choson Bay, a couple of hours at top speed, to make landfall.

Bucher (and the United States) cannot have it both ways. If *Pueblo* was where claimed, then Bucher had large reaches of sea in which to maneuver. If his maneuvers were restricted, then he wasn't where he claims he was. If *Pueblo* was in the radar shadow of Yo Island, near where the North Koreans say they seized it, then *Pueblo* does indeed have restricted room. To the west lie Yo and Ung Islands. If Bucher goes north he will parallel the Hado Peninsula, but remain in North Korean waters. He has room to the south, but he will "inevitably"—within a few miles—reach the southern rim of Choson Bay. His best way out is to go in an easterly direction.

To continue with Bucher's narrative, while he weighed the risks of more right rudder, the subchaser "suddenly" opened fire with a "long-sustained burst" of cannon fire.

To Bucher, the "muzzle-blast of the SO-1's cannon came as a delayed series of dull popping concussions." He heard the shells "screaming overhead, exploding with peculiar crackling sounds against the radar-mast, the whine of splinters drilling through the lucite windscreen of the flying bridge." To Murphy the shooting happened with a "horrendous roar, the twin cannons of the SO-1 belched fire, the shells whistling high overhead." Quartermaster Law told Brandt it was a "popping noise." Armbrister describes it as "Ba-roooom, Ba-roooom, Ba-roooom . . ."

The nature of the gunfire—and certainly the extent of it—is unclear from the various accounts. Murphy speaks of a "second volley," the machine gun bullets rattling against the sides of the ship "like hail," and an "earlier salvo." Schumacher refers to a "shell from the first salvo, or the next one" and says "glass zinged around like shrapnel." Brandt writes of a "first shell" and a "second shell."

Bucher tries to describe the scene more fully. "The [first] salvo lasted for perhaps five or six seconds, blasting to shambles not only my bridge—but also all the high-level briefings which had been my guidelines for this mission." He told the Court of Inquiry, "They fired between six to 14 individual shells from what I believe were 57 mm cannons. Most of the shots went over the ship. At least one hit the radar mast."

Apparently this succession of six to fourteen shells is what is meant by a salvo, for Bucher told Armbrister (p. 56): "He [the subchaser] continued to fire salvos at approximately thirty-second to one-minute intervals, six to fourteen shots in a continuing sequence." Bucher told the Court of Inquiry there were "approximately 10 to 14 or 15 salvos altogether" directed at his ship and "something in the neighborhood of 1,000 to 2,000 rounds of light machine gun fire from four torpedo boats." In other words, anywhere from 60 to 210 shells were directed at *Pueblo* during the seizure, according to Bucher. A 57-millimeter shell is roughly two and three-eighths inches in diameter.

It is difficult to visualize the shooting. Murphy has the twin cannons belching fire, the shells "whistling high overhead." He asks, "A warning, or bad aim? As if in answer, the second volley crashed into the radar mast, demolished Bucher's plexiglass windshield, and shattered all over the pilothouse (which lies below)." This seems to indicate two shells passing overhead, followed by two more shells which hit the bridge, not the long-sustained burst of six to fourteen shells lasting five or six seconds, as Bucher describes.

What constitutes a salvo? The answer is important, for most accounts separate the firing into salvos. Sometimes there was quite a lengthy separation. While Bucher told Armbrister the salvos came in thirty-second to one-minute intervals, Law told the Court of Inquiry that "20 to 25 minutes" elapsed between the first and second salvos and Hayes estimated "45 minutes to an hour" elapsed between the second burst of fire and the boarding.

Trying to figure out what really happened is not easy. There can be no doubt *Pueblo* was fired upon. The shells, at least initially, were aimed high. Many passed harmlessly overhead. Hayes said in his interview that they were aiming at the antennae—and we will come to a reason for that soon. The radar mast and the ship's stack were hit first. Bucher came to the conclusion they were directing their fire at his flying bridge, which is to say at *him*. Obviously, the North Koreans were not trying to sink the ship. No one below decks was wounded in the initial firing. Hayes said one of the radio antennae was knocked out, but the ship was not badly damaged during the seizure. For his part, Bucher portrays a ship under merciless fire and sustaining considerable damage.

The initial salvo (or salvos) brought casualties. All accounts report that, but exactly who was wounded, by what, and in which part of the anatomy is in dispute. Bucher writes that he was on the flying bridge with Signalman Leach and CT3 Steven J. Robin. What was a CT doing on the flying bridge? Armbrister asked the question and there is no sure answer. Bucher says he was "manning the telephone." But there was no telephone on the flying bridge. Brandt and Murphy say Robin was called to the bridge to aid in ship identification, although it would seem all the North Korean ships ought to be familiar by now. Were there other ships about? Bucher says Lacy and Tim Harris had gone down to the pilothouse before the shooting and mentions Law rushing up after the hit to ask if anyone was hurt. In his account to Brandt, Law places himself on the flying bridge.

Bucher writes (p. 187): "Even as I threw myself down on the deck to dodge the lethal hail of shattered steel and plastic, I felt pieces slashing into my legs and buttocks. A sliver of shrapnel seared squarely up my rectum with a red-hot shock of pain." He said both his companions on the bridge were "hit by shrapnel"; Robin was hit in the neck and Leach "had splinters in a leg."

Brandt's version is different (p. 42). "Law thought it was a machine gun firing and hit the deck with Steve Robin behind the captain's chair. Bucher and Leach dived behind the metal signal desk. Law looked up and realized that the captain's chair was raised a step off the deck and he and Robin weren't hiding behind anything but canvas. Before he could move to a safer place, he heard louder booms, and realized the Koreans were shooting their 57-millimeter cannon at the *Pueblo*. He heard a crashing noise as a shell hit the stack about ten feet behind him and then heard Robin shout: 'They got me!'

"A second shell tore through the Plexiglas screen on the bridge and exploded on the signal desk hood about six feet from where Law and Robin were lying. Law turned over on his side, frightened, and saw Robin trying to take off his jacket. Law helped him, then called to Bucher that Robin had been hit in the arm but it didn't seem too bad. Bucher replied: 'Well, they got me in the ass.'"

Whether it was the neck or arm, Robin was wounded. Or was he? Schumacher was on the wing of the pilothouse, he writes (pp. 90-1), thinking about what to put into a third Pinnacle message, which apparently was never written or sent. Hayes approached with his arms loaded with "secret message files" and asked Schumacher for "permission to commence emergency destruction." No one had started the process but Hayes was "sensing disaster," according to Schumacher. At that moment the firing began. "A shell from the first salvo, or the next one—I couldn't tell which—shattered the windows in the pilothouse," Schumacher writes. "I hit the deck, along with the others. . . .

"Almost immediately, the word came down through the voice tube from the bridge, to be passed over the 1 MC: 'Commence emergency destruction.' I called the CT's in crypto and told them to send off their Critic message. They said it had already gone." (This was surely difficult since there was no phone line between the pilothouse and the interior of the SOD-Hut. In my opinion, Schumacher is still trying to account for the Critic messages, not realizing, as Armbrister learned, that they never came from *Pueblo*, but were sent from Japan.)

Schumacher continues: "Then I unlocked all the small safes we had on the bridge containing classified publications. Grabbing an armload of them, I headed for the ship's small incinerator on the starboard deck.

"The Captain, who had been standing on the exposed flying bridge, was slightly wounded by that first salvo. He quickly left the bridge and came down into the pilothouse, as did Law, Robin, and . . . Leach.

"Robin and [CT1 Michael T.] Barrett were at the incinerator, tearing pages out of secret publications, when I arrived there." Schumacher goes on to describe their conversation, the "almost complete detachment" with which they "watched the bullets work their way aft from the pilot-house, past the stack, and then over our heads and into the whaleboat." He thought it time for "some quick prayers." He gave his lighter to Robin to use to start the fire. "Maybe it was our smoke that caught the eye of the Korean machine gunners. A burst came at us, denting the stack just above where our heads had been before we hit the deck." Barrett took a ricocheting bullet in his arm. There is not a syllable about a wounded Robin.

(If anyone can figure out how Robin got from the flying bridge to the incinerator before Schumacher, I'd love to hear the explanation—along with how he was wounded either in the neck or arm in one place but not in the other. Sorting through all the conflicting information requires patience. I admire the men of *Pueblo* and am not trying to make them look foolish. I am only trying to discover what really happened aboard that ship. My belief is that a cover story was imposed on the men of *Pueblo*. But only the broad lines of the cover story were made known to them. In attempting to flesh out the story with details which sound authentic, the men of *Pueblo* simply made up details which ultimately make no sense and destroy the cover story. Robin is merely one instance of many.)

Murphy writes that just before the firing started he was trying to raise Japan on the HICOMM (there are various spellings), an insecure voice circuit to be used in emergencies. When he hit the deck, as the firing began, he still had the phone in his hand. In his ear he heard the operator in Japan repeating, "Stand by to change frequencies." Murphy writes (p. 134): "Talk about bad timing, this was the worst possible! Frequency shifts on the Hi Comm occurred only twice a day. At the very moment we most needed to get through, we'd caught one of them! I couldn't believe our bad luck. 'Stand by to change frequencies.' I tried repeatedly to break in, but the operator wouldn't stop talking long enough to give me a chance." It does sound very similar to the experience of Hayes the night before, doesn't it?

Bucher writes that his first act after being wounded—even before inquiring about the wounds of Robin and Leach—was to call down the voice tube: "Commence emergency destruction of all classified pubs and gear! Be sure the word is passed on down to Lieutenant Harris in the SOD-Hut!"

Murphy, who was below in the pilothouse, says (p. 136) Bucher's first words were, "The bastards shot me in the ass!" Then he said: "Get on the 1MC and order 'Prepare to commence emergency destruction.'

"*'Prepare to commence'* when they were firing at us? [Murphy's emphasis]

"We relayed the order, in the excitement forgetting, as obviously had Bucher, that there was no loudspeaker for the 1MC in the SOD-Hut. Since there were also no portholes, Steve Harris and his technicians were completely out of touch with what was going on."

Prepare to commence. To clarify the difference between "prepare to commence" and actually commencing emergency destruction, I spoke to persons familiar with ELINT ship operations. They explained that destruction of classified equipment and papers occurs in three stages. In a Yellow Alert, explosive devices installed in equipment are armed—of which more later. In Red Alert, certain highly classified materials, such as current codes and messages, are destroyed. In Emergency Destruction everything goes. These sources further state that just operating off unfriendly shores, *Pueblo* would have been in a constant state of Yellow Alert. Thus, the term "prepare to commence" suggests the CTs went to a Red Alert. Barrett told the Court of Inquiry that when the subchaser signaled HEAVE TO he recommended that CTs "prepare for emergency destruction." Does Barrett mean the first or second time the subchaser raised the HEAVE TO signal? If it was the first time, then *Pueblo* was in a state of Red Alert from very early in the encounter.

As reported previously, Bucher did use a term similar to "prepare to commence," but not at this juncture. Just as *Pueblo* got under way to escape, he writes, "I ordered the word passed over the ship's 1MC to prepare for destruction of all classified material." After the first shells hit, Bucher's first order, he says, was to "commence" emergency destruction. He wanted the word passed to the SOD-Hut. Murphy says he ordered someone in the pilothouse to get on the loudspeaker and order "prepare to commence." Again, two men, two Navy officers, two stories. Add a third officer, Schumacher. His story supports both Bucher and Murphy. The order was "commence emergency destruction" all right, but it was to be "passed over" the loudspeaker. He says nothing about phoning or dispatching a messenger.

So how and when did the SOD-Hut get the order to commence emergency destruction? Destroying top secret gear, codes, messages, and intercept tapes was the most important single activity on the ship. Bucher, standing on his flying bridge, accompanied only by a signalman and a CT, out of contact with subordinates except by voice tube to the pilothouse below, orders, "Commence emergency destruction." He does not follow through. Murphy hears "prepare to commence" and gives that order over the loudspeaker, forgetting the sound does not reach the SOD-Hut. He doesn't follow through either. Schumacher hears Bucher's order, dutifully opens safes, and carries an armload of paper to the incinerator and hands his lighter to Robin to start a fire. It apparently never occurs to Schumacher to race to the SOD-Hut to alert it to the crucial order.

Emergency destruction *did* begin in the SOD-Hut. How did it happen? A person can read Bucher, Murphy, and Schumacher in vain for an answer. From his interviews, Armbrister fortunately provides an answer—and a sharply different set of events. He writes that when the "first salvo" of cannon fire hit the bridge, Schumacher was on the "wing of the signal bridge." This has to be a misstatement by Armbrister. He has to mean the wing of the pilothouse, for Schumacher looked up to the bridge and said, "Everybody all right?" Bucher yelled down, "I'm okay. Just got some glass in my ass."

As Bucher "staggered to his feet," Armbrister writes (p. 50), his first thought was "of ordering flank speed—an extra .6 knots," but he didn't want to risk overloading his engines. Besides what good would it do? There was no possibility of outrunning the North Korean vessels.

Armbrister continues (p. 51): "*Pueblo* was already maintaining a course of 110 degrees." Bucher said he started out on 080 and ordered two right rudders of ten degrees, which would make a heading of 100. There must have been a third right rudder. "He couldn't order the ship any farther to the right without jeopardizing his chances of reaching the 100-fathom curve. Too much of a turn, in fact, and he'd be heading toward the North Korean coast. Still, he had to do *something* [Armbrister's emphasis]."

(This business of the hundred-fathom curve is a red herring introduced at the Court of Inquiry. Bucher was asked by the admirals why he didn't scuttle his ship to keep it from falling into North Korean hands. He replied that the ship was in thirty fathoms of water. Divers could easily recover the top secret gear from that depth. Thereafter, this matter of water depth became a part of the cover story, thrust into every written account. Steve Harris couldn't throw documents overboard because the water wasn't deep enough, or he lacked enough "weighted bags" to sink them. Bucher uses it here to tell Armbrister he wanted to reach the hundred-fathom curve. Why? Was he planning to reach deep water and scuttle his ship? If not, then a hundred fathoms wouldn't matter. Besides, Bucher also told the Court how difficult it would have been to scuttle his ship and the great risk the frigid waters would have held for his men. This reference to water depth is an effort, I believe, to "explain" his difficulties in maneuvering because he was really much closer to Yo and Ung islands.)

Armbrister writes that Bucher "leaned over the brass voice tube. 'Right to one-two-zero.'" Thus, Bucher's first order was not "commence emergency destruction" but a course correction. He apparently was still trying to present a smaller target.

Armbrister discusses the problem with the HICOMM circuit, then considers the matter of emergency destruction in the SOD-Hut. He writes (p. 51): "When the SO1 first signaled 'Heave to,' Communications Technician First Class James A. Sheppard had been standing on the bridge. He ran to the research spaces and asked Steve Harris if he could begin emergency destruction."

Armbrister continues: "'I said we couldn't do it because we didn't have permission yet,' Harris remembers. 'I thought, "Well, we'll just barrel on out of here. Let's hurry up and do it," you know. I mean, we couldn't just go ahead and start destructing by ourselves. Suppose we got away and all the stuff was smashed up and the skipper had never said, "Yes, do it"? Where would I be? I knew it was getting tight, though, and I was hoping that somebody up there would remember to give the order.'"

This statement by Steve Harris is amazing in view of all the reports of quarrels between Bucher and himself over who commanded the SOD-Hut. By all accounts, Harris insisted his was a "detachment," under separate command, even obtaining a letter to that effect. Now, in his statements to Trevor Armbrister, he eschews responsibility and can't order emergency destruction except on command of his captain.

Armbrister continues with his account of how emergency destruction began: "Sheppard stepped into the aft berthing compartment. He said a prayer. When he returned to the [research] spaces, the firing had already started. Everyone had hit the deck. Surely this was the time to start emergency destruction. He looked for Harris.

"Chief Communications Technician James Kell was one step ahead of him. He and Sheppard urged Harris to give the order immediately.

"Harris telephoned the pilot house and spoke to Murphy. Then he turned to the two CT's. 'We don't have permission yet,' he said.

"Kell didn't even stop to think that he was disobeying an officer's command. 'At that point,' he remembers, 'I took it upon myself to give the order to destruct.'"

Brandt tells the story this way (p. 38): "A thoughtful observer to all this was James A. Shepard,* twenty-seven, of Williamstown, Massachusetts, a communications technician on his first sea duty despite nearly eight years in the Navy. A top expert in his particular electronics field, he had taken five other CTs to Fuchu near Tokyo to give them some special training while the *Pueblo* was in Yokosuka. He had been asleep when the subchaser first approached the ship and had gone to the bridge on awakening. When he saw the order from the subchaser to heave to, he went below to the research space and asked Lieutenant Harris if they should prepare for emergency destruction of the hundreds of pounds of classified material aboard, as well as the equipment. Harris called the pilot house but was

---

*What is the man's name? Armbrister spells it Sheppard; Brandt spells it Shepard in his text but Shephard in his crew list; Bucher spells it Shephard in his crew list; Schumacher spells it Shepard in his list.

told to wait a while, that the situation was still considered harassment. Shepard went back to his bunk and prayed."

Later, when the firing began, Shepard got up from his bunk and "ran" to the SOD-Hut (p. 43). "When he arrived he found everyone lying on the deck and no one making a move to start destruction. The men had heard the firing but not the general-quarters calls, since the 1MC didn't extend into the research space.

"Shepard asked Lieutenant Harris again about emergency destruction. Harris called the pilot house and got another 'No,' but before he put the phone down he got a loud 'Yes!'

"Sergeant Hammond, standing near Sergeant Chicca, who was trying to listen in on North Korean transmissions, thought he heard Lieutenant Harris in a low voice give the order to destruct. Others in the space heard only Chief Kell and Jimmy Layton give the orders to begin destruction."

Murphy gives some support to Brandt's version of events. He writes (p. 136): "By this time [after the second salvo] one of the CTs had reached the SOD-Hut and told Steve Harris what was happening. Steve called the pilothouse and asked permission to start emergency destruction. The question was relayed to Bucher, who replied with a flat 'No,' hesitated for what seemed a full minute, then said, 'Yes.'

"'Commence emergency destruction,' I yelled over the phone and the loudspeaker."

These stories told by Armbrister, Brandt, and Murphy—and it should be noted that Bucher never mentions any of this, indeed never indicates how emergency destruction began in the SOD-Hut other than by his order—must be suspected of containing a degree of fabrication as part of the cover story. As evidence, I cite testimony before the Court of Inquiry. It released a summary of closed-door testimony which read, according to the New York *Times*: "Kell stated that he gave the word to commence emergency destruction in the research spaces. He further testified that at no time during the destruction attempts did he receive an order from Lieutenant Stephen Harris or did he hear Lieutenant Harris give an order."

In its report on the summary of closed-door testimony, the *Times* wrote: "In their testimony, the petty officers clearly indicated that it had been the enlisted men, and not Lieutenant Harris, who ordered the destruction of secret material in the intelligence area.

"The Navy summary said that Communications Technician 1st Cl. Michael T. Barrett 'recommended on his own initiative that personnel in the research space prepare for emergency destruction.'

"He made this decision about the same time that the [North Koreans] signaled, 'Heave to or I will open fire,' the summary said.

"Communications Technician 1st Cl. James D. Layton 'told his men to start [destroying] the top secret material and work down,' it said.

"The summary went on:

"'He stated that Lieutenant Harris walked in shortly after the firing started, but had no orders nor messages to be released and that he never saw Lieutenant Harris participate in the destruction of materials.'"

Here we have—in sworn testimony—a far different tale. It is one of senior enlisted men, petty officers, forthrightly ordering emergency destruction on their own. Not even Harris, let alone Bucher or any other officer, was present. If this is correct, then there is no possible way the various tales of Harris phoning the pilothouse, getting a No and then a Yes, can possibly be correct. (I have no doubt Armbrister and Brandt, both reporters, were *told* this information by persons they interviewed. They did not, however, compare these stories against testimony before the Court of Inquiry.)

There are two possible conclusions from all this. One is that United States Navy officers, at least those aboard *Pueblo*, were inept and a rather sorry lot when it came to the crucial matter of ordering emergency destruction. I really don't believe this and opt for the second conclusion, which is: None of the *Pueblo* officers, most especially Stephen Harris, commanded the SOD-Hut. It was run by NSA personnel masquerading as enlisted men. Harris was a figurehead and knew it. He let the "enlisted men" order emergency destruction. It was simply another of the command decisions they had been making all along. My own very strong feeling is that Harris, who I understand is still in Naval Intelligence with the rank of commander, should not have the can tied to his tail for what happened aboard *Pueblo*—any more than Bucher should.

After ordering emergency destruction to commence, Bucher faced what many feel was his most important command decision: Should he go to General Quarters and Battle Stations? He writes (p. 188): "This command was on the tip of my tongue, but I choked it down. There were in fact no Battle Stations on *Pueblo* and General Quarters really meant nothing more than manning Damage Control. Our 50 [*sic*] caliber machine guns were no match for 57-mm automatic cannons, could only be reached by crossing exposed decks that would be raked by many machine guns from 30-yard range concentrating from both sides against our mounts while our gunners unlashed frozen tarpaulin covers, opened ammunition lockers, and attempted to bring into action their totally exposed weapons. It was certain death to even try to shoot back."

Bucher uttered this view repeatedly in interviews and before the Court of Inquiry. Others testified that *Pueblo*'s guns were not iced over. Gunner's Mate Kenneth R. Wadley said he had inspected the guns the morning of the seizure, removing the ice. He felt the guns would be ready to shoot in five to ten minutes. He also said the guns had no protective shields and anyone firing them "wouldn't have survived." If called upon, he said, "I think I would have gone up to man them. I think I would have done it."*

Bucher cared about his men. He saw no advantage in casualties in a hopeless cause. So he shouted down the voice tube: "Set a *modified* [his emphasis] General Quarters! Nobody to expose themselves topside! I have the deck as well as the conn. *Left full rudder, all ahead full!* [My emphasis]." He adds, "Even if I could not fight back, I was damned if I would give up. As futile a gesture as it might seem, I ordered Leach to haul a protest flag to our yardarm, and pressed my ship on toward the open sea." (Brandt reports the protest was, "You are interfering with my right of free passage." Bucher never mentions this. Perhaps it is the protest Leach referred to but couldn't remember.)

There are conflicting versions of these events. Armbrister's is the most detailed (pp. 54–5): "Seconds before, Lacy had suggested sounding general quarters. Bucher had hesitated. 'I did not want to give these people cause for attacking us,' he remembers. [*Pueblo* was already under attack, having sustained one salvo, according to Bucher, or two salvos, according to Armbrister.] 'I really felt strongly about my orders in connection with not provoking an international incident.' But that incident had already begun. He leaned over the voice tube. 'Sound general quarters.'

"He felt his first responsibility was to keep his superiors informed of what was happening. Bailey was taking care of that on the teletype. His second task was to complete emergency destruction. 'Yet I did not want to come under such severe attack,' he says, 'that it would have been impossible to destroy the classified material. I did not feel there was any point in attempting to go to war with the group of ships. I was completely and hopelessly outgunned. Those guys were between thirty-five and fifty

*It never occurred, of course, but what would have happened if *Pueblo* had fought back? The .50 caliber machine gun is no match for a 57-mm cannon, as Bucher points out, but it isn't exactly a pea shooter, either. There would surely have been casualties among *Pueblo* gunners, but if the pair of machine guns had been manned and fired, it is at least possible the torpedo boats, with their men more exposed on deck, could have been driven back, especially if the Thompson submachine guns were brought out and fired. This might have gained *Pueblo* enough time to escape, although it seems certain the cannon on the subchaser would have caused heavy damage and casualties. One thing is certain: This is what the five "fighting" admirals on the Court of Inquiry wished had happened.

yards away. There was just no way to get to our guns or even to get the ammo lockers open.'

"At that point—just ten or fifteen seconds after ordering GQ—Bucher made the decision which was to render inevitable every other decision he made that afternoon. He yelled into the voice tube, 'Set modified GQ. Pass the word to all hands to stay clear of the weather decks. Repeat, no personnel are to come topside.'

"The men who had been rushing toward the machine guns stopped in their tracks."

Bucher's order for a "modified" general quarters is surely strange, especially when he orders no one to come topside. He had already given such an order! Recall that it was just about his first order when the sub-chaser appeared at noon.

Murphy's version of these events (p. 137) is similar to Armbrister's: "Gene Lacy again asked Bucher if he should order general quarters. Bucher hesitated, then gave the order, which I relayed over the 1MC. But almost immediately he changed his mind: 'Make that a *modified* GQ, all personnel except those already topside to remain below!'"

Murphy makes two comments about the order. "I still have no idea what, if anything, Bucher was thinking," he writes. "He would give a command, then, as quickly, either qualify or countermand it. Probably, like the rest of us, he was still in a state of shock." Murphy also calls the order for modified GQ "strange," adding: "What drills we had conducted were for naught. Since the sod-hut was topside, it meant those CTs not already there couldn't carry out their destruction assignments. It also meant that the pilothouse, the very nerve center of the ship, would not be properly manned. For example, lacking a phone talker, who ordinarily would have manned the 1JV circuit, we would have to rely on hand-held phone sets. It was the old daisy-chain concept; if one man does not show up to replace another, he can't replace the man he's assigned to replace, and so on down the line. I could visualize the confusion below. For a moment I thought of arguing with Bucher, then decided against it. As I'd learned over and over again, the hard way, he not only discouraged, he resented advice." What this says about Murphy and his relations with Bucher needs no comment here.

To recap, Bucher has the first salvo landing near the flying bridge, wounding Leach, Robin, and himself. He immediately orders emergency destruction to begin, then a modified general quarters. He does this while standing on the bridge, before the second salvo arrives.

Apparently writing on the basis of interviews with Bucher, Armbrister records a different set of events. Armbrister has Bucher alone being wounded in the first salvo, saying the "pain in Bucher's ankle was bearable" and the "pain in his rectum was excruciating." Bucher sees the two MIGs wheeling to make another pass. The torpedo boats are firing at point-blank range. The subchaser is "churning" closer. Armbrister writes: "Bucher expected another salvo in a few seconds. And now it occurred to him that there were too many people on the flying bridge. They had no protection at all. He would stay there with Leach, his signalman, and Robin—what the hell was Robin doing there anyway?—and Law, his quartermaster." Others were ordered below to the pilothouse.

Armbrister: "Up to this point he had refrained from ordering emergency destruction. 'I didn't know what their intentions were, whether they would follow me out to sea.' But now 'I realized that these people intended to make a full-scale incident out of this.' Unaware that Kell had already passed the word, he yelled into the voice tube, 'Commence emergency destruction.'"

Armbrister then describes what was happening in the SOD-Hut as Bailey was sending out his SOS, WE ARE HOLDING EMERGENCY DESTRUCTION message. Then his account returns to the pilothouse. He writes: "From the port side of the pilot house, Communications Technician First Class Michael T. Barrett was watching the SO1. Suddenly he shouted, 'They're swinging their guns; they're swinging their guns. Everybody down.'"

Yes, it is the same man! Schumacher has him out by the incinerator helping Robin and him start a fire, and then being wounded. The Court of Inquiry says he was recommending emergency destruction in the SOD-Hut. Now he is in the pilothouse warning everybody to get down.

Armbrister writes: "Ba-roooom, Ba-roooom, Ba-roooom . . . The second salvo ripped into the ship. A cannon shell burst through the window behind the captain's chair, missing Tim Harris' head by inches, streaking out of the window just in front of him. Incredibly, it didn't explode. But flying glass was everywhere. Harris felt a sharp pain at the back of his neck. He reached up to touch it. He drew his hand back and saw blood. He picked up the narrative and stepped into the chart room."

Ed Brandt also interviewed Ensign Harris. This is what he reports (p. 42): "Ensign Harris had just finished drawing a diagram of the PT boat criss-crossing in front of the *Pueblo* when he heard firing. He was vaguely aware that everyone else in the pilot house had hit the deck at the first sound of shots, but he was too engrossed in his chore to move. He saw smoke but thought the North Koreans were just firing across the bow of the *Pueblo*. When he heard still another explosion, however, he dived out of the chair and onto the deck. He lay there for a moment, unaware that he was in a bed of broken glass, and continued to log the shots. He turned on his side to look around and saw a jagged hole in the glass directly in front of where he had been sitting, about head high. Then he saw his torn pants and blood on his knees, from where he had been cut by glass. Still bewildered and a little scared, he said: 'What the shit is this!'"

I can't explain the differences other than that Tim Harris told Brandt one thing, then later, being interviewed by Armbrister, moved his blood from his knees to his neck, surely a more threatening and thus heroic location. I'm sure he deserved a Purple Heart at either spot.

Armbrister continues: "Steve Robin had come to the flying bridge to deliver a message and had remained there out of curiosity [another explanation]. Now he was hugging the deck. He felt something like a hot poker jab at his left elbow. A few feet away Wendell Leach was lying behind the flag box. He realized dumbly that pieces of shrapnel had entered his thigh and right calf. He remembers feeling very cold."

(On the surface the matter of why Steven J. Robin was on the flying bridge would seem to be inconsequential to the story, yet I can't help but wonder why all these different reasons for his presence are given. Bucher says he was manning the phone, but there was no phone on the flying bridge, only a voice tube. Brandt and Murphy say he was aiding in ship identification. Armbrister says he had come to deliver a message and remained "out of curiosity." To stand exposed on the flying bridge during a cannonade indicates a truly powerful curiosity. Again, why all these various reasons? Why not just flat out state what Robin was doing on the bridge? To offer my opinion: Armbrister is correct. Robin was a messenger between the SOD-Hut and the bridge. To have said so would have shown there was no telephone link from the bridge and pilothouse to the SOD-Hut, thus proving the fabrication involved in all the alleged phone conversations between Harris, Bucher, Murphy, Hayes, Schumacher, and others. It is by such details that the cover story is unraveled.)

Bucher has Robin, Leach, and himself wounded on the first salvo, not the second. Bucher's version of what happened then is as follows (pp. 188–9): "Perhaps forty seconds had gone by since the first salvo, and now came the second. A stream of shells yowled through the rigging, some of them bursting against the masts and scattering another shower of shrapnel downward; others could be heard slamming through the stack and superstructure. And the torpedo boats cut loose with their machine guns at the same time, stitching through the pilothouse from both sides.

All four of us [Law had rushed up to the bridge after the first salvo] flattened ourselves on the deck and as soon as the cannon fire let up, I shouted: 'Clear the flying bridge!' When I raised myself to scramble for the ladder, I noticed a large hole in the deck where my chin had just been and wondered how the hell I had escaped having the piece of shrapnel go through my head.''

Bucher is the only person to report that any North Korean shells landed in the superstructure at this time. As we will see, Bucher belies this when he later states there was no damage below decks.

Bucher does, however, provide us here with a most important clue to what really happened during the *Pueblo* seizure. An enemy round makes a "large hole in the deck" near where Bucher's chin had been and he wonders how he escaped a serious shrapnel wound. Indeed he should wonder! *Pueblo* was made of steel. It would take a powerful shell to make a "large hole" in the deck. A shell from a 57-millimeter cannon could do this. Yet it didn't explode and cause casualties among men standing nearby. Recall that a shell hit the metal signal desk. Another hit the stack. Yet the wounds to Bucher, Robin, and Leach were minor, caused by flying glass and splinters. There was no shrapnel at this point. Apparently the subchaser was not firing explosive shells—or if it was, they weren't doing much damage or causing serious casualties. All this becomes vital information when we come to the death of Duane Hodges.

Bucher writes that Law, Robin, and Leach jumped for the lower bridge and landed in a heap. His own attempt "to make a more dignified retreat" was "given a precipitous impetus by bullets that missed me by inches." But even as he dropped down, he glanced at the torpedo boat and saw it had "unmasked its port torpedo tube and was training it outboard for a shot that could hardly miss blowing *Pueblo* sky-high." (There are no written reports of torpedos being fired at *Pueblo*.)

Bucher told Armbrister all this occurred on the third, not the second salvo. Bucher, as quoted by Armbrister (p. 56), says: "The SO1 had closed to a range of 900 yards on my port quarter. He continued to fire salvos. . . . After about the third salvo it occurred to me that most of the firing was being directed toward my flying bridge. All of the windows in the canopy had been shot out or were holed in two or three places. One shell had also struck the captain's chair three feet to the left of the voice tube. I was standing at the tube. I decided it would be prudent to clear the flying bridge." (There were no near-miss holes in the deck in what Bucher told Armbrister.)

Bucher writes (p. 189) that when he reached the "flimsy protection" of the pilothouse he found the "entire bridge-watch lying prone on the deck with the wheel tended from that awkward position." He had to cringe himself while ricocheting bullets and bits of glass flew around. But when the machine guns stopped firing, he yelled, "Everybody on your feet!"

Everybody obeyed "except my Executive Officer, Lieutenant Murphy, who remained prone on the deck, his spectacles askew on his nose as he whined at me:

"'But sir . . . they are still shooting at us! . . . '

"'No kidding, Ed! So get off your ass and start acting like my XO!' When he did not instantly react, I gave him a kick that brought him more or less upright."

(Murphy makes no reference to such an incident at this time. But he describes something similar that supposedly occurred much later, after 1415, when *Pueblo* was about to be boarded. Under "sustained, concentrated" fire, Murphy ordered everyone in the pilothouse to hit the deck and "stay down until they stop shooting." In came Bucher. "You sons of bitches," Bucher screamed. "You cowards! Get up off the deck!" Murphy writes: "Later Bucher would say that the men were all lying in a pile, quivering with terror, that no one was manning the ship. Not true. Some of us were crouched, a few were prone, but each man knew his assigned task and was doing it; we retained control of the ship throughout, albeit from less exposed positions. Bucher would also state that when I didn't get up he helped me to my feet with a well-placed kick astern. This, too, never happened. And, for Bucher's sake, it is perhaps best it didn't, for I was in no mood to become a scapegoat for his ill-conceived actions.")

Bucher goes on: "Now that some order had been restored to the bridge, it came uppermost in my mind to make sure the emergency destruction of the especially sensitive material kept in the cryptographic room and the SOD-Hut be accomplished with all possible speed." He phoned Steve Harris and received the following report:

"'Emergency destruct is in progress, Captain, and our communications are open with Kamiseya.'

"'Good! Keep up the destruct, but don't destroy today's crypto codes until I give the orders. I'll have another CRITIC message to go soon.'

"'Yes sir.'"

Bucher says Harris's "tone was a little shaken, yet sounded as if he understood what had to be done and was prepared to do it."

Having "temporarily reassured" himself that matters were being taken care of in the SOD-Hut, Bucher writes, "I returned my full attention to the bridge." He checked his speed, all ahead full, and his course—"(still angling out to sea at 135 degrees)."

Two large questions must be asked: *How* did Bucher get on this heading, and *why* did he? Bucher's own report of his course commands offers no explanation of how he reached course 135, which is southeast. He says *Pueblo* got under way at 080. He ordered ten degrees right rudder, which would make 090, then another ten degrees right rudder, which would make 100. Then, he says, he ordered, "Left full rudder!" This would take him almost due north, yet he ends up on a 135 heading—southeast. This is utterly impossible unless he steamed in a circle.

Armbrister also reports course commands. After the first salvo Bucher has his ship on course 110 and was worried about "heading toward the North Korean coast." Nonetheless, Armbrister reports, Bucher ordered "right to one-two-zero." After ordering emergency destruction and modified GQ, "Bucher bellowed new course changes into the voice tube: 'Right to one-three-zero; right to one-four-zero. . . .' *Pueblo* was steaming almost parallel to the coast. The SO1 was still trying to force her back toward shore." Armbrister makes no mention of Bucher's command for "Left full rudder!"

Murphy refers to the 080 heading and the two orders to "come right ten degrees." He writes (p. 133): "Bucher was trying his best to extricate us, but every time he ordered a course change, the faster SO-1 compensated. Moreover, the positions he gave were gradually turning us back toward land." The shelling occurs. Then Murphy writes a sentence (p. 138) which greatly adds to the confusion: "We were still well outside them now, but the SO-1 and the P-4's were gradually forcing us in closer."

If *Pueblo* is where the United States, Bucher, Murphy, and everyone say it was, 15.8 miles north and east of Ung Island, then it is in open water. Land is hardly visible. As observed earlier, if *Pueblo* headed due west or southwest toward Wonsan, more than an hour of hard steaming would be required to make landfall. In any other direction, it would take many hours and even days. Worries about heading toward the North Korean coast seem thin indeed.

From that location, *Pueblo* can sail in any direction. Bucher heads east, which is the direction of escape. To present a smaller target, he says, he orders right rudder until he reaches 135. This doesn't make a lot of sense. His right rudders haven't prevented the subchaser from firing at him from his port side. Why persist in futile maneuvers that only slow down his escape? To go southeast on 135 takes him obliquely past Wonsan, keeping him in peril longer. Escape is due east.

If *Pueblo* is in the radar shadow of Yo Island, a course of 135 doesn't make a lot of sense either. Again, escape is due east. But it must be said that a heading of 135 would bring *Pueblo* "almost parallel to the coast"— the southern coast of Choson Bay.

Even this possibility is destroyed by Murphy's statement that "we were still well outside them now" yet being gradually forced "in closer." If *Pueblo* is on a course of 135 and "outside" the subchaser, this can only mean the North Korean vessel is on *Pueblo's* *starboard*. Every account, including Murphy's, has the ship shooting from the port side.

There is one clear, simple explanation which straightens out this muddle of directions and course changes. It persuades me of where *Pueblo* really was and how it maneuvered.

The pilot-navigator was correct in guessing that Bucher "doctored" the evidence by simply adding ten minutes of a degree—a single digit—to the actual position. The actual coordinates were 39 degrees, 15.2 minutes North, 127 degrees, 45 minutes east. This locates *Pueblo* in the radar shadow of Yo Island, 7.6 miles from Yo, well inside territorial waters. It also places *Pueblo* roughly 15.8 miles from *shore*, not from Ung Island.

Bucher gives the correct maneuvers in his book. Dead in the water, headed north, he gets under way and turns in a wide circle on a 080 course, the best direction for escape. Bucher goes right ten degrees to 090 and another ten to 100. The subchaser fires from his port side, wounding Bucher. He then orders, as he writes, "Left full rudder, all ahead full!" There can be only one reason for this. Recall how Commander Clark of *Banner* had escaped harassment by aiming *Banner* right at the nearest ship. In a similar situation, Bucher emulates him, ordering "Left full rudder," aiming *Pueblo* directly at the subchaser. It is a good, bold maneuver, presenting the subchaser with a smaller target and forcing it to take evasive action.

The subchaser easily evades the oncoming *Pueblo*—I suspect by going right full rudder. This leaves *Pueblo* "well outside" the subchaser, as Murphy writes, as the ships head north "almost parallel to the coast" of Hado Peninsula.

Pueblo's left full rudder does one other thing. In a very short time, it takes *Pueblo* to 39 degrees, 17.4 minutes North, 127 degrees, 46.9 minutes East—where the North Koreans say they boarded.

I strongly believe that Bucher's reference to a 135 heading—recall that it was placed in parentheses, suggesting it was added by the censor—is untrue. Bucher never explains in his book how he went to left full rudder from a heading of 100 and arrived at 135 simply *because there is no possible explanation*. Wanting to lead the reader away from the real happenings, the man with the blue pencil added the 135 course and Bucher was stuck with it. In one of those tiny but crucial human errors, the censor missed Bucher's reference to the "Left full rudder!" command, which occurred some pages earlier in the middle of a long paragraph.

I believe that in interviews with Armbrister—and stuck with the 135 course—Bucher neglected to mention the "Left full rudder" command and told Armbrister he went to 110, 120, 130, and even 140 (for good measure), all of which makes extremely limited sense. Once more Bucher is caught in the position of not being able to have it both ways. He can't have that "Left full rudder" command, which takes him almost due north, and end up sailing southeast.

The narrative continues: In the pilothouse, having determined his ship was on the correct heading of 135, Bucher observed that destruct procedures were going on. Hayes and Crandall, the radiomen, were "initiating their Destruction Bill by carrying out files from their cubicle and rushing them to the incinerator located behind the stack." He saw "swirls of smoke smelling of burning paper" which told him "that primitive destruct equipment was functioning." Law, Leach, Robin, and the "now useless lookouts and photographer" were passing out "an amazing amount of classified matériel and documents from our cramped spaces, all of them aware of the importance of keeping these from falling into Communist hands."

Bucher warned, "Watch yourselves out there and take cover behind the whaleboat if the shooting gets hot. But keep that stuff burning . . . burning . . . burning to ashes!" He took time to put down Murphy, who still couldn't raise anyone on the HICOMM. "Well, never mind the goddamned HIGHCOM," he told Murphy. "What about the plot of this action that I ordered a while back?" Clearly, Bucher is indicating that Murphy's level of incompetence is such that he could only stand there and hold a useless telephone—and perhaps rub his sore ass where Bucher had kicked him.* Lacy reported, *"No damage below, sir, except minor hits*

*In this truly obscene feud between these two Navy officers, Murphy has his innings, too (p. 138): "It seemed they had us every which way. Four ships [not Bucher's six] to one. We couldn't out-maneuver or outrun them. Because the guns were unmanned, we couldn't even fire back. With one misstep after another we had blundered into a stalemate from which there seemed no way out except to stall for time until help arrived. Bucher's sole contribution as CO at this point was to wander from one side of the pilothouse to the other, muttering strings of curses at the North Koreans."

above the waterline [emphasis mine]." Bucher replied, "Okay, Gene. We're still afloat and under way. We'll keep trying to bull our way through." He picked up some papers off the chart table and shoved them into the arms of Crandall as he "rushed another load toward the incinerator."*

Bucher writes (p. 191): "Then the KORCOMs opened up another salvo that was accurately aimed directly at *Pueblo*'s bridge." I assume he means pilothouse, as distinct from the flying bridge above. He had left that. One round passed "within inches" of Lacy's head and scorched Tim Harris's left ear before "zinging into the sea a hundred yards beyond the ship. If it had exploded, we would all have been killed then and there." (This makes a third part of Tim Harris's anatomy said to have been wounded.) Everyone hit the deck, Bucher writes, "listening for the following pizzicato of machine gun bursts to let up before returning upright."

Bucher: "I was stunned by Gene Lacy's wild-eyed look as he dragged himself back to his feet and suddenly yelled at me:

"'Are you going to stop this son-of-a-bitch or not?'

"There was only a fraction of hesitation before he reached out himself and yanked the handles of the annunciator to ALL STOP. The blindly alert engineers isolated three decks down instantly rang the answering bells. There followed an abrupt break in the wheezing exhaust throb of our perforated stack, then a rapid deceleration downward of our 12-knot speed. I kept staring at Gene in utter disbelief for another fifteen seconds. Fifteen seconds that brought the stark realization that my most experienced officer, my most trusted friend aboard this ill-starred little ship, had robbed me of the last vestige of support in my efforts to save the mission, leaving me alone with an Executive Officer who had proven to be unreliable and two very young and inexperienced junior officers on my bridge. Suddenly the complete uselessness of further resistance flooded my brain. It would only result in our being shot to pieces and a lot of good men killed to no avail, because the North Koreans would in the end get most of our secret documents. Instead of lunging for the annunciator and racking it back to ALL AHEAD FULL, I turned my back on it and Gene, and walked out on the starboard wing of the bridge."

As can be imagined, Bucher takes his lumps for his statement that

---

*I attach significance to Bucher's saying he picked up papers off a chart table and had them burned. He is endeavoring to undermine Murphy's statement that he preserved logs, charts, and other indications of *Pueblo*'s position. Murphy didn't preserve them, Bucher seems to be saying, because he, Bucher, destroyed them. Recall that Law told Brandt that he destroyed them.

his friend Gene Lacy, not Bucher himself, surrendered the ship. Murphy hammers him for it. (Murphy wrote his book after Bucher, so he can comment on it.) He writes (pp. 423–4): "At this point the real villain of Bucher's book appears. Throughout our detention and during the Court of Inquiry, Bucher had vainly sought to avoid one inescapable fact: given his first command, he had surrendered the ship. There was something very pathetic in his search for an alternative to this unpleasant truth, a quest that had taken him from the explanation that the ship had been seized by superior force to the justification that the *Pueblo* obviously hadn't surrendered because she had never lowered her flag."

(Murphy's words here are startling. The context is that Murphy is suggesting that *Pueblo* was *not* seized by a superior force. As noted, Murphy saw only three torpedo boats and one subchaser, not the six vessels which Bucher saw. Murphy never had paid much attention to the MIGs. Throughout his book, Murphy maintains that Bucher placed *Pueblo*'s machine guns in the wrong position. They were mounted as if on a submarine, not the appropriate way for a surface ship. Murphy was dismayed that the guns were not manned. He objected to the modified GQ. Most of all, recall Murphy's statement, quoted earlier, that Bucher increased the amount of shells fired on *Pueblo* "tenfold." He seems to be suggesting that *Pueblo* was not "seized by superior force" and need not have surrendered.)

Murphy continues: "Now, finally, Bucher finds his answer, and his chief scapegoat.

"In a sudden turnabout, Bucher admits that the USS *Pueblo* was indeed surrendered.

"But he, Commander Lloyd M. Bucher, didn't surrender her.

"*The guilty party was Chief Warrant Officer Gene Lacy*! [Murphy's emphasis]"

Others are less outraged than Murphy, but agree with him in substance:

Armbrister: "Then Lacy suggested stopping the ship. Bucher nodded. Lacy ordered, 'All Stop.'"

Brandt: "Everyone hit the deck again. As Gene Lacy got to his feet, he yelled, 'Let's stop this goddamn ship before we all get killed!' Bucher said, 'Okay,'" and ordered all stop. Lacy rang up the emergency stop himself."

Schumacher quotes Bucher's own testimony to the Court of Inquiry, which was: "Mr. Lacy asked if we should stop the ship—I presume in order to have the firing stopped in order that we might more successfully continue with our destruction. I nodded to Mr. Lacy, and Mr. Lacy rang up all stop. As the ship stopped, the firing stopped."

According to Murphy's book, Wallace Turner of the New York *Times* set out to contact the men who had been on the bridge. He couldn't. Berens refused comment and others were unavailable—a condition which persists to this day. But Turner did reach Lacy, who said: "I don't know whether he's [Bucher] grasping at straws or what the hell the deal is on it. He was kind of wild-eyed, which was normal under the situation. He walked back and forth across the bridge, didn't say anything to anybody, and I asked him if he was going to stop the ship." Bucher then "nodded assent to me, and I did bring the annunciator back." (Quoted from Murphy, page 443). Murphy also says an "anguished crewman" called him in the middle of the night, just having read Bucher's book, to say, "How could he do that to Gene Lacy, Mr. Murphy?"

In this context, recall from Chapter One the efforts reported by Murphy and Bucher to prepare a cover story, especially Bucher's description of Lacy's "depression" after discovering that he had "blacked out" and couldn't remember surrendering the ship.

All this is extremely distasteful. All I'm trying to do is discover what really happened aboard *Pueblo*. I have no interest in personality clashes or guilt. I am not assessing blame on anyone. It is to me most regrettable that bickering, name-calling, and fault-finding ever had to enter into the matter. All were serving their country.

After letting Lacy stop the ship and after being flooded by the "complete uselessness of further resistance," Bucher writes:

"The shooting had stopped. From 40 yards off our starboard quarter, the KORCOM torpedo boat was bobbing along, its machine gunners staring back at me with grimly impassive oriental faces over the sights of their weapons. Farther behind them, their SO-1 subchaser dropped apace as we coasted to a stop, its smoking cannon still aimed at our vitals, and a new signal rising to her yardarm:

"FOLLOW ME—HAVE PILOT ABOARD."

At last, the signal everyone else, save Murphy, had reported occurring much earlier shows up in Bucher's book. (Observe that Bucher looks at the torpedo boat "off our *starboard* quarter," then "farther behind" the subchaser "dropped apace as we coasted to a stop." *Starboard*? All along the subchaser has been firing from the *port* side.)

Bucher does not give a time for this. He does not say how far or for how long *Pueblo* traveled, but the impression given by his writing and all that happened is of a lot of elapsed time.

The radio transcript is precise. At 1337 *Pueblo* reported, "WE ARE LAY-ING TO AT PRESENT POSITION." Armbrister says *Pueblo* stopped at 1337. So does Murphy. *Pueblo* got under way to escape at about 1315, perhaps a minute or two later. Thus, it sailed for no more than twenty-two minutes. At full speed it might have gone four miles, but with all the maneuvers—two right rudders and that "Left full rudder!"—chances are that it wasn't more than two or at the most three miles from where it started.

Of those twenty-two minutes of flight, most were uneventful. *Pueblo* left the subchaser behind, perhaps by as much as three thousand yards, as it radioed for instructions. At 1326 *Pueblo* reported, "AND THEY PLAN TO OPEN FIRE ON US NOW." The first shells landed on *Pueblo* at 1330, the same time *Pueblo* radioed that it was being boarded and holding emergency destruction—or perhaps a minute or so before.

Pueblo was under fire for no more than seven minutes before it stopped at 1337. A lot of shells can be fired in seven minutes, but no one suggests the North Korean subchaser cannonaded *Pueblo* for that long. There were "shells," "salvos," "bursts," separated by periods in which men visited the incinerator or started fires on deck. Bucher himself said the salvos came in thirty-second to one-minute intervals.

How much North Korean fire was aimed at *Pueblo*? Quartermaster Law, a veteran sailor in a position to know, told the Court of Inquiry that twenty to twenty-five minutes elapsed between the first and second salvos. If that is so, it means only one salvo was directed at *Pueblo* before it stopped. Ed Brandt, having interviewed fifteen crewmen, including Tim Harris and Law, does not describe a great deal of firing, although he is not specific about salvos.

Bucher, Murphy, Armbrister, and Schumacher all describe a great deal more firing. Schumacher is not specific about salvos. He was busy going to and from the incinerator. At one point he says shells were "thudding into us with a ba-wham, ba-wham sound." They were hitting above his level. Another time he says the "subchaser kept pumping shells into the *Pueblo* as she ran for the open sea." Murphy and especially Bucher and Armbrister are more precise in counting salvos. Careful reading indicates there were no more than four salvos and possibly only three.

Four salvos, especially if each consisted of six to fourteen shells, as Bucher states, can do a lot of damage. But apparently they didn't. The flying bridge and the pilothouse had the windows shot out or holed. An antenna for the HICOMM was damaged. There was no damage below deck, as Bucher informs us. The ship was functioning, its engines running, and it was still in communication with Kamiseya. There were casualties from flying glass and spent bullets. There is dispute about who they were, but the list of anyone hurt at all is Bucher, Tim Harris, Leach, Robin, and Barrett. All wounds were slight. Apparently the services of medical corpsman Herman "Doc" Baldridge weren't required. Every one of them would suffer far more grievous injuries in captivity.

In his account of the seizure, Bucher tries to portray his ship as surrendering under merciless fire from a vastly superior enemy force. This may have played before the Court of Inquiry, but it won't now. The facts are that *Pueblo* had sustained minor damage and no serious casualties. Except for the SOD-Hut, where emergency destruction had occurred, it was a fully functioning ship. There were all manner of options open to Bucher other than stopping in surrender.

It doesn't make any sense. The ship was under enemy fire for only seven minutes. Fewer than sixty shells—and that is the absolutely outside figure, very much open to dispute—were fired. They were only two and three-eighths inchers. Most missed the ship.

With minor damage and casualties, *Pueblo* stopped in surrender.

That's what Bucher and others say happened. It is hard to believe—almost as hard to believe as what they say happened next.

10

COVER STORY: THE BOARDING

Pueblo **did not obey** the FOLLOW ME order immediately. Rather, the ship remained stopped for eight minutes. At least that is what the radio transcript indicates. The "WE ARE LAYING TO" message came at 1337; the "WE ARE BEING ESCORTED INTO WONSAN" transmission came at 1345.

What happened during those eight minutes? The most logical assumption is that the ship was boarded at that time. It fits all the known actions of the North Koreans. They radioed at 1306 that they were going in to board *Pueblo*. They formed the boarding party on a PT boat and came within a few feet of *Pueblo*. Bucher evaded boarding by getting his ship under way. The North Koreans opened fire and *Pueblo* came to a stop. The most logical assumption would be that the North Koreans would now board the vessel. This fits the transcript—we are being boarded, holding emergency destruction, laying to, being escorted into Wonsan. It certainly was the Pentagon's belief in its original announcement that *Pueblo* was boarded at approximately 1345.

But that is not the story told by Bucher and the others. Bucher does not refer to the eight minutes and really gives no indication of what happened during that period.

After Lacy rang up ALL STOP, Bucher writes (p. 193) that he stood on the starboard wing of the bridge "for perhaps ten seconds" in what he says "seemed like a prolonged agonizing purgatory." None of his officers "came forward with a single word of advice" and he had a feeling of "utter loneliness" which was "so overwhelming" he wanted "to cry out for help from anybody with a sensible suggestion" about what to do.

He looked at his officers. Lacy was "glowering vacantly." Murphy was "swaying unsteadily" and "silently blinking through his spectacles while alternating fearful squints with ferocious frowns that signified nothing but indecision and total lapse of initiative." Tim Harris was "staring at me with a lost expression which asked *me* to give him something more significant to do" than keep the now-useless narrative log. Schumacher's "eyes pleaded with me for something more positive . . . to do" than write another Pinnacle-Critic message and burn publications. Bucher concluded, "It was all up to me, and me alone." His decision: "We will stall as long as we can so as to complete destruction." He ordered everyone to the task, burning, throwing over the side, anything to get rid of secret documents. With that, Lacy "roused himself from his torpor" and Bucher "admonished" him, "Hang in there and do the job right."

Bucher writes that he then went to the SOD-Hut and was "shocked by what I found." There were fires and smoke and lots of documents lying around, but the CTs were all "flattened" to the deck. (Bucher's is only one of several references to CTs becoming prone to avoid the firing. This has the aspect of fiction. The SOD-Hut was not only protected by the deck of the ship, it was itself made of armor plate. It had no portholes. The CTs were probably in the safest place in the ship. With no portholes or outside communication, it is doubtful they even knew when they were being fired upon—which may account for the fact the radio transcript makes no mention of actual firing.)

Bucher continues, yelling "Everybody on your feet! The shooting has stopped, so get off your asses and get on with the destruction down here!" To Steve Harris, who had wedged himself behind a rack of radio receivers for protection, Bucher said, "Come out from there, Steve, and make your men move, damn it! We're going to be boarded and every second counts. Destroy everything you can, any way you can!" Steve Harris came from behind the rack, "his face gray as he coughed and wheezed, 'Yes sir, captain . . . we're getting it done!'" But his "actions were dazed and uncoordinated, like those of a man on the brink of panic, and it forcibly struck me that here in the SOD-Hut, as well as on the bridge, leadership was failing me in the emergency." (Bucher's reference to Steve Harris wedged behind radio receivers shows that the SOD-Hut did indeed have transmission capabilities separate from the ship's transmitters manned by Hayes. Bucher would have been referring to R-90 transceivers, which both transmit and receive.)

Bucher says he then returned to the pilothouse. He saw the North Koreans "impatiently threatening us with their guns" and pointing to the FOL-

LOW ME flag hoist. Bucher ordered a slow all ahead one-third and a course to drag along behind the subchaser.

In his interview with Armbrister, Bucher gave a radically different account of his actions. After *Pueblo* stopped, Bucher told Armbrister, he gave the conn to Lacy and rushed down to his stateroom. "He searched through the file cabinet and locker above his desk but couldn't find any message folders pertaining to *Pueblo*'s mission." He did find some official correspondence which he gave to a sailor to burn. Then he remembered his personal sidearms and gave them to a sailor to throw over the side. When he left his stateroom he saw fires burning. There was a lot of smoke but it wasn't "hindering destruction." He returned to the pilothouse and resumed the conn. He ordered Berens, the helmsman, all ahead one-third. Armbrister: "If he [Bucher] was going to capitulate, he might as well do so in as slow and dignified a manner as possible." There is not one word here indicating Bucher's put-downs of all his officers and his going to the SOD-Hut.

In his book, Bucher gives a colorful description of frantic efforts to hold emergency destruction. There are several fires. The incinerator is "belching smoke." Tools, Mack's camera equipment, even galley utensils are thrown overboard. (He later refers to the galley as intact, lunch still on the stove.) He is surprised by how much material there is to be destroyed on the bridge and realizes the SOD-Hut has "fifty times" as much, all of it more sensitive. He realizes, "We need more time!"

Lacy says to him, "Captain, they are signaling us to put on more speed."

Bucher replies, "To hell with 'em." Leaving the annunciator on one-third speed, he now goes to his stateroom. He disposes of some correspondence, letters from home, and personal photographs, then his personal sidearms.* During the trip to and from his stateroom Bucher rallies his men. "Hang in there troops! Keep smashing and burning! Don't leave those bastards anything they can use."

Then comes a key and highly disputed development. Bucher (p. 201): "When I reached the pilothouse, I was astounded to find that the annunciator had rung up ALL AHEAD, TWO-THIRDS and we were now making 8 knots in the wake of the KORCOM subchaser leading us toward Wonsan. I felt my temper boiling over and did not try to belay it as I furiously asked, 'Who the hell ordered more speed?'

*What ought to be the simplest factual detail seldom is. Bucher says his sidearms were "a pair of .22 pistols." Armbrister says Bucher's weapons were "a .22 Ruger Black Hawk pistol and a .38 Smith & Wesson revolver."

"Gene Lacy met my accusing glare with a glassy stubborn look of his own. 'The Koreans ordered it, sir,' he answered with a dead flat tone of voice.

"'Those fucking Koreans aren't commanding this ship, Mister Lacy—I am!' I yelled in his face with no consideration for his obviously over-wrought state. 'Now, ring down one-third and keep your goddamned hands off that annunciator until I give you orders differently.'"

Bucher then writes: "In a desperate attempt to emphasize my point and to take back whatever time the Koreans had just gained, I reached out for the annunciator and rang up ALL STOP."

Then the subchaser "opened fire with its cannon from off our starboard bow, pumping a long salvo of shells which could be heard bursting inside our hull." This happened, he says, without "warning signals."

This same story is radically different in Armbrister, who describes Bucher as worrying about the lack of communications with the research spaces. "Did silence mean that the CTs were succeeding in their destruction efforts? Or did it mean that they were encountering serious problems?" He would "inspect the spaces himself." He'd "need more time. Perhaps he could feign some sort of mechanical difficulty. He picked up the microphone for the 1MC. 'All stop,' he ordered. It was almost two o'clock."

Armbrister says the subchaser, which had gotten about three thousand yards ahead, "spun around in a swirl of foam and raced back toward the ship. The P-4's opened out to 100 yards."

The difference in the two stories is cardinal. Bucher tells of his confrontation with Lacy, his worrying about time, and his stopping the ship. The SO-1 opens fire without warning. Armbrister, writing on the basis of interviews with Bucher, says nothing about *Pueblo* having speeded up to two-thirds. Rather, Bucher orders all stop, hoping to feign mechanical difficulties. And there is lots of warning. The subchaser has to return nearly two miles and the torpedo boats must move away so the cannon can be fired.

Murphy says of this event that Bucher "decided to gamble again," adding: "Wanting to see what would happen, he later stated, he ordered the *Pueblo* brought to FULL STOP. The answer came quick enough. Dropping back, the SO-1 fired a heavy barrage of shells that smashed into the center part of the *Pueblo* on the starboard side, the area from which most of the smoke was coming."

Brandt writes (p. 48) that the firing came about 2 P.M. "The shell was the result of a delaying maneuver by Bucher, and it had fatal consequences. After fifteen minutes of sailing toward Wonsan, Bucher ordered all stop on the engines, deciding to feign a casualty and play for time. The subchaser fired a salvo the moment it saw the *Pueblo* slow down.''

Still another reason for stopping the ship came in testimony before the Court of Inquiry—from Bucher himself: "I had second thoughts about the destruction of classified pubs that was going on. I decided that I would stop the ship and make an inspection." This was quoted by Schumacher. Murphy asks in his book a question the admirals did not. Why did Bucher need to stop the ship to inspect the SOD-Hut?

Thus, in the versions of Armbrister, Murphy, Brandt, and Schumacher there is nothing about the ship going to two-thirds speed and the confrontation with Lacy.

The reason the ship was stopped is important, for that action brought on the casualties. Duane Hodges was mortally wounded. His buddy, Fireman Steven Woelk; Robert Chicca, the Marine interpreter; and radioman Charles Crandall were badly injured, others less so.

Bucher's response to the shelling was to ring up ALL AHEAD, ONE-THIRD. Bucher then describes a bloody scene in which Baldridge, the medical corpsman, tries to help the wounded—the morphine hadn't even been broken out. Bucher describes it as a "scene of carnage."

Burning is still going on but there is still an incredible amount of undestroyed material. Bucher refers to "these mountains of paper."

Several writers describe the scene in the SOD-Hut as one out of Dante's *Inferno*. Most devote several pages of highly vivid prose to describing the frantic efforts at emergency destruction. Brandt (p. 44): "Hammond, Ginther, and Shepard picked up eight-pound sledgehammers and began hitting the equipment, packed in bays along the walls, while others began carrying armfuls of paper outside. Ginther attacked the two $60,000 tape recorders first, but they were encased in heavy metal covers and his hammer bounced off. The others were having the same trouble in the narrow space. The equipment was screwed tight to protect it from the roll of the ship. Almost all of the equipment had heavy metal covers protecting the fragile inner works. It would have taken too long to unscrew them, so the men simply tried to hammer them out of shape. When a man's arms got tired, he turned the sledgehammers over to someone else and assisted in the burning of material.''

Bucher (p. 204): "The SOD-Hut was still the scene of frenetic destruction activity with fire axes and hammers pounding equipment to pieces and piles of discouragingly large amounts of pubs and papers being shoved toward the fires. CT1 Peppard was in the Communications Office stoking a pyre of documents in a wastebasket. Steve [Harris] was ripping apart whole files with fearful, nervous bursts of exertion, his face flushed and grim. What appeared to be two large mattress covers stuffed with paper were laying in the middle of the deck.

" 'There's still too much stuff left, Steve,' I admonished him. 'Get all of it out of here over the side.'

" 'We're doing it as best we can, Captain! We're doing it!'

" 'Never mind the shallow water now. The fires can't keep up with these mountains of paper, so don't hesitate to throw the rest overboard.'

" 'We're doing it! . . . ' "

These two accounts (and others might be cited) provide contrasting images. Where Brandt is told the sledgehammers are bouncing off, Bucher has axes and hammers "pounding equipment to pieces." He later describes seeing gear reduced to "powder." And Bucher's reported conversation with Steve Harris is highly suspect. CT1 James D. Layton, the "watch supervisor," told the Court of Inquiry (according to the New York *Times*) "that Lieutenant Harris walked in shortly after the firing started, but had no orders nor messages to be released and that he never saw Lieutenant Harris participate in the destruction of materials." Brandt reports that "Bailey turned the transmission duties over to McClarren so he could help in the destruction. He nearly fell over Lieutenant Harris, who was kneeling and praying in the middle of the ten-by-fifteen-foot space. Bailey said: 'I'm going to have to get busy and destroy this gear, sir. You're going to have to get out of the way.' Lieutenant Harris got to his feet and left."

Such discrepancies might be attributed to differing memories or literary styles, except that there is sharp evidence that emergency destruction was of short duration. Bucher told the Court of Inquiry that "close to 100 per cent" of the gear was destroyed within a few minutes. The Court of Inquiry summarized the secret testimony of Communications Chief Kell as follows: "Kell estimated that burning of publications only lasted 10 to 15 minutes and was accomplished by using three or four wastebaskets. He did not use the ship's incinerator because it was on the open deck and would have exposed the men to gunfire from North Korean boats." The Court summary also stated that "Kell said burning of classified documents ceased when he received word from someone to stop burning. He couldn't remember who gave the word." Kell later told Armbrister that he couldn't remember who gave the order but it was someone with "competent authority."

Kell's sworn statement to the Court sharply belies the image of destruction drawn by every other account, which is of a protracted period during which *Pueblo* sailed along behind the subchaser—except for stopping once and drawing gunfire—while the crew started many fires, jettisoned materials, and hammered equipment to pieces.

The radio transcript suggests exactly how long this process went on. At 1345 *Pueblo* sent its WE ARE BEING ESCORTED INTO WONSAN message. Thereafter it remained in contact with Kamiseya until 1432, when it sent: "HAVE BEEN DIRECTED TO COME TO ALL STOP AND BEING BOARDED AT THIS TIME. BEING BOARDED AT THIS TIME." Its last actual message was: "FOUR MEN INJURED AND ONE CRITICALLY AND GOING OFF THE AIR NOW AND DESTROYING THIS GEAR".

That indicates that forty-seven minutes elapsed while *Pueblo* followed the subchaser, performing emergency destruction. But did they? Kell, a communications chief, a senior man, thirty-two years old, says he was ordered by someone to stop burning after ten to fifteen minutes. Nor was Kell alone in this declaration. The Court of Inquiry summary, as quoted by the New York *Times*, says: "CT1 David L. Ritter told the Court how he destroyed various publications and pieces of equipment, but *like many of the other crew members* [emphasis mine], did not remember who passed the word to 'stop burning.' He said he saw Lieutenant Harris in the research space, but no one was 'really supervising' destruction."

The five admirals, having heard this sharp discrepancy in testimony, then proceeded to do nothing about it. One would think they would have wanted to learn whether the senior petty officers were correct in stating emergency destruction lasted only ten to fifteen minutes, or whether it went on for forty-five minutes to an hour, as the ship's commissioned officers testified. But they didn't.

They didn't because they couldn't, for the duration of emergency destruction is the very heart of the cover story concocted by the Navy and the NSA. If a long, drawn-out destruction process is not believed, then the entire cover story falls apart.

Bucher maintained before the Court, in interviews with Armbrister, and in his own book that (1) *Pueblo* contained no emergency destruct devices and his men had to use sledgehammers and axes to destroy top secret gear; and (2) there was a "mountain" of classified documents aboard *Pueblo* which could only be disposed of by burning and jettisoning.

I will treat these claims separately. Persons familiar with ELINT ship operations state unequivocally that it is unthinkable that *Pueblo* was sent on a mission near Soviet and North Korean waters without automatic destruct mechanisms on top secret equipment. These devices were described to me as follows: Atop the equipment is a tab which a CT pulls. It sets off a device similar to a blasting cap. This in turn ignites a phosphorous grenade or thermite. The guts of the machine melt in seconds. These devices can also be wired in such a way that a single person can activate all of them at once. These automatic destruct devices are built in by the manufacturer and are largely tamper-proof.*

These statements are corroborated by early Pentagon announcements after the seizure. These stated that it was "believed" Duane Hodges was mortally wounded when his leg was blown off in a "destruct explosion." Hedrick Smith, military correspondent for the New York *Times*, writing a few days later (February 4, 1968) and quoting unnamed Pentagon sources, referred to "built-in destructive mechanisms for all her [*Pueblo*'s] highly secret electronic devices." As we will see, immediately after the seizure top aides to President Johnson were told *Pueblo* was equipped with destruct devices.

Vietnam War pilots, including a retired Navy wing commander, tell me that their aircraft were equipped with automatic devices. Upon ditching in the sea, top secret devices in the cockpit were said to "melt right before your eyes." If bailing out, the pilot was to pull a tab which activates the mechanisms.

That the U.S. Navy and the National Security Agency would send into hostile waters the *Pueblo*—or any ship—containing not just top secret equipment but a set and operable U.S. code machine, not to mention code cards and the codes themselves, without automatic destruct devices is unthinkable. And if by any remote chance it happened, heads should have rolled. National security could not possibly be more jeopardized.

Nonetheless, the five admirals on the Court of Inquiry accepted with equanimity (and straight faces) Bucher's testimony—and it was among the first things he spoke about on the first day of hearings—that his ship had no destruct mechanisms and his men had to use hammers and axes to destroy top secret gear. This became elaborated on, as we have seen, until arm-weary men are flailing away at steel boxes. Somehow it worked, for as Bucher told the Court, "close to 100 per cent" of the equipment was destroyed. But it took time, the forty-five minutes during which Bucher sailed behind the subchaser stalling for time. This is the heart of the cover story.

---

*Recall that the Court of Inquiry never questioned anyone from the equipment manufacturers or from the Naval Ship Support Command, which installed the equipment.

It is simply not true. The words which belie the cover story, already printed twice in this book, lie in the radio transcript of *Pueblo*'s last messages, a transcript prepared by the Navy and given to Congress, a transcript which the Court of Inquiry suppressed and which Bucher tries to ignore. At 1331 *Pueblo* transmitted, "WE ARE HOLDING EMERGENCY DESTRUCTION." At 1337 *Pueblo* sent, "WE ARE LAYING TO AT PRESENT POSITION. AS OF YET WE NO LONGER HAVE GOPI [WESTPACOPINTEL broadcast]. THIS CIRCUIT ONLY CIRCUIT ACTIVE ON SHIP."

Emergency destruction lasted six minutes. It began at 1331 and by 1337 Bailey's teletype was the only circuit open on the ship.

Those (principally Murphy and Armbrister) who take note of the radio transcript dismiss it as "mistakes" by Bailey. He *thought Pueblo* was being boarded at 1330 but he was *wrong*.

It won't wash. It is conceivable that Bailey was misinformed and in error about the 1330 boarding, but there is no possibility of his being in error about the emergency destruction. He was sitting in the SOD-Hut and could see it with his own eyes, something neither Murphy or Armbrister (or any other *Pueblo* writer) could do. Even Armbrister says smoke in the SOD-Hut confused Bailey. And Bailey was thirty-six years old, an expert on radio transmission, sent over from Kamiseya for this one voyage for the sole purpose of straightening out *Pueblo*'s transmission difficulties. If he transmits to Kamiseya that his is the only circuit active on the ship, I must believe him. He certainly knew more about the transmission capabilities of *Pueblo* than either Murphy or Armbrister.

Again, emergency destruction began at 1331 and by 1336 all circuits but one were destroyed. *Pueblo* no longer had contact with Western Pacific Operational Intelligence. It took six minutes. Whether this destruction was performed by automatic devices which melted the equipment or by men swinging sledgehammers, the destruction was of short duration.

Then there are all those classified documents. Capt. John H. D. Williams, described by the New York *Times* as an "emergency destruction expert for the Chief of Naval Operations," told the Court there was a ton of classified documents aboard *Pueblo*, a figure he later reduced in closed door testimony to six hundred pounds. Ten bags of documents were said to have gone undestroyed and fallen into North Korean hands. Bucher said there were whole mattress covers stuffed with them. He couldn't believe it and had no idea where the documents came from. He certainly hadn't signed for them. His actions in following the subchaser were designed to permit destruction of this paper. The incinerator was inadequate and fires were started all over the deck, even in the mess hall. Crewmen "waded" through documents, some of them soaked with the blood and guts of wounded men and thereby unburnable.

Where on earth did all these documents come from? *Pueblo* was a small ship, so overcrowded with eighty-three men on board that the crew had to eat in three shifts and a toilet had to be used as a makeshift darkroom. There were no roomfuls of typists turning out classified documents. Indeed, Yeoman Canales was so overworked he was seven months behind in his mail, as we have learned. And who wielded the Secret and Top Secret stamps on all this paper? As noted earlier, the CTs in the SOD-Hut *recorded* on magnetic tape—did not write down—electronic signals. Yet the paper *was there.*

If the men of *Pueblo* could not have produced this mass of classified documents, then the Navy or the NSA had to physically carry them aboard. Did they?

In a manner of speaking, yes. Persons familiar with ELINT ship operations explain that the SOD-Hut on every intelligence-gathering vessel has bags of documents stashed in compartments behind and above the operating gear. These "documents" look official. They bear "Secret" and "Top Secret" stamps. But they are fraudulent, phony. In intelligence parlance they are called "confetti."

As it was explained to me, in emergency destruction the CTs are to carry some of the bags of confetti outside and throw them overboard. It is hoped that boarders will jump into the water to retrieve some of it, thus being delayed. Other bags of confetti are to be used to start fires on deck. CTs are to throw them on mattresses and ignite them. The aim is twofold: to make smoke to conceal the real activities of destruction, and to delay boarders by causing them to busy themselves stamping out fires to retrieve the "documents." Hopefully, the boarders will believe some of the disinformation printed on the "documents." This use of confetti was described to me as a prearranged system in which CTs are supposed to be regularly drilled. If so, the CTs aboard *Pueblo* apparently executed these maneuvers to perfection. Even Bucher tells us he saw burning mattresses.

Worthless documents? *Confetti*? Can this be true? By way of corroboration I can report this story told me by Radioman Hayes during his interview. Apparently the North Koreans didn't place much value on the unburned documents from *Pueblo*, for they were placed in a hut at the camp where the men of *Pueblo* were imprisoned. Hayes said, "I know it is hard to believe, but one day a bird flew into the mess hall at dinner with a piece of paper in its mouth, which it dropped. One of the men picked it up. It was a corner off one of our documents. The word 'secret' was stamped on it in red. A Korean guard saw him, assumed he'd gotten it from the hut, and beat the shit out of him."

Better corroboration would seem to come from the senior enlisted men who told the Court of Inquiry they were ordered to stop burning after ten to fifteen minutes. This would seem to indicate they knew the documents weren't of much value. And if the unremembered "competent authority" who told them to stop burning was Bucher, Steve Harris, or another of the ship's officers, it would seem to indicate they also knew the documents were worthless confetti. But I cannot subscribe to this, because we will soon discover who the "competent authority" really was.

We will also discover other evidence that the period of emergency destruction was indeed of short duration, as the senior enlisted men swore to the Court of Inquiry.

Bucher insists the destruction went on for forty-five minutes to an hour. It was during this period before boarding that Bucher says he went to the SOD-Hut, saw the "frenetic" activity there, and had his conversation with Harris, as quoted. Then he pushed his way to the crypto center where "CT Bailey was nervously concentrating on his teletype machine whose lively chattering told me we had maintained contact with Kamiseya. From over his shoulder I could read a message coming in: . . . LAST WE GOT FROM YOU WAS 'ARE YOU SENDING ASSIST?' PLEASE ADVISE WHAT KEY LISTS YOU HAVE LEFT AND IF IT APPEARS THAT YOUR COMM SPACES WILL BE ENTERED."

This is the first time Bucher refers to any material that appears in the radio transcript. (Actually, he still does not refer to the existence of a transcript.) He explains that "key lists" refers to "our classified communication," adding: "Evidently the Naval Security Group had awakened to the danger of these falling into unfriendly hands." He tapped Bailey on the shoulder and told him he was coming on the line. "Bailey was too nervous, so McClarren manned the keyboard. His fingers flew over the keys, alerting whichever high-ranking officer who had the deck at Kamiseya that the captain of *Pueblo* was sending the following personal message . . ." Bucher said he had "no time to compose any dramatic verbiage, only compress into a very few words all the essential information about the situation and my intentions in dealing with it."

Bucher's message: "HAVE 0 [zero] KEY LISTS AND THIS ONLY ONE HAVE, HAVE BEEN REQUESTED FOLLOW INTO WONSAN, HAVE THREE WOUNDED AND ONE MAN WITH LEG BLOWN OFF, HAVE NOT USED ANY WEAPONS NOR

UNCOVERED 50- CAL. MAC . . . DESTROYING ALL KEYLISTS AND AS MUCH ELEC [electronics] EQUIPT AS POSSIBLE. HOW ABOUT SOME HELP. THESE GUYS MEAN BUSINESS. HAVE SUSTAINED SMALL WOUND IN RECTUM, DO NOT INTEND TO OFFER ANY RESISTANCE."

Bucher reports that "within a few seconds" Kamiseya's answer came back: "ROGER, ROGER. WE DOING ALL WE CAN. CAPT. HERE AND CNFJ ON HOTLINE. LAST I GOT WAS AIRFORCE GOING HELP YOU WITH SOME AIRCRAFT BUT CAN'T REALLY SAY AS CNFJ COORDINATING WITH I PRESUME KOREA FOR SOME F-105. THIS UNOFFICIAL BUT I THINK THAT WHAT WILL HAPPEN." Bucher says he answered "ROGER YOUR LAST. ROGER YOUR LAST," and "after reflecting on nothing for a moment, hurriedly left the Crypto Center."

All this is highly suspect, so much so there is doubt it ever happened. First, recall that Bucher says he told Harris not to destroy codes except on his order. Apparently they were destroyed, for Bucher says he is using the only one left. Second, his description of McClarren's fingers flying over the keys to send his message and receiving a reply "within a few seconds" does not fit what we know about how the teletype machine operated. As Schumacher informs us, and the transcript itself reveals, the operator (either on *Pueblo* or at Kamiseya) first cut a tape which sent the message in code. This process took several minutes. Recall that in the transcript Bailey said he had a message coming but it wasn't ready yet. The tape was being cut. And a minute or two elapsed after a message was sent before Kamiseya said it had been received. A tape was being cut at that end. Bucher's description of the process of sending the message is not accurate with what we know about the method. Third, consider Bucher's alleged line, DESTROYING ALL KEYLISTS AND AS MUCH ELEC EQUIPT AS POSSIBLE. He began his message by saying he had zero keylists and "this only one have." Now he is destroying "all keylists." He supposedly transmits that he was also destroying as much electronic equipment as possible. Recall that he told the Court of Inquiry that close to 100 percent of it was destroyed quickly. Fourth, it is hard to believe that in this situation Bucher would refer to his rectal wound when he had seriously wounded men. It is also highly uncharacteristic of him to write "after reflecting on nothing for a moment." Throughout his book, Bucher offers total recall of his actions and his thoughts at all times.

Ed Brandt, who interviewed both Bailey and McClarren, but obviously had not seen the radio transcript, gives a different version. Bucher entered and McClarren sent the message. It is quoted from memory but is essentially the same as that in the transcript. Then Brandt writes (p. 50):

"Bucher left as abruptly as he came, and McClarren sent the message twice. Then McClarren added on his own, repeating three times: 'How about some help out here?'" The transcript does not show this. Brandt writes: "The answer came back in seconds. 'Roger your last. This is Captain Pierson. Try to hold out as long as you can. ComNav 4, Japan, talking to ComNav 4, Korea, about getting some 105s out there. Good luck.'" These words are not in the radio transcript; rather, it is as Bucher quoted. If Brandt is correct, Bucher had left and couldn't have seen the reply from Captain Pierson. And it is McClarren, not Bucher, who transmits, "How about some help?" receiving the reply from Pierson. And Pierson talks about Navy fighters, not Air Force. Completely lost from either Bucher's story or the transcript are the words, "Try to hold out as long as you can."

Who do you believe? There is one certainty. Bucher's alleged message to Kamiseya matches the radio transcript, so he must have seen the transcript he otherwise ignores and contradicts. Or is it a certainty? I strongly believe the censor added the message to Bucher's book. As we will see, there is grave doubt the message was ever sent.

The radio transcript gives no precise time when Bucher sent his alleged message, but it comes at the end of a variety of transmissions said to have been sent between 1345 and 1409. This would indicate there was still another twenty-three minutes before boarding.

How did Bucher spend this time? He writes that he returned to the pilothouse, along the way expressing his "agonizing frustration by kicking at several fittings and throwing curses at the KORCOM ships bobbing close to our quarters as they herded *Pueblo* toward their lair like a fat cow to the slaughterhouse." He saw the Korean coastal mountains were "reappearing solidly ahead after having almost vanished during our abortive run to the sea." He noticed the "intense" cold, with temperatures plunging down to zero "during the past fateful two hours."

This is one of the few references to time Bucher provides in his account of the seizure. His reference to two hours agrees approximately with the transcript, since he has just returned from sending his message at 1409. Since he writes that only thirty minutes elapsed while the North Korean ships approached and he got under way to escape boarding, he has to be indicating that his period of flight, the shelling, the stopping, and following the subchaser consumed an hour and a half. This is not supported by the radio transcript or any other published account.

In the pilothouse Bucher noticed that Murphy had left and that the annunciator was set at ALL AHEAD, ONE-THIRD. Berens worked the wheel with "steady competence" and Radioman Hayes was "turning inside out" the contents of the radio shack "while Crandall kept demolishing equipment with his hammer." (Every other account has Crandall below deck seriously wounded in the shelling that killed Hodges. The report of Hayes's activity is also suspect. How did the ship's radio shack accumulate so much to be burned? *Pueblo* was supposedly on its maiden voyage and Hayes, by his own admission, could not receive messages and sent only "weather reports and such.")

Bucher says the "traffic from below to feed the incinerator was continuing," and has Yeoman Canales staggering up from below on "his tenth long tortuous trip from the bilges to the bridge." (The ship's office where Canales worked was in the bilges?) Tim Harris noted Bucher's return in his narrative report, and Bucher told him: "Okay, Tim! Now put down there that the captain orders the narrative log destroyed—then destroy it!" He describes Ensign Harris tearing it into pieces and throwing them out a "shot-out window to scatter like confetti in our wake." He notices that "surprisingly," torpedo boats "steamed right through that flotsam of secret documents without paying attention to it." (Tim Harris mentions none of this in interviews with Brandt.)

Bucher then writes that Steve Harris phoned from the SOD-Hut: "I request permission, sir, to send a message to Kamiseya telling them we will be unable to destroy all our classified publications, that some of them may be compromised."

Bucher says he barked, "Like what?"

"Mostly technical pubs and such. We simply can't get to them all, sir, but. . . ." Bucher says Harris's voice "faded into an agitated whimper" as he added, ". . . but I think we've gotten rid of everything else."

Bucher replied, "Permission granted to send the message if that's the situation as you see it. But we've still got time, so don't let up on your destruction."

This conversation, like many of those alleged to have occurred between Bucher and Harris, is strange. Recall that earlier Bucher chafed because Harris had authority to send messages which he knew nothing about and which might reflect "adversely" on *Pueblo*. Enlisted men testified that Harris did not participate in emergency destruction. He told the Court that ten bags went undestroyed, not that "I think we've gotten rid of everything" but "technical pubs and such." Bucher himself testified that when the boarders took him on a tour of his ship he was surprised to see a mattress cover full of documents undestroyed in the SOD-Hut. Then, again, there is the mysterious order to stop burning after ten to fifteen minutes.

I cannot explain this alleged conversation between Bucher and Harris except as fiction designed to enhance the cover story and aid screenwriters who would soon work on the script for the movie.

After talking to Harris, Bucher writes, "a couple of minutes later" the subchaser "ran up a new signal which ordered us to stop." He says, "I had no alternative but to order Gene to ring up ALL STOP and to stand by to receive boarders."

He says Lacy reminded him about the Military Code of Conduct. Bucher writes: "The pertinent suggestion calmly spoken took me somewhat by surprise after the way he had been acting during the past hour. It was in its way reassuring that he was yet able to function rationally." Bucher told him to make the announcement, saying, "I'll greet the bastards in person."

As he departed the bridge, he heard Lacy say over the loudspeaker: "Now hear this! Now hear this! All hands are reminded of our Code of Conduct. Say nothing to the enemy besides your name, rank and serial number. Repeat: Nothing besides your name, rank and serial number! Deck watch will now lay aft to receive boarders!"

Murphy's version of these events is so different, it is hard to believe the two officers were on the same ship. Murphy's account is laced with the contents of the radio transcript, set in boldface type. It reads as though someone stuck in the transcript, which bears no relationship to what Murphy is writing about from his own knowledge.

When the subchaser opened fire the second time, Murphy went below to check on the wounded. Bucher also came down to look at Hodges. Murphy (pp. 146–7): "On seeing the captain had left the bridge, I started back topside. The SO-1 was no longer firing now, but the P-4's were." No one else mentions such firing. "As I came out onto the 01 level, I could see paper scattered all over the deck on the port side just aft of the pilothouse. I recognized the sheets. They were from ship identification pubs and were stamped SECRET. I guess someone had dropped them when the firing resumed. There was a P-4 off our starboard quarter nearly astern of us. It wasn't firing, but I knew it could do so at any moment. Crawling on my hands and knees, but keeping a nervous eye on the P-4, I started picking them up."

At this point a long excerpt from the radio transcript is inserted. Then Murphy writes: "With a big sigh of relief, I grabbed the last sheet. Then to my dismay I saw a mass of pages, at least fifty of them, underneath the boat davit. To reach them I'd have to crawl toward the P-4. Hoping no one aboard was looking, I inched forward, then grabbed as fast as I could.

With the last one in hand, I hurried to the side and threw the documents overboard. At least a few of our secrets wouldn't fall into enemy hands.''

(If a person assumes something like this did happen, and there is grave doubt of that, it remains rather pathetic. In the 1960s, as perhaps today, the U.S. government was involved in what can only be referred to as "classification mania." Astounding things were classified Secret; newspaper clippings, personal letters, transcripts of public testimony, Civil War records, credit ratings—indeed, just about anything which a bureaucrat could construe as possibly embarrassing. The motto was: When in doubt, classify. Here we have a Navy officer supposedly risking his life to save official secrets. But what were they? The technical publications and ship identification manuals he refers to were available in libraries, even published in trade journals. The Secret classification applied to such a hodgepodge of material it was virtually meaningless. Top Secret and higher classifications were something else. The simple fact is that the really valuable, highly classified material and equipment aboard *Pueblo* were destroyed within a minute or less, when emergency destruction began. Unfamiliar with SOD-Hut operations, Murphy portrays himself as risking his life to destroy what are in reality not very valuable materials—if he destroyed any at all. As we will see, it is extremely doubtful that Murphy or anyone else, other than the CTs in the SOD-Hut, destroyed much of anything.)

Murphy continues: "One of the P-4's resumed firing. I couldn't see which one, but guessed it was my nearest neighbor, as I could hear the splatter of the machine-gun bullets all around me. I felt no pain and was convinced they had missed. All the same, I wanted to put as much steel as possible between me and them. I dashed back across the deck.

"It was then I saw the captain. He had come back topside while I was gathering the classified pages. He was standing on the port wing, frantically waving his white stocking cap. 'Stop firing, you bastards!' he yelled over and over.

"Seeing him waving the white emblem of surrender, I realized for the first time that Bucher intended to give up the ship, that he was, in fact, at this very moment doing exactly that."

All this is so radically different from any other account that it defies comment.

On the next page (p. 148), Murphy begins a new chapter with these words: "Perhaps because the North Koreans had no way of knowing that Bucher was the *Pueblo*'s captain, the firing didn't stop. Moments after I returned to the pilothouse, the SO-1 let loose another barrage."

No one else refers to any firing upon *Pueblo* after the rounds that wounded Hodges, Woelk, Chicca, and Crandall. Indeed, Bucher writes (p. 202), "As soon as *Pueblo* started moving again, the shooting stopped." I simply cannot explain such discrepancies in works of nonfiction.

Murphy goes on to describe the scene, quoted earlier, in which Bucher entered the pilothouse, called the crouching men cowards, and supposedly kicked Murphy in the derriere, which Murphy denies ever happened.

Murphy continues (pp. 148–9): "After a few minutes the firing subsided, then stopped. But Bucher's mood was little improved. And it grew worse when Steve Harris called to report that there was just too much paper and too little time. He asked Bucher to tell Japan that at least some of our classified pubs would probably be compromised.

"Bucher favored Steve with an even choicer set of swear words.

"I again checked our navigation—we were still a good distance outside the twelve-mile limit—then helped Schumacher start drafting a new message to Japan. One of the men asked if he could destroy the main transmitter. Negative, I replied; that should be the very last thing to go. I did give him permission to destroy the one for the Hi Comm network. By now we had discovered it was inoperative.

"There was no need for both the captain and the exec to remain on the bridge. With Bucher's consent, I decided to go below to see if I could help in the destruction or [in the] care of the wounded." More of the transcript is inserted here. "As I started below, I happened to look aft through an open door and saw the P-4 with the boarding party come alongside on our starboard quarter. I didn't see the message the SO-1 hoisted about this same time, but later learned they had ordered us to come to all stop. I did feel the change in the engines, as, following Bucher's instructions, Lacy pulled the annunciator back. And I heard, over the 1MC, a message that sent a wave of nausea from my stomach to my throat, Bucher ordering: 'Lay aft to the starboard quarter to assist the boarding party.'

"It wasn't enough that we had to surrender; we had to help the bastards aboard too."

Murphy then describes Klepac, Bussell, and Commissaryman Lewis going to assist the North Koreans and Lacy coming on the loudspeaker with his name, rank, and serial number message. Murphy went below to check on the wounded. He picked up some documents and tried to flush them down the toilet (p. 151): "There was a chair next to the john. I collapsed into it. I was physically and emotionally drained. Had I tried, I doubt seriously if I could have summoned the strength to get up. I just sat there staring dumbly ahead. There wasn't anything more that could be done. It was all over."

Murphy prints the final portions of the radio transcript, then writes that Bucher "laid below to his stateroom to put on long underwear, an extra pair of socks, his flight jacket, and commander's cap. I just stared at him as he dressed for the formal surrender."

Astonishingly, Murphy writes (pp. 151–2): "I felt sorry for all of us, the whole crew of *Pueblo*, but most of all, oddly enough, for Bucher. His first command, and he'd lost his ship. A number of his men were wounded, one dying. He cared about his 'boys.' What had happened to Hodges must have deeply shaken him. I could feel nothing for him now but sympathy. Not since reporting aboard the *Pueblo* had I felt as close to him as I did at this moment. It was as if all our differences had been obliterated by the North Korean gunfire. We were no longer adversaries. We were, literally and figuratively, in the same boat. And that boat was now the proud possession of a hostile nation. . . .

"I just sat there watching Bucher. It didn't seem there was anything more to say, but, incredibly, for several minutes we exchanged small talk. The words have since faded from my mind, but not the impression they made. It seemed inconceivable that we could be talking like this, about such inconsequential things, considering the enormity of what was happening.

"When he finished dressing, Bucher went topside. I sat there for a few more seconds, then wearily rose and started to follow him. As I stepped into the passageway I almost collided with a North Korean soldier. His dark Oriental face was the opposite of inscrutable; hatred was written all over it. He pointed his bayonet-rigged automatic rifle straight at my stomach."

To borrow a word Murphy used, all this is *incredible*. At the very moment *Pueblo* is being boarded, Lieutenant Murphy, the second in command, goes down to his stateroom, sits in the toilet, deeply depressed, then watches his captain change clothes and engages in unremembered "small talk" for "several minutes." Bucher leaves. Then in "a few more seconds" Murphy leaves, only to have a North Korean point his rifle at him.

As incredible as it reads, it apparently happened! Bucher reports something similar (pp. 207–8): "I estimated that it would take another three or four minutes for *Pueblo* to come dead in the water and for the KOR-COM torpedo boat to maneuver itself into position to board us. I used that time to make another dash to my stateroom with the purpose of exchanging my tasseled ski cap for regulation headgear that would mark me as a senior officer of the U.S. Navy and captain of my ship. I also took the opportunity to hastily pull on some heavy woolen underpants as protection against the increasingly bitter cold, and to wrap a sock around my blood-soaked ankle. The doors connecting to the bathroom I shared with the Executive Officer's quarters were open and I saw Murphy standing in there, sort of listlessly fumbling about over nothing in particular, then looking surprised at seeing me, [saying], 'What shall we do now, sir? What happens next?'

"I thought it had been a long time since he left the bridge without being specially missed. I felt almost sorry for him and wished to hell for both our sakes I had requested his transfer "for cause" and sailed into the Sea of Japan one officer short. But there was no more time left for another of our private talks. I could only tell him, 'I am going to meet the KOR-COMs who are now making to board us. You had better go topside and stand by for whatever develops. You might as well brace yourself for the worst, Ed, and try to measure up.'"

It is difficult, but try to set aside this obscene feud between Bucher and Murphy and concentrate on what *both* say happened. After *Pueblo* had obeyed an order to stop and after men were ordered aft to receive the boarders, both Bucher and Murphy went below. While Bucher changed his attire, the two men had some type of conversation. How long did this take? Bucher says "three or four minutes" while Murphy indicates a longer period of time. Even if Bucher was a rapid dresser, it would seem the incident must have taken several minutes. All this indicates that Bucher was not topside greeting boarders, as we will see he says he was. And if Murphy is correct that he followed Bucher seconds later, only to have a North Korean point a rifle at him, then it must be concluded that both the captain and the executive officer of *Pueblo* were below decks chatting at the very moment their ship was boarded and seized.

On page 77 of his book Armbrister refers to the incident below decks in this language: "Suddenly Bucher remembered he was wearing a ski cap. He ran to his cabin to find his Navy hat with the gold braid on its visor. He put on some long-handled drawers and boots and wrapped a pair of black socks around his bleeding ankle. Then he saw Murphy and asked, 'How's Hodges?'

"'He's resting,' Murphy said.

"'How did the rest of the destruction go?'

"'Real good, I think.'

"Murphy left. Schumacher came down to get his hat and foul-weather jacket. Bucher started back toward the bridge." Thus, in this account Murphy left before Bucher.

Bucher, however, says he was on deck when *Pueblo* was boarded. He rushed topside to the fantail where "a party of sailors under Boatswain's Mate 1st Class Klepac was making ready to receive the lines of the approaching torpedo boat."

Bucher writes that the torpedo boat's fenders thumped against *Pueblo*'s stern and "suddenly a detachment of eight or ten Koreans swarmed over the railing, brandishing automatic weapons with fixed bayonets. They were led by two officers with red and gold shoulderboards attached to their dark green jackets. One of them came right at me with a pistol aimed at my head."

Bucher shouted at him: "I protest this outrage! We are a United States ship operating in international waters and you have no damned right to attack us like this. As captain, I order you to get off my ship at once and let us go our way in peace." Bucher writes that there was "not a flicker of understanding on his sullen face."

Ed Brandt interviewed fifteen key people and what he learned from them is shockingly different from Bucher's story. More importantly, it casts the entire boarding in a different light.

Brandt (p. 52): "Tim Harris went to the port side of the pilothouse, where Lieutenant Schumacher was standing and looking out. A few yards away a North Korean PT boat was jockeying for position alongside the still-moving *Pueblo*. Boatswain's Mate Willie C. Bussell, twenty-two, of Hopkinsville, Kentucky, one of the two Negroes aboard the *Pueblo*, and Norbert J. Klepac, thirty-four, of San Diego, California, were on the port quarter, apparently waiting to receive a line from the PT boat."

Pueblo was *still moving* when boarded. It had not come to a stop.

Brandt continues: "Even though he could see the Koreans coming, Tim Harris was shocked when he heard Bucher say over the 1MC: 'Prepare to take on boarding party.'"

Bucher, according to these eyewitnesses, is not greeting the North Korean boarders, having a pistol thrust at his head, protesting an outrage, and ordering them off his ship. He—not Lacy—is in the pilothouse, speaking over the loudspeaker, ordering his men to prepare to take on a boarding party.

Schumacher's version of the boarding has the PT boat backing down "along our port side"—not the starboard, as Murphy writes, or stern, as Bucher says. About ten armed men and two officers were intent "on stepping across the foot or so" that separated the ships. Tim Harris came alongside him on the wing of the bridge. "Looks pretty bad," Harris said. Schumacher replied, "Yeah, it does."

According to Schumacher it was Lacy in the pilothouse who "passed the word" to "prepare to receive boarders." He also reminded crewmen of the Code of Conduct, but Schumacher admitted, "I didn't hear any of the last part. I seemed to be deafened by my bewilderment over what I was watching but not believing." (Perhaps another reason he didn't hear is that he was below decks getting his hat and foul-weather jacket, as Armbrister states.)

Bucher was standing "near the ladder that led from the deck below, where the Koreans would board. Tim and I watched with disbelief as, after missing the first time, they threw a line from their small boat onto our deck. Mechanically, a sailor slipped the hated line over a bit."

The North Koreans moved about the ship "as if they had rehearsed this hijacking," Schumacher says. First on board was an officer carrying a .45. "The Captain went up to him and presented himself as the commanding officer of the U.S.S. *Pueblo*. With the revolver pressed against the Captain's head, the Korean waved him into the pilothouse, with the rest of the boarding party following. Berens was still at the wheel. The Koreans directed him, Tim, and me, along with the others in sight, to the fantail."

This version differs from others. It is Lacy, not Bucher, who gives the order to receive boarders, although Schumacher admits he wasn't listening too well. He has boarders intent on jumping across a foot or so—yet they throw a line which was received. Bucher presents himself as commanding officer. Berens, along with everyone else save Bucher, is herded to the fantail. Bucher and others write that Berens remained at the helm.

It is difficult to visualize the boarding as described by Schumacher. He refers to the torpedo boat as coming alongside and describes men jumping over from a "small boat." The P-4 is smaller than *Pueblo*, but not really that small. It is extremely difficult to believe the North Koreans would tie their high-speed, highly maneuverable PT boat to *Pueblo*. *Pueblo* could tow the smaller craft, thereby placing it in jeopardy. It could easily be damaged against the side in a swell. And the PT boat commander had to fear that with his boat thus immobilized he was at risk of U.S. sailors jumping into his craft and seizing it. It is simply easier to believe Brandt's version that the North Koreans jumped aboard the *still moving Pueblo* and did not tie up to it. (It is obvious to me that the reason Schumacher has the line being thrown over to *Pueblo*—a nonsensical action on the North Koreans' part—is that it was testified to in the Court of Inquiry where the five admirals also bought it. Klepac told the Court, "They threw me a line and came aboard." According to the New York *Times*, Rear Adm. Marshall W. White asked, "When they threw you the line, did you have any impulse to throw it back?" The *Times* said "the sailor paused a moment," then answered, "I didn't want to receive the line—let's put it that way." The illogic of the PT boat tying up to *Pueblo* never occurred to Admiral White.)

Brandt (p. 52): "Seven or eight soldiers, dressed in heavy olive green quilted jackets and square fur hats each with a big red star in the middle, began jumping aboard, carrying submachine guns with bayonets attached. An officer, in a black greatcoat and fur hat, was carrying a pistol."

The key issue in this paragraph is not whether there were seven or eight, as against eight or ten, or whether there was one officer or two. The key word in the paragraph is *soldiers*. *Pueblo* was boarded by soldiers, not sailors or marines or people familiar with ships.

Brandt (p. 52): "To [Ensign] Harris, the Koreans all looked slant-eyed and short. He thought they were the perfect stereotypes of Orientals as they jumped the low railing on the fantail one at a time. The officer waved his pistol at Harris and Schumacher, motioning them to come to the fantail and sit down. In a few moments they were joined by about a dozen other crewmen. Harris was too dejected to look up to see who his companions were as he sat down on the cold deck. For the first time, Harris was getting scared. He figured that if the Koreans were going to shoot them, they would do it now. His fears increased ten minutes later when Bucher walked up, followed by a Korean officer holding a pistol.

"Bucher carried blindfolds torn from a bedsheet and his face was very grim as he passed them out and said in a low voice: 'They want you to put these blindfolds on.'"

Ed Brandt also interviewed Quartermaster Law. Brandt describes what he learned (p. 53): "Charlie Law had gone back to the mess deck for another cup of coffee when he heard Bucher call over the 1MC for Klepac and Bussell to go to the fantail to receive a boarding party. He didn't hear a 'repel boarders' call and he knew that there was not going to be any resistance. Shortly after, Law heard Lacy's voice on the 1MC warning the men that they were required to give only their names, ranks, and serial numbers."

Brandt says Law went to his quarters for thermal underwear and his foul-weather jacket. "On the way, he noticed some members of the crew ripping their insignia from their left sleeves. . . . Law ran into Donald

Peppard, who was also drinking a cup of coffee. Peppard said it might be the last one he would get for a while. They were talking about the situation when they heard Bucher over the 1MC order all hands except those necessary to operate the engine room to go forward to the well deck. . . . So the crew began wandering, bewildered and a little frightened, from all parts of the ship toward the well deck forward.''

All this is astounding. Law is drinking coffee when *Pueblo* is being boarded by North Koreans. He goes to his quarters for "thermal underwear"—which means he had to strip down and re-dress, which had to take a few minutes—and his warm jacket. He runs into Peppard, who is also drinking coffee, and they talk over the situation until ordered by Bucher to report to the well deck. The impression given is that not only did *Pueblo* surrender without resistance, it did so calmly, matter-of-factly, almost as though it were routine.

Brandt writes (p. 54) that Don Bailey and Chief Bouden were still in the crypto center. "Bailey was keeping the line open to Kamiseya with operator's chatter when he suddenly became aware that he wasn't getting any more information from the research space. He got up and walked into the passageway, puzzled by the sudden silence, and choking in the dense smoke. He rounded a corner and almost walked into a North Korean guard, who, fortunately, was looking the other way and shouting something in Korean. Bailey turned, ran back to the crypto center, and told Bouden that the Koreans were already aboard. Bailey sat down and requested permission of Kamiseya to secure the circuit and destroy the gear. Kamiseya answered: 'Permission granted. Good luck.' Bailey immediately began destroying the equipment with Chief Bouden's aid. Bailey, hard of hearing, was smashing the working parts inside the crypto cabinets when he felt a tap on his shoulder. He turned and saw a crewman, followed by a stocky, expressionless North Korean armed with a submachine gun. The crewman told Bailey he had to get out of there and go to the well deck.''

To a person coming along twenty years later and trying to discover what really happened during the seizure, Bailey's words, as told to Ed Brandt, leap off the page. Bailey is sitting in the SOD-Hut, choking, when he is puzzled by the "sudden silence." The SOD-Hut, once so crowded, is now empty except for Senior Chief CT Bouden—and a Korean guard, who doesn't see him. Bailey runs back to the crypto center, telling Bouden they are boarded. He asks and receives permission from Kamiseya to destroy his gear. I am not doubting Bailey's veracity or Brandt's accuracy, but this exchange does not show up on the transcript, which is heavily edited at this point anyway. The closest thing is Bailey's statement that he is going off the air and destroying his gear. He did not ask permission on the transcript. *Nor did he inform Kamiseya that the North Koreans were already aboard. Surely he would have, yet that is not in the transcript.*

It is significant that Bailey told none of this to Armbrister, who reports (p. 210): "Don Bailey climbed to the main deck and saw a North Korean directly in front of him, pointing an AK-47 at his chest. He had been kneeling beside the teletype so long that his feet 'felt like two-by-fours.' He noticed ice on the deck; he hoped the guard wouldn't slip and accidentally squeeze that trigger. The guard prodded him toward the fantail. 'I couldn't get this one question outta my mind,' he says. 'Where the hell is the rest of the Navy? Where is the Air Force? When are they gonna get here?'" Since Armbrister interviewed Bailey after Brandt did, I can only conclude that Bailey was briefed in the interim on what not to say. I cannot conceive that Armbrister, if he had heard the information Bailey gave to Brandt, would have omitted it as unimportant.

Returning to Brandt's account, Bailey was in the process of "smashing" his gear—we will come to evidence the teletype was not destroyed—when he "felt a tap on his shoulder." He turned and "saw a crewman" accompanied by a North Korean. The crewman told Bailey to go to the well deck.

Who is the crewman and why doesn't Bailey identify him? It is most unlikely that Bailey doesn't know who he is. He doesn't want to say— much like all the crewmen who can't remember who ordered them to stop burning after ten to fifteen minutes. If the North Korean soldier wanted Bailey out of the SOD-Hut, he didn't need a crewman to tap Bailey on the shoulder and tell him to leave. He was quite capable of using his AK-47 to herd Bailey to the well deck.

Who is this crewman and, more importantly, why is he aiding the North Koreans? Was the crewman there because he spoke Korean and was forced to act as an interpreter? Is he unidentified because there was supposedly no one on board who spoke fluent Korean? Or was some other language being spoken?

The real reason Bailey's words to Brandt leap off the page is that they indicate that Bailey is still on the teletype with Kamiseya *while the North Koreans are already on board.* No time is given in this paragraph. Even Bailey's asking permission to destroy his gear doesn't show up in the transcript. There is no indication of how long Bailey, somewhat hard of hearing, has been bent over his teletype before he realizes he is getting no more information, goes to check, and finds out the North Koreans have boarded. Is it a minute? Ten minutes? Longer? How long has Bailey been messaging Kamiseya without realizing the North Koreans are aboard?

Wouldn't it be logical to assume that Bailey, still unseen by the North Korean, would jump back inside and close one of the doors?

If so, when Bailey gets the tap on the shoulder from a crewman, it makes a little sense, because the crewman could have punched the cipher lock and let himself and the North Korean in. Or did he? Read the following excerpt from the New York *Times* coverage of the Court of Inquiry, January 31, 1969:

> Commander Bucher said that, after the *Pueblo* was captured, he walked through the ship accompanied by several North Koreans.
>
> "We finally arrived in the research space," he recalled. "The door was opened, and upon walking inside. . . ."

The door *was opened*, which is entirely different from saying the door *was open*. Could Bucher, forced at gunpoint to conduct the North Koreans on a tour of his ship, come to a locked door in the SOD-Hut and simply pound on it to gain entry, as he had so often done in the past? If Bouden opened it, could it have been Bucher who tapped Bailey on the shoulder and told him to go to the well deck?

What is important is not *who* told Bailey to leave, but rather *how long* Bailey remained in contact with Kamiseya before the unidentified crewmember told him to surrender and go to the well deck. At the very least, we have in Bailey's words to Brandt a means of solving the mystery of how *Pueblo* could be boarded and in enemy hands by 1345 yet remain in contact with Kamiseya until 1432.

A far different picture than Bucher offers is now beginning to emerge. But we need first to learn what Bucher says happened.

He notes (p. 209) that "although the Korean Communists who boarded us looked more like ground troops than sailors, they did not act out of their element or hesitate in their actions." He says the North Koreans "forced my men on the fantail to sit down on the deck with their hands above their heads." In contrast, Armbrister reports (p. 224): "Suddenly, one of the guards squeezed off a burst of automatic rifle fire. It passed directly over the men on the fantail. They hit the deck. The North Koreans told them to sit there with their knees tucked up against their chests." (Since the rusty Chicca and Hammond were the only Americans with any knowledge of Korean, one wonders just how they were *told* what to do.) Bucher writes that "others [North Koreans] immediately moved through the rest of the ship, looking for more of the crew whom they roughly herded forward and made to sit on the well deck in the freezing cold."

Bucher says nothing about coming on the loudspeaker to order his men to prepare to receive boarders. He has the North Koreans rounding them up.

Bucher: "They [the North Koreans] produced lengths of rope to tie the prisoners' hands and tore up strips of sheets with which to blindfold them." There is no word of Bucher approaching his men with the torn sheets and telling them to blindfold themselves. Most other reports say the hands of the men were not bound until much later, when they left the ship at Wonsan.

Bucher says he was forced at gunpoint toward the bridge. Only he and Berens were allowed to remain there. (Armbrister reports that Berens was at first herded to the fantail with the other crewmen. In searching him, the North Koreans discovered he was the helmsman and sent him back to the pilothouse.)

Bucher: "One of the Korean officers pointed at their subchaser who was again flying its FOLLOW ME signal and then indicated the annunciator with some vigorous motions [of his] head. I rang up ALL AHEAD ONE-THIRD and ordered Berens to steer in the wake of the subchaser." Armbrister reports something different (p. 226): "*Pueblo* got under way again at one-third speed. Berens stood at the helm flanked by North Korean guards. An officer was using the 1MC to talk to the SO1 on the ship's port side. The SO1 veered off and sped toward Wonsan. The officer motioned for Berens to follow in her wake. Berens turned and looked at Bucher." Armbrister does not report what Bucher said or did.

Bucher: "The other officer had entered the radio shack which was in shambles except for one transmitter that had been left intact and still turned on. When he indicated to me that he wanted it turned off and I adamantly shook my head, I received my first blow, a sharp crack with the barrel of his pistol to the side of my head. Yanking me out of the way, he tore out the transmitting key from its base and the power connectors out of their jackboxes, thus severing our last communication with the outside world." This is not correct. There was still a link, which Bucher himself reports shortly. This passage indicates, however, that Hayes was incorrect when he says he destroyed his equipment with an ax.

Thus the first acts of the North Koreans were to (1) herd everyone except Berens and Bucher to the fantail and well deck and blindfold them; (2) get the ship under way; and (3) disconnect the radio.

Bucher says neither of the officers could speak English, but one of them could write a few words: "Picking up a scrap of paper among those littering the deck, he printed the words MANY MANS, thrust it in my face and made a querying gesture.'' Bucher says he stalled for time by shouting down to Yeoman Canales on the well deck. "After we decided there were eighty-three men on our roster, I scribbled down that figure."

Armbrister's version is different (p. 224): "In the pilot house Bucher was alone with his captors. [Where was Berens?] One of the junior officers drew heads with long noses on a sheet of paper and placed a question mark beside them. How many men were aboard ship? Bucher stepped out on the 0-1 level and shouted to Canales below.

"'About eighty,' Canales replied.

"'What do you mean, "about"?' Bucher snapped. 'Don't you know?'

"'Eighty-three,' Peppard said.'' (I read into this that there had been so many last-minute replacements aboard his ship that Bucher was uncertain how many men were under his command.)

Bucher said the North Koreans "stared" at the figure "with an incredulous expression that turned into irritated disbelief." The point here is that the North Koreans couldn't believe this tiny ship actually had eighty-three men crammed aboard it.

Bucher writes that Berens was left in the pilothouse with a guard, while he was "prodded at pistol point" to the .50-caliber machine gun mount located aft. "There I was given the sign to unlash the tarpaulin covering the weapon. It had, as usual, frozen solid in the intense cold and that gave me an excuse to again adamantly shake my head in refusal. Again I received a blow from the pistol barrel. The lieutenant then assigned the job to two enlisted troopers."

Add this to the order of North Korean actions, which now reads boarding, capturing and blindfolding the crew, getting the ship under way, disconnecting the ship's radio, and uncovering the ship's weapons. This is reinforced by Brandt, who writes (p. 59): "Bucher asked Gunner's Mate Wadley for the keys to the ready locker, which held the ammunition for the machine guns. Wadley pointed to a guard and said, 'I've already given them to him.'" Armbrister also describes Wadley giving the keys to the North Koreans.

In understanding what really happened aboard *Pueblo*, a truly significant question must be asked: Why would one of the first acts of the North Koreans be to uncover and arm *Pueblo*'s weapons—something *Pueblo* had never done? After all, *Pueblo* was already captured. Why now arm the vessel? Who were they going to shoot at?

Bucher writes (p. 211) that one lieutenant left to "take over things below," leaving Berens and himself in the pilothouse guarded by an "enlisted Korean trooper who kept a finger on the trigger of his submachine gun." Bucher then pens perhaps the most preposterous passage in his book:

"*Pueblo* was moving along at her one-third speed of 5 knots, following her escorts of KORCOM warships toward the walls of Korean mountains which were turning a reddish purple in the early winter twilight; the island of Hado Pando stood out sharply with its distinctive shape that reminded me of Rio de Janeiro's famous Sugar Loaf. We were getting close to the hostile mainland, but I had learned during the past twenty-four hours to fairly accurately estimate the ranges of this area and judged us to be barely within the Korean's own twelve-mile territorial limit and still a full twenty miles from Wonsan harbor."

All of this is utterly impossible on several grounds. For starters, how on earth did it get to be "early winter twilight"? By Bucher's own admission, the ship was boarded at 1432 (2:32 P.M.). According to his description of events, North Koreans can only have been aboard a few minutes, certainly less than an hour. It can't possibly be "early twilight." Sunset, according to the Navy, was at 1734 and total darkness set in at 1806. Early twilight would be around a quarter to six in the evening, not three or three-thirty in the mid-afternoon.

If it was indeed twilight, the mountains weren't going to be "reddish purple." The sun sets in the west. He is east of Wonsan and the mountains would have been backlit. Then there is his reference to the "island of Hado Pando." If he is as familiar with these waters as he claims he is, he simply has to know Hado Pando is a peninsula. Indeed, the word *pando* means peninsula in Korean. Finally, if Bucher is twenty miles from Wonsan, Hado Peninsula is perhaps twelve miles away, backlit. Even if it were an extremely clear day, and other descriptions suggest it wasn't, Bucher would have been lucky to see Hado, let alone compare it to Rio's Sugar Loaf.

There are three possible conclusions from this: (1) Bucher and his collaborator Mark Rascovich simply made it up; (2) Bucher, an intelligent man and a Navy commander, forced to write a cover story, was deliberately writing something so obviously incorrect as to enable readers to see through his own story;* or (3) he did see something like this at early twi-

---

*By all accounts Bucher and the entire crew of *Pueblo* engaged in a great deal of this sort of activity while captives in Korea. Forced to write letters home and to appear at "press conferences," they made nonsensical references to American trivia to indicate to those back home that they were being forced to make statements. For example, they referred to Navy officers by such names as Buzz Sawyer and Barney Google. They became quite clever at this sort of thing.

light, but simply moved it three or four hours earlier in time. If (3) is the case, then it must be asked: What was *Pueblo* doing for all that time if it approached Hado Peninsula at twilight?

After describing his visual impressions, Bucher then writes: "Even with the two pairs of suspicious eyes watching my every move and keeping me covered with a pistol and a cocked submachine gun, I still had some freedom of movement on my bridge. The Korean lieutenant urged more speed, but somehow accepted my gestures of refusing to comply without administering any more punishing blows. Perhaps, after all, he was an infantry-type who had been thrust into an unfamiliar role by his Communist superiors and could not really judge what could or could not be done by a ship at sea. Perhaps he had to still rely on *me* to a certain extent."

I believe these words by Bucher to be highly significant in understanding the *Pueblo* seizure. Bucher understood that infantry soldiers had seized his ship. They were unfamiliar with not just this ship, but any ship. He felt he had some freedom of movement. How did he use it? He says he used it to pace back and forth, then at gunpoint broadcast over the loudspeaker, "All hands muster forward and stand by on the welldeck." (It would be interesting to know how the North Korean, not speaking English, managed to indicate to Bucher that he wanted him to make the announcement. It certainly would have been easy for Bucher to indicate that he didn't understand what he was to do. Both Armbrister and Brandt [and, recall, even Bucher] indicate that the herding of crewmembers to both the fantail and welldeck commenced as soon as the North Koreans boarded.)

Bucher writes that "twenty–thirty minutes went by" in this fashion and they "drew within about nine miles" of the coastline when "the Korean lieutenant grabbed the annunciator and placed it at STOP."

Recall the "early winter twilight" passage. At that time *Pueblo* was twenty miles from Wonsan harbor. How, moving at one-third speed of four or five knots, it came within nine miles in "twenty–thirty minutes" is not explained.

After *Pueblo* stopped, a new cluster of boarders came from a torpedo boat. Bucher: "This was a high-level personage and his staff who had evidently decided the situation was now secure enough for him to make a personal intervention on the scene. He swaggered up to my bridge with red shoulderboards reflecting the rays of the setting sun from clusters of gold stars."

Sunset, again, was at 1734 hours. And "twenty–thirty minutes" earlier it was "early winter twilight." Now we have the "setting sun." Bucher's day is moving backward.

Bucher writes that "I didn't know what they [the gold stars] signified—a full colonel, at least. His face and neck were disfigured by the prominent scars of a veteran campaigner."

With him was an interpreter who spoke "letter-perfect textbook English" and a civilian pilot who went to the pilothouse and "unceremoniously rang up ALL AHEAD FLANK SPEED." Berens was shoved away from the helm and escorted below with the rest of the crew.

Bucher was forced to give the officer a tour of the ship. They went to the mess hall, deserted now except for piles of ashes, then to the engineroom where Chief Goldman and Engineman Blansett were running the engines under a "watchful Korean trooper."

Bucher says the officer, who became known to crewmen as "Colonel Scar," showed surprise when he entered the SOD-Hut. This surely indicates the time when Bucher says the door to the SOD-Hut "was opened." "He quite obviously never expected this small ship to carry such an elaborate electronic intelligence system." Bucher says he was "relieved to notice all the visible coding equipment had been smashed," then he writes: "But the power was still on and the teletype machine was faintly humming with an occasional random twitch of its keys that left odd, meaningless letters typed on the teletype paper. I was ordered to shut it down and when I refused with an ignorant shrug, received a hard blow to the back of my neck. . . . The interpreter proceeded to kill the teletype by yanking out its power connector."

These details are significant. *The teletype was still running.* It had not been destroyed by Bailey. And the teletype had a separate power supply and did not run through the transmitters in the ship's radio shack. It also indicates the eagerness of the North Koreans to cut off all communications between *Pueblo* and the outside world. Who didn't they want *Pueblo* to contact? The crew was captive. There were no Americans to send messages. Why shut down the radio transmitter and the teletype? And recall that the North Korean broadcast picked up at 1306 said they planned to board the ship and shut down the transmitters. Why was this so important?

Bucher showed them the forward berthing compartment, where the men were now being held, then was placed in the passageway near Hodges' now dead body. Bucher was helpless and out of any involvement, a prisoner like his men. He writes that "an hour dragged by" and "about two and a half to three hours after the seizure" he saw the lights of Wonsan through a porthole. Bucher's story of the seizure ends here.

There is another vital piece of evidence. Again it comes from Ed Brandt (pp. 54–5): "Most of the crew, meanwhile, had reached the well deck. When Law arrived, about sixty crewmen were standing around, quiet and subdued, most of them with their hands in their pockets. [Their hands were not tied!] A Korean stood at the 0-1 level about eight feet above their heads, his submachine gun pointed at them. He was trying to count the crew, but [Fireman] Mike O'Bannon kept moving. The guard yelled at him and pointed his gun. O'Bannon took his helmet off, waved it in the direction of the guard, and bowed. But he remained in place. When the guard yelled at him a few moments later as he lit a cigarette, O'Bannon bowed again. As he flicked the cigarette over the starboard side he looked up, and a tingle of excitement ran through him. *A large ship was on the horizon and coming fast* [emphasis mine]. O'Bannon was certain it was a U.S. Navy destroyer. He suppressed a shout.

"*Like most of the rest of the crew* [emphasis mine], O'Bannon thought help was imminent and strained his ears for sounds of jet planes. Don Bailey stood near the railing, ready to go over the side if the Koreans started shooting. So was Charlie Law, who saw the same ship O'Bannon had spotted. *His more experienced eyes told him it wasn't a U.S. Navy ship* [emphasis mine], but he kept hoping. He couldn't believe they wouldn't get help. If someone would take care of those ships out there, he was certain the crew could overwhelm in seconds the half-dozen or so guards on board."

Brandt (p. 59) makes a subsequent reference to the ship on the horizon. ". . . a soldier came down to the well deck and ordered the crew to sit. He was holding a couple of bedsheets, and he began tearing them into strips and passing the strips among the crew. He made it plain he wanted them to blindfold one another. There was some whispering among the men as the blindfolds were passed out. They didn't like what was happening and they were frightened. It was getting colder, and as someone behind Law blindfolded him, Law took one last glimpse at the ship he had seen on the horizon. *It was definitely not American* [emphasis mine], and Law lost all hope of rescue."

This report of a large warship "coming fast" occurs in no other account of the *Pueblo* incident. Again, I attach significance to the fact that Brandt interviewed crewmen *first*, shortly after they came home, before they were briefed thoroughly on what not to say.

What was this ship the men saw? It was obviously a warship, for they mistook it for a U.S. destroyer. It was coming fast. From where? For what purpose? And what did it do after it got there? It also seems to me that Quartermaster Law, an experienced man able to recognize that "it definitely was not American," would have had some idea whose ship it was. After all, the previous night he had in the darkness recognized Russian radar on a passing ship.

One more key question remains and it involves *time*. By all accounts the North Korean subchaser approached at noon, 1200 hours. It is in dispute whether *Pueblo* was boarded at 1330 or 1432, but in either case it was boarded in the early afternoon. Most of the stories say it took two and a half or three hours (as Bucher did) to reach Wonsan. Most say it was dark when they arrived there.

It simply won't wash. Two and a half to three hours makes it about 1700 hours, five o'clock, when *Pueblo* reached Wonsan—a figure given by Steve Harris in his book. It wasn't dark at five o'clock! Sunset was at 1734 and absolute darkness—according to the Navy's own figures given in the radio transcript—came at 1806, six minutes after six in the evening.

The Navy says *Pueblo* was moored at the pier in Wonsan at 2030 hours—8:30 P.M.! Recall the statement Radioman Hayes made to me: "It seemed to take forever to reach Wonsan. I still had my watch and it was after eight o'clock."

Even if the boarding occurred as late as 1432, another six hours elapsed before *Pueblo* reached Wonsan—and remember, Bucher has the North Korean pilot cranking the ship up to *flank speed*, over twelve knots an hour. There is no way *Pueblo* could have taken six hours to reach Wonsan at that speed. Even if it was twenty-five miles from Wonsan, as claimed, the voyage would have taken no more than two hours, three at the outside.

What was going on that took six hours?

These then have been the various stories of the seizure as told by participants and reporters who interviewed participants. The stories vary so widely it is hard to believe at times that the men were on the same ship, let alone witnessing the same events. Every one of the stories omits details a person cries aloud to know, while including events and descriptions which are extremely hard to believe and sometimes impossible.

If, as the United States claims, *Pueblo* was on an innocent passage in international waters when the North Koreans came out and seized the ship in an act of piracy, then there ought to be one, clear, simple story of those events, a story in which the facts are in some essential order, which fits the actions of participants, which gets the compass directions straight, which fits the Navy's transcript of *Pueblo*'s radio messages, which accounts for elapsed time.

No such story exists. We have, instead, several highly confused stories. One thing is certain: Not all can be correct. It is conceivable that *one* of them is, but which one? It is simply easier to believe *none* of them is wholly correct.

There has been a cover-up. It began in captivity and stretched through the Court of Inquiry, which suppressed the radio transcript and other evidence that belied its own findings. Why? What happened during the *Pueblo* seizure that we are not supposed to know about, even twenty years later?

The men of *Pueblo* tried to tell us what happened as best they knew. Certainly they gave us the information to enable us to figure out, if not precisely what happened to them, at least enough to state unequivocally that the cover story is false.

Consider just two key pieces of information. Both are from Ed Brandt's book. Recall that he interviewed fifteen crewmen *first*, in mid-May, 1969. They gave him information they would later neglect to mention to Armbrister.

They told Brandt that just before their blindfolds went on they saw a large warship on the horizon "coming fast." They first thought it was an American destroyer, then recognized that it wasn't. Their hopes for rescue faded. In a telephone interview I asked Ed Brandt if he had any idea whose ship it was. He replied, "I assumed it was North Korean. Some of the men did speculate that it was Russian, but I didn't see how that was possible."

It couldn't have been North Korean. They had no ship that size. And if it had been North Korean, Bucher, who had to have seen the ship, would have mentioned it as another, larger warship out to menace *Pueblo*. After all, he went to great lengths to describe *Pueblo* as being outgunned. He saw six ships—two subchasers and four torpedo boats—when Murphy saw only one subchaser and three torpedo boats. If a North Korean destroyer or light cruiser had come out, Bucher would surely have mentioned it as evidence of the hopeless state he was in.

It might perhaps be suggested that the "large warship" was the second North Korean subchaser that Bucher refers to. He reports the presence of the second subchaser early in the encounter, saying it was "coming out to join in the fun." Murphy makes a big point that he never saw a second subchaser or a fourth torpedo boat, but Schumacher supports Bucher when he says he "could just make out a second subchaser on the horizon." He did not report the vessel in the Pinnacle message he drafted, however. No one has this second subchaser firing on *Pueblo* or even participating in the seizure. Could this second subchaser have been the "large warship" coming fast?

To answer in the affirmative takes a reach of imagination. A subchaser is 133 feet long, a third smaller than *Pueblo* itself. It is extremely difficult to believe that an experienced seaman such as Charles Law would mistake a subchaser for a destroyer in broad daylight, especially when a similar vessel was in clear view for comparison.

Then whose ship was it? There really aren't very many choices. It couldn't have been Japanese. Disarmed since World War II, the Japanese Navy had no vessel as large as a destroyer. Not until the 1980s would the Japanese possess such a ship. Nor could it have been South Korean. They had such ships, but South Korea obtained the vessels from the United States. The warship would have looked like an American destroyer, certainly at a distance. And, it must be assumed, if a South Korean destroyer was operating this close to Wonsan, it would have made some effort to rescue *Pueblo*—recall that *Pueblo* still flew the U.S. flag—or, failing in that, told the world they had at least tried to.

The same logic applies to ships belonging to the British, French, Dutch, Filipino, or some other of the world's navies. They would have mentioned their involvement and they did not. Nor could it have been a destroyer from one of these nations just passing by, paying no attention to the cluster of small ships. The men of *Pueblo* clearly saw a "large warship" of destroyer size "coming fast" *toward* them.

By a process of elimination, there really are only two choices as to whose ship it was. It had to belong to either the Union of Soviet Socialist Republics or the People's Republic of China.

Which? The men of *Pueblo* also told us that.

Again Ed Brandt reported the absolutely key information (p. 52), as already quoted: "Seven or eight soldiers, dressed in heavy olive green quilted jackets and square fur hats each with a big red star in the middle, began jumping aboard, carrying submachine guns with bayonets attached."

These are *not* North Korean uniforms.

The uniforms worn by North Koreans in that period were a gray khaki. The insignia in the front of their hats was a small round disk with a small star in the center.

"Heavy olive green quilted jackets and square fur hats each with a big red star in the middle" are the uniforms worn by soldiers of the People's

Army of the People's Republic of China. They are Red Chinese uniforms (see figure 1).

There is a paucity of description of the appearance of the men who boarded *Pueblo*—and one would expect that to be noted and cemented in the men's minds. Murphy and Schumacher speak of "helmeted" troops in the PT boat. They are alone in having them wear helmets. Even Steve Harris refers to fur hats. Armbrister describes "dark blue" uniforms, but I strongly believe that by the time he conducted his interviews he was being led away from the truth. And who wears dark blue uniforms? Certainly not the North Koreans.

Other than Brandt, the best description comes from Bucher. As already quoted, he said that among the first boarders were "two officers with red and gold shoulderboards attached to their dark green jackets." *Dark green.* Brandt writes *olive green.* Shades of color lie in the eye of the beholder and are hard to describe in words. An official of the Communist Chinese Embassy in Washington was asked if their uniforms were "olive green." He didn't understand "olive green," but said his country's military uniforms were "yellowish green." His confusion is surely understandable. Color television pictures from Red China show soldiers of that country in green uniforms. Having written for thirty years, I hesitate to characterize what shade of green it is. But the uniforms are *green*, not the gray khaki worn by the North Koreans.

There is evidence other than descriptions of uniforms that suggests that Red Chinese, not North Koreans, first boarded *Pueblo*. Recall that Marine sergeants Hammond and Chicca were inept translators of the Korean language. On the twenty-second, Chicca had to go for his dictionary to read the words "Rice Paddy" on the sides of the fishing boats that surveyed *Pueblo*. The final word on the ineptness of the two translators can come from Bucher, who writes on page 196 of his book:

"I interrupted our two Marine language experts, Sergeants Chicca and Hammond, who were monitoring the North Korean's tactical communication network for the purpose of keeping me informed as to their intentions against us. I had so far received no such intelligence whatsoever out of our supposedly sophisticated capability. 'Well, what about it?' I asked. 'Haven't you guys been able to make out anything they are saying out there?'

"They both shook their heads and Chicca made an aggrieved confession, 'It's nothing but a lot of fast gibberish which we can only identify as Korean. We're just not proficient enough at the language, sir . . .'

"'You can't understand a word of it?' When they helplessly shrugged,

The photograph (top) is of Communist Chinese soldiers in uniform. Below are North Korean soldiers in uniform. Note that the Chinese have a big star in the middle of their square fur hats, while the North Koreans have a round disk. (UPI/ Bettmann Newsphotos)

I exclaimed in disgust to Steve [Harris], 'Some damned linguists they sent us. If they'd been qualified, they could probably have warned us out of this mess hours ago. You might as well turn them to destructing.'"

But *Pueblo was* warned. At 1306, as Schumacher informs us, the North Koreans were heard to say they planned to go in, board *Pueblo*, shut down the radio, and tow the ship to Wonsan—a piece of information Bucher studiously avoids mentioning. At 1326 *Pueblo* radios Kamiseya, "AND THEY PLAN TO OPEN FIRE ON US NOW." This can only mean *knowledge of intentions*. Somebody was listening to the North Korean tactical channel and understood what was being said.

If Chicca and Hammond were such inept interpreters that the Korean they heard was "gibberish," then some other language was spoken over the tactical channel, a language understood aboard *Pueblo*. It cannot be argued that someone other than Chicca and Hammond understood Korean, for if there was, there would have been no point in placing them aboard at the last minute. As far as is known, the Marines had no purpose aboard the badly overcrowded ship other than to interpret Korean.

There is other evidence the boarders spoke some language other than Korean. Recall the unnamed crewman who entered the SOD-Hut accompanied by a boarder and tapped Bailey on the shoulder and told him to go to the well deck. As noted previously, this suggests the actions of a crewman acting as an interpreter. By all accounts, none of the first boarders spoke English, yet Bucher was able to obey commands to get his ship under way, to produce keys for the ammunition locker, and to order men to the well deck. Conceivably all this could have been done in sign language; still, one wonders if someone wasn't interpreting.

There can be no doubt there were Chinese-speaking crewmen on *Pueblo*. Steve Harris is said to have spoken four languages, only one of which was identified: Russian. The NSA is known to train its personnel in four languages, of which two are Russian and Chinese.

I have no doubt that most *Pueblo* crewmen *thought* they were boarded by North Koreans. After all, they came from North Korean ships. Most Americans, especially in a time of stress, cannot readily differentiate between Koreans and Chinese. Which language was spoken would be meaningless to those unfamiliar with either language. And certainly, being sailors, most of the Americans would not be able to distinguish Red Chinese army uniforms from those worn by North Korean soldiers.

The men who first boarded *Pueblo* wore Red Chinese uniforms. Among their first acts, as we have seen, was to *arm Pueblo*. The weapons were uncovered and the keys to the ammo locker obtained. The question was asked before: Why arm a ship that was already captive? After all, there was a certain risk that the Americans, outnumbering their captors ten to one, might seize those .50-caliber machine guns and turn them against their captors, especially now that they were uncovered and set to fire. It would only have taken seconds. Why take this risk on a ship being held by ten men?

There is only one logical answer. There was a large warship "coming fast" and to protect their prize the boarders needed all the firepower they could muster. Even at that, a subchaser, torpedo boats, and poor *Pueblo* were no match for a destroyer or light cruiser in broad daylight.

If the men who first boarded and seized *Pueblo* were Red Chinese—and they did wear Red Chinese uniforms—then the large warship coming fast, which the Chinese wanted to defend themselves against, can only have been Soviet.

11

WHAT REALLY HAPPENED

To understand the *Pueblo* surrender, we must put it in the context of other events of the time.

We didn't then, and understandably so. We were distracted by the war in Vietnam. The Tet Offensive, one of the largest battles ever fought by American forces, began eight days after the *Pueblo* seizure. We were shocked by the heavy casualties occurring in a war we had been led to believe was almost won. Opposition to the war escalated with street demonstrations and riots. President Johnson lost the New Hampshire primary and stepped out of the race. Our quadrennial nominating process began. Then came the riots at the Democratic National Convention in Chicago and the close, hard-fought election. The Naval Court of Inquiry began its deliberations on inaugural day for Richard Nixon, a more newsworthy event than the *Pueblo* seizure.

These distracting events are not terribly important to the *Pueblo* story. For the important ones we need to go back a bit further in time. In the wake of World War II, Joseph Stalin accomplished for the Soviet Union what the czars had only dreamed of. Estonia, Latvia, Lithuania, and part of Poland were annexed into the USSR, providing a generous outlet on the Baltic Sea. Archenemy Germany was laid waste and divided, apparently permanently. Communist governments were established in the countries of Eastern Europe, providing a buffer zone of satellite nations. These governments gave the Soviet Union virtually total control of the warm water ports in the Black Sea, as well as access to Mediterranean ports in Yugoslavia and Albania. Russia's only warm water port in the

Pacific remained Vladivostok, and it was shallow, developed ice floes in winter, and was hardly ideal for submarines. Then Nationalist China fell to Mao Tse-tung, a Communist. All of a sudden, the Soviet Union had access to a plethora of warm water ports on the China Sea. With the Soviet sub base at Wonsan, North Korea, the Russians were in the submarine business in a big way.

There was a problem. The Russian brand of state socialism called Communism isn't a very salable product. It doesn't work very well and few want it if they can help it. Political leaders in the Soviet satellites, like politicians everywhere, were motivated by staying in power. This involved some undercutting of the Russian brand of state socialism and a certain amount of encouragement of nationalist feelings. The Soviet Union has had trouble with just about every one of its satellites except Bulgaria, where the people really do like the Russians. Marshal Tito led Yugoslavia into a break with the Soviet Union, despite numerous armed threats— hindering, especially when Albania turned Maoist and hostile, Soviet access to ports on the Mediterranean Sea. East Germany was a horrendous problem, at least until the Berlin Wall was built. Rumania survived by toeing the mark politically and in foreign affairs, while altering its economic system. Hungary and Czechoslovakia were kept in line by armed invasion, as Afghanistan has been in the 1980s. Poland, with its "subversive" notions of Solidarity, has had several changes of communist leadership. There are few who doubt that if Polish Communists loyal to Moscow fail to maintain control, Soviet tanks will roll. The pattern is clear. The world needs no lesson about the Soviet Union's determination to do whatever is required to control its satellite nations.

It was also clear in 1967. The Soviet Union would not invade Czechoslovakia until the summer of 1968, but it had already put down the "freedom fighters" in Hungary—where the Soviet ambassador was Yuri Andropov.

The Soviet Union's problems with its Eastern European satellites paled before its difficulties with China. Mao not only led the most populous nation on earth, he considered himself something of an ideologue, advocating and eventually exporting a brand of communism that was not only heretical to the Soviets but downright subversive. Mao had strong nationalistic ideas and was, to make an understatement, an extremely poor puppet. He had firm control of China, perhaps even some popularity, and he was not a man to be easily controlled and subverted by Russian "advisers" and political cadres.

Any Soviet hopes of subverting and controlling China, as it had its

European satellites, was lost when Mao declared his "Cultural Revolution" in 1966. He recruited and unleashed thousands of young men and women called "Red Guards" who were to cement the Maoist Revolution by eradicating all influence of "foreign devils." In the United States (being perhaps a trifle self-centered) we assumed the movement was aimed at the West. Perhaps, but it was also aimed at the Soviet Union. China became a bad place to be a Russian.

In 1967, Moscow protested when Communist Chinese "hooligans" stormed the Soviet freighter *Svirsk* in the port of Darien, overpowering the crew and destroying equipment. Premier Kosygin, in a virtual ultimatum, demanded a halt to the violent acts against *Svirsk* and the release of the captain, crew, and ship. Chinese Premier Chou En-lai replied by threatening to break trade relations with the Soviet Union. The ship finally sailed on its way in a few days—but the whole incident has a familiar ring.*

Other incidents between the two "allies" might be cited, but the major one occurred in January and February, 1967. It was front-page news in the United States. Thousands of Red Guards demonstrated in front of the Soviet Embassy in Peking, allegedly protesting "police brutalities" against Chinese students in Moscow. Effigies of Brezhnev and Kosygin were burned outside. Insults were hurled over a loudspeaker. A bonfire was kept continuously lit at the embassy gates. It went on for eighteen days.

Tass, the Soviet news agency, reported the USSR was preparing emergency evacuation of dependents at the embassy and all Chinese employees were discharged. The Russian dependents were allowed to leave, finally, but did so under the jeers and threats of the Red Guards. The Soviet Union charged the Chinese government with fanning "hostile anti-Soviet hysteria" and causing "direct physical encroachment" on the embassy. Tass said the Chinese tried to lynch Soviet diplomats and advisers returning from Vietnam to the USSR. The demonstrations at the embassy were "without precedent in the history of diplomatic relations," Moscow protested.

The situation became ominous, with Soviet diplomats virtual prisoners inside the embassy. For their part, the Russians formed their own mobs at the Chinese Embassy in Moscow, at one point actually invading it. The USSR threatened to take "necessary . . . measures" unless the riots

*Full accounts of these events involving the USSR, China, and North Korea may be found in the New York *Times* of the period.

stopped in Peking. U.S. experts saw the demonstrations—all foreshadowing later events in Tehran—as a calculated move by Mao to force a break in diplomatic relations with the Soviet Union. It didn't happen, but relations between the two countries were in such disarray it would be a long time, if ever, before they were mended.

An extremely large question being asked in capitals around the world, most especially in Washington, was whether the Soviet Union would calmly lose China as a satellite—indeed, would it accept an inimical nation along a large common border (not to forget loss of all those ports)—or would it do as it had in Hungary: invade? Soviet troops would be up against more than "freedom fighters," but China was a "paper tiger," its economy in disarray from Mao's Cultural Revolution. The USSR could expect to lop off China's northern provinces at least and perhaps replace Mao with a more docile puppet. In 1967, the risk of war between the USSR and China was real. The situation was volatile.

North Korea, tiny, impoverished, was caught in the middle. It had a long border with China, its ally in the Korean War in the 1950s. China had kept U.S. troops from overrunning North Korea and ending the regime. Since North Korea had only a minuscule border with the Soviet Union, the choice should have been easy—except that North Korea badly needed the wealth, trade, and technical assistance of that country. Russia could do a lot more for North Korea economically than China could.

In 1966, Kim Il Sung, the North Korean leader, cemented his hold on the country by purging opposition and "reorganizing" the Communist Party—as they say. He also proclaimed North Korea's independence from both the Chinese and Soviet leadership. This independence was proving difficult to maintain, however, for the Red Guards also put Kim on their list of enemies. Posters were erected in Peking scoring Kim and his "clique" for slandering the Chinese Cultural Revolution. He was showing "ingratitude." The North Korean embassy in Algiers charged the Red Guards were conducting a "campaign of calumny" toward North Korea and demanded its halt.

The Soviet Union stepped in, wooing North Korea. On March 6, 1967, less than a month after the embassy siege was lifted in Peking, the USSR and North Korea signed a new mutual defense pact which included cooperation in economic, scientific, and technical fields. Another term for such a pact is "subversion."

With China lost, North Korea now assumed paramount importance for the Soviet Union, if for no other reason than its sub base at Wonsan. The subversion of North Korea into a puppet regime for the Soviets was fast moving. Two months after the pact a campaign was opened to glorify Kim Il Sung. A registry of the entire population was seen in the West as a prelude to a political purge. A North Korean military delegation held secret talks with Soviet defense officials in Moscow in July. By this time bright young North Korean men and women were already in the Soviet Union for "technical training"—read *indoctrination*. And there was a substantial flow in the opposite direction, with Soviet "technical advisers" subverting the North Korean military and assuming control of its communications system. North Korea was not going to be another Yugoslavia or China. It was moving in the fast lane toward becoming another Bulgaria. If that didn't work, it could always become another Hungary.

In understanding the *Pueblo* seizure, it is important to realize that North Korea was in no position to stand against its two powerful neighbors, Red China and the Soviet Union, either of which could have stamped it out of existence in a fortnight. In its precarious position, North Korea's hope for independence, even existence, rested on cooperating with both China and the Soviet Union. The North Koreans had to do what either nation wanted and hope for the best.

With this in mind, consider the one "inexplicable" question always asked about the *Pueblo* incident: Why did the North Koreans seize the American ship?

It never did make much sense. North Korea was a poor country with horrendous economic and social problems. It had been all but eradicated (an estimated 500,000 killed out of a population of less than 10 million, most of its cities, industry, and infrastructure destroyed) in one war with the United States. To the south it faced hostile South Korea, growing economically and militarily more powerful daily. Why on earth would it want to provoke another war by firing on a U.S. Navy vessel, causing casualties, then seizing the ship and imprisoning the crew—historically, all acts leading almost inevitably to war?

If the North Koreans were annoyed by *Pueblo,* as assuredly they were, they had alternatives. Under international law, they could have stopped *Pueblo,* sent officers aboard to inspect it, and ordered Bucher to remove his ship from their waters. If he refused, the North Koreans had the right under international law to arrest Bucher, tow the ship to port, try the captain, and impose fines. This had happened several times in the world. The United States had done it with Soviet "fishing trawlers."

No Soviet or U.S. ELINT vessel had ever been seized anywhere in the world and dozens, perhaps hundreds of them, had been operating for years. Indeed, Rear Adm. Frank L. Johnson, who commanded the fleet of ELINT vessels in Japan, expressed in dramatic terms to the Court of Inquiry his dismay that the North Koreans had seized *Pueblo*. It was unthinkable to him.

USS *Banner* had made previous trips into these waters and was harassed, but not seized. As cited, there is considerable evidence *Pueblo* itself had made previous trips into North Korean waters. If so, it was not seized then. Why was it on January 23, 1968?

One reason was offered by President Johnson in his memoirs, *The Vantage Point* (see appendix). He suggested that the North Koreans, by seizing *Pueblo* and conducting raids and other hostile acts along the border with South Korea, were trying to provoke the South Koreans into removing their contingent of troops from Vietnam prior to the Tet Offensive. If so, this indicates that North Korea was acting at the behest of China or the Soviet Union, both of whom backed the North Vietnamese in the war. Mr. Johnson's reasoning must be questioned, however. The Tet Offensive came eight days after the *Pueblo* seizure, which hardly allowed enough time for the South Koreans to recall their troops from Vietnam had they wanted to.

The most popular answer given at the time was that the North Koreans, in their hatred for the United States, were so stupid and irrational that they would risk war with the United States in total violation of their own self-interest. This thesis of self-destructive irrationality may be correct, but it is easier to ask other questions: Did the North Koreans actually seize *Pueblo*? And if they did, did they act alone?

We know they did not. There was a contingent of Red Chinese soldiers aboard the subchaser which came out to *Pueblo*. These soldiers transferred to a PT boat and ultimately boarded *Pueblo*.

For some reason—which we will consider shortly—the Red Chinese were interested in *Pueblo*. Since China lacked a port on the Sea of Japan—their naval vessels would have had to sail around the Korean peninsula from the China Sea—they "persuaded" the North Koreans to use their subchaser to ferry them out to *Pueblo*.

Let us now reexamine the events of the seizure.

Where was *Pueblo* at noon, 1200 hours, on January 23, 1968? As said previously, it really doesn't matter where *Pueblo* was, but the preponderance of evidence suggests that *Pueblo* was not 15.8 miles from Ung Island, as the United States claims.

In twenty years, the NSA and the Navy have offered no "proof" that *Pueblo* was in that location. The charts and logs of *Pueblo* were never recovered, but the NSA had satellite photographs and other means to pinpoint *Pueblo* within three feet of its location on the planet. Such information has never been made public. Instead of proof, the world has been given a variety of "revised" locations from those aboard *Pueblo* and in the Pentagon. Bucher himself said evidence was "doctored" to make it look as if *Pueblo* was in international waters when it wasn't. I believe that "doctoring" consisted of adding ten minutes of a degree to *Pueblo*'s true location—which was about 7.6 miles west of Ung Island, where *Pueblo* hid in the radar shadow of Yo Island.

I cannot, of course, *prove* this location any more than those aboard can *prove* any of the *various* locations they gave for the ship. I don't believe the matter of *Pueblo*'s location—once more, not an issue of paramount importance—will ever be settled until the NSA and the Navy permit an impartial examination of their records.

Wherever *Pueblo* was, the North Korean subchaser comes out and circles the American ship. Even though the North Koreans are at battle stations, this causes no particular alarm among Bucher and his men. They had been approached the day before (and the day before that) yet returned to approximately the same spot where North Korean vessels had detected them the previous afternoon. Bucher is actually pleased, for, as he writes, "according to our orders" he is to have the opportunity to "test" North Korean intentions. Although Steve Harris is nervous and wants to get out of there, CTs in the SOD-Hut are pleased. "The presence of an enemy ship" is what they "had been hoping for."

When the subchaser approaches, it sends a message at 1210, which the NSA intercepted. Doubtlessly, CTs listening to a tactical channel aboard *Pueblo* did also. It quoted the North Koreans on the subchaser as reporting the ship was GER-2 and they were "American guys."

Clearly, the subchaser was sent out with orders to determine the exact numerical identity of the ship—GER-2, not GER-1, the *Banner*'s number—and its nationality. Recall that the subchaser's first query was to ask nationality and that *Pueblo* raised the biggest ensign it had aboard.

Now, having determined *Pueblo* is the GER-2 and American—the ship they want—the subchaser hoists HEAVE TO OR I WILL FIRE. To the Americans this is confusing because *Pueblo* is already dead in the water. It is under orders to remain that way to monitor North Korean harassment procedures. The HEAVE TO signal indicates a lack of originality on the part of the North Koreans, perhaps, but it was the standard signal used in all such instances. Bucher knew the Soviets had used it with *Banner*. And the HEAVE TO signal really isn't so strange. Since

Pueblo is already dead in the water, the signal most likely means for *Pueblo* to remain that way, as Murphy figured out.

Bucher and others say he replied with his I AM IN INTERNATIONAL WATERS signal. I go along with Signalman Leach, Ed Brandt, and the two Pinnacle messages from *Pueblo* that he didn't raise the signal (at this time at least)—because he wasn't in international waters. I accept Brandt's statement that he raised a signal I AM HYDROGRAPHIC and, perhaps, Murphy's, who says he raised INTEND TO REMAIN IN AREA UNTIL TOMORROW. Considering that the North Korean subchaser wanted *Pueblo* to remain where it was, that message must have comforted it.

Minutes drag by. What is the subchaser waiting for? The answer comes with the arrival of the three North Korean torpedo boats at 1244 hours. They come on a bearing of 160 degrees. This is *southeast,* so the torpedo boats could not have come from Wonsan, as Bucher says, which is to the *west.* A bearing of 160 can only mean the PT boats were out in the Sea of Japan. What were they doing there? Could they have been on a scouting mission, returning at high speed to report there was a large warship out there "coming fast"?

About this time Bucher finally starts his engines. The North Koreans see the smoke, lower their HEAVE TO signal, and raise—as the Pinnacle messages and every source save Bucher and Murphy tell us—flags that read FOLLOW ME—HAVE PILOT ABOARD. I submit this is a peaceful signal. The North Koreans could have flown FOLLOW ME OR I WILL FIRE but they did not. The HAVE PILOT ABOARD signal suggests that the North Koreans did not want a confrontation but simply wanted *Pueblo* to go to Wonsan for some reason. Bucher ignores the signal. The North Koreans, figuring that perhaps this American captain doesn't understand international signals or appreciate the danger he's in from that warship out there, put a man on top of the subchaser's pilothouse with red flags which he waves frantically, trying to get *Pueblo* to go to Wonsan.

Having failed to get *Pueblo* to go to Wonsan, the captain of the subchaser—or more likely the Chinese officer aboard the vessel—decides to carry out his orders to bring *Pueblo* to Wonsan any way he can. At 1306, as Schumacher tells us, the subchaser radios: ". . . according to present instructions we will close down the radio, tie up the personnel, tow it and enter port at Wonsan. At present, we are on our way to boarding. We are coming in."

The first priority of the North Koreans (or Red Chinese) is to "close down" *Pueblo*'s radio. The first assumption is that they don't want *Pueblo* to alert U.S. forces to its danger, but the encounter has been going on for over an hour. It has to be assumed the North Koreans know the United States has already been alerted to what is happening to *Pueblo,* as indeed it has. A second assumption is more logical. The North Koreans want to close down *Pueblo*'s radio to prevent the approaching warship from learning *Pueblo* was already seized or indeed from hearing any messages from the American ship.

When, at about 1315, Bucher sees the boarding party scamper from the subchaser to the torpedo boat and it backs down toward his stern, he finally gets his ship under way. The argument between Murphy and Bucher over how fast *Pueblo* moved is really unimportant, although it seems to me Bucher would have tried to move as fast as possible. But there were those "Nansen bottles" cast out by Tuck and Iredale, the oceanographers. If that's all they were, the lines would have been cut. We must assume the gear was too important (and secret) to be lost in shallow waters, and, as Murphy says, valuable time was lost bringing it in. But Bucher gets his ship to its top speed of twelve knots as fast as he can.

In getting under way, Bucher takes *Pueblo* into a wide turning circle to assume a course of 080, almost due east, heading for the open sea. From the viewpoint of the North Koreans and Red Chinese, this is sheer idiocy. There is a warship—a destroyer, perhaps a light cruiser—out there.

Bucher's maneuver does evade the boarders and he heaves a sigh of relief. Even the subchaser falls behind. Perhaps he will get away. As *Pueblo* steams eastward, the subchaser awaits instructions and receives them. They are heard aboard *Pueblo*. Bailey teletypes at 1326: "AND THEY PLAN TO OPEN FIRE ON US NOW."

What is important here once more is *time*. If *Pueblo* is under way at 1315 and learns it is to be fired on at 1326—eleven minutes later—*Pueblo* has moved about two miles. This is roughly the three thousand yards Bucher says the subchaser fell behind. If the subchaser received its orders to open fire at 1326, it would have taken the forty-knot ship about three, at the most four, minutes to catch up to *Pueblo*. Thus, at 1328, *Pueblo* repeats, "NORTH KOREAN WAR VESSELS PLAN TO OPEN FIRE." The subchaser has not yet fired, but it is moving up at high speed and in a menacing manner. It has lowered its FOLLOW ME signal and again hoisted HEAVE TO OR I WILL FIRE. There can be no confusion about its meaning this time.

At 1330, two minutes later, *Pueblo* radios that it is being boarded. At 1331 it is holding emergency destruction. At 1337 it is laying to at its present position and Bailey's teletype is the only circuit open on the ship. Emergency destruction is largely complete. At 1345 *Pueblo* is being escorted into *probably* Wonsan.

In reconstructing the events of the seizure, this transcript must govern. Those (Murphy and Armbrister) who say that Bailey, as advised by Watch Captain Layton, was mistaken have a most difficult claim to prove. Certainly the Pentagon believed *Pueblo* was in enemy hands by 1345 and so stated in its initial announcements. Not until the Court of Inquiry convened a year later was the 1432 boarding put forward.

It should be recalled that at about 1315 the North Korean torpedo boat backed within a few yards of *Pueblo* with its boarding party. The facial features of the boarders were seen. Crewmen heard them cocking their rifles. Bailey did not make a "mistake" at this time and report *Pueblo* was being boarded. Yet it is argued that Bailey made a mistake fifteen minutes later. Perhaps. There is a circumstance in which Bailey and Layton could have thought they were being boarded when they weren't. We will come to that in a moment.

But, to repeat for emphasis, it is inarguable that Bailey is mistaken when he says emergency destruction is being held at 1331. Bailey is in the SOD-Hut. He can see the destruction with his own eyes. When he transmits at 1337 that *Pueblo* is laying to at its present position, there seems little chance for error there. And there is virtually no possibility of his being wrong when he says his is the only circuit open on the ship. Bailey is thirty-six years old, an expert on communications placed aboard to straighten out *Pueblo*'s transmission difficulties. Again, I will not say he is mistaken when he says his is the only circuit open. Murphy, or certainly Armbrister, is hardly in a position to even know the transmission capabilities of *Pueblo*. Bailey was.

To believe the story which Bucher and others told (more correctly, I believe, were *forced* to tell) of a 1432 boarding, a person must accept not only the "mistakes" of Bailey, but a truly bizarre series of events. It is necessary to believe that the North Koreans, having decided at 1306 to board the ship, having formed a boarding party on the PT boat which backed to within a few yards of *Pueblo* before Bucher got under way, and having fired upon *Pueblo* to stop it, now sail alongside *Pueblo* while crewmen start fires on deck and dump gear overboard in emergency destruction—for forty-five minutes to an hour. It is worse than that. If Bucher's story of a 1432 boarding is believed, not only do the North Koreans not try to board the smoking ship for all that time, but when Bucher stops it, they open fire (killing Hodges) to get it moving again.

Having gotten *Pueblo* under way, they continue to follow the burning ship for another half hour before ordering it to stop and finally, at long last, boarding at 1432. If, by stretching the imagination to encompass this series of improbable events, a person is willing to believe the North Koreans did follow the smoking *Pueblo* without boarding, there is no rationale for them to stop it and board at 1432. Their actions have been those of people trying to get *Pueblo* to sail to Wonsan—for some reason. *Pueblo* is doing just that. Why stop and board it, delaying its progress, especially if they are worried about that large warship "coming fast"?

It is far more difficult to accept the notion of "mistakes" by Bailey and a whole series of irrational acts by the North Koreans than it is to accept the accuracy of the Navy's own radio transcript and the Pentagon's early announcements.

Bucher and the others did not lie about the 1432 boarding. *Pueblo* was indeed boarded at 1432—*for the second time.* Omitting the 1330 boarding and referring only to the 1432 boarding offered great advantages to the cover story. It meant an hour less daylight, making it more plausible that no U.S. planes came to rescue *Pueblo*. And a 1432 boarding made it easier for the Navy to save face. The hour was spent, supposedly, with *Pueblo* under heavy bombardment, being overwhelmed by a superior force. A 1330 boarding meant a U.S. Navy ship was captured effortlessly by ten or so foot soldiers. Finally, and most importantly, a 1432 boarding enabled the NSA and the Navy to hide, hopefully forever, what really did happen during the *Pueblo* seizure. If a 1330 boarding is believed, then the entire cover story collapses and what really happened to *Pueblo* becomes obvious.

How did the 1330 boarding occur? While prevented from describing a 1330 boarding, the men of *Pueblo* tried to tell us what happened. I believe Bucher maneuvered his ship as he said he did in his book—except for the 135 heading added by the censor—and the events of the boarding said to have happened at 1432 really occurred about an hour earlier.

Bucher, a "taxi driver," is endeavoring to follow "to the letter" orders that specify where his ship is to be stationed. Thus, on the morning of the twenty-third, he is dismayed that his ship has drifted so far off station and blurts, "Let's get back in there." His orders also require him to "test" North Korean intentions. So, when the subchaser appears, he remains stationary, engines down. He doesn't leave the area, as *Banner* had done, nor does he obey the frantic signals from the subchaser to go to Wonsan. When the torpedo boats appear, the situation worsens, but Bucher still doesn't leave. When the MIGs buzz his ship, Bucher realizes his ship is in real danger and the situation is getting out of hand. Indeed, as Armbrister reports, Navy officers in Japan began taking the situation seriously when the MIGs appeared. This had never happened to *Banner.*

As Brandt tells us, Bucher leaves the bridge and goes to the SOD-Hut, informing Kamiseya of the worsening situation and that he may have to disengage and leave the area. Again, he cannot leave his station without permission. About this time, the 1306 transmission is heard. The North Koreans—or Chinese—plan to board *Pueblo.*

Bucher returns to the bridge. He looks over the situation, but, even though he is aware of North Korean intentions, he still doesn't leave for another nine minutes. Why? The answer is simple. Boarding a ship is not that unusual. The procedures are established under international law. A couple of officers come aboard, ask to see the ship's papers, and tell the captain he is suspected of being in territorial waters. Normally, the boarding officers tell the captain to leave, but they also have a legal right to arrest the captain and tow his ship into port.

This is the worst Bucher expects to happen. But when he sees the boarding party of eight or ten armed soldiers forming on the PT boat, which backs down toward *Pueblo,* he realizes he faces seizure, not a legalistic boarding and warning. He gets his ship under way. Headed north, he makes a wide turning circle and heads for the open sea on a course of 080. The subchaser lags behind awaiting instructions. But it seems to me that the commander of the PT boat, under orders to board *Pueblo,* would have persisted. Coming alongside and matching *Pueblo*'s speed—especially if *Pueblo* was delayed to bring in "Nansen bottles"—would not have been difficult. Recall that Murphy said that as the bottles were brought in, the PT boat again tried to back down to *Pueblo*'s stern.

It is not difficult for Bucher to thwart the attempted boarding. He orders ten-degree right rudders and performs other maneuvers to keep the torpedo boat away. Then, when the oceanographic equipment is aboard, he goes to full speed. He heaves a sigh of relief. Maybe he will escape. As Brandt tells us, he orders Signalman Leach to semaphore AM IN INTERNATIONAL WATERS—DEPARTING THE AREA. Even if he actually wasn't, he was moving in that direction. He tells Law to look for a reply.

Meanwhile, the subchaser has received its orders. These are heard aboard *Pueblo*, which transmits: "AND THEY PLAN TO OPEN FIRE ON US NOW." Bucher sees the subchaser racing up on his port side. It again signals HEAVE TO OR I WILL FIRE. Law has his reply. The PT boats move away from the ship. *Pueblo* is in imminent danger.

Listening to the tactical channel inside the SOD-Hut, the CTs are perhaps better informed than Bucher. They know of the intentions to seize *Pueblo* and take it to Wonsan and they know of the plan to open fire. Senior enlisted men, veteran NSA personnel, do what they must. The set and operating code machine, codes, and other top secret gear cannot possibly be allowed to fall into Communist hands. They order emergency destruction. Tabs are pulled. Equipment melts. "Confetti" is brought out and fires started to make smoke. Perhaps in their inexperience some CTs bring out hammers and axes to flail away at metal-encased gear, not realizing the guts of it are already gone. Or perhaps they seek to destroy R-90 transceivers, teletypes, and other unclassified equipment not outfitted with destruct mechanisms.

From his flying bridge, Bucher looks down and sees the door to the SOD-Hut open, men rushing out, starting fires. He hears explosions from inside. There is smoke everywhere. What on earth is going on?

The subchaser opens fire, aiming high at the antennae, for the first priority is to shut down *Pueblo*'s radio. A shell hits the stack. Bucher is wounded by splinters and flying glass. In pain, enraged, a fighter and battler by nature, Bucher does the only thing he can. He emulates Commander Clark of *Banner* and orders "Left full rudder!"—aiming *Pueblo* directly at the subchaser. It easily evades. Perhaps it fires again.

Another set of events is possible. Seeing that the subchaser plans to open fire, Bucher could have ordered his "Left full rudder!," heading for the subchaser and presenting a smaller target. The North Korean ship evades and then opens fire. From the stories told by participants, I cannot decide which is correct—and it really doesn't matter.

Pueblo has been fired upon. There has been minor damage and casualties. In the pilothouse, Chief Warrant Officer Lacy, a veteran sailor, the most experienced officer aboard *Pueblo,* asks Bucher if he is going to stop the ship. Bucher hesitates. Common sense overrides the fighter in him and he nods assent.

Why stop *Pueblo?* There are several good reasons. Bucher really is outgunned. The subchaser and torpedo boats can do an awful lot of damage and cause many casualties. And he can't outrun or outmaneuver them. From a purely tactical standpoint, he is in a hopeless position. Then, particularly if he is in territorial waters, he has no right either to fight back or to disobey a legal order to stop. Furthermore, he is under instructions from his admiral not to break out his weapons or start a war. It seems to me there was another good reason to stop. Surely *Pueblo*'s radar had picked up the fact that there was a large warship coming fast.

Bucher doesn't know what ship it is, but clearly the situation is getting out of hand rapidly.

Still believing—or at least hoping—that this is a routine boarding that will result in a warning, Bucher orders Klepac and the others aft to receive boarders. He'll treat them courteously, do this by the book. Meanwhile, he rushes below to get his commander's cap and has some sort of conversation with Murphy.

But Bucher has misjudged the Red Chinese. While he is below, they jump aboard the *still moving Pueblo,* brandishing their AK-47 rifles, herding the topside men to the fantail, and seizing the pilothouse. Lacy, seeing the ship is being seized, not just formally boarded, grabs the loudspeaker and warns his men to give only name, rank, and serial number. Bucher races topside and is captured. A despondent Murphy follows a few seconds later, but the Red Chinese are already below deck and thrust a bayonet at him.

This series of events may not be precisely correct. From the radio transcript and the various accounts of the seizure it is difficult to decide. Something different may have occurred—but not too different. *Pueblo* got under way at 1315, or shortly thereafter, and *Pueblo* learned of the plan to fire on the ship at 1326. It repeated THEY PLAN TO OPEN FIRE ON US NOW at 1328. The first shelling of *Pueblo* probably occurred at about 1330. I suspect Murphy and Armbrister are correct when they say Bailey was mistaken when he sent the WE ARE BEING BOARDED message at 1330. Bucher managed to evade that with his "Left full rudder!" command. But his tactic brought only a brief respite. By 1337, as the transcript informs us, *Pueblo* had stopped, emergency destruction was complete, and Bailey's was the only circuit open. Bucher has gained perhaps seven minutes before the ship was boarded.

Again, the 1432 boarding was not put forward until the Court of Inquiry. To sustain it, the five admirals were forced to ignore and suppress the Navy's own radio transcript. They (like Bucher) ignored, at least in public testimony, any reference to the 1330 boarding. Instead, they accepted Bucher's testimony that there were no destruct mechanisms aboard *Pueblo* and that the crew used hammers to destroy top secret equipment.* They also accepted the notion there were six hundred pounds of classified documents aboard *Pueblo,* all of which had to be burned. The lack of destruct mechanisms—belied by the radio transcript, which

*Descriptions of this process reach their apex in this statement Steve Harris made to Armbrister (p. 75): "I saw those guys smashing up this great equipment, and I said, 'Why, why?' Axes going into the guts of that precision equipment—it was hideous."

reveals destruction were completed by 1337—and the burning of documents were concocted to "explain" what went on for an hour so as to justify the 1432 boarding.

This story, farfetched at best, is truly denied by the testimony of Kell and the other senior CTs. They swore they were ordered to stop burning after ten to fifteen minutes but couldn't remember who gave the order. Displaying considerable wit, Kell told Armbrister that the order came from someone with "competent authority." Yes. The someone was a Red Chinese soldier—technically, Kell didn't know who he was—and his "competent authority" was the AK-47 attack rifle in his hands.

Pueblo was first boarded at 1330 or, certainly, by 1337. Emergency destruction, begun at 1331, was completed by 1337. The burning phase begun at 1331 was ordered stopped by someone with "competent authority" within ten or fifteen minutes. The fires were stamped out. In other words, emergency destruction was all over, the crew rounded up, and *Pueblo* on its way to Wonsan by 1345—as the Pentagon first told the world.

The Chinese "grunts" who boarded *Pueblo* didn't know a SOD-Hut and an ELINT operation from a rice paddy. Their prime objectives were to get the ship under way to Wonsan, to turn off the ship's radio, and to take the crew captive. None of them spoke English, but with motions of their rifles it was rather easy for them to round up the men visible topside and move them to the fantail. Among those visible were Kell and the other CTs who were burning "documents." They were ordered to stop and sent to the stern.

Amidst the smoke and confusion, the Chinese missed Bailey, who was deep inside the SOD-Hut hunched over his teletype, and Senior Communications Chief Ralph Bouden. I believe the story Bailey told Brandt. Hard of hearing, he looks up and realizes he is alone. He gets up, goes to the door, and sees a "North Korean" soldier, who doesn't see him. Contrary to what he told Brandt, I believe Bailey shut and locked the door, thus remaining inside with Bouden and continuing to transmit to Kamiseya.

Evidence for this exists in the story by Hedrick Smith of the New York *Times*, which was already mentioned. Smith endeavored to re-create the events of the seizure shortly after it occurred, when almost nothing was known. He talked to unidentified informants at the Pentagon who sought to explain how *Pueblo* could be boarded at 1330 and remain on the air till 1432. They told Smith they believed the CTs had locked themselves inside the SOD-Hut for forty-five minutes, carrying out emergency destruction after *Pueblo* was boarded.

If Bailey and Bouden did lock themselves inside the SOD-Hut, when and how did they emerge? They couldn't remain there forever and may simply have opened the door. Recall that Bouden testified that he was the last person to leave the SOD-Hut, surrendering his keys. It is also possible that some member of the crew who knew the combination to the lock was forced to open the door. Either possibility could explain Bucher's statement that the door "was opened" to him.

Even a casual reading of the radio transcript (see appendix) shows that its nature was changed after 1345. I believe the transcript to be reasonably accurate up till 1345. Thereafter it was heavily edited and perhaps even fictionalized by someone who didn't know a lot about radio transmissions. From 1345 to 1409 all transmissions are lumped together, with precise times, given earlier, omitted. At least half the transcript records what Kamiseya sent, not *Pueblo*. The whole transcript after 1345 is much too brief for a forty-five-minute period during which *Pueblo* is supposedly fired upon, sustains casualties, and engages in prolonged emergency destruction. If the cover story is correct, Bailey would have reported a great deal more information than is on the transcript. Messages that Bailey and McClarren told Brandt they sent do not show up in the transcript.

Other evidence might be cited, including Bailey's whereabouts as reported to Brandt. He told Brandt that he remained in the SOD-Hut, transmitting to Kamiseya, until tapped on the shoulder by an unidentified crewman and told to go to the well deck. Later Brandt writes that Bailey was standing at the railing of the well deck thinking of jumping overboard when the large warship coming fast was sighted by the crewmen. This would indicate Bailey remained inside the SOD-Hut in contact with Kamiseya no more than twenty to thirty minutes after the boarding—which would make the last half hour of the transcript pure fabrication.

My belief is that the transcript after 1345 is at best only partially accurate. A key question, of course, is whether Bucher went to the SOD-Hut and dictated the message which he says he did and which shows up in the transcript. To state the matter frankly, Bucher was required to say so much that was clearly untrue in defense of the cover story that I have great doubt the message was ever sent. From the first of ultimately scores of readings, the message has an unreal quality. It is not the sort of thing a ship captain would report. It reads like a condensation of the cover story. I believe someone in the NSA or the Navy composed it to enhance the cover story. Bucher was required to add it to his book (or someone else added it), where it became the only reference to the radio transcript.

The actions of the Chinese after they boarded *Pueblo,* as described by

Bucher and other writers, are mostly correct—only they occurred roughly an hour earlier. The boarders spread over the deck and seize the pilothouse. Murphy, Schumacher, both Harrises, and Lacy, along with topside crewmen and CTs, are herded to the fantail and well deck, leaving Bucher and Helmsman Berens (along with two guarded men in the engineroom) to get the ship under way to follow the subchaser. Bucher and Berens are under enemy weapons.

An attempt is made to get Bucher to turn off Hayes's transmitter. He refuses and a Chinese jerks out the wires himself. Keeping *Pueblo* from contacting the approaching warship is paramount and, perhaps, the boarders didn't want the United States to know that Chinese, not North Koreans, had seized *Pueblo*. Knowing nothing about ELINT ships, the Chinese infantry officer is unaware that inside the SOD-Hut Bailey is still on the teletype to Kamiseya. Did Bailey know the boarders were Chinese and did he so inform Japan? It is a question I cannot answer. I can only guess that he did not.

Bucher is led to the .50-caliber machine guns and told to uncover them. He refuses, receiving a blow. In so doing—a fact the Court of Inquiry never noted—Bucher was obeying Navy Standing Orders not to cooperate with an enemy. The North Koreans put two of their own men to stripping off the frozen covers. The key to the ammo locker is obtained from Gunner's Mate Wadley. As observed earlier, this action of arming *Pueblo* can only mean that the Chinese intend to defend their prize from the Soviet warship "coming fast."

Then the Chinese officer writes on a piece of paper MANY MANS—or draws a picture of faces with big noses. How many men are on board? Doubtlessly he is surprised, as Bucher relates, to learn that eighty-three Americans are crammed into the tiny ship. Under threats, Bucher uses the loudspeaker to order all hands to the well deck. This is followed by the pantomime of counting. The crew is blindfolded. The exceptions are Bucher and Berens in the pilothouse and Goldman and Blansett in the engineroom. All have AK-47s aimed at them.

The question was asked before: Why blindfold the crew and take them below deck? It is possible the blindfolds were an aid in subduing the Americans, who greatly outnumbered the boarders. But if that was the purpose, they ought to have been tied up. Despite Bucher's statement that they were, every other account says they were not tied until they left the ship at Wonsan. Therefore it must be assumed the men of *Pueblo* were blindfolded to keep them from seeing something. What?

As noted, the men of *Pueblo* had already seen it—the large warship coming fast from the horizon. They saw it was not an American destroyer coming to rescue them. It was a Soviet warship—which, as Brandt said in his interview with me, some of the men suspected.

What did this Soviet ship do when it arrived?

For an answer, consider again the reported events of the boarding. Six to ten soldiers, led by officers, jump onto *Pueblo*. They quickly herd the crew to the fantail and well deck, then blindfold them. They get *Pueblo* under way—in a great hurry—shut down its transmitter, and break out its weapons.

How long did this take? It can't have been long, especially if the boarders were in a hurry. A reasonable estimate is "twenty-thirty minutes," a phrase used by Bucher in another context. This same time span was used by Quartermaster Law in testimony before the Court of Inquiry when he said twenty to twenty-five minutes elapsed between the first and second salvos.

Another way to judge the elapsed time is by Law's statement to Brandt that he drank some coffee, changed into his thermal underwear, drank some more coffee, then was ordered to the well deck. Near the end of this period, Law sees the warship approaching fast and recognizes it is not American. Then he and the others are led below where they can't see.

With *Pueblo* boarded at 1330 or a few minutes thereafter, it is reasonable to figure that by 1400 or a few minutes thereafter the men of *Pueblo* are either below deck in the forward berthing compartment or in the process of being led there.

Recall the cover story. To support the 1432 boarding, Bucher maintains that after the first shelling, he followed the subchaser to gain time so emergency destruction (that mountain of paper) could be carried out. After inspecting the SOD-Hut, he returned to the pilothouse, saw that his friend Gene Lacy had moved the annunciator to two-thirds speed (an acceleration Bucher alone refers to), chewed him out, and then, to make up the time, brought the ship to ALL STOP. Recall, also, that everyone who writes about this gives a different reason for stopping the ship—to make an inspection, to feign mechanical failure or a casualty, or "just to see what would happen," as Murphy suggests.

The more likely explanation for this confusion is that none of these people really know because they were blindfolded and below deck. The only persons who know are Berens and Bucher.

The cover story has it that when Bucher brought *Pueblo* to ALL STOP, the North Koreans fired upon it, killing Hodges and seriously wounding Woelk, Chicca, and Crandall. Bucher then got under way again at one-third speed and after a half hour obeyed an order to stop and the boarding occurred—at 1432.

It was, is, and always will be unbelievable. Aside from the total illogic of it, as already pointed out, there are other serious problems. Why would the North Koreans, having aimed high at the masts and antennae of *Pueblo*—and gotten it to stop—now lower their sights and fire into the bowels of the ship? At no time have the North Koreans given any indication they want to destroy or sink—or even damage—*Pueblo*. Their actions have been those of people trying to get *Pueblo* to go to Wonsan. They didn't fire on the ship for an hour and a half, then aimed high. They put a man on their pilothouse waving flags. They lofted a signal, FOLLOW ME—HAVE PILOT ABOARD. That the North Koreans would fire into the superstructure of *Pueblo* just to get it moving again is extremely hard to believe—especially if it were already boarded.

Even if it is argued that the "irrational" North Koreans would fire on *Pueblo* the second time just to get it moving, there is another reason to disbelieve it ever happened. How was Duane Hodges killed? I could quote here the various versions with their discrepancies and conflicting information, but we truly have had enough of that. It isn't pleasant reading, and I see no sense in imposing unnecessary grief on the Hodges family.

There is general agreement that the casualties occurred in the wardroom (some say mess hall) or the passage leading to it. What is significant is the cause of the casualties. Bucher speaks of "several Korean cannon shells exploding there." Armbrister is more specific (p. 71): "One shell struck forward by the laundry. A second hit the mainmast and showered debris on the deck. A third exploded inside the starboard passageway, splattering blood and pieces of flesh on the bulkheads and deck."

Armbrister's reference to one shell causing the casualties is supported by Ed Brandt (p. 49): "*One shell* went through the hull near Bucher's stateroom on the starboard side. It struck Duane Hodges in the right thigh and hip and blew his leg nearly off. The young man fell back, stunned and moaning, unaware that Chicca was on the deck next to him with a hole about the size of a silver dollar in his thigh and that his good friend Steve Woelk had been badly hurt by *the same shell* [my emphasis]."

The casualties themselves strongly suggest that the *Pueblo* crewmen were in the process of being rounded up and led below decks when the fatal shell struck. All were from widely separate areas of the ship. Hodges and Woelk were from the engineroom below decks. Crandall was a radio operator from the bridge. Chicca, the Marine interpreter, worked in the

SOD-Hut. It is impossible for one shell to have wounded them all unless they had gathered together.

My point is simple. The 57-millimeter shells from the subchaser which fell on the bridge—making a hole in the deck near Bucher's head, hitting the metal signal desk, striking the ship's stack above the bridge, holing glass and plastic, etc.—did not explode, send large pieces of shell fragment flying, or cause any but extremely minor casualties in a surrounding area. Hodges had his leg blown off and Chicca and Woelk were seriously wounded by a single large shell from a bigger gun. As Murphy says, it made "a gaping hole" in the ship.

Recall that Law told the Court of Inquiry that twenty to twenty-five minutes elapsed between the first salvo and the second. Recall also that all accounts have the second shelling occurring at 1400 hours or shortly thereafter. Both statements are correct. *Pueblo* was boarded at 1330 and twenty to thirty minutes later was fired on again.

About 1400 hours on January 23, 1968, the USS Pueblo was fired on by a Soviet warship, a destroyer or light cruiser; one American sailor was killed and three others seriously wounded.

There are details about the shelling a person cries aloud to know. How close did the Soviet ship come? My guess is not too close. It didn't want to be positively identified as Soviet and with its big guns it didn't need to be close. Did it raise a warning—HEAVE TO OR I WILL FIRE? Did Bucher try to stop his ship, only to be thwarted by the Chinese aboard it? Did the Chinese call the Soviet bluff, keeping *Pueblo* on course for Wonsan? Did the North Koreans move their vessels away, leaving *Pueblo* a helpless target? My guess is that they did. The North Koreans wanted no quarrel with the Soviets any more than they did with the Red Chinese. Did the Soviet gunners fire a warning or aiming salvo, or did they just fire one salvo with deadly accuracy? Recall Armbrister's report that three shells— suggesting a three-gun mount—hit *Pueblo*. Were there Chinese casualties as well as American? What risks did Bucher take to stop his ship and save his men from certain death? (Recall Bucher's statement that while on the bridge with Berens and a soldier after the seizure, he realized that the soldier was "an infantry-type" who "could not really judge what could or could not be done by a ship at sea. Perhaps he had to still rely on me to a certain extent." The question was asked: What did Bucher do with his newly realized freedom of action? He reports only that he used the loudspeaker to order all hands to the well deck, something which others report had long since occurred. It is to me not unreasonable to speculate that Bucher, despite the weapon aimed at him, found some way to stop the ship or take other actions to save his ship and crew during the Soviet bombardment.) Above all recall Bucher's words uttered shortly after his release from captivity that it was "nothing but a slaughter out there." Yes.

Only two Americans aboard *Pueblo* saw what happened and know the answers to these questions. Helmsman Berens has refused most interviews and has been extremely circumspect in what he says. Trevor Armbrister lists Berens among the three hundred persons he interviewed for his book, but he does not quote Berens directly and indeed refers to him very little, especially to his activities while alone on the bridge with the boarders. As mentioned earlier, Berens refused to be interviewed by Wallace Turner of the New York *Times* about events in the pilothouse during the seizure. Commander Bucher has been required to tell a cover story.

Pueblo did stop after the Soviet shelling and was boarded for the second time at 1432. Who formed the second boarding party? The first assumption is that the Soviets, having fired on *Pueblo* to stop it, would now board it. But I think not. Firing on an American Navy vessel, causing casualties, is such a provocation for war—at the least the Soviet Union had to expect the United States to retaliate against its own numerous ELINT vessels—that the USSR would attempt to conceal what it had done. Most likely the Soviet warship did not fly the hammer and sickle or get close enough to be positively identified. And the Soviets would be extremely hesitant to show their non-Oriental faces on board an American ship they had just shelled.

Nor did they have to. They used the North Koreans, just as the Chinese had done. A party of North Koreans, summoned from Wonsan, came out in a PT boat. As Bucher tells us, he was of high rank, a veteran campaigner, and heavily scarred. The men of *Pueblo* became familiar with him (and the interpreter they called Max) in captivity and called him Colonel Scar. The second boarding, then, was made by North Koreans acting on orders from Moscow. Recall that Bucher says he saw six ships. Murphy insists there were only four and accuses Bucher of exaggerating the force arrayed against *Pueblo*. It is quite possible both men are correct. Murphy saw one subchaser and three torpedo boats. Then *Pueblo* was boarded and Murphy was blindfolded and taken below decks, as he himself describes. But Bucher is still on the bridge with Berens. He now sees a fifth ship, the Soviet destroyer, and a sixth ship, the fourth torpedo boat which ferried Colonel Scar and his party out to *Pueblo*.

The greatest significance may be attached to the fact that no reference to the second boarding, by Colonel Scar—or any of the events said to have then occurred—is to be found in Brandt's book. All of the fifteen crewmen he interviewed were blindfolded and below decks and didn't see the second boarding.

Bucher writes that Berens was taken below and that he was forced to conduct Colonel Scar and interpreter Max on a tour of *Pueblo*. At the SOD-Hut, as he told the Court of Inquiry, the door "was opened." Inside, the teletype to Kamiseya was *still running*. Bailey had not destroyed it. Max disconnected it.

Then Bucher is led below decks to sit with his dead and wounded. He does not say that he was blindfolded. If he is not, perhaps he has an opportunity to peek out a porthole later and see "early winter twilight" turning the mountains "reddish-purple" so that Hado Peninsula reminds him of Sugar Loaf. In any event, he is now below decks, out of it, a prisoner like his men.

Thus, there is no one aboard *Pueblo* to tell us what happened during the next six hours until *Pueblo* reached Wonsan at 2030 hours, 8:30 P.M. that night.

There are three major questions to be asked about the *Pueblo* seizure. They are:

1. Why would the Red Chinese seize the ship and take it to Wonsan and why would the Soviet Union fire on *Pueblo* to stop them?

2. What happened during the six hours before *Pueblo* reached Wonsan?

3. Why did the NSA and Navy concoct the elaborate cover story to conceal the actions of Red China and the Soviet Union?

We consider these in the next chapter.

12

NEED TO KNOW: THE INFORMANTS' STORY

Of all the visual images associated with the *Pueblo* surrender, one is foremost: the famous photograph in which *Pueblo* crewmen defiantly give "the finger" not at their North Korean captors but at their fellow Americans who put them there, as Bucher informed the world in his first press conference after his release.

Bucher's exact words, as quoted by Armbrister, were, "They were trying to tell you that we'd been had. We realized that if we were discovered, it was going to be 'Katie, bar the door,' but we felt it was important that we get that information out. So there would be absolutely no room for doubt in your minds, the American people's minds, that we'd been had."

It was an act of immense courage. Knowing what would happen to them if discovered, they went ahead and sent "the finger" to America anyway. And they *were* discovered. The North Koreans learned from *Time* what the gesture meant, assuming, as everyone else did until Bucher told us differently, that the obscenity was aimed at them. The result was "Hell Week," as the men of *Pueblo* called it. They were savagely beaten. Their captivity, hardly bearable at best, turned far worse. They had to want to send the message very badly to knowingly bring on Hell Week.

The key words in Bucher's statement are *we'd been had*. In American slang "to be had" means to be tricked, taken advantage of, or victimized by a confidence game, which is to say "conned," lied to, deceived, bilked in a "sting." To know you've been "had" after the fact is to say that you now realize you have been fooled, deceived, and taken advantage of. You know you are a victim of another person's deception.

This is the famous photograph in which eight *Pueblo* crewmen sent the finger home to America to show they had been "had." Seated left to right: Fireman Howard Bland, CT Donald Peppard, CT James Layton, and Chief Engineer Monroe Goldman. Standing, left to right: Boatswain's Mate Ronald Berens, civilian oceanographer Harry Iredale, Engineman William Scarborough, and Quartermaster Charles Law. This photo is the most widely known, but the finger was displayed in other photographs. Bucher writes that he originated the gesture, and Murphy says he also used it in photo sessions. (Wide World Photos)

One expects some reporter to have asked, "What do you mean by had? How were you had? Who did what to you and what makes you think so?" If these questions were asked, I have been unable to find the answers. In their absence, a person coming along twenty years later must assume that the men of *Pueblo* felt somehow betrayed. They felt deceived and victimized, enduring an arduous captivity for reasons not of their own making.

By the time the photograph was taken, the men of *Pueblo* had been in captivity several months. They had had the opportunity to talk among themselves. They received some letters from home, as well as press clippings chosen by the North Koreans. They were forced to answer questions at carefully staged "press conferences." One of these was even attended by an American "journalist." My point is that the men of *Pueblo* had at least some idea of what the world believed about the *Pueblo* seizure. As a protest they sent "the finger" so "there would be absolutely no room for doubt in your minds, the American people's minds, that we'd been had."

What did they know which provoked them to use the obscene gesture? At the very least they were protesting the fact that the world's most powerful Navy and Air Force had made no effort to aid them, although more than eight hours elapsed when they could have. Were they also saying to Americans that what we believed about the *Pueblo* seizure was simply not true? Were they saying their ship was first boarded by Chinese and not North Koreans, that Russians were involved? Surely they knew. Among the men in the photograph were Peppard and Law, both of whom told Brandt they saw the large warship coming fast and suspected it was Soviet. Also in the photograph was Helmsman Berens, who other than Bucher was the only man topside, unblindfolded, and able to see what that large warship did. Quartermaster Charles Law acted as OOD, navigated the ship, and was on the bridge during the seizure. Civilian Harry Iredale was on deck and saw what happened. Chief Engineer Goldman was unblindfolded and forced to man the engines by the Chinese. CT James Layton was watch captain in the SOD-Hut and knew first-hand what happened there. Make no mistake, this is a group of truly important and knowledgeable enlisted men.

Of those in the photo William D. Scarborough died shortly after his return from captivity under circumstances that are certainly strange, even mysterious.

In his book Murphy refers to Scarborough's death as a "suicide." The police department in Anderson, South Carolina, his hometown, label the death of Scarborough, known to his family and friends as Douglas, as an accidental death. His body was found about 7:30 A.M. on February 26, 1970, in the front seat of his sister's car, which he had been repairing, inside an Amoco station in Anderson, a station Scarborough had acquired three days previously. The official cause of death was carbon monoxide poisoning.

Chief Jim Burris of the Anderson Police Department, who investigated the death as a lieutenant, told me that although the circumstances suggested suicide, the death was labeled accidental because Scarborough left no suicide note and had not been despondent. Lacking a motive for suicide, Burris concluded that the victim had been working under the dash of the car. It was a chilly evening and he must have run the motor to keep warm, thus accidentally taking his own life.

Scarborough's brother John and his sister, Mrs. Ann Sutherland, vehemently insist their brother, whom they were close to, was neither a suicide nor an accidental death but a murder victim. They point to the following evidence: Douglas was not working on the car but seated in the front seat; there were no apparent marks on the body; he had not been robbed of money, but a packet of papers he carried with him at all times, even to the bathroom, was missing and never found; his .32 caliber pistol was on the seat beside him; federal investigators, who Burris said were not FBI, entered the case and the vital organs were shipped to Washington for autopsy, the report of which has not been released except to state carbon monoxide poisoning as the cause of death; the county coroner has no copy of the autopsy report; puncture marks were found at the base of the victim's skull; he had been ill with diarrhea and vomiting "greenish foam"; he had no soles on the bottom of his feet and walked with difficulty; a skilled mechanic, he would never have run the car engine within an enclosed garage; he had taken his sister's car to do a brake job and there was nothing wrong under the dash; the car engine was not running when the body was found, but the car started at once and was backed out of the service bay, indicating the points on the car had not been fouled by carbon monoxide; nor had it run out of gas, for Mrs. Sutherland drove the car home.

The brother and sister cite other evidence of foul play, but they can think of no motive. They believe his death is in some way related to his service aboard *Pueblo* but they cannot think how. Douglas spoke very little of his *Pueblo* experiences and had offered no information damaging the *Pueblo* cover story.

What else had the men of *Pueblo* figured out during their lonely hours of captivity? The thirty CTs who worked the SOD-Hut were by training and experience—there were numerous men of high enlisted rank, chief and first class petty officers—familiar with normal ELINT operations. They had to know *Pueblo* had not performed as *Banner* had. After all, *Pueblo* was berthed next to *Banner* at Yokosuka, and the captured crewmen knew *Banner* had disengaged under harassment and sailed away to safety, while they had orders to remain dead in the water. Certainly Bailey and McClarren had to know what messages they actually sent to Kamiseya and what orders were received from there. Other CTs were operating esoteric equipment capable of monitoring all existing signals in the area. They just had to know what was happening and what the intentions of the North Koreans and Chinese were. From what they knew, the men of *Pueblo* reached a conclusion: "We'd been had."

A most difficult question must be asked. Were the men of *Pueblo* trying to tell us that their ship was deliberately surrendered?

We have seen a lot of evidence which sure makes it look as if it was. *Pueblo* was sent off on a "minimal risk mission" when it clearly wasn't, and warnings to that effect were "lost" and never reached *Pueblo*. A greener crew is hard to imagine. Hardly anyone had ever been to sea before. More than 10 percent, at least nine of eighty-three men, were brought on at the last moment for this specific voyage. Vital security clearances were not obtained—why send uncleared men aboard to navigate?—and makeshift navigators had to be pressed into service. It does look as though it was arranged so most of the ship's navigators were so ignorant of navigation they couldn't be sure where the ship really was.

Then there is the extremely strange matter of the weapons aboard *Pueblo*. The individual crewmen were disarmed. While on duty, CTs normally carry a .45 pistol as a sidearm. This is to prevent unauthorized entry into the SOD-Hut and access to the code machine and codes. These weapons were taken away. In normal operations, the SOD-Hut contains a cache of arms, such as automatic weapons, grenades, and grenade launchers, so that the CTs can put on a defense of the SOD-Hut in case of attack. These weapons were taken away. Key members of the regular crew also carried sidearms, but these were also taken away, as Radioman Hayes informs us. There were the captain's weapons—automatic rifles, pistols, and grenades—but they were kept locked up and never broken out until the Chinese did so. Thus, the *men* of *Pueblo* were disarmed, unable to defend themselves.

Paradoxically, *while the men of Pueblo were disarmed, the ship was armed*. Just prior to this last voyage, a pair of .50-caliber machine guns

214 ■ THE PUEBLO SURRENDER

was brought aboard *Pueblo* and *mounted*. The same weapons were brought aboard *Banner*, but Commander Clark was told to keep them in the hold and not mount them. Historically, ELINT ships were not armed, and Clark told the Court of Inquiry he opposed arming his ship because it would make *Banner* more provocative and subject to harassment. Admiral Johnson also opposed the arming of *Pueblo*.

Why disarm a crew while arming a ship for the first time? The answer is apparent. Under international law, an unarmed ship, even a naval vessel, which intrudes into territorial waters cannot be considered a threat and fired upon. A nation intruded upon can stop the ship and order it to leave, even arresting the captain and towing the ship to port if it refuses to leave. But an *armed* ship is in another category. Because it is armed, it poses a threat of invasion and may be attacked, which is what supposedly happened to U.S. destroyers *Maddox* and *Turner Joy* in the Gulf of Tonkin in 1964.

The facts are beyond dispute: *Pueblo* was sent on a mission off unfriendly shores, having been armed for that specific mission while the crew were disarmed and unable to defend themselves.

There is much more. *Pueblo* was clearly spotted the day before the seizure. Yet when it tried to alert Kamiseya to that fact, it was unable to make contact for seventeen hours—this on a ship pregnant with eight antennae and possessing the most esoteric communications gear in the world, including the capacity to "key a bird" and send messages by satellite. The next morning, an hour before the seizure began, the same equipment which had "failed" for seventeen hours worked just fine. "Change frequencies, change frequencies." As we have seen, those words were almost a litany among the NSA operators in Kamiseya when *Pueblo* tried to contact them.

Early on the morning of the seizure, as Schumacher informs us, Bucher is dismayed that his ship has gotten "so far out" and orders, "Let's get back in there." He returns *Pueblo* to approximately where it had been spotted the day before, as Navigator Murphy tells us. This must be read in the context of Bucher's position as a "taxi driver," taking his ship to where the CTs in the SOD-Hut, who themselves take orders from the NSA, tell him to go and remaining there until told to leave. Clearly, *Pueblo* was ordered to return to the location of maximum danger.

When the subchaser comes out, Bucher is pleased, for at last "according to our orders" he has the "unexpected opportunity to really test . . . their reaction to our presence . . ." (How it could be "unexpected" when he had been spotted in the same location the afternoon before he does not explain.) In any event, the confrontation was desired, fulfilling his "orders." As we have seen, CTs also wanted the "presence of an enemy ship."

The subchaser, much more heavily armed than *Pueblo*, is at battle stations, yet Bucher makes no effort to remove *Pueblo* from the scene for seventy-five minutes. This is in sharp contrast to *Banner*, which, as Bucher, Murphy, and others report, was always under way during harassment so it could "disengage" and take itself from danger. *Pueblo* did not "disengage," as Murphy clearly expected it to do. It is so apparent as to be obvious: Bucher had "orders," unlike those of *Banner*, to remain stationary under harassment. He did not leave when threatened, nor did he obey the FOLLOW ME signal from the subchaser. He just stayed where he was. Recall the statement by Radioman Hayes that prior to the Court of Inquiry, Bucher and others told the crew not to mention "secret orders to remain in the area to see how much harassment the North Koreans would give us."

Not until the boarding party is formed and gets within a few yards of *Pueblo* does Bucher get his ship under way to escape. By then it is too late. From first to last, Bucher maintained that he followed his orders "to the letter." If so, then he was under orders to remain on station in the face of enemy harassment, and he did so for seventy-five minutes—until it was too late. Who on earth would write such orders? And for what purpose? Particularly if *Pueblo* was in North Korean territorial waters, and a great deal of evidence suggests it was, then the orders would appear to have had the *intent* of placing the ship in a position in which it was likely to be captured. Ordering Bucher to keep his ship stationary under harassment—unlike *Banner*—surely placed him in a situation from which he was extremely unlikely to extricate himself and his men.

When *Pueblo* finally got under way to escape, its flight—despite Bucher's attempts to make it appear otherwise—was of short duration, no more than twenty-two minutes, as the Pinnacle messages and the radio transcript reveal. *Pueblo* was fired upon by machine guns and cannon firing two and three-eighths inch shells. But the shots were aimed high. Most missed the ship. Damage was slight, casualties incidental. Yet Bucher stops his ship in surrender. If he followed his orders "to the letter," what were those orders? He says only that he was under instructions not to start a war.

Questions must be asked. Was *Pueblo* under orders that put it in a position of almost certainly being captured? Were the men of *Pueblo* trying to say that when they risked Hell Week by sending "the finger" back home?

I can imagine nothing more *unthinkable* than that the National Security Agency and the United States Navy, both of which shared command of *Pueblo*, would deliberately sacrifice a vessel and its crew. If by any remote possibility they did so, it had to be for an extremely important reason of state.

To understand the *Pueblo* surrender, we must think about the *unthinkable*. Could there be any possible reason that would justify the deliberate surrender of a U.S. Navy vessel and its crew?

This brings us to the three questions posed at the end of the last chapter: Why was *Pueblo* seized by the Chinese and fired on by the Soviets? What happened during the more than six hours between the seizure and the ship's reaching Wonsan? Why did the NSA and the Navy cover up Chinese and Soviet involvement?

These are most difficult questions to answer. To mix some metaphors for emphasis, we must cross uncharted terrain and enter a thorny thicket where we open a can of worms. Thus far I have relied almost exclusively on printed material to discover what really happened during the *Pueblo* seizure. But I can find very little in print—just hints and a single enigmatic sentence by Lyndon Johnson—which even suggests Chinese and Soviet involvement. After all, everything was blamed on the North Koreans. The cover story was very successful for a long time.

I do have other information, a great deal of it, that suggests both *how* the *Pueblo* surrender was arranged by the NSA and *why*. But I hesitate to use it because it comes from the celebrated "informed sources." I know, unnamed sources of information are omnipresent in newspapers and radio and television news broadcasts. But I hated using them when I was a journalist and I like it even less today. But in this case there is a most cogent reason for keeping the sources of information unnamed—the Executive Order of President Reagan imposing harsh penalties on any person who identifies intelligence personnel. I could not name the sources even if they wanted me to.

By its very nature, information from unidentified sources—indeed, it is the reason most are unnamed—can be neither proved nor disproved. The careful reporter passes it on as useful information to the reader, listener, or viewer, but does not claim truth for it. Such is most definitely the case here. I have spent thousands of hours interviewing these informants. I have gone over their story hundreds of times and in the most minute detail, comparing its every nuance with printed sources of information, challenging it constantly in terms of logic and reasonableness. There is some corroboration for the story in the pages of this book and in other printed material. Readers will quickly spot it. But in my opinion it is not enough. Their story is simply not subject to proof or disproof at this time, perhaps never. Nonetheless, I believe readers should possess the information so they may judge its accuracy for themselves.

For what it is worth, having played the role of the proverbial doubting Thomas for so long, I have with great reluctance come to believe the story. It holds up under scrutiny, it makes sense, and it does explain a lot about the *Pueblo* seizure. But I am mindful of a line from this book: "Belief in truth does not create truth. Conviction, no matter how fervently believed, is not truth." I will not claim truth for this story or even defend it. I will not invoke a double standard. If I state that other "sources" were misinformed about the *Pueblo* seizure, I cannot now claim veracity for my "sources." What they do have is the right to be heard.

It is proper to ask why I have delayed so long in reporting this information in this book. The answer is that the story told by informants mostly relates to why *Pueblo* was surrendered, and this is the proper place for the information. For a long time informants never described the seizure itself, saying it "wasn't important." When pressed, they finally admitted, "There are things about the *Pueblo* seizure which can never be known."

Their silence and my determination to discover what could "never be known" led me down the long path which the reader has already followed. I should point out that all along the way, as I discussed each new discovery with informants, they kept throwing up smokescreens, doing all they could to direct me away from what could never be known: Chinese seizure of *Pueblo* and Soviet naval gunfire. I was able to figure it out only when I stopped talking to my "sources" for a long time and wrote the previous pages of this book. Only after I had figured it out did informants confirm Chinese and Soviet involvement, adding some pertinent information—apparently on the theory that if I was going to write it I might as well get it right.* They remain, however, not very happy with the fruits of my labors. This is not the book they wanted.

For a long time I excluded all information obtained from informants. After all, they had been no help in discovering what happened during the

---

*One detail they reported is that the shells fired by the Soviet ship were about four inches in diameter. They were armor-piercing shells, which burst through the hull, hurling shrapnel and causing the casualties. The Soviet ship did not fire incendiary or explosive shells because the Soviets did not want to cause an explosion and fire aboard *Pueblo*. They did not want the ship sunk or even badly damaged. They wanted to search it.

seizure. To answer the question of why the Chinese seized the ship and the Soviets fired on it, I used some logic, which the reader will encounter shortly. Then an editor of a celebrated publishing house said to me, "You have proved beyond doubt that a lie was told, but everyone knows the government lies. There is nothing remarkable in that. What you have not proved is why."

The depth of cynicism which permits a person to accept official governmental lies with equanimity needs no comment here. One need not agree with orator Wendell Phillips that "eternal vigilance is the price of liberty." Unfortunately, the editor did not read the last chapter of this book, which pursues the question of whether, in the *Pueblo* incident, our visible elected and appointed government leaders lied—or were lied to.

But the editor was perceptive. Other than by logic, I cannot prove, certainly from printed sources, that the Soviet Union planned to invade China, that the NSA intercepted a message relating to that fact, that it led the Chinese and Soviets to believe such a message was aboard *Pueblo*, thus inducing them to try to stop and search *Pueblo*, if not actually seize it. Such statements are not even subject to proof, unless the Soviet Union, China, and the NSA choose to admit it. The *Pueblo* literature will not tell us, for there was no one aboard *Pueblo* when it was seized who had any knowledge of such an intercepted message.

To me, why *Pueblo* was seized—or surrendered—is only of secondary importance. The main theme of this book (see last chapter) is that the National Security Agency, through control of coded information, was able to conceal Chinese and Soviet participation in the *Pueblo* incident from our visible leaders, and that the NSA has thereby assumed awesome power, greatly altering our constitutional form of government. If this has indeed occurred, the *why* of the *Pueblo* seizure pales to insignificance.

Nonetheless, as a result of the editor's comment, I realized I have an obligation to report to the reader all information I have which may help in understanding the *Pueblo* seizure and its significance. The story told by informants surely does that.

According to informed sources, what became the *Pueblo* surrender on January 23, 1968, began in Vietnam in the summer of 1967. Two highly trained NSA operatives, both cryptography experts, both possessing what was then the highest security classification in the land—Top Secret Category Three, Cryptographic Code Word Three, a classification I'm told no longer exists—were aboard the USS *Jamestown* off Vietnam. A converted liberty ship, *Jamestown* was a larger ELINT vessel, a sort of mother ship to vessels such as *Pueblo* and *Banner*. It was sister ship to the USS *Georgetown* and the so-called USS *Liberty* which the Israelis bombed in the summer of 1967. (I write "so-called" because this class of ship is always named after cities.)

Both men, one white and one black, held the rank of Navy lieutenant, but were on detached service to the NSA. Their uniforms bore no insignia of rank or specialty. Indeed they mostly wore T-shirts and dungarees. Those aboard *Jamestown* knew them only by first names. They had no idea who they were or what they did, other than that they obviously had something to do with U.S. intelligence.

It was explained to me that the two *Jamestown* operatives held extraordinary power. They were part of a short-lived NSA experiment in which a small group was specially trained and its members given the highest security classification to act as sort of supernumeraries in the field. They reported directly to the huge NSA underground headquarters near Washington. They possessed the "Red Card." With it they could open any door, look at any file, learn any information they had need to know, requisition any manpower or equipment, and issue orders to any officer of any rank, including admirals and generals, with absolute assurance they would be obeyed. Informants said the experiment was quickly abandoned because the Code Word Three agents came to know too much and acted too independently of supervision.

Informants state, most emphatically, that power in the United States (and in the Soviet Union and most other countries) is not derived from rank, title on the door, money, popularity, or anything other than security classification. They state that it is people who are most impressed by rank and position who are easiest to manipulate.

This becomes easier to believe when it is realized that codes developed by the NSA (and the KGB) exist in a hierarchy. A person with a security classification can read a message in a code for which he is cleared—and all those below him, but none above. A person cleared for S1, Secret, might be suitably impressed with his cryptographic knowledge, but what he perhaps didn't realize was that there were in 1968 at least ten codes higher than his. A person classified Top Secret One could read all messages in his own code and those classified Secret, but there were still a lot of codes higher than his. Indeed, the same transmission might contain messages in several different codes. The person classified "Secret" saw his message but did not realize there might be a "Top Secret" message therein. And this person did not realize there might be a Cryptographic Code Word One message there also.

In the summer of 1967, the two NSA operatives aboard *Jamestown* were the only two men in the field in the Western Pacific with the capability of reading all messages sent in inferior codes, while the messages they sent in their code could be read only at NSA headquarters. Said another way, the two operatives were privy to all information known to others, but no other persons in the field could break their codes and learn what information they possessed. They were aware of what others knew, thought, and did, while no others had any idea of what they knew, thought, and did—or even who they were, for that matter.

This situation created opportunities for endless manipulation. To give an example, it was really quite easy, indeed routine, for the two operatives to control the mission and movements of *Jamestown* without the captain or anyone else aboard knowing it. All they had to do was send a Code Word Three message, which no one else aboard could read, to NSA saying what they wanted done. This message was then "recycled," which is to say reduced to inferior and appropriate codes, and sent to the ship captain, communications officer, and anyone else it might apply to. The orders looked as if they came from official Navy or NSA channels. As it was explained to me, a lieutenant commander, classified Code Word Two, who commanded all the SOD-Hut operations aboard *Jamestown*, shared an office with the two operatives. He often discussed his newly received orders with them, never once realizing the orders had originated with them. Why didn't they simply tell him to his face? Because it would have blown their cover. Identified, at least in terms of security classification, they would have been useless in further assignments.

If this information is correct and a person begins to extrapolate the possibilities of such manipulation in terms of generals, admirals, cabinet officers, presidents—and where they obtain information—it becomes very disturbing, even frightening.

The assignment of the two operatives aboard *Jamestown* was to find a way to speed up the breaking of the tactical codes used by the North Vietnamese. NSA computers could break the codes, but they were about three weeks behind. The North Vietnamese were being exceedingly clever. They changed codes every four hours or sooner. They sent a massive amount of transmissions—Chairman Mao's little red book, speeches by Ho Chi Minh, tracts, manuals, pages from newspapers, anything—in the midst of which was an important coded message, or part of one, for the message might be sent part in one code, part in others. Those acres of NSA computers were inundated and overmatched, running behind. And three weeks in a war situation was considered an eternity with the North Vietnamese planning what became known as the Tet Offensive.

The operatives led a series of clandestine raids on North Vietnamese communications bunkers in the demilitarized zone, hoping to find code books and other materials to speed up the decoding process. The raids failed to locate useful material. Then, in desperation, the operatives came up with a scheme which ultimately became the *Pueblo* surrender.

I'm told—like Ripley, believe it or not—that the *Pueblo* surrender originated when the two operatives were drinking beer and letting off steam at a beach party on Vung-tao Island, off Vietnam. Six other NSA operatives were in attendance and all, half in the bag, began to brainstorm the problem of breaking the North Vietnamese codes. Someone suggested that the way to do it was to get the North Vietnamese to use a code machine which had been rigged so that one letter was always transmitted by the same signal. This "constant" would enable NSA computers to break out the codes within seconds. Fine, but how could anyone get the North Vietnamese to "accept delivery" of the rigged code machine? Someone suggested floating it in from a submarine. The drunken brainstorming broke up in hilarity when someone suggested mailing it to them through the U.S. Postal System—only it would get there too late to do any good.

The next morning, back on *Jamestown*, presumably not too overhung, the two operatives realized that this scheme of the rigged code machine had merit. The North Vietnamese, who had lots of Soviet code equipment—much of it U.S.-made and given to the Soviets in World War II—would never fall for it. But the North Koreans, who used the same codes supplied by the Soviet Union, just might. Forgotten, hard up for any sort of modern equipment, they might "accept delivery" of a rigged code machine and use it—especially if they "found" it aboard a U.S. Navy vessel which they had "captured."

The scheme was too classified ever to be transmitted, so one of the operatives, the black man, flew to the underground NSA headquarters to propose it. The plan was approved. The two operatives were ordered to carry out the plan applying the rules of Need to Know. They were to interfere with normal routine as little as possible. And they were to use the ship on station.

As it was explained to me, Need to Know is a highly systematized process by which U.S. intelligence practices deception and maintains secrecy during operations. A person is told only what he needs to know to do a specific task. That person has no Need to Know how that task may or may not relate to anything else that is happening and so does not know. It is as if the entire intelligence operation is a jigsaw puzzle. A person is given a single piece of it. He has no knowledge he has the piece or even that there is a puzzle. He has never seen the picture on the puzzle and cannot relate his piece to anything else. The number of people who have seen the picture on the puzzle and know how the pieces relate to one another is extremely small. I'm told that in the *Pueblo* seizure, those who had seen the picture on the *Pueblo* puzzle consisted of the two operatives on *Jamestown* (and eventually they would be in the dark, too, when the puzzle changed) and a few high-ranking officials at NSA—less than a dozen people in all. As the informants' story of the *Pueblo* seizure unfolds, it is possible to see that, although many persons were involved, Need to Know kept them from even realizing that an intelligence operation was in progress, let alone its nature. To the participants everything looked highly routine, even boring.

But Need to Know is far more than a jigsaw puzzle. As practiced by the NSA it is an exceedingly clever process by which the beliefs and actions of a person can be manipulated. It is a mind game. It is magic. It is mirrors. What you see happening with your own eyes or hear with your own ears isn't happening at all. What you know for certain is a fact isn't a fact at all. Need to Know is a disaster for empiricists. Bucher sees undestroyed "classified documents" when he really is looking at worthless confetti. He sees Steve Harris as commander of the CT detachment when he really is a figurehead. CTs see "repairs" being made to equipment and do not realize it isn't broken. Naval officers in Japan see coded messages that *Pueblo* is surrounded by ships at battle stations and file it on the "interest board." Air Force pilots hear distress calls and believe "the Navy is overdoing it this time."

All of these people were victims of Need to Know as perfected by the NSA. The simplest way to understand Need to Know is to realize a person is told *whatever he can be made to believe.* The NSA takes what you already know, then provides you with additional information (what you have Need to Know) to alter your thinking and beliefs. This new information is invariably quite plausible, highly reasonable, thoroughly believable. It makes sense. What it often really is is the classic American tall tale, the albino alligators in the New York sewer system.

Need to Know, as practiced by the NSA, is so foreign to human nature it is difficult to understand and certainly to accept until you are a victim of it. Perhaps a couple of illustrations from my own experience will aid understanding.

One of the early announcements by the Pentagon after *Pueblo* was seized was that it was believed Duane Hodges had his leg blown off and lost his life in a "destruct explosion" while destroying classified gear in the SOD-Hut. This was important to me because it belied the sworn testimony of Bucher and others to the Court of Inquiry that there were no destruct devices or explosives aboard *Pueblo* and sledgehammers and axes had to be used to destroy the gear.

Informants picked up this bit of information which I had learned and used it to form the smokescreen over the events of the seizure. They explained about the destruct mechanisms on the equipment, how a tab is pulled, setting off thermite which melts the guts of the machine. When I said it didn't sound like much of an explosion occurred, they replied, "Thermite is dangerous stuff. Some of it has been in the equipment a long time." Made sense. Highly believable.

Later, after further research and thought, I said that Hodges was a fireman working in the engineroom, a member of the regular crew, who were forbidden entrance to the SOD-Hut. What was he doing in the SOD-Hut destroying Top Secret gear and getting his leg blown off? Answer: "He was a striker [a Navy term for a person in training for another job]. CTs fresh out of CT school in Pensacola aren't permitted full access to the SOD-Hut. They're hidden among the regular crew, tested, and trained in the SOD-Hut before getting their CT stripe." Made sense. What do I know about how they train CTs? It's all classified.

Further research produced the information that Woelk, Crandall, and Chicca were injured in the same explosion. Chicca was in the SOD-Hut, but were Woelk and Crandall also strikers? It was an awfully big explosion. How come others weren't hurt? Eventually even the most obtuse and naive can recognize that a smokescreen was being thrown over Hodges' death. Why? How was Duane Hodges killed? It became a key question to me. Eventually I came to know the answer, but not from informants.

Another illustration: From the outset, informants insisted the North Koreans *towed Pueblo* into Wonsan. This belied all the testimony and writings of Bucher and everyone else that *Pueblo* was boarded and *sailed* into Wonsan. Informants even said there was a satellite photograph which shows *Pueblo* being towed. They'd try to let me see it. (I never did.) The weather was rough. They made only one knot an hour. And of course this towing information was supported by the intercepted 1306 message that the North Koreans planned to board *Pueblo* and tow it into Wonsan.

For a long time I believed *Pueblo* was towed into Wonsan. I could think of no reason for informants to insist so vehemently that the ship had been towed if it hadn't been. I thought they were just providing evidence that

Bucher had lied and that there had been a cover story about the seizure. Only later, after I had learned what could never be known, did I realize the towing story was vital to "explain" why it took six hours for the ship to reach port.

Again, under Need to Know a person is told whatever he can be made to believe. When I finally learned about the "large warship" which was "coming fast" and was not American but suspected of being Soviet, informants produced their last tall tale about the seizure: "It was a Mexican standoff. There were both a Soviet and a Chinese cruiser out there at battle stations. Both wanted *Pueblo* but both were afraid to fire on the other and start a war. To settle it, Colonel Scar was sent out to search *Pueblo*. He found no message, all the tapes destroyed, so the Chinese and Soviet ships simply left." Oh, I loved it! It made so much sense I thought I had finally been told the truth. Only later when I discovered that the Chinese, not the North Koreans, have a big red star in the middle of a square fur hat did I realize that Need to Know had struck again.

I was fortunate that so much had been written about the *Pueblo* incident, allowing me to seek corroboration for the informants' story and thus discover when the mental manipulation of Need to Know was being applied to me. And, of course, they had already described in juicy detail how Need to Know was applied in the *Pueblo* surrender. As a result of my experiences, I will never again rely solely upon interviews to obtain a story. It is precisely because of my experience with the mental manipulation of Need to Know that I refuse to claim truth for any utterance from informants.

In my first interview with informants I made this statement: "I always believe anything anyone tells me until I have a reason to believe otherwise." This brought scoffing laughter. Apparently they didn't hear the second part of the statement. A little later on I said, "I don't want to know, let alone write any national secrets. If there is something I shouldn't know, just don't tell me. But please don't lie to me." They agreed. And, of course, they did lie. Much later, after I'd learned what could never be known, I threw this up to them. One replied: "You must understand now why we had to lie to you. We had to do all we could to lead you away from the truth."

Writers and journalists are particularly susceptible to manipulation by Need to Know simply because we depend so much for our information upon interviews and "informed sources." It is axiomatic in our business that when we want to know something we seek out the person with information and authority, ask him, then print or broadcast what he says.

We've done our jobs. Often the person being interviewed is the sole source of information we have. We believe and trust the source. He would not risk his reputation for veracity by lying now. It is simply very difficult to come to grips with the situation in which the person being interviewed isn't lying. He's telling the truth as he knows it—only it isn't the truth because this person is a victim of Need to Know. Where did he or she get the information? Has the person been told something he could be made to believe?

Government officials and military leaders are also highly susceptible to Need to Know machinations simply because they depend heavily on highly classified and encoded information from intelligence agencies. Presidents and cabinet officers, generals and admirals receive almost daily "intelligence briefings." Where did the persons briefing them get their information? Are those persons victims of Need to Know? Have they seen the picture on the puzzle or do they just hold a piece of it, performing their small role in a larger plan?

To aid in the better application of Need to Know, I'm told, the NSA employs significant numbers of psychologists and other such practitioners. They are said to busy themselves preparing "psychological profiles" that offer insights into the background, attitudes, and "mind set" of important, influential, and useful people with special emphasis on what they already believe, where they obtain information, and whom or what they are likely to believe. All this is said to be an aid in their manipulation.

As informants continue with their *Pueblo* story, it will be possible to see how the NSA used Need to Know, both as a jigsaw puzzle and as thought manipulation, to induce Bucher to do the one thing he would never do: surrender his ship without a fight.

Banner was the ship on station off North Korea. Planning proceeded for *Banner* to be surrendered. (The men of that ship might be interested to learn just how close they may have come to *Pueblo*'s fate.) At the eleventh hour *Banner* was replaced by *Pueblo*, which had been in training in the area for several months. Informants do not know why *Pueblo* replaced *Banner*. They say it may have been entirely routine. *Banner* had been on station a long time and was due for crew replacement and refitting. Or it may have been because the crew of *Banner* was too skilled and experienced to be lost. Among the ELINT fleet, *Pueblo* had a reputation as a "foul up" crew. On one occasion they had misadjusted the directional antenna and beamed their transmissions directly to Vladivostok. I'm told the operatives were displeased with the switch to *Pueblo*, for it posed a risk that the North Korean transmission over the rigged machine might be lost.

About four o'clock on a fall morning, *Pueblo* rendezvoused with a U.S. submarine in the Sea of Japan and the two *Jamestown* operatives came aboard from a rubber boat to activate their plan. The first order of business was to rig one of the two code machines aboard *Pueblo*. Accompanying the two operatives was a CET—Communications Electronic Technician. Although highly skilled in the inner workings of electronic gear, he had been carefully selected because he was by nature a chronic complainer who only wanted to get a job done as quickly as possible. He was capable of figuring out what was being done to the machine, but the two operatives stood by, cracking jokes, distracting him, so that he attached no significance to the "repairs" he was asked to make to the machine.

When he finished, the operatives "tested" the machine. It worked exactly as desired—the single letter always transmitted with the same signal—but they declared it still didn't work right. It would have to be returned to the factory to be worked on. They literally slapped a red "out of order" sign on it so it wouldn't be used. This was imperative, for if the *Pueblo* CTs had used the rigged machine, the Russians would have broken out U.S. codes just as quickly as we hoped to break out theirs. The CTs on *Pueblo* were to use the second code machine.

(I am not certain this is precisely how the machine was rigged. I am apparently incapable of understanding modern codes and code machines. I perhaps spent more time questioning informants about code construction than about any other subject and simply became more confused. Finally in disgust one informant said: "Why don't you go to cryptography school?" In any event, informants claim the machine was rigged in some fashion so that it always gave a "constant"; that is, a single letter or squiggle or pulse or signal was always the same.)

As it was explained to me, there was nothing out of the ordinary in having a "broken" code machine on board. Equipment breaks down and is taken out of service. More importantly, an out-of-service code machine was not considered classified equipment. The United States manufactured and sold code machines all over the world, one reason being that it aided codebreakers. English has only twenty-six letters, unlike the longer alphabet of the Soviet Union and certainly unlike Chinese. The code machine became valuable, indeed priceless, only when it was set and operable by insertion of a code card. It was explained to me that the code machine in use at that time, which somewhat resembled a stereo amplifier, was hooked to a random scrambler. The effect of the code card, which looked something like a U.S. Treasury check, was to harness the random scrambler into something which made sense. I was told the random scrambler was esoteric and classified. The NSA hated to give it up, but considered it part of the price to be paid for what would be gained if the North Koreans used the code machine.

The hope was that when the North Koreans (no one was thinking Chinese or Russians at this time) seized *Pueblo*, they would find the out-of-order code machine, insert one of their own code cards, and use it. To ensure that the machine would remain intact, the *Jamestown* operatives posted new "destruct orders" in the SOD-Hut. These specifically eliminated the rigged machine from equipment to be destroyed. As further insurance they disconnected the automatic destruct device inside the machine.

The biggest problem facing the two operatives, I was informed, was how to get Commander Bucher to do the one thing he would never do—that is, surrender his ship without a fight and not (hopefully never) realize that that was precisely what he was supposed to do. If given a direct order to surrender his ship, Bucher would have disobeyed, and rightly so. Any Navy ship captain would have done the same.

Bucher was manipulated into doing the one thing he would never do through Need to Know. Through control of codes, the two operatives knew exactly what information Bucher possessed and thereby believed. It was a simple process to feed him a little more information (tell him what he had Need to Know) to get him to surrender his ship without a fight.

The two operatives met with Bucher in the Space Two aboard *Pueblo*. This was a courtesy visit. They told him that *Pueblo*, having successfully completed its training, was now going "on line, real time," replacing *Banner*. Congratulations. They also left him sealed, "his eyes only" orders to be opened at a later date, then destroyed.

Those orders, most carefully drafted by the two operatives while aboard *Jamestown*, then recycled, reduced to the code Bucher was classified to read, and made to look as though they came through official Navy channels, were the heart of the deception. The operatives knew Bucher had talked to Commander Clark of *Banner*. Bucher knew that *Banner* had made many trips into North Korean waters, the radar shadow of Yo Island, and been harassed. But *Banner*, except for the one time when its engines broke down, had always been under way and sailed away to safety.

The orders left for Bucher (I'm told no copy exists, making all this utterly unprovable) told him that he was to remain on station, dead in the water, and make no effort to leave. This was to be a test of North Korean reactions to the continued presence of an American ship. By monitoring the North Korean radio transmissions it would be possible to discover whether the North Koreans were taking orders from the Chinese or the Soviets. This would provide valuable intelligence information. And, of course, with the rapidly changing political situation in North Korea, this was true. The NSA did want to know whether China or the USSR was dominant in North Korea.

Bucher's orders further told him that he was not to provoke an international incident. The orders actually contained these words: DO NOT RESIST BOARDERS. Informants told me that the operatives knew that including those words in the orders was a risk. It might well tip off Bucher as to what was really going on. But they counted on Bucher to believe that since no ELINT ship had ever been seized anywhere in the world, the term "boarding" meant a legalistic visit by a couple of North Korean officers who would order him to remove his ship from their territorial waters.

After meeting with Bucher, the operatives met with the chief CT, an enlisted man, a Code Word One NSA operative, who actually commanded the SOD-Hut. He controlled the code machine and thus the ship. I'm told this is true in any military or governmental installation outfitted with a code machine—and that the KGB operates on the same principal. Only persons with very high security classifications are permitted to use a code machine—or even have access to it. The machine is kept under the tightest security in a "cryptospace," a "Space Three." Standing orders are that any unauthorized person attempting to enter the cryptospace is to be shot on the spot, no questions asked. No message may be sent or received over the crypto machine—indeed, in normal operations it is impossible to do so—without the knowledge of the one person who commands the set and operating code machine. His security classification, always the highest on the ship or other installation, permits him to read all inferior codes. He is thus aware of what all others know and of what their orders are. Although he (or she) may be only an enlisted person for reasons of deception, he commands the entire installation, manipulating "superiors" by having his own orders recycled and re-cut through NSA headquarters. So effective is this system, I'm told, that even persons of very high rank, responsible for large commands, have no idea they are being manipulated, let alone by whom, most especially an "enlisted man." To repeat, I'm told true power lies not with rank or position, but with security classification and access to coded information.

To clarify the organization of the SOD-Hut, NSA personnel refer to the places where intelligence activities occur as "spaces." Aboard *Pueblo*, the regular crew spoke of the "SOD-Hut," while the CTs referred to the place where they worked as "spaces." As it was explained to me, the spaces on *Pueblo* and any other intelligence-gathering installation are secure. Access is tightly controlled. There is no communication between "spaces" and any insecure place.

On *Pueblo*, entry was gained through a triple-locked outside door. A person then entered a small vestibule where a Marine guard was always on duty. If authorized beyond that point, a person passed through a second, cipher-locked door into the Space One, the largest area where the surveillance and intercept activity was performed. The Space Two was a locked, soundproof room containing, on *Pueblo*, the files and safe for code cards, orders, important papers, and reels of magnetic tape containing intercept. All were equipped with automatic destruct devices. There was communication *into* Space Two, but not from it. Anything said in Space Two was totally secure. The Space Three was the crypto room. There was no communication in or out of it. Only one person knew the combination to the cipher lock. Only one other CT was authorized to enter, and then only briefly twice a day. He was authorized because two men, possessing two keys and two combinations, were required to open the code machine and insert a new card. Given this situation I asked informants how the North Koreans managed to open the rigged machine, insert their own card, and use the device. They say they are uncertain exactly what the North Koreans did. They say obtaining the keys and combinations would not have been difficult. With enough time it was also possible for North Korean technicians, trained in the Soviet Union, to dismantle the machine and get inside.

Greatly experienced, the chief CT was the one person aboard *Pueblo* who was capable of figuring out what was going on, at least after the fact. In the Space Two, the operatives congratulated him on doing such a fine job in training the *Pueblo* CTs. His tour of duty was up. He would leave the ship by bosun's chair during the next rendezvous with a tanker, after which he would be reassigned. They gave the chief sealed orders which were to be left in the safe for his replacement. The two operatives were going to great pains to see that the old chief and the new never met or exchanged a single word—most especially about how *Pueblo* and *Banner* had operated previously.

When the new chief came aboard he found sealed, "his eyes only" orders. Their contents were in sharp contrast to those given to Bucher, but neither man was permitted to confer with the other to discover that. Thus, I'm told, was the dual command aboard *Pueblo* used to lead it into surrender. The new chief CT was from NSA headquarters, highly knowledgeable about communications and electronic intercept, but he had never set foot on an ELINT ship before. He had no firsthand knowledge of how ELINT ships normally performed.

He read what appeared to him to be normal "intercept orders," a listing of map coordinates where the ship was to take station on certain days and the type of intercept to be performed. These coordinates repeatedly took *Pueblo* into the radar shadow of Yo Island. Like Bucher, the new chief CT was ordered to remain on station under enemy harassment. He was to monitor and record North Korean radio to see whether they took orders from the Chinese or the Russians.

Then came the sharp contrast with Bucher's orders. The chief CT was told that if faced with boarding, he was immediately to order emergency destruction in accordance with the posted "destruct orders." Thus, Bucher was not to resist boarders, while the CTs, when faced by boarding, were to emergency destruct—blowing up gear and destroying the working code machine, code cards, files, safe, reels of tape, tape decks, and the rest. They were to haul out confetti and start fires on deck. The intent of the orders was to create a situation in which the North Korean boarders, even if just a pair of officers issuing a warning, would be greeted by explosions, fires, and general hubbub and thus go to investigate. Because of the fires aboard, the North Koreans would doubtlessly tow the "burning" ship into Wonsan where the rigged code machine would be discovered and used.

After the operatives left *Pueblo* by submarine, they set up the rest of the plan. They arranged for the crew of *Pueblo* to be disarmed when the ship next returned to Japan. I'm told this action, while unusual, was not unheard of. *Banner* had been disarmed on trips into hostile waters precisely to prevent provocation for seizure and an international incident. It was imperative that every peep from *Pueblo* be received and recorded, so that when the North Koreans used the rigged code machine the message was not lost. Toward this end, NSA ground stations at Kamiseya, Japan, and Adak, Alaska, were to constantly monitor *Pueblo*, as were ships and planes. Even a submarine, as a last resort, was stationed in the Sea of Japan with orders to surface on command and record messages from *Pueblo*. It was then to sail at full speed to Japan with the message. In addition, to ensure that no ship or plane attempted to rescue *Pueblo*, Air Force and Navy units were told a "training exercise" was under way in the Sea of Japan. They were to operationally ignore all distress calls.

After Thanksgiving, *Pueblo* was sent into the radar shadow of Yo Island. The NSA hoped to have it captured before Christmas. Although

Pueblo performed admirably, lingering, drawing harassment from North Korean patrol craft, the North Koreans simply would not seize *Pueblo*. It was a time of acute frustration for the NSA and the operatives aboard *Jamestown*. The North Vietnamese offensive was known to be approaching. If *Pueblo* was not captured soon, and the rigged code machine used, there would be no point to the whole operation. New orders were sent to *Pueblo*, in effect telling Bucher and the chief CT to remain on station longer and to act more provocatively so that North Korean pride would overrule their self-interest and cause them to seize the ship. They would not. (Instead they registered the protests reported in Chapter One.)

Then, on the ship's penultimate voyage, the CTs aboard *Pueblo* intercepted and recorded a message from the Soviet Union to its cadre in North Korea. I was not told the content of the message, only that it pertained to Soviet plans to invade China and that it was a message China was most eager to know about and which the Soviets were equally anxious to keep them from knowing. The message was sent in the premier Soviet diplomatic code (not the tactical codes used by the North Koreans and North Vietnamese), which had long since been broken by the NSA, although the Soviets were unaware of that. Informants said that if *Banner* had been on station, its very experienced CTs would have recognized the importance of the intercept and sent the message, encoded in "real time," to Japan immediately. The inexperienced crew of *Pueblo* attached no special significance to the intercept, continued its routine mission, and returned to Japan on schedule. The intercept tapes were routinely flown to NSA headquarters, where the importance of the Soviet message was instantly appreciated.

What had begun as an operation to speed the breaking of North Vietnamese tactical codes now took on a whole new meaning. Not even the *Jamestown* operatives knew of the intercepted Soviet message or of the extraordinary steps the NSA now took to virtually guarantee capture of *Pueblo*. *Pueblo* was sent back to Wonsan. (Informants are uncertain whether the .50-caliber machine guns were mounted for this voyage or earlier ones to give the North Koreans the legal right to seize the ship.) *Pueblo* was to stay well away from Soviet shipping and attempt to remain undetected. It was to observe EMCON, or radio silence. The purpose of all this was to keep the Soviet Navy from boarding *Pueblo* before it reached Wonsan and access to the Chinese and North Koreans. Also, it was hoped that the Chinese and Russians might not realize that *Pueblo* had returned to Japan and that the intercepted Soviet message was long gone from the ship.

For this last voyage it was also necessary to make numerous replacements in the *Pueblo* crew. All CTs who had any knowledge of the intercepted Soviet message had to be replaced, including the chief CT and various operational CTs. This was necessary, I'm told, to ensure that there would be no person aboard *Pueblo* who had any conception of a reason for surrender of the ship. Then Bailey was sent aboard to ensure that *Pueblo* communications worked perfectly and that all communications went directly to his buddy Haizlip at Kamiseya, which is to say NSA.

All that remained to seal *Pueblo*'s fate was to alert the Chinese and Soviets that there was a message both wanted aboard *Pueblo*. Informants will not state what information was given to the Soviets and Chinese or how the information was leaked. They will say only that both countries were alerted. (In my opinion one or the other, conceivably both, received the information when the North Koreans raided the presidential Blue House in Seoul, South Korea, on January 21, two days before the *Pueblo* seizure.)

From the viewpoint of the NSA, the whole operation was a howling success. The only thing that went wrong was that Bucher did not follow his orders not to resist boarders. When he saw the boarding party of armed soldiers, he got his ship under way to try to escape, thus delaying the seizure and forcing the North Korean ships to fire on *Pueblo* to stop it. The CTs performed emergency destruction to perfection, leaving the rigged code machine intact. Bucher surrendered his ship without realizing that was what he was supposed to do or certainly why. I was told the NSA's original estimates were that three on board *Pueblo* would be killed. Only one was. I was also told that NSA was prepared to lose the entire crew. The loss of eighty-three men was considered a minuscule price to pay for the thousands of lives that would be saved in Vietnam.

Important corroboration for the informants' story came in March 1986 at the espionage trial of Jerry A. Whitworth in San Francisco. A man identified as Earl D. Clark, Jr., and said to be an ''expert in communications security for the National Security Agency,'' admitted that a U.S. code machine had been captured by the North Koreans when they seized the USS *Pueblo* in 1968.

At that same trial Master Chief Thomas F. Bennett, a Navy radioman for twenty-five years, according to the New York *Times* coverage of the trial, told the jury that used coding and decoding materials are ''of such importance that they were the first items to be destroyed should a ship be in danger of being captured.''

Informants had earlier told me that used code cards, messages, and such are normally shredded on ELINT ships, then burned twice a day in accordance with a regular schedule. That's what the incinerator was aboard *Pueblo* for. They pointed out that if the *Pueblo* CTs had followed the schedule they would have been burning at 1300 hours, just prior to the seizure. It is at least conceivable that the smoke from this incineration is what provoked the attempted boarding at 1315.

When Colonel Scar and the Soviet-trained cadre came out to inspect *Pueblo*, they found no reels of tape bearing messages. But they did find an undestroyed U.S. code machine. They inserted their own code card and used the machine to ask instructions from the Soviets, turning *Pueblo* so its directional antenna was aimed toward Vladivostok. That message was intercepted by the NSA. The tactical codes used by the North Koreans and North Vietnamese were broken out within seconds.

The informed sources provide some addenda to their *Pueblo* story. The two operatives aboard *Jamestown* were decorated. I was shown a photograph of two young men, one white, one black, receiving congratulations from an Army officer in full uniform aboard a ship, itself a somewhat unusual occurrence. Gen. William C. Westmoreland, commander of U.S. forces in Vietnam, went to Washington where, I'm informed, both he and President Johnson were told the North Vietnamese codes were broken. Neither man was given any indication this had anything to do with the *Pueblo* seizure, however. General Westmoreland was briefed on North Vietnamese plans for their offensive. (As it turned out, the Army already had a complete set of plans obtained from a dead officer. But Army intelligence had dismissed the plans as a plant.) Before returning to Vietnam, General Westmoreland met with reporters to express his confidence that any attempted offensive by the enemy would result in their resounding defeat.

Informants said the Army needed about two weeks to prepare defenses for the offensive. Thus it was imperative that the North Vietnamese receive no hint that their codes had been broken. All military actions were to appear normal. Nothing unusual or provocative was to occur.

Aboard *Jamestown*, the two operatives, who had the capacity to listen to any message being transmitted throughout the fleet, heard an admiral order a chopper strike against a North Vietnamese SAM (anti-aircraft missile) site which had never been attacked previously. The admiral had been deliberately ordered into the backwater of the war just to prevent such an air strike. When the strike order was overheard, the *Jamestown* operatives ordered the admiral to abort the strike. Perhaps frustrated by inactivity, perhaps upset by the loss of Navy pride symbolized by the

Pueblo surrender, he ignored the order (actually, he asked for authority for the order—who sent it) and launched the choppers. At this point, so I am told, the operatives sent a one-word coded message to the admiral. Because of the need for speed it was sent enciphered, but not encoded, over a tactical channel which could be easily intercepted. Thus an entire system of codes was compromised and had to be changed. The one-word message meant in effect, "I am God, you will obey." A blanched admiral immediately recalled the choppers, but it was too late. The attempted strike had alerted the North Vietnamese. They launched the Tet Offensive the next day, the eighth following the *Pueblo* seizure. The North Vietnamese were not ready, and neither was the United States. The Tet Offensive ended up in a bloody stalemate. I'm told the admiral's next command was over a desk.

Even though the immediate results of the *Pueblo* operation were a disappointment, I'm told its long-term effects cause the NSA to consider the *Pueblo* surrender one of the greatest intelligence coups of modern times.

Soviet belief that *Pueblo* had intercepted their message meant that their premier diplomatic code had been broken by NSA. I'm told that within a few days Soviet cryptographers, examining the North Korean messages sent from the *Pueblo* machine, realized it had been rigged and that their codes used for communication with their satellite nations were also compromised. (I'm told the Soviets immediately ordered the North Koreans to stop using the *Pueblo* code machine, but they kept on doing so for quite some time.)

Informants say the KGB "overreacted" to the *Pueblo* seizure. Believing that the breaking of their codes gave the NSA detailed knowledge of their past and present intelligence activities, they began a complete overhaul of those activities, changing codes, agents, methods, operations, and plans. Since this would take years, during which the KGB perceived itself to be in a position of weakness vis-à-vis the NSA, the Soviet government launched its policy of détente with the West, courting better relations with the United States, buying time for the KGB overhaul.

Informants said one of the minuses of the *Pueblo* surrender was that the KGB immediately changed codes and agents, leaving a number of U.S. agents exposed and in jeopardy in the middle of operations. A number of American agents lost their lives thereby.

Again, this was considered an acceptable price, I'm told, for what was gained. As one person put it, "The KGB was set back for years as a result of the *Pueblo* seizure. We are still reaping the fruits of that operation."

This story, told with a great deal more elaboration and detail than I have related here, offers some answers to various *Pueblo* mysteries. To repeat, there is some corroboration for it in printed material, but because of the covert nature of the operation, the fact so few knew of the entire plan—only two operatives in the field and no one aboard *Pueblo*—makes the story most difficult to prove or disprove, although I believe the future may provide opportunities to do so.

I do not defend the story. The first person who declares it poppycock will get no argument from me. What I will defend is the right of the American people to know the story and judge its present and future accuracy for themselves.

If a person disbelieves the story told by informants and ignores it, as I try to do, there still remains an answer to the question of why China seized *Pueblo* and the Soviet Union fired on it—an answer based on logic.

There was a terrible risk of war with the United States for both nations. To take such a risk, both nations must have wanted *Pueblo* very badly. There was, or they believed there was, something of great value to them aboard *Pueblo*. It wasn't just another American ELINT ship to them, none of which had ever been seized (although the Israelis had bombed *Liberty*) anywhere in the world. And they wanted this specific ship. Recall the North Korean message, "The ship is GER-2 and they are American guys."

Since the first to board and seize *Pueblo* were Red Chinese, since the warship which arrived to shell *Pueblo* was Soviet, since *Pueblo* was an ELINT ship, carrying no cargo, and having no other purpose than to intercept communications, the Chinese and Soviets had to believe *Pueblo* had intercepted some message of great importance to both of them. Since these two superpowers were involved, the message had to pertain to the two countries. It doesn't really matter what the message was, but since both China and the USSR wanted it so badly, it may well have pertained to Soviet plans to attack China. And if the Soviets wanted *Pueblo* badly enough to open fire on it with a destroyer or light cruiser, then they indeed had to have sent such a message and they indeed had to be desperate that it not fall into Chinese hands.

One more piece of logic. Since Red Chinese first boarded and seized *Pueblo* and since the Soviets fired on *Pueblo* to stop it from reaching Wonsan, then the NSA had to have alerted both the Chinese and the Russians that there was a message of great importance aboard GER-2. It wouldn't have been difficult. As the code-making and code-breaking arm of the United States government, NSA could easily have "leaked" information about a message on board *Pueblo*. The NSA could have made the leak in a code which they knew had been compromised and which they knew both China and the Soviet Union could break. It certainly would not have been difficult for the NSA to arrange for both China and the USSR to intercept the "leaked" information.

Consider the seizure one more time. The subchaser comes out, waits for scouting torpedo boats to arrive, then frantically signals *Pueblo* toward Wonsan. FOLLOW ME—HAVE PILOT ABOARD, they say. *Pueblo* doesn't move. Finally, in desperation, Red Chinese foot soldiers board. But they know nothing about ELINT ships and communications. They try to sail *Pueblo* to Wonsan—until stopped by Soviet gunfire.

The men of *Pueblo* were truly "had." They were sitting ducks, under orders to remain stationary, disarmed, ordered not to defend themselves, trapped. No wonder they gave "the finger" to those who did it to them. It is the human reaction of angry, suffering, disillusioned men who feel betrayed.

The second question—what happened during the six hours before *Pueblo* reached Wonsan—is even more difficult to answer. The men of *Pueblo* were blindfolded and below decks. There is no one to tell us. I can find no printed material which discusses the question. My informants say they do not know.

Let's begin with the *known* and try to approach the *unknown*. The six hours are a *fact*. I was alerted to it during my interview with Lee Hayes. He still had his watch. It was after eight o'clock when *Pueblo* reached Wonsan. He could not believe all that time had passed and no American planes or ships had come to their rescue. Hayes's estimate is validated by the Navy's radio transcript. It concludes with "Analysis—What actions were possible?" Then the following sequences of time were given. The numbers are in Korean time. The first two digits are the date, followed by the time in military hours.

Time to act before dark. 231330 to 231806 = $4^h\ 36^m$

Time to act before seizure. 231330 to 231435 = $1^h\ 5^m$

Time to act until *Pueblo* abeam Ung Do island. 231330 to 231645 = $3^h\ 15^m$

Time to act until *Pueblo* moored at the pier. 231330 to 232030 = 7^h

This is of course incorrect, as the transcript itself reveals. The seizure began at 1200 hours, making eight hours and thirty minutes in which "to act"—more than a third of a day. In eight hours, a destroyer could have traveled in excess of two hundred miles. We need not even consider how far a military jet could fly during that time. It should also be noted that the "time to act" is calculated from 1330. Why, particularly when "seizure" was said to have occurred at 1435? In this "analysis," what significance is the Navy attaching to 1330? They don't say. I believe we all know now.

Despite the fact the Navy says *Pueblo* was moored at the pier at 8:30 P.M., Steve Harris manages to write on page 13 of his book: "By five o'clock on that dismal January 23, 1968, we were moored to a pier in an alien and hostile land." Five o'clock fits Bucher's estimates, for he writes (p. 217): "It was about two and a half to three hours after the seizure that I saw outside lights flashing through the porthole. . . . I could feel the ship . . . begin berthing maneuvers. Old *Pueblo* showed her resentment over foreign handling by banging hard against a dock." No! Two and a half to three hours makes it five or five-thirty. There could have been no "outside lights flashing through the porthole" at that time. As the Navy informs us, it wasn't dark until six minutes after six. And it *was* dark when the ship arrived. There is a photograph showing the men being led off *Pueblo* in darkness.

Why write five o'clock when the fact of eight-thirty is incontrovertible? It is a puzzle. I can only conclude that something happened out there in Choson Bay which had to be concealed by collapsing six or seven hours of time into two or three.

Beginning with the *known* again, we may state as fact that there *was* a cover story. At risk to the patience and eyeballs of the reader, 186 pages have been spent unraveling it. The public cover story began on the first day of hearings by the Court of Inquiry when Bucher said *Pueblo* had no destruct mechanisms and the crew had to destroy top secret gear with hammers. It continued through suppression of the radio transcript and by ignoring the sworn testimony of enlisted men which contradicted their officers. We have encountered a bewildering variety of discrepancies, omissions, contradictions, and impossibilities in written accounts, no two of which are alike. We have heard enough "mistakes" and "can't remembers" to last a lifetime.

Why tell a cover story, and such a poorly conceived and far-fetched one at that? (At one point I suggested to informants that the cover story was ridiculous, that a sixth grade child could have done better. Their answer: "The problem is Need to Know. The censors weren't permitted to know what had really happened. They knew they were covering up something but didn't know what.") There can be only one answer. A cover story is told to conceal something.

What? Again we begin with the *known* revealed by the men of *Pueblo* in Ed Brandt's book. Those who first boarded *Pueblo* wore Red Chinese uniforms. Unless a person is willing to believe that for some inconceivable reason North Koreans dressed up in Red Chinese uniforms, then it must be assumed the boarders were indeed Red Chinese. And the men of *Pueblo* also saw, before being blindfolded, a large warship "coming fast" which they knew was not American. Since the Red Chinese were already aboard and had armed *Pueblo* to defend it, that warship, by a process of elimination, had to be Soviet.

To my knowledge no one has ever hinted at, suggested, or even breathed a misspoken syllable about Soviet and Chinese participation in the *Pueblo* seizure. The only mention of the Soviet Union is that the United States asked the Soviets to help gain release of the crew and received a "chilly" negative in reply. There is even less mention of the Red Chinese. (We will see shortly that President Johnson suspected the Soviet Union had prior knowledge of the seizure.)

Isn't that strange? North Korea was closely allied with both Red China and the Soviet Union. Indeed, North Korea was created by the Soviets in the wake of World War II. From the Korean War, it owes its existence to Red China. It may be said that North Korea is a puppet regime for Red China and the Soviet Union and indeed exists only by sufferance of both nations.

Looking back with the hindsight of twenty years, it is hard to believe that anyone ever conceived that North Korea acted alone in seizing *Pueblo*. There just had to be *some* involvement by Red China or the USSR.

And there was. A more accurate news story would have read: "The North Koreans, aided by Red Chinese foot soldiers and Soviet warships, today seized the USS *Pueblo* off Wonsan, North Korea." That "lead" was never written on any story. Instead, the world was given an elaborate cover story which never mentioned Red Chinese and Russian involvement.

Why? In search of answers, return to Choson Bay a little after 2 P.M. on January 23, 1968. There floats a Soviet warship, the muzzles of its guns still smoking from the shells which it dispatched into the helpless *Pueblo*, a United States Navy vessel. In a nuclear age, this is a monstrously serious situation. It is a crisis of the first magnitude.

There has been an act of war. Nobody really intended for it to happen. And nobody wants the war. But there it is, smoking guns and dead and wounded Americans. What can be done about it? There really are only two choices: either start the missiles flying or find some way to cover it up. Thank God they chose the latter.

There is no one to tell us how it was done. Oh, of course, *there is*, but it is hard to believe that even after twenty years anyone will relate the details. I can only speculate that it was crisis time in Washington, Moscow, and Peking. I imagine that for the NSA and the Pentagon the first priority was to ground every plane and moor every ship that might possibly rescue *Pueblo*. If a single U.S. jet had appeared and attacked the Soviet warship, the situation would obviously have gotten out of hand and we might all be living in caves right now.

Then, I suspect, the United States had to send a very clear message to Moscow and Peking that it wasn't going to do a blessed thing about it. This could have been done rather easily, by referring only to North Korean involvement. *Pueblo* was fired upon and seized by *North Koreans*. If no mention is made of Red Chinese or Soviets, even the most obtuse among them must have gotten the message: Blame it on the North Koreans.

(Some provocative questions must be asked, if only in a vain hope for eventual answers. What did the KGB tell Leonid Brezhnev and the other visible Soviet leaders in the Kremlin? Did the KGB tell the Politburo that a Soviet vessel had fired on *Pueblo*, or did they cover it up as the NSA did?

It seems to me that the Soviet Union could have said it fired on *Pueblo*, concocting some story to justify the action. They might even have achieved some propaganda value by making the United States look warlike, attempting to provoke armed conflict. But the Soviet Union said nothing, nor did the Chinese.

Question: Did the NSA and the KGB collaborate in the cover-up of the *Pueblo* incident? It can have been no more difficult for the KGB to silence those who did the shooting than it was for the NSA to silence those who were shot at. Did the KGB want to conceal its activities from the Kremlin just as the NSA did from the White House, Pentagon, and Congress? To have collaborated is not even an intimation that the NSA is disloyal in any way to this country—or the KGB to the Soviet Union, for that matter. The two intelligence agencies have often reached accords; for example, to exchange captured agents. Like all super-secret agencies, their first priority is to maintain their own secrecy, their own integrity. When that is threatened, the needs of the governments they serve become secondary.

Question: To what extent is the long-standing, planet-threatening and hugely costly antipathy between the Soviet Union and the United States the result of the intelligence activities of both nations? I ask the question because of the oft-repeated statements by my informants that the intelligence wars between the KGB and the NSA are a "game," played endlessly, using nearly identical methods, for no conceivable purpose other than continuation of the game and the sense of power, the "thrill" those in charge of the game receive. What is the "prize" for the winner of the game? I'm told he gets to play again.)

But regardless of who was told what in the Soviet Union and China, there must have been a great sigh of relief in Moscow and Peking. It can't have been hard for the Soviets and the Chinese to persuade the North Koreans to "accept delivery" of *Pueblo* and imprison the crew. I'm sure solemn promises of mutual aid were made in case the United States attacked North Korea to recover the ship and crew. Captivity was necessary, for both the Chinese and Soviets had to try to find out exactly how much the men of *Pueblo* knew about the intercepted message. And the North Koreans were eager to obtain confessions and apologies all around, so as to have at least the appearance of independence and viable nationhood.

Did the NSA also want the captivity as part of the cover-up? I don't know, but it is not unreasonable to speculate that the NSA needed time to concoct the cover story and arrange for the crew to be sequestered and silenced upon its return. It seems to me that if the North Koreans had promptly released the ship and crew and it had sailed back to Japan, blabbing about Chinese uniforms, suspected Soviet ships, secret orders, and a whole lot more, then the cover story would have been impossible. The NSA and the Navy would have been asked a lot of embarrassing questions. Time was needed to find out what exactly had happened and what the men of *Pueblo* actually knew, and to concoct the cover story. I have evidence that the crewmen were contacted in captivity by at least one NSA operative. Murphy also declares that their activities while in captivity were known to American authorities at the time.

While these high-level decisions were being made in Moscow and Peking—and it had to take some time—my guess is that Colonel Scar and other North Korean technicians searched the SOD-Hut aboard *Pueblo* and informed both the Chinese and the Russians that there wasn't any message there, not even an intact reel of magnetic tape containing intercept. That's what they were looking for. I doubt if anyone of importance was fooled by the U.S. "confetti."

There is no one to tell us, so I don't know how long the Soviet warship remained at the scene. But eventually it left. It would be interesting to know whether the Russians gave the captain a medal—or command of an ice floe in northern Siberia.

My guess is that it was the latter, for the Soviet Navy needed a scapegoat just as much as the U.S. Navy did. The *Pueblo* surrender was a disaster for Soviet intelligence. They were "had" by U.S. intelligence—royally. Believing an interception of one of their own messages was aboard *Pueblo*, a warship was sent under orders to stop and search *Pueblo* and get the message back. The Soviet Navy vessel arrived too late. Red Chinese had already seized the vessel and were headed for Wonsan. At a stupendous risk of war with the United States, the Soviet captain opened fire. He sent Colonel Scar aboard to search—and discovered that if there ever had been such a message, it was no more.

The damage to the Soviet KGB—whose head by this time was a fellow named Yuri Andropov—was awesome. The very act of shelling *Pueblo* confirmed to the Red Chinese, as no words ever could, the accuracy of what they believed. There had been a message and the Soviets were prepared to stop at nothing to prevent the Chinese from knowing about it. The act of shelling *Pueblo* warned the Chinese of their peril. They took defensive measures. The element of surprise gone, the Soviets were forced to scrap their plans for invasion. Even the North Koreans had to be aware of what their northern neighbor was doing to them.

More damage to the KGB. If the United States had intercepted their message—and again, the very act of shelling *Pueblo* confirmed its accuracy—then the KGB's highest-level codes had been broken and the American NSA was privy to knowledge about its agents, methods, and plans. A whole lot more than codes would have to be changed. I suspect that ice floe in Siberia became well populated.

Again, all this is speculation on my part. I don't know what happened during the six or seven hours before *Pueblo* reached Wonsan, and without access to information buried deep within the bowels of the National Security Agency, I have no way to learn. There are few who do have such access.

I do not sit in judgment on the NSA. The *Pueblo* surrender was a covert U.S. intelligence operation, performed I'm sure for good and sufficient reasons that were appropriate to national security. I believe, for reasons already stated, that the covert operation was aimed at thwarting Soviet plans to invade Communist China and subvert North Korea. A potential nuclear conflict between the USSR and Communist China bore such a risk to world peace—could the United States have stayed out of such a war?—that any action to prevent even the remotest possibility of it was surely justified.

The *Pueblo* surrender was brilliantly successful, yet things went awry. I do not know if the NSA, which controlled the movements and uses of

Pueblo, intended for the ship to be captured. Perhaps not, but they surely did put it in a position and make it operate under orders which made it highly likely it would be stopped, boarded, and searched. And, of course, it *was* seized, the crew imprisoned.

I find it impossible to believe that the NSA intended for the Soviets to fire upon *Pueblo*. That just had to be a miscalculation. After it happened, the NSA had no choice but to concoct the cover story to conceal the true events. Why? That is the third key question of this chapter.

The ostensible answer is that the role of Red China and the Soviet Union had to be concealed to prevent a war among the three superpowers. There is some justification for this. After all, the United States had magnified its involvement in Vietnam after the North Vietnamese fired upon American destroyers in the Gulf of Tonkin in 1964. What would have happened if President Johnson had announced that the Red Chinese had seized *Pueblo* and the Soviet Union had fired upon it, causing American casualties? Doubtlessly there would have been outrage at home and calls for war. But surely cooler heads would have prevailed—just as they did when we believed the North Koreans had acted alone. We didn't attack North Korea, surely a more viable target than either China or Russia.

Indeed, announcing the participation of Red China and the Soviet Union might have offered a great advantage to the United States. It would have confirmed to American public opinion that China and the USSR were a serious threat, actively hostile to the United States. Surely greater expenditures for national defense would have been approved and opposition to the war in Vietnam defused. None of this happened.

Why the cover-up of Red Chinese and Soviet participation in the *Pueblo* seizure? One possibility is that the NSA wanted to keep those two nations from knowing exactly what had happened to maximize its great gains from the covert operation. Telling the full truth might have provided too much information to those countries about the intelligence capabilities and methods of the NSA.

Perhaps, but surely the Soviet KGB knew it had been "had." Their chilly response to American entreaties for help in gaining release of the crew indicates they were extremely unhappy with events. They must have realized very quickly what had happened—the snooping *Pueblo*, leaked messages about non-existent tapes. They fell for it and were had. If the United States had reported Chinese and Soviet involvement, it would have provided them with little information they didn't already know. That we had the capacity to intercept and decode Soviet messages—and they ours—was hardly a secret to them.

Again, why the cover-up? Another possibility is that the cover-up was for domestic consumption. Knowledge of the true events would surely have led high government officials and members of Congress to ask some extremely difficult and probing questions about the role of the NSA in American life. This had to be prevented. We will consider this matter in the next chapter.

The men of *Pueblo* didn't realize it at the time—indeed, they may not until they read this—but just think of what they accomplished through their sacrifice:

• Red China was warned of Soviet intentions. A potentially planet-destroying war between Red China and the Soviet Union was averted. Chinese hostility toward the United States lessened and rapprochement began. Four years and one month after the *Pueblo* surrender Richard Nixon was making rice wine toasts in Peking.

• Its schemes in the Far East thwarted, the KGB in disarray—it would take years for the KGB to replace agents, methods, and plans—the Soviet Union launched a policy of détente with the West, the ramifications of which still reverberate throughout the world.

The *Pueblo* surrender was perhaps the greatest intelligence coup of modern times. It changed the world in which we all live.

There were negatives. Young Duane Hodges lost his life. Three sailors were seriously wounded. Eighty-two men suffered harsh captivity. Commander Bucher, and to a lesser extent all the men, endured a certain amount of calumny—that whispered word, "coward"—and were required to mouth an absurd cover story. On the international scene, the *Pueblo* surrender doomed Czechoslovakia. When those valiant people made their bid for freedom in the summer of 1968, the Soviet Union didn't hesitate. Their tanks rolled. Afghanistan faced a similar fate a decade later.

From the standpoint of the NSA, all this was a minuscule price to pay for what was gained. Again, I do not sit in judgment on them. That is for others to do. All I've tried to do is to figure out what happened to the men of *Pueblo* and to offer them the recognition they deserve—and to set the historical record straight.

The *Pueblo* surrender was a brilliant success for the NSA. It changed the world. Doubtlessly, the agency is proud of it, as they well might be.

But there is one element to the *Pueblo* surrender that ought to give Americans, indeed the whole world, cause for concern. We consider this in the last chapter.

13

AN AWESOME GRANT OF POWER

Travel back in time to nine o'clock on the morning of December 23, 1968. United States Maj. Gen. Gilbert H. Woodward takes a seat at a round table at Panmunjom, the place where the armistice ending the Korean War was signed in 1953. He nods at his North Korean counterpart, Maj. Gen. Pak Chung Kuk, and begins to read a statement.

"The position of the United States Government with regard to the *Pueblo* . . . has been that the ship was not engaged in illegal activity, that there is no convincing evidence that the ship at any time intruded into the territorial waters claimed by North Korea, and that we could not apologize for actions which we did not believe took place. The document which I am going to sign was prepared by the North Koreans and is at variance with the above position. My signature will not and cannot alter the facts. I will sign the document to free the crew and only to free the crew."

Armbrister (whose description of events I am using) writes that "Pak shuffled some papers. Woodward glanced down at the North Korean document." It read:

"The Government of the United States of America, acknowledging the validity of the confessions of the crew of the USS 'Pueblo' and of the documents of evidence produced by the representative of the Government of the Democratic People's Republic of Korea to the effect that the ship, which was seized by the self-defense measures of the naval vessels of the Korean People's Army in the territorial waters of the Democratic People's Republic of Korea on January 23, 1968, had illegally intruded into the territorial waters of the Democratic People's Republic of Korea on many occasions and conducted espionage activities of spying out important military and state secrets of the Democratic People's Republic of Korea,

"Shoulders full responsibility and solemnly apologizes for the grave acts of espionage committed by the U.S. ship against the Democratic People's Republic of Korea,

"And gives firm assurance that no U.S. ship will intrude again in the future into the territorial waters of the Democratic People's Republic of Korea.

"Meanwhile, the Government of the United States of America earnestly requests the Government of the Democratic People's Republic of Korea to deal leniently with the former crew members of the USS 'Pueblo' confiscated by the Democratic People's Republic of Korea side, taking into consideration the fact that these crew members have confessed honestly to their crimes and petitioned the Government of the Democratic People's Republic for leniency.

"Simultaneous with the signing of this document, the undersigned acknowledges receipt of 82 former crew members of the USS 'Pueblo' and one corpse.

"On behalf of the Government of the United States of America,

Gilbert H. Woodward,
Major General, United States Army
23 Dec., 1968."

Armbrister then tells what happened: "He [Woodward] signed his name and handed the paper across the table.

"Suddenly, Pak announced that he could not release the crew. The United States had 'insulted the entire Korean people' by its premature disclosure of a settlement. Therefore, the return would have to be 'renegotiated.'

"'Do you now repudiate the agreement we made just yesterday? I will repeat that agreement for your benefit.' And Woodward did.

"'You've twisted my words,' Pak replied.

"Woodward glared at the North Korean contemptuously. He could not believe that Pak was serious. There had to be some way to test his intention. 'I felt like saying, "What the hell are you trying to prove?" he remembers. 'I decided to give him the needle instead. I said, "Is there anything I can do to assist you? If you are having administrative delays, if you cannot release the crew at eleven o'clock, then eleven-thirty would be acceptable. But I will need a receipt."

"Silence. The North Korean saw that his cruel ploy wasn't succeeding.

Finally, he reached for the paper and filled in the time of return: eleven-thirty. Then he tossed it across the table."

Thus were the men of *Pueblo* held captive a half hour longer.

This scene at Panmunjom is unsettling to an American. Frankly, it isn't pleasant to think about, let alone write. But we live in an uncertain world. We are at constant risk of miscalculation in a nuclear age. We are best served, not by an ostrich mentality, but by facing our problems with realism.

What really happened at Panmunjom on December 23, 1968? What did major generals Woodward and Pak know about the *Pueblo* seizure? Did they know the incident was a covert operation by the intelligence agencies of the United States, Soviet Union, and Red China? Did they know of Red Chinese and Soviet involvement in the seizure? Did they have any idea that North Korean participation was minor and done at the command of Red China and the Soviet Union? Did either man have any idea that he wasn't telling the truth?

Our concern here is not Pak, but Woodward. His actions and words described above, as well as those uttered in other interviews, suggest he sincerely believed *Pueblo* was seized by the North Koreans in an act of piracy. His outrage seems genuine. Since there is not a shred of evidence that General Woodward is anything other than a truthful and honorable man, we have to assume he sincerely believed he was uttering the truth.

But he wasn't. Belief in truth does not create truth. Conviction, no matter how fervently believed, is not truth. And since the facts of the *Pueblo* seizure were buried deep within the bowels of the NSA, General Woodward had no capacity to learn the truth and therefore cannot even be said to be intellectually dishonest.

My point is this: Whether General Woodward knew it or not, the United States was not telling the truth at Panmunjom, and at least some in the North Korean government knew it. The Soviets knew it and so did the Chinese. Because of the *Pueblo* incident—if nothing else—we have a reputation as liars, very clever liars because our representatives, such as General Woodward, sincerely believe they are telling the truth and thus can lie with total conviction. One immediately thinks of Adlai Stevenson, an honorable man, twice candidate for President and then ambassador to the United Nations, standing before that body to passionately deny that U.S. planes were involved in the Bay of Pigs—then being personally destroyed when he discovered shortly thereafter that our planes were involved.

Because of *Pueblo*, the Bay of Pigs (and how many other incidents?), when our representatives sit down with those of other nations to discuss arms limitation or any type of international accord, they carry with them a certain reputation—the same reputation we ascribe to the Soviets—which surely makes it difficult to negotiate those agreements which would encourage world peace and prosperity. To put the matter in the frankest terms, trust is a rare commodity among people who perceive one another as liars.

In this sense, *Pueblo* added to our international difficulties.

Question: If General Woodward, the U.S. representative at Panmunjom, was not fully informed about the *Pueblo* seizure, who else was likewise uninformed? In search of an answer let's borrow that famous question Sen. (later Majority Leader) Howard H. Baker, Jr., of Tennessee repeatedly asked during the Watergate hearings in the summer of 1973: "What did he know and when did he know it?" Senator Baker was trying to discover what President Nixon knew about the Watergate break-in and when he knew it. (Murphy reports in his book that shortly after the Court of Inquiry, he was summoned to the White House, where he spent several hours briefing aides to Richard Nixon on the *Pueblo* incident. Did he tell them something different than he had the Court of Inquiry? His book, written later, was certainly at variance with his testimony. No other crewman reports receiving a White House summons, but it is difficult to believe Murphy was the only one questioned. Why did the newly inaugurated Mr. Nixon conduct an independent investigation into the *Pueblo* seizure immediately after the Navy's? Murphy does not say.)

What did members of Congress know about the *Pueblo* seizure and when did they know it? Virtually every senator and representative issued statements following the seizure. They varied from outrage and demands for immediate war to words of caution (such as Senator Kennedy's) suggesting we first learn what really happened during the seizure. But all the statements have two things in common. Every member of Congress was obviously surprised by the seizure, and everyone believed the North Koreans had seized the ship; they made no reference to participation by Red China and the Soviet Union.

We may safely conclude that members of Congress were either not informed of the true events of the seizure or that, to a person, they joined in the cover-up. I have no doubt the former is correct.

Who did know and when did he know it? How about Defense Secretary McNamara and Secretary of State Rusk? As reported in Chapter One, both men told the press they had not known of the *Pueblo* mission but "their representatives" had. They declined to identify their representatives. It must be assumed this is correct. Secretaries McNamara and Rusk, the two highest ranking members of the Cabinet with direct responsibility for war and peace, did not know in advance of the *Pueblo* mission. It is also to be assumed that Secretaries McNamara and Rusk were extremely perturbed that "their representatives" had not informed them that *Pueblo* was on a high risk mission acting under orders which made the ship likely to be boarded. That failure to inform them left both officials unprepared for the international incident and the risk of war that followed.

How about the White House? What did President Johnson know about the *Pueblo* seizure and when did he know it? In *The Vantage Point,* President Johnson writes that he was first informed of the seizure via a phone call from the White House Situation Room, at 2:24 A.M. on January 23. The initial Pentagon announcement said *Pueblo* was seized at 11:45 P.M. (January 22) Washington time, which was 1345 aboard *Pueblo* in Korean waters. Thus, President Johnson was apprised of the attack upon and loss of one Navy vessel under his command two hours and thirty-nine minutes after the event. No one was in a great hurry to tell him.

Trevor Armbrister sought to trace who knew what about *Pueblo* and when. His book makes informative reading. He reports that the first of *Pueblo*'s Critic messages—those Pinnacle messages which were upgraded to Critic in Japan—arrived at the Defense Intelligence Agency in the Pentagon "shortly before midnight." It arrived at the State Department and at the White House at about the same time, where Andrew J. "Bud" Denner received it. He told Armbrister the time and location were garbled. "All we got out of it was the name of the ship, *Pueblo*. Normally, if there's a garble on a critic, you'll get a follow-up in one or two minutes. It didn't happen in this case." Denner also told Armbrister he tried to find out "what type of ship this was." At first he didn't have much luck. "I couldn't find any people in the Pentagon who'd ever heard of *Pueblo*," he said to Armbrister.

President Johnson was annoyed that he was not informed of the seizure until more than two and a half hours after it occurred. Armbrister quotes Arthur J. McCafferty, White House aide: "He [Johnson] was concerned about the safety of the men, and he was mad as hell. One time he asked me, 'Why wasn't I called immediately [when the first critic arrived]? You know you can call me anytime. I was still awake.' And the only answer I could give him was, 'Mr. President, we could have called you and said, "Sir, here's what we have. But please don't ask questions. We just don't know the answers."' "

In *The Vantage Point*, President Johnson discusses the *Pueblo* seizure with extreme brevity. Most illuminating is this paragraph (p. 535): "There was another reason that persuaded us that the seizure was not an impulsive act. As soon as I learned that the *Pueblo* had been seized, I instructed Ambassador Llewellyn Thompson in Moscow to ask Soviet officials for assistance in obtaining the release of the ship and the crew. Ambassador Thompson received the Soviet reply almost immediately, a very negative and chilly response. The Soviets could scarcely have obtained the necessary information regarding the incident from the North Koreans, conferred about it, and taken a position so quickly without prior information.

"We believed that the capture of the *Pueblo* was premeditated. But what did the North Koreans hope to accomplish?" Mr. Johnson goes on to suggest the North Koreans hoped to force removal of South Korean troops from Vietnam.

This paragraph from Mr. Johnson's memoirs suggests that he was aware that the Soviet Union had "prior information" about the seizure, but he does not suggest that the Soviet Union or Red China actually participated in the seizure. He blames it entirely on the North Koreans. What did Mr. Johnson actually know? Something other than he wrote in his memoirs? Regrettably, he is not alive to tell us.

The person most responsible for briefing Mr. Johnson about the *Pueblo* seizure was Walt W. Rostow, his national security adviser. Armbrister interviewed Rostow and gives this report (pp. 237-8): "Rostow had called the President shortly after two o'clock [in the morning] to give him an 'advisory'; he hadn't been able to supply too many details.

"For there were still so many unanswered questions. The ship had maintained radio silence for a full ten days, had not submitted position reports until just prior to the incident. Had she at any time violated waters claimed by North Korea? This was one of the first questions the President had asked. And Rostow hadn't been able to say. *It was difficult enough from reading those confused messages to ascertain Pueblo's position at the time of boarding* [emphasis mine]. But why hadn't she made a run for it? Why hadn't she fought back? Throughout the night, *Pentagon aides had insisted she carried destruct devices* [emphasis mine]. So why was Bucher saying that destruction had been 'ineffective,' that several publications would be 'compromised'? Which ones? There was no sense trying to guess about that. Already, the word had gone out to United States posts around the world: Change codes immediately. Rostow trimmed the report to one page and sent it upstairs."

Armbrister reports that McNamara left his home and went to the Pentagon to meet with military and civilian advisers. "' There was a sort of stunned silence,' remembers Richard C. Steadman, the Deputy Assistant Secretary of Defense for International Security Affairs. '*Pueblo* was in port. Nobody really knew what had happened or what to do about it. He [McNamara] told us to reconstruct the incident, prepare a chronology of events.'"

Stunned silence among the nation's top defense officials! Nobody knew where *Pueblo* was, what had happened, or what to do about it!

There is more. Four-star Admiral John J. Hyland, commander in chief, Pacific Fleet, was hosting a dinner party in Hawaii when he learned of *Pueblo*. He later told Armbrister: "*Pueblo*'s presence in the Sea of Japan was in my consciousness. I knew she was there, but if someone had come in before all this happened and asked me, 'Where is she now?' I'm not certain I'd have been able to say."

Vice Adm. William F. "Bush" Bringle, commander of the Seventh Fleet, was aboard the USS *Providence* in the Gulf of Tonkin. Armbrister writes (p. 217): "The white-haired admiral was stunned by the news. He kept rubbing his hands against the sides of his head. *Pueblo* was only one of hundreds of ships which at one time or another fell under his operational control. He was 'not personally aware of the specifics of [her] mission,' and did not know that she was operating off Wonsan. Incredibly, instead of dispatching a copy of her sail order to him through normal communications channels, COMNAVFORJAPAN had relied on the Armed Forces Courier Service. That sail order wouldn't arrive for another four days."

Many, many other sources could be quoted, but the pattern is clear. Vice admirals and full admirals in charge of fleets of ships, the secretary of defense, the national security adviser to the President are all "stunned" and surprised by the *Pueblo* seizure. If they had even heard of the ship, they didn't know where it was or what it was doing.

It is understandable, perhaps, that persons of such high rank would be unaware of the activities of the small, obscure *Pueblo*. But surely lower-ranking officers with direct operational control knew where *Pueblo* was and what it was doing? Not exactly.

In a superior job of reporting, Trevor Armbrister traces (pp. 61-6) the actions of Navy and Air Force officers in Japan as the distress calls arrived from *Pueblo*. He describes a scene of confusion and a certain amount of disarray. Key personnel were out to lunch or involved in conferences. Security was so tight around *Pueblo* and its mission that key intelligence officers had difficulty even informing commanders of the attack. When Lt. Ed Brookes sought to inform Naval Operations in Japan of the attack, he "looked for someone who possessed a high enough security clearance to hand-carry the message." Finally he discovered Lt. Anthony J. Celebrezze, now attorney general of Ohio.

Rear Adm. Frank L. Johnson, commander of naval forces in Japan, was in Tokyo to give the welcoming address at the annual Pacific Command Tropical Cyclone conference in the Sanno Hotel. When his chief of staff, Capt. Forrest A. "Buster" Pease, tried to reach him there, he did so on an insecure phone and therefore "had to talk in riddles." Pease told the admiral, "Looks like *Pueblo*'s had the course. She may be gone." Johnson didn't understand, thinking *Pueblo* was caught in a storm or had engine failure. He asked if Sea-Air Rescue units had been alerted. Pease said that wouldn't be sufficient and suggested his admiral return to Yokosuka. The Navy had no helicopters available to fly him back. The Army thought it might have one in about an hour.

When, at close to 1400 hours, Navy officers sought to inform the Air Force of *Pueblo*'s seizure, they reached air officers who had never heard of *Pueblo* or Ichthyic One—and indeed believed this was just another mock alert and that "the Navy was overdoing it this time." (All quotes are from Armbrister.)

Coming along twenty years later, one is left with several impressions. First, the reactions of Navy and Air Force personnel to *Pueblo*'s plight hardly constituted the finest hour of U.S. defense forces.

Second, no Navy officers with direct authority over *Pueblo* had any inkling the ship was in danger. Its first messages were filed on the "interest board." Intelligence and operations personnel were out to lunch, thinking of shopping for a hibachi, reading magazines, or nibbling a pork chop sandwich brought from home. Admiral Johnson was giving an address in Tokyo. Captain Pease, the chief of staff, was entertaining two Japanese admirals making a courtesy call. The state of mind of these officers was best expressed by Admiral Johnson in testimony before the Naval Court of Inquiry: "I would like to assure the court and Commander Bucher and the crew that, had I been convinced that ship was in jeopardy, I would never have sent the ship on that mission without proper protection." He cited sixteen other missions by ELINT ships, including two other visits to North Korea. There had been no trouble. Then he testified, "If you were a betting man, the odds a bookmaker would have given you on that happening [the seizure]—the odds would have been so fantastic that not even a man as rich as Howard Hughes could pay off."

Third, ignorance about *Pueblo* extended throughout the chain of command. The vice admiral commanding the Seventh Fleet was "not personally aware" of *Pueblo*'s mission or that it was operating off Wonsan. A four-star admiral in charge of the Pacific Fleet was vaguely aware *Pueblo* was in the Sea of Japan but was not "certain" just where. The Pentagon official in charge of international security affairs thought *Pueblo* was in port. The secretary of defense is "stunned" and wants more information. The national security adviser to President Johnson reads "confused messages" and desperately tries to gain information to pass on to the chief executive and commander in chief.

But *somebody* knew where *Pueblo* was and what its mission was. Somebody drafted the orders that Bucher followed "to the letter," remaining on station to "test" the reactions of North Korean ships at battle stations. Somebody gave orders to the CTs that made them "hope for" the "presence of an enemy ship." Somebody kept *Pueblo* in the area where it had been detected the day before. Somebody provoked the *Pueblo* crewmen to give the finger because they had been "had."

That *somebody* was the National Security Agency. The NSA controlled *Pueblo* and all other ELINT ships. It trained CTs and issued security clearances to them. It issued orders telling *Pueblo* where to go and what type of signals to monitor. It was in charge of communications to and from the ship. It reduced Navy personnel to "seagoing chauffeurs," as Bamford said in *The Puzzle Palace,* and "taxi drivers," as Murphy informed us.

Therefore, to understand the *Pueblo* surrender, we need to look at the National Security Agency. That is not an easy task. The NSA was formed in November 1952 by Executive Order of President Harry Truman. That order has remained highly classified for over thirty years; thus, the exact nature of the agency and what it is empowered to do—other than some involvement with national security—has never been publicly known.

In 1952 and for some years thereafter hardly anyone, certainly not the public, knew the agency existed. The index of the New York *Times,* for example, lists no news report on the agency's formation. For years the agency was not listed in any government directory. Nor was it included in the federal budget.

The first dent in the agency's armor of secrecy came in 1967 with publication of David Kahn's *The Codebreakers.* He devoted a long chapter to the agency, providing some of its history, identifying directors, and informing the public about some of its functions, such as interception of all electronic transmissions and its codebreaking and codemaking activities. Kahn's book remained just about the only source of information about the agency until 1982 when James Bamford published *The Puzzle Palace*, which offered a great deal of previously unknown information.

The aura of non-existence fostered at the agency's outset soon became difficult to maintain. An immense headquarters was built for it at Fort George G. Meade in Maryland, outside of Washington. It was a structure nine stories high with the longest (980 feet) unobstructed corridor in the country. Many thousands of people were employed. Chances are the agency parking lot was visible from the moon. (On page 4, Bamford calculates the agency controlled 68,203 people in 1968, "more than all of the employees of the rest of the intelligence community put together." He says the number of agency employees was down from the 95,000 employed during the Vietnam War—when *Pueblo* was seized.)

After a few years, claiming non-existence for the agency was like trying to hide an elephant in the White House rose garden. So the agency went public—sort of. Someone concocted a statement about its activities which was a model for saying absolutely nothing: "The National Security Agency performs highly specialized technical and coordinating functions relating to national security." (That priceless sentence of gobbledegook was used for many years, but it has been replaced today. The agency listing in the *U.S. Government Manual*, published by the *Federal Register*, says it is "responsible for centralized coordination, direction and performance of highly specialized technical functions in support of U.S. Government activities and to protect U.S. Communications and produce foreign intelligence information." That, I submit, does not tell much more than the first statement. The full listing for the agency is somewhat longer and just as meaningless.)

Since its existence was now admitted, the agency had to find a place in those nice organizational charts bureaucrats are fond of drawing. So, the agency became part of the Department of Defense. It was said in 1965 the agency was headed by a director who reported to an assistant secretary of defense who served as deputy director of defense for research and engineering. This individual supposedly reported to the secretary of defense, who sat on the National Security Council along with the President, vice president, secretary of state, and director of the Office of Emergency Planning, which handled civil defense and civil mobilization. The organizational charts also showed the agency as parent organization of the CIA (Central Intelligence Agency). The CIA was famous, or maybe infamous, the world over. Its parent organization was so shrouded in secrecy it was all but unknown. (This organizational structure has since been changed. Charts in the *U.S. Government Manual* show the NSA is still part of the Department of Defense, but its director reports directly to the secretary of defense and his deputy. There is no link to the National Security Council, nor is the CIA shown to be subsidiary to the NSA. Just how limited DOD control of NSA is was revealed by Caspar Weinberger, the secretary of defense during the Iran-*contra* hearings. He held up and read from an NSA document, explaining that he wasn't supposed to see it but had.)

There can be no doubt the agency's place in organizational charts was meaningless. An agency director let the cat out of the bag when he said (as quoted by Kahn) that his organization was "within but not part of the Defense Department." In other words, it was autonomous, operating alone, so deeply secret its budget wasn't even included in the Defense Department's.

How this was managed was explained by Kahn in *The Codebreakers* (p. 689): "Among the agency's deep secrets is its annual budget. [It] does not appear in the federal budget. All its funds, like those of the C.I.A., are cunningly concealed by adding a few million dollars to each of several line items in other parts of the budget. The chiefs of the agencies whose budget figures are thus padded know only that the money is for a classified project, but in many cases Congress is told in executive sessions what the figures are for these projects. The secretary of defense can legally shift funds from one unit to another, within certain limits. Unlike the C.I.A., N.S.A.'s finances are audited by the Government Accounting Office. The results, however, have not been shown to Congress, G.A.O.'s boss." (This practice of hiding billions in secret funds among appropriations for other agencies doubtlessly accounts for some of the difficulties encountered in cutting the federal budget.)

If the agency's budget is unknown, there can be no doubt it is large— billions annually. And the agency has come to dominate the American intelligence community. Bamford charts the dwindling influence of the CIA in intelligence affairs, quoting the Senate Intelligence Committee as saying the director of the CIA "controls less than ten per cent of the combined national and tactical intelligence efforts." The committee said the CIA director was reduced to the role of an "interested critic." Despite this finding, the Senate committee and the nation's press continue to treat the CIA as the premier U.S. intelligence agency, both seeking information from it and blaming it for operations that go wrong. My informants describe the CIA as so controlled by the NSA, so manipulated by Need to Know, that it is little more than a front for NSA activities.

Even today it is difficult to comprehend the secrecy attending such a large organization as "No Such Agency" or "Never Say Anything," as residents of the nation's capital came to say its initials stood for. On page 688 of his book, David Kahn wrote: "The veil . . . thrown around the agency at its very birth has cloaked it to this day. N.S.A. is even more still, more secret and more grave than the C.I.A., whose basic functions are set forth in the 1947 law that created it. C.I.A. officials have occasionally issued statements to the press and have more often leaked favorable publicity. N.S.A. officials never have. The National Security Agency thus remains the most reticent and least known organ of the entire hush-hush American intelligence community."

The NSA is reticent indeed. Throughout its history it has rarely issued any public statement other than "No Comment." An exception occurred in the early 1980s when the agency director was Vice Adm. Bobby R. Inman—who as a then-commander in naval intelligence testified before the *Pueblo* Court of Inquiry. Inman appeared on television and was quoted in the press more than all his predecessors combined. He testified before Congress and gave public speeches and even the only formal, carefully proscribed press interview in the history of the agency. His knack for headline grabbing may have had nothing to do with it, but Admiral Inman was replaced in 1982 by Lt. Gen. Lincoln D. Faurier. He has kept a low profile.

General Faurier has since been replaced by Lt. Gen. William E. Odom. Since its founding in 1952, the NSA has had eleven directors, all lieutenant generals and vice admirals rotated among the Army, Air Force, and Navy. The average tenure has been a little over three years, suggesting they have hardly had time to become overly acquainted with the functions of the huge agency.

The July 4, 1983, issue of *Newsweek* printed a sidebar on the recently retired Admiral Inman as part of its cover article on supercomputers. *Newsweek* wrote of Inman: "By the time Inman resigned last year—partly to earn enough money to put his two sons through college, partly because *he disagreed with some covert-action schemes* [Emphasis mine]—his reputation had soared. . . . Inman's straight talk and lack of political deviousness made him a darling of Congress." If *Newsweek* is correct, it indicates that Admiral Inman was unable to control the activities of the agency he directed. The deputy director under both Inman and Faurier was Ann Z. Caracristi—since replaced by Charles R. Lord. He is the tenth deputy director of the agency.

No other names than those of the director and deputy director are listed.

There is no breakdown in the *Federal Register* or *Congressional Directory* of assistant directors, division chiefs, bureau heads, press officers, etc., as there is for other government agencies, such as the Defense Department. With the exception of the director and deputy director, the people who work for the NSA are utterly nameless and faceless. That is in compliance with a 1959 Act of Congress. Bamford commented on this as follows (pp. 88-9):

"Below the level of deputy director, NSA's organizational structure has always been one of the Agency's closest-guarded secrets. Unlike the CIA, which has never hidden most of its upper framework, the NSA quietly arranged to have Congress pass, in 1959, a statute forever sealing this information under a blanket of secrecy. Section 6 of Public Law 86-36 provides: 'Nothing in this Act or any other law . . . shall be construed to require the disclosure of the organization of any function of the National Security Agency, of any information with respect to the activities thereof, or of the names, title, salaries, or number of the persons employed by such Agency.' Thus, under the little-known law, NSA has the unusual authority virtually to deny its own existence."

My informants also offer information about the National Security Agency. They describe an organization unlike any other in our society: monolithic, all-powerful, extremely authoritarian, and utterly unknown and unknowable because it scrupulously applies the rules of Need to Know. Such an organization is so foreign to our thinking, so different from what we are accustomed to, that it is difficult even to comprehend it.

In search for understanding, return to the USS *Jamestown*. Anchored off Vietnam, it was a sort of "mother ship" or headquarters ship for the ELINT fleet in the area. The *Jamestown* was in a way the NSA in microcosm. There was a ship captain with the rank of commander. Like Bucher, he was a "taxi driver," taking the ship to where it was supposed to be. He was in charge of the operation of the ship, keeping it seaworthy and seeing that the complement was housed, fed, disciplined, and entertained during very dull duty.

He had virtually nothing to do with the seventy-five or so CTs who performed the real functions of the ship. Indeed, he had little knowledge of what they did. In charge of all these men and their operations was a communications officer, a Navy commander, with the extremely high NSA security clearance of Top Secret Category Three, Cryptographic Code Word Two.

Aboard the ship came two men wearing black uniforms, sans insignias of rank or specialty. They met with the communications officer in the ship's Space Two and exchanged "recognition signals" which told him only that they came from higher authority. He had no knowledge of who they were, where they came from (other than NSA), or what they were there for. But they were obviously his superiors and thereby took over command of the code machine from him. (I'm told he was miffed at first, but came to accept the two operatives.)

No one aboard ship knew who the two men were or where they came from, except that they were obviously in the Navy. Their identity was the subject of endless speculation aboard the ship. Most figured they were Naval Intelligence, which they were not. (I'm told one man came too close to the truth. The operatives arranged for his immediate transfer to Pensacola, Florida, where he could be watched. He probably didn't mind at all.) Both men held the rank of lieutenant. A phony record jacket was maintained giving various duty assignments. But the Navy didn't really know the names they were now using or what they were doing. They might be *in* the Navy, but they did not work *for* the Navy. They were NSA operatives of the highest rank, which is to say security classification. Very few persons within the NSA knew who they were or what they did—or even that they existed.

The extent of the deception about these two operatives is mind-boggling, considering the fact they were aboard a U.S. Navy vessel and not on some deep cover mission behind the Iron Curtain. The two operatives were there under aliases. Also aboard *Jamestown* were two men using as aliases the real names of the two operatives, although they didn't know that. Anyone in the KGB—or the Navy—checking up on the operatives under their real names would have discovered they were indeed aboard *Jamestown*. Only those weren't the right two men.

I can suggest a reason for all these machinations. In a brief conversation with a former government official about the *Pueblo* incident, he said the NSA is forbidden to hire operatives. If that is so, then the NSA circumvents that by using personnel from the military and, presumably, other government agencies as operatives. Again, the operatives were in the Navy but did not take orders from the Navy. They were, however, paid by the Navy and had a Navy record. Any link to the NSA could not be proved.

All this was made possible by codes. As Cryptographic Code Word Three agents they sent and received messages in codes which no one on the ship, no one in Southeast Asia, indeed very few in the NSA itself could read. Their transmissions in their own codes went unread until they reached high-ranking persons at the NSA who had the security clearance and the capacity to read Code Word Three messages from these specific agents. The reverse was also true. Thus, the very existence of the operatives and what they were doing was known to only a few people within the NSA. Because codes are so compartmentalized—the *Jamestown* operatives had no capacity to read codes used in Europe, Africa, or even somewhere else in Asia which they had no Need to Know about—it is conceivable that only a single person within the NSA knew what they were doing.

Understanding of how the NSA is organized is enhanced when it is realized that the two *Jamestown* operatives had no idea at all who their superior was. They couldn't even guess who read their Code Word Three messages and who sent them orders. They knew only that their contact was cleared for Code Word Three and knew the "address" which identified them. To their knowledge they had never met him and wouldn't know him* if they did.

When the black operative from *Jamestown* went to Washington to propose the scheme that became the *Pueblo* surrender, he did not go to the visible NSA headquarters at Fort George G. Meade, Maryland. He entered a vast underground complex near Washington, one of five such NSA facilities in the United States, where its most sensitive codemaking, codebreaking, and covert operations are conducted. The place is said to be impregnable and impenetrable. To enter, the *Jamestown* operative had to be authorized for entry and then pass through multiple elaborate security devices which assured his identity.

After passing through various cipher-locked doors, he entered a Space Two. There he met with a "debriefer," a thoroughly impersonal individual whom he did not know and would never meet again. Nor did the debriefer have any idea who he was speaking to. No notes were taken, no recordings made. The debriefer was trained to memorize the words spoken by the operative. The operative spoke mostly in code words that had no meaning to the debriefer. This person simply passed along the words until they reached someone to whom they had meaning. When the plan was approved and the operative returned, he met this time with a different person, called a "briefer," who passed on the orders through meaningless code words—meaningless to the briefer. (This description applies to the usual procedure when NSA operatives go to headquarters. Informants say that in the *Pueblo* case, because by its very nature the scheme could

---

*I write *him* because informants say the very highest security clearances are reserved for males. The NSA is not too big on the feminist movement.

not easily be reduced to code words, the *Jamestown* operative was probably debriefed by someone of extremely high rank within the NSA who possessed the same security classification he did. He may well have been their contact.)

All of this is exacting application of Need to Know. No one has any need to know anyone else so they don't. Identities are controlled through aliases and code names. Information, the lifeblood of the agency, is tightly compartmentalized and controlled through codes. Power and rank lie solely in security clearances and which codes a person has the capacity to read. Even then, a person of high security classification may spend his life knowing only top level messages from the Indian subcontinent, Scandinavia, East Africa, or some other part of the world and possess no information about what is happening elsewhere. He may be consulted for information about his area of expertise, but he will have no idea how that information may relate to anything else or what use is made of it. (Informants say that information is jealously guarded within the agency, for it is *what* you know and not *who* you know that leads to promotion and power.)

Thus, informants describe the NSA as an organization which is a hierarchy, a pyramid, but one based on security classification and access to encoded information.

Who is at the top of the hierarchy of information? Who runs the NSA? Informants state most emphatically that the agency is not run by the director and deputy director. They perform administrative and housekeeping functions, much as the captain of *Jamestown* did, or Bucher aboard *Pueblo,* but they have virtually no information about the covert intelligence operations of the agency. They are told only what they Need to Know to brief the President, cabinet officers, and other government and military leaders. Their ignorance is considered mandatory simply because they are the two people in the agency who are identified publicly. They are at risk of being seized by enemy agents and "chemically debriefed," which is to say forced to tell all they know. They are not permitted access to sensitive information involving national security. They can identify no one of importance. They are figureheads.

Informants state that no one knows, even within the agency, who runs it. But it is widely believed throughout the agency that the NSA is controlled by "The Committee." The group is believed to have five members because the NSA divides the world into five intelligence zones: North America, South America, Europe, Asia, and Africa. The persons who head each zone are believed to join together to form The Committee, which supervises all agency activities and both concocts and approves covert operations, such as the *Pueblo* surrender.

They meet in secret in the Space Three deep underground in the secret headquarters complex. It is said to be impregnable at ground zero and capable of sustaining the lives of its occupants for up to a year. There are no communications in or out. No notes or recordings are made. What is said there is known only to members of The Committee.

Who appoints The Committee? Informants state that no one does. They appoint themselves. NSA veterans, they have over the years accumulated and jealously guarded so much information about past and present world-wide intelligence that no decision can be made without their information and consultation. When one of them dies or retires, he is replaced by the next most knowledgeable person in the zone.

If this information is correct—and by its very nature it is unprovable—then the NSA is run by a group of nameless, faceless, wholly unidentified persons—not only to the public and the rest of government, but even within the NSA. According to this description of the NSA, if the President or a committee of Congress wished to summon these persons for questioning about their activities, they wouldn't know who to subpoena—or whether the people who showed up were the right people.

Return to the *Pueblo* surrender. We traced as best we can the knowledge of *Pueblo* and its mission through Navy lieutenants in Japan all the way to full admirals in Hawaii, a "stunned" secretary of defense, and a "confused" national security adviser to President Johnson. As we have seen, even Commander Bucher and others aboard *Pueblo* couldn't believe what was happening to them.

This is of profound importance. The organizational chart of the Pentagon in 1968 showed the director of NSA reporting to the assistant secretary of defense who reported to the secretary of defense who sat on the National Security Council whose other members were the President, vice president, secretary of state, and director of the Office of Emergency Planning. As we have seen, Defense Secretary McNamara was stunned by the seizure. Secretary of State Rusk didn't know of the *Pueblo* mission. President Johnson wasn't even informed of the seizure for two hours and thirty-nine minutes, principally because he would ask questions for which his national security adviser, Rostow, had no answers.

Clearly, the National Security Agency, which issued orders to *Pueblo* and controlled its mission, did not correctly inform the President, secretaries of defense and state, and other members of the National Security

Council—which supposedly had oversight of the NSA—of *Pueblo*'s mission *in advance,* of its orders to remain stationary under North Korean harassment, of the interest of the Red Chinese and Soviet Union in the ship, and much more. This lack of advance information extended from the White House down through fleet admirals to lieutenants with operational control of *Pueblo.*

Question: If national leaders and Navy officers were not told in advance of *Pueblo*'s mission, what were they told *after* the seizure? Were they told only that the North Koreans seized *Pueblo,* or were they told of the actions of Red China and the Soviet Union? Did they knowingly participate in the cover-up to prevent hysteria and possible war? To put the matter in the simplest, most direct language, did these people lie—however virtuous the reasons—or were they lied to?

In search for answers we need to reconsider the functions of the National Security Agency. Thanks largely to the work of authors David Kahn and James Bamford, what the NSA does is not as unknown as it used to be. The major functions of the NSA are as follows:

1. The NSA is massively equipped to literally eavesdrop on the planet. Via ships, planes, satellites, and powerful ground stations, it has the capacity to intercept, record, and listen to virtually any and all messages sent through the atmosphere or space, through the oceans and over wire. In *The Puzzle Palace,* author Bamford describes how a minor adjustment in a satellite receiving dish enabled the Agency to listen to a phone conversation between Honolulu and Colorado. Few conversations, certainly by phone and even orally, are secure if the Agency wants to hear them.

2. The NSA is massively equipped with ''acres'' of computers to break codes used by other nations. The Agency is the largest single buyer of computers in the world, and the needs of the Agency play a signal role in the development of computer technology. It is no accident that Vice Admiral Inman became head of the company which hopes to develop ''supercomputers'' that ''think.'' (He has since resigned.)

3. The NSA is empowered to develop codes for use by U.S. government departments and agencies—including the Armed Forces and itself. It is hoped that the codes thus developed are unbreakable by other nations.

4. The NSA is empowered to develop and provide to the United States government all information important to national security. Toward this end, it is authorized to conduct both overt and covert intelligence operations aimed at garnering such information and indeed to carry out operations important to national security. It is authorized to recruit and train persons to conduct the overt and covert operations.

This list of functions—and there is not one that has not been generally known to the press and the public for many years—indicates that the NSA is authorized and equipped to accumulate all information even remotely connected to national security. It can do this by any means it chooses, including intercepting messages, breaking codes, and employing intelligence agents in the field. National security is a very large umbrella and the Agency, as its very name indicates, holds the handle.

But the greatest—the truly awesome—power of NSA is that it can easily control dissemination of information through its codebreaking and codemaking powers.

To give an example, if the Soviet Union sends a coded message and the NSA is able to decipher and read it—an ability possessed by no other agency in the U.S. government—it is able to control who has knowledge of that message. The NSA is the only one that knows the message was sent and has the capacity to break the code, read the message, and know its content. It can then encipher the message into a code developed for its own use—a code no other government agency has the ability to break—and easily restrict knowledge of the message to an extremely small group of people of its own choosing, for whatever purpose it may decide. It can inform the President, the secretaries of defense and state, the joint chiefs of staff, key members of Congress, and others to whom the message might be of interest—or it can tell some of them and not others, it can tell none of them, it can report only part of the message to some of the people, or it can give an entirely erroneous message. Who is to know the difference?

I said *can* or *could*. The paramount question is *does it?* Return to the Sea of Japan and the USS *Pueblo*. There can be no doubt the National Security Agency controlled the movements and mission of the ship. There can be no doubt the NSA controlled communications to and from the ship. Recall that Bucher was upset that he did not receive his own radio messages, which came through the SOD-Hut and were often delayed. He fought with Harris over these delays. Recall that Radioman Hayes, a member of the regular crew forbidden to enter the SOD-Hut, did not receive incoming messages and was restricted in what he sent to "weather reports and such." Recall that for seventeen hours *Pueblo* could not report that it had been detected, which it was supposed to report when it happened, yet that report reached the NSA base at Kamiseya through the SOD-Hut, not the ship's transmitters operated by

AN AWESOME GRANT OF POWER ■ 263

Hayes. Recall that only highly classified, authorized personnel were permitted to enter the SOD-Hut.

My point is this: It was eminently possible, indeed rather easy, for the NSA, by controlling communications both aboard *Pueblo* and at Kamiseya, to restrict the amount of information known about the *Pueblo* seizure, including who boarded it and who fired upon it.

Did they? We are left with some inescapable facts. No United States plane or ship came to the rescue of the men of *Pueblo,* although eight hours elapsed when they could have. Vice admirals, full admirals, secretaries of defense, and White House aides, interviewed by Trevor Armbrister a year and a half to two years after the *Pueblo* seizure, expressed in frank terms their ignorance about the *Pueblo* mission, their surprise and dismay that a Navy vessel was captured. At the time and ever since, there was no inkling that others than North Koreans participated in the seizure. The role of Red China and the Soviet Union remained unknown until now.

We are left with two choices. Either the United States Navy is indifferent to the lives and safety of its men who go down to the sea in ships, and the elected President and the men he appoints as aides and cabinet officers, as well as members of Congress, are callous to the men in service and willing to cover up events—or *they didn't know.*

Question: Is the NSA tail wagging the United States governmental dog? I have found two knowledgeable men who have stood up, been counted, and replied yes. In the article quoted earlier from the Denver *Post,* former CTs T. Edward Eskelson and Tom Bernard wrote: "We find it unnerving that these offensive capabilities [aboard the RC-135 flying near Russian territory during the shooting down of the Korean airliner in 1983] *are under the exclusive control of an agency, the NSA, which operates unchecked by our elected representatives and beyond all traditional restraints* [emphasis mine]."

This statement is supported by information from informants. They describe how the NSA is able to influence, if not actually control, the beliefs and actions of our visible leaders in national security affairs. The NSA's power stems from its combined eavesdropping, codemaking, and codebreaking functions together with its application of Need to Know.

To illustrate, suppose an ambassador transmits a highly classified report in a premier diplomatic code to the secretary of state. Perhaps he even labels it "his eyes only," to be read only by the secretary. Unless it is hand-carried to Washington, the NSA is almost certain to have intercepted the message. Reading it would be effortless, for the NSA developed the codes used by the State Department and everyone else in government.

Knowing the information now possessed by the secretary of state, the NSA is in a position to encourage or discourage belief in the ambassador's report by making additional information available in "intelligence briefings." Said another way, the NSA is in a position to provide the secretary with what he has Need to Know to think and perhaps act in a way desired by the NSA.

Informants say this sort of mental manipulation through the withholding and altering of information and the spreading of disinformation is routinely applied to members of Congress, cabinet officers, generals and admirals, and presidents. They further state that the persons being manipulated do not realize the NSA is the source of their information or disinformation. Most of the intelligence briefings are conducted by directors or staff of the Central Intelligence Agency or the Defense Intelligence Agency. They believe what they are telling the president or other leaders, but they are victims of Need to Know. They were themselves manipulated. If they report incorrect or incomplete information, they have no capacity to know it, for the correct or full information is locked up in codes inside the NSA, codes which they have no ability to break.

Informants state that because only two members of the NSA are publicly identified, the NSA has virtually free rein to conduct whatever covert operations it chooses—such as surrendering a naval vessel without the crew, the Navy, or anyone else in government knowing that was what was supposed to happen. Informants report that most of these covert operations are performed without anyone in government realizing they were covert operations or certainly that the NSA was involved. But on occasion, in certain types of operations, it is necessary to have the President sign a "blank authorization." He takes responsibility for an operation but doesn't know its nature, unless something goes wrong with it.

Informants are uncertain just how this blank authorization is obtained. They believe the CIA and/or DIA director, perhaps even the NSA director, approach the President to seek authorization for an operation, the nature of which they do not know themselves. The President is told the operation involves national security and is highly classified and sensitive. The chief executive is in a position of asking questions that have no answers—at least no answers that are complete and correct. Informants state that the authorization may not actually be blank, but may contain the same sort of gobbledegook about "technical assistance" and "national security" as the NSA uses in its public description of its activities. (When first told about blank authorizations I scoffed, asking how anyone could get the President to sign something he knew nothing about. One cold-eyed informant replied, "I'll give you a one-word answer: *pressure*. No, I'll give you a two-word answer: *lotsa pressure*.")

As bizarre and hard to believe as they are, there is some evidence to support these extraordinary statements about presidential manipulation. Dwight Eisenhower was so upset by the U-2 incident, saying the CIA had lied to him, that he told his aides he never wanted to meet alone again with CIA Director Allan Dulles. John F. Kennedy was so upset by CIA lies during the Bay of Pigs fiasco that he ordered ambassadors to supervise CIA operations and appointed an aide to oversee this attempt to control the CIA. He further named his brother Robert Kennedy (saying he was "wasted at Justice") to oversee the entire U.S. intelligence apparatus. Richard Nixon summoned the heads of all U.S. intelligence agencies, including the NSA, into the Oval Office and sharply criticized their work because he was not receiving full and correct information. Thereafter he created the so-called "White House plumbers" in an effort to obtain better information. Mr. Nixon conducted an independent investigation of the *Pueblo* incident immediately after the Court of Inquiry. He also set up a secret system to record all conversations in his office. To transcribe the White House tapes, it was necessary to make copies of them to be passed around the steno pool. Who possessed the originals and made the copies? NSA, the National Security Agency. Remember the famous and unexplained eighteen-and-a-half-minute gap? The June 27, 1972, tape, the so-called "smoking gun" tape that led to impeachment charges against Mr. Nixon and his resignation, contains these cryptic words uttered to his aide H. R. Haldeman: "They play for keeps." Who are *they?* It may not be correct, but it is eminently possible to read that entire tape today and achieve a whole new meaning from it, in light of informants' statements about NSA activities.

In more recent years, Jimmy Carter sent his most trusted aide, Hamilton Jordan, on secret missions aimed at gaining release of the U.S. hostages held by Iranians, missions usually performed by intelligence or diplomatic personnel. He also ran the secret and failed rescue attempt from the White House. Ronald Reagan said he knew nothing about the siphoning of funds from the sale of arms to Iran into secret Swiss bank accounts. He also encouraged the Senate Intelligence Committee to conduct a full investigation so he could find out what had happened for himself. CIA Director William Casey told the committee under oath that he knew nothing about shipments of arms to Iran or the siphoning off of funds.

I am not claiming accuracy for informants' statements about presidential manipulation. I am simply suggesting that enough evidence exists to warrant serious study and investigation into the role of U.S. intelligence agencies in national security affairs.

Informants vehemently defend the NSA's manipulation of visible leaders as an absolute necessity. They argue that the President is elected for only four years and cannot serve more than eight; in that time, they maintain, no President can possibly learn enough about past and present activities to make an intelligent decision about what they see as a worldwide communist menace orchestrated by the Soviet KGB. He must therefore be provided with information which he has Need to Know to made a decision desired by the NSA. It is further stated that the White House, certainly Congress, cannot be trusted with highly classified information. All government agencies except the NSA are considered a sieve of leaks. The White House, Congress, and federal departments are easily infiltrated by foreign agents. Therefore, the information they possess must be severely restricted—and a great deal of disinformation put in place. Finally, it is maintained, presidents and members of Congress are politicians, surrounded by persons motivated only by self-interest and staying in office. The NSA believes the national security of this country cannot be decided on the basis of what is "good politics." Therefore, the NSA is performing a "patriotic duty" by manipulating the knowledge, thoughts, and actions of people who are not as wise and experienced in various foreign menaces and national security affairs. Informants made this statement: "The last President who made decisions affecting national security was Harry Truman—and he made such an ungodly mess of things no President has been permitted to do so since." The NSA was created in November 1952, just before Mr. Truman left office.

Informants further state that the same situation of manipulation is true in the Soviet Union, China, Britain, France, Israel, and any other viable nation one can think of. It has been so throughout time. Genghis Khan, various Roman caesars, Napoleon, Hitler, and Stalin were all manipulated by intelligence services. The United States was simply late in arriving at what other nations have done for a long time. "If you think the president runs this country, or Gorbachev the Soviet Union or the prime minister England, then you are a fool."

I report these statements not as truth, but as evidence of prevailing attitudes within the NSA. It is a very cocky organization. It has been highly successful for thirty-five years and is now deeply entrenched with personnel, equipment, methods, and philosophy to carry out what it perceives to be its mission.

Return to the *Pueblo* surrender. Consider once again the key question posed earlier: Why the cover-up? If Red Chinese and Soviet participation were made known, if Commander Bucher, Helmsman Berens, and other crewmen of *Pueblo,* as well as other officers in the Navy and intelligence services, were able to speak frankly of what they knew before a truly impartial fact-finding inquiry into the loss of *Pueblo,* then the NSA would have had to answer some terribly difficult questions.

It must be remembered that in 1968, the time of the seizure, or 1969, when the Court of Inquiry convened, the NSA (let alone what it did) was virtually unknown. Most Americans had never heard of it, and perhaps at least a few of those who had, confused it with NASA, the National Aeronautics and Space Administration, which was sending a man to the moon.

An impartial inquiry would have ferreted out that *Pueblo* was controlled by the NSA, which defined where it went and what functions it performed; that the NSA had exclusive control of communications to and from *Pueblo* so that even top Pentagon officials thought it was still in port; that orders were issued keeping *Pueblo* under harassment by a ship at battle stations for seventy-five minutes; that *Pueblo* was armed and made more provocative while its crew was disarmed; that the men who boarded *Pueblo* wore olive green uniforms with a big red star in the middle of a fur hat; that a large warship was coming fast—and much, much more.

At the very least, President Johnson, Pentagon officials, and Navy admirals would have asked, why was *Pueblo* sent on this mission? Why was it under orders that kept it in maximum danger and made escape difficult? Why were no U.S. planes and ships alerted to *Pueblo*'s danger so our men could be protected? Why was Red Chinese and Soviet participation not made known? Why were we not given information vital to national security? As military commanders and diplomats, how can we perform our functions if we are not informed of the true events of the *Pueblo* seizure? Why were we not informed in advance of the nature of *Pueblo*'s mission so we could have been prepared for the outcome?

These and a great many other questions surely would have been asked. The role of NSA in national life would have been exposed. The ability of NSA to collect and then withhold information from even top governmental officials, both military and civilian, would have become known. From the standpoint of the NSA, the cover-up was essential. One is tempted to say it was vital.

We as a people and as a government have bestowed a grant of awesome power on the National Security Agency. The unknown, and by act of

Congress unknowable, men and women of the NSA have the capacity to both collect vital information and control its dissemination through codes which they develop. Control of information by nameless, faceless individuals is unlimited power. We are all left to hope they use it wisely.

Certain it is that the American people were not told the truth about *Pueblo*. We were told an elaborate cover story designed to mask the true events. Inevitably our perceptions of that seizure, of ourselves, and of the world situation were manipulated.

This sort of manipulation is lethal in a self-governing republic. We have to trust our leaders, at least until the next election. Without that trust, we have anarchy or dictatorship. As a people we understand that we don't have to know *everything* that happens, particularly in matters relating to national security. But we assume as a matter of course that our visible elected and appointed leaders are informed about national security and participate in the decision-making process.

There is, therefore, something extremely distasteful and unsettling in images of Senator Kennedy saying he'd like to know what happened during the *Pueblo* seizure before deciding on a course of action. Or of Senator J. W. Fulbright, then chairman of the Senate Foreign Relations Committee, also urging caution because the Senate was just finding out what happened in the Gulf of Tonkin in 1964. There is something unsavory when Major General Woodward sits down at Panmunjom to negotiate the release of eighty-two courageous American sailors and makes fallacious statements which he is convinced are utterly true. There is something alarming when spokesmen for the White House, Pentagon, and State Department stand before the public and make a statement, perhaps under oath, sincerity and conviction shining in their eyes, which is absolutely wrong. It is dynamite in a democracy if trusted officials truly *believe* their falsehoods because the truth is hidden within the NSA, leaving the officials with no possible way to discover it. If this occurs, it is a profound alteration of our form of government.

The *Pueblo* surrender was a covert intelligence operation of the National Security Agency, hidden behind a cover-up that went on for twenty years. As such, was it an isolated instance, a one-of-a-kind-never-to-occur-again event?

Several other seemingly inexplicable events of the last thirty years suggest that is was not. We need to ask questions. What other crimes were committed? What other national property was lost? What other events seemed inexplicable and subject to a cover-up? What other formal boards, committees, and commissions conducted investigations which many people found incomplete and unsatisfactory? What other crises were trau-matic for the American people and took a long time to resolve? In what other events did persons in authority assume responsibility for events which they maintained they knew nothing about? What other persons were accused of crimes, then never tried for them? Who else had calumny heaped upon them and were forced to abandon careers they wanted above all things, even being forced to leave national life despite personal denials of culpability? What other events were said to involve national security, thus restricting the flow of information to the public? What other events involved some form of eavesdropping, leaked information, and large amounts of classified documents which fell into unfriendly hands? What other events involved a person who refused to speak publicly about his involvement? By way of answer, I will say only that there are several events in the past thirty years which bear a striking resemblance to the *Pueblo* surrender.

I am not condemning the National Security Agency. Without doubt, it is staffed by dedicated men and women. I believe they have made great sacrifices, personally and collectively, of lives and veracity to defend national security, sacrifices which remain unrecognized. The very act of secrecy causes them to be unknown, their accomplishments unsung except among themselves. None of us know the debt we owe them.

I believe that NSA, having accumulated immense power over national life through its eavesdropping, codebreaking, and codemaking func-tions, which enable it to control the collection and dissemination of information, has put in place an internal security system to guard against its own subversion. At least I hope so. I also believe the NSA has in place a fail-safe system to guard against abuse of its own power. Again, I hope so. I believe the NSA is extremely careful and circumspect and doesn't often make the sort of miscalculations that led to the superpower confrontation in the Sea of Japan which was the *Pueblo* surrender. Again, I hope so.

I believe the accumulation of power within the National Security Agency is natural, inevitable, and probably necessary. Since ancient times, kings, despots, and democratically elected leaders have depended upon intelligence information obtained by aides and employees and have had to assume its accuracy. The power of intelligence agencies to collect and disseminate information existed prior to 1952 and will continue to exist into the foreseeable future. The NSA has simply systematized, doubtlessly with great effectiveness, power which has always existed and always will exist. If the NSA were disbanded tomorrow, it would simply re-create itself the next day—and probably be far less effective and disciplined.

Intelligence information is especially valuable in the modern ideologically dissected world. The Soviet KGB is far larger than the NSA, the CIA, and other U.S. intelligence agencies combined. The personnel of the KGB are just as well-trained, well-equipped and dedicated as the men and women of the NSA. As the KGB and the NSA confront each other around the world, they engage in a sort of Mexican standoff, each side notching temporary victories, a *Pueblo* here, a Nicaragua there. It apparently is destined to continue into the foreseeable future.

This poses a problem in an American context. By its very nature, the success of an intelligence operation, such as the *Pueblo* surrender, depends upon extreme secrecy—surely difficult when there are 535 members of Congress, scores in the White House, and thousands in the Pentagon, State Department, and other agencies. To achieve any success at all in defense of national security, NSA must keep knowledge of its activities restricted to as small a group of utterly trustworthy people as possible.

On the other hand, the United States of America is a republic, governed by a Constitution created by our forefathers and designed to protect individual liberty and a democratic form of government for all time. That Constitution, and the form of government that evolved from it, for all its faults, is both our birthright and our most marketable asset in worldwide confrontations with totalitarianism. What we truly have to offer other peoples of the world is the ideal of liberty, and hope.

The United States Constitution is replete with checks and balances—the Bill of Rights, procedures for government by law, an independent court system to enforce the law and the Constitution—all designed to protect individual liberty and collective security. We have civilian control of the military, a free press, and an impartial court system. Congress still passes laws, still has the power to tax and to appropriate. For all the faults and limitations of Congress, it remains our greatest safeguard of the republic.

In the midst of government is created a supersecret intelligence agency, created not by Congress but by presidential order, the text of which few have ever seen. It employs scores of thousands of people, only two of whom (by act of Congress now) can be publicly identified. It spends billions of dollars annually that Congress does not realize it is appropriating, let alone for what purpose. The agency is in a position both to collect information and to control its distribution. Knowledge is power. All of us are the sum of the information in our brains. We think and act upon the basis of what we know. A person who can control what we know can manipulate our thoughts, our beliefs, our actions. Very little knowledge of history is required to realize the possible effects of this.

Thus, we have a problem. By their very nature, to be effective intelligence agencies must work in secret. Yet the very existence of a secret organization able to control information and manipulate the beliefs and actions of a people and its government is lethal in a republic. Our forefathers would not have approved.

If we need and want the NSA, which we undeniably do, and if we want to protect ourselves from even the *possibility* of subversion of our form of government and our own beliefs through manipulation of information, then we must find a solution to the problem.

Oversight of the NSA is supposedly provided by the intelligence committees of the two houses of Congress. There is not one speck of evidence suggesting those committees knew of the *Pueblo* operation in advance or what really happened to *Pueblo* after the event.

At least in the *Pueblo* incident, oversight of the NSA was less than effective. Was it an isolated breakdown? Or have there been other instances in which presidents, cabinet officers, military leaders, and members of Congress acted upon the basis of incomplete and even erroneous information provided by the NSA? It is simply too easy, because of the combined codebreaking and codemaking powers of the NSA, for a small group of legally unknown persons, or even conceivably a single individual, to withhold or falsify information vital to national security.

My point is simple. I am suggesting that the procedures for oversight of the NSA be re-examined by appropriate bodies in the legislative and executive branches of government. Unsurprisingly, informants scoff at even the notion of it. Said one: "Do you really believe the amateurs in Congress are going to find out anything by investigating the pros at NSA? And if by chance they do, they will simply drive the NSA deeper underground."

Yet I cannot conceive that the effectiveness of NSA would be greatly damaged if it were required to prove that it has in existence fail-safe methods of internal security that prohibit any possibility of its own subversion, as well as a system of internal audit for monitoring its own activities. I find it difficult to believe that national security would be threatened if NSA activities and the accuracy of the information it imparts were subject to a review by impartial civilians and military officers possessed of extremely high security clearances and undoubted trustworthiness. The whole world wouldn't have to know of mistakes, miscalculations, and excesses, but at least the NSA would benefit from outside, impartial criticism. Disagreement and fresh viewpoints can only help improve the NSA while conforming to the system of checks and balances inherent in our form of government. Perhaps greater oversight of NSA appropriations, perhaps even some reorganization of the agency with greater separation of its eavesdropping, codebreaking, and codemaking functions, would be useful.

I offer these as ideas—only. I am neither expert nor arrogant enough to know how to solve the problem created by an autonomous, supersecret intelligence agency in control of information in a self-governing republic.

No one wants to damage national security. At the same time no one wants to damage the form of government created by our forefathers. Surely we who follow are no less capable of preserving both.

APPENDIX 1
Pueblo's Radio Transmissions

DEPARTMENT OF THE NAVY
OFFICE OF THE CHIEF OF NAVAL OPERATIONS
WASHINGTON, D.C. 20350

IN REPLY REFER TO
Op-03Pl: gm
Memo 457-69
13 March 1969

UNCLASSIFIED

MEMORANDUM FOR MR. FRANK SLATINSHEK (STAFF COUNSEL, SPECIAL SUBCOMMITTEE, *Pueblo* INQUIRY)

Subj: *Pueblo* Incident (U)
Encl: (L) Chronology of Radio Transmissions to and from the *Pueblo* pertinent to the seizure

1. Enclosure (1) is forwarded herewith as requested.

(s)

LESLIE J. O'BRIEN, JR.,
Rear Admiral, U.S. Navy
Special Assistant to the Chief of Naval Operations
for *Pueblo* Matters

UNCLASSIFIED

Chronology of all radio transmissions to and from the *Pueblo* pertinent to the seizure commencing the day before the seizure through the time *Pueblo* went off the air.

1. Background

a. The first record of contact by *Pueblo* with a shore station is approximately 0920Z/22 JAN (1820 local). At this time *Pueblo* broke radio silence and called NAVCOMMSTA JAPAN on primary CW ship to shore (1306 KHz) and requested activation of 100 wpm ORESTES covered communications with Kamiseya. This was in accordance with her communications instructions.

b. Communications from ship to the shore in this area is sometimes difficult due to the propagation conditions which vary with the different times of the day. According to the reports from the commanding officer of the Naval Communication Station in Japan, communications to some of the areas from the Sea of Japan are not always satisfactory. That is, selection of the proper frequencies vary for use at different times throughout the day. It is necessary that ships have available to them a selection from a wide range of frequencies in order to maintain communications reliably under those poor propagation conditions. Thirteen different frequencies were tried prior to establishment of a two-way circuit with *Pueblo.*

c. The circuit was established at 1054 Korean local time on 23 January 1968. This circuit was a 100 word-per-minute, simplex (one-way reversible), crypto-covered, high frequency radio teletype circuit. The circuit was activated continuously from 1054 until 1432 when *Pueblo* went off the air to destroy the crypto equipment.

d. The following chronology picks up with *Pueblo*'s transmission of SITREP 1 at 231100 Korean time. Korean local time is used throughout except date-time groups are given in GMT(Z) and Korean local time.

2. *Chronology*

Korean
Local

Time	*Transmissions*	*Actions Taken*
1100	*Pueblo* completed transmission of SITREP 1 (DTG 220915 Z). This report was addressed to AIG 7622.	CNF (CTF-96) Watch Officer Intelligence read/filed on interest board.
1135	*Pueblo* completed transmission of Intel/Tech Rpt #1 (DTG 220820 Z/221720 Korean). Precedence was Routine and message was addressed to fifteen activities.	Routine patrol; no action required.
1140	*Pueblo* completed service message (a request for missing COPI broadcast numbers) (DTG 221126 Z/222026 Korean).	Routine action taken to re-broadcast missing numbers requested.

1150 *Pueblo* completed transmission of SITREP 2 (DTG 230150 Z/231050 Korean). This report had Priority precedence and was addressed for action to CTF-96 and to the following for information:

COMMANDING GENERAL, FIFTH AIR FORCE

COMMANDER IN CHIEF, PACIFIC

COMMANDER IN CHIEF, PACIFIC AIR FORCE

COMMANDER IN CHIEF, U.S. PACIFIC FLEET

CHIEF OF NAVAL OPERATIONS

COMMANDER, FLEET AIR WING SIX

COMMANDER SERVICE FORCE, U.S. PACIFIC FLEET

COMMANDER, SEVENTH FLEET

DIRECTOR, NAVAL SECURITY GROUP

FLEET AIR RECONNAISSANCE SQUADRON ONE

HEADQUARTERS, NATIONAL SECURITY AGENCY, PACIFIC

JOINT CHIEFS OF STAFF

NAVAL FIELD OPERATIONS INTELLIGENCE OFFICE

NAVAL SECURITY GROUP ACTIVITY (KAMISEYA)

OCEANOGRAPHER OF THE NAVY

CNFJ (CTF-96) Watch officers in Intelligence read/filed on interest board.

1200 *Pueblo* operator stated he had another message being prepared for transmission and that there was "COMPANY OUTSIDE."

1210 *Pueblo* transmitted INTEL/TECH REPT number 2 (DTG 230206 Z/231106 Korean). For period 220001 Z-222400 Z. Precedence was Routine and message was addressed to several (15) intelligence activities.

Routine patrol; no action required as indicated.

1210–
1244 Exchange of transmissions between *Pueblo* and Kamiseya operators regarding garbled or misunderstood portions of four messages sent by *Pueblo;* reruns of parts of

messages, checks of routing indicators assigned, etc. At approximately 1230, *Pueblo* operator advised, "DON'T WANT TO GO DOWN YET. WE STILL GOT COMPANY OUTSIDE. WILL ADVISE ASAP."

1244 *Pueblo* operator advised, "WE ARE FINISHED FOR NOW BUT GOT COMPANY OUTSIDE AND MORE COMING SO WILL HAVE TO KEEP THIS UP FOR A WHILE. WILL ADVISE ASAP."

1245– Exchange of transmissions between
1249 operators, primarily personnel chatter, such as; sea duty is rough, be glad to get back, see you about 7 FEB, etc. At end of period, *Pueblo* operator sent, "I AM TRYING TO FIND OUT WHAT THE OIC WANTS (Garble) NOW BUT EVERYONE IS TOPSIDE WORRYING (Garble) HAVE RIGHT NOW WILL ADVISE ASAP." This was followed shortly by, "CHANGE YOUR TAPE AND GOT A FLASH COMING FOR YOU NOW. AM GETTING IT READY NOW, STANDBY FOR FLASH."

1250– *Pueblo* transmitted OPREP
1254 3/PINNACLE 1 message (DTG 230352 Z/231252 Korean) twice and Kamiseya receipted at 1254. Kamiseya advised, "FLASH GONE." indicating message was being relayed.

1255– *Pueblo* operator advised, "GOT
1315 SOME MORE COMING SOON SO WILL
HAVE TO STAY UP. WILL ADVISE WHEN
WE GET READY FOR YOU." Kamiseya
acknowledged this and requested a
rerun of a line from a previous
message. *Pueblo* complied. Kam-
iseya acknowledged and sent, "DO
YOU HAVE ANYMORE TRAFFIC? HOW
IT FEEL TO BE THREATENED?" *Pueblo*
response was, "GOT SOME MORE
COMING IN A MINUTE BUT DON'T HAVE
IT IN COMM YET. WILL PASS IT AS SOON
AS I GET. IT IS WORSE OUT HERE NOW,
GOT MORE COMPANY AND NOT DOING
SO GOOD WITH THEM SO WILL HAVE TO
KEEP THIS CIRCUIT UP, WILL ADVISE
ASAP AND PLEASE STAY WITH ME ON
CIRCUIT."

1315– Kamiseya acknowledged the above
1317 and sent, "KNOW WHAT YOU MEAN
ABOUT THAT COMPANY AND WILL
STAY DOWN SO YOU CAN COME TO ME.
HOW TO PUT ON TEST ON YOUR NEXT
START UNTIL YOU GET YOUR TRAFFIC
SO WE CAN KEEP FREQ FAIRLY
CLEAR?" *Pueblo* complied and ran a
test tape for about a minute.

1318– *Pueblo* transmitted OPREP
1321 3/PINNACLE 2 message (DTG
230415 Z/231315 Korean) once
and Kamiseya receipted. *Pueblo*
voluntarily retransmitted the
message. This message was the first
indication that more than
harassment was involved.

PINNACLE 1 was received
by CNFJ at 1313 and hand-
delivered to Chief of Staff by
Intelligence watch officer.
Also delivered to OPCON-
CENTER Harassment
reported was no worse than
expected nor as bad as
previously experienced by
Banner (AGER 1).

Kamiseya relayed message to
CNFJ, who received at 1322.
Intelligence watch officer
hand-delivered to Chief of
Staff who ordered, "RELAY
INFO TO 5th AF AND PUSH THE
BUTTON FOR CONTINGENCY
ACTION."

1322– No transmission between *Pueblo*
1325 and Kamiseya other than repeats of
PINNACLE 2.

1326– *Pueblo* sent, "AND THEY PLAN TO
1327 OPEN FIRE ON US NOW, THEY
PLAN TO OPEN FIRE ON US NOW,
THEY PLAN TO OPEN FIRE ON US
NOW."

Kamiseya received at 1328 and relayed it CNFJ who received at 1329. Based on this and PINNACLE 2, CNFJ prepared to send a special procedure message.

1328 *Pueblo* again commenced sending
PINNACLE 2 but interrupted to
send, "NORTH KOREAN WAR VESSELS
PLAN TO OPEN FIRE, SHIP POSIT
39-25.5N, 127-54.9E, SHIP POSIT
39-25.5N, 127-54.9E." Kamiseya
acknowledged this and asked,
"HOW MANY FLASH HAVE YOU SENT
US?" Kamiseya continued to
acknowledge receipt of *Pueblo*
posit info, and invited *Pueblo* to
transmit.

Kamiseya was now relaying all *Pueblo* transmissions in near real time to CNFJ by secure teletype circuit. At 1330 CNFJ initiated first phone call (secure) to 5 AF HQ for assistance.

1330 *Pueblo* transmitted, "WE ARE BEING
BOARDED," five times followed by
two repeats of previous ship's
position, and two repeats of, "WE
ARE BEING BOARDED." "SOS" was
then sent thirteen times, followed
by two transmissions of a revised
ship's position, "39-34N,
127-54E," eighteen more SOSs and
the new position once more.
Kamiseya acknowledged receipt of
all these transmissions and invited
Pueblo to continue sending.

1331 *Pueblo* resumed transmitting a few minutes later with, "WE ARE HOLDING EMERGENCY DESTRUCTION. WE NEED HELP. WE ARE HOLDING EMERGENCY DESTRUCTION. WE NEED SUPPORT. SOS SOS SOS. PLEASE SEND ASSISTANCE (sent four times), SOS, SOS, SOS. WE ARE BEING BOARDED. HOLDING EMERGENCY DESTRUCTION." Kamiseya acknowledged and again invited *Pueblo* to continue sending.

At 1335, CNFJ transmitted a special procedure message based on contents of PINNACLE 2 and "chatter" from *Pueblo*.

1331– At about 1337, *Pueblo* advised,
1337 "WE ARE LAYING TO AT PRESENT POSITION. AS OF YET WE NO LONGER HAVE GOPI (WESTPACOPINTEL broadcast). THIS CIRCUIT ONLY CIRCUIT ACTIVE ON NIP. PLEASE SEND ASSISTANCE. WE ARE BEING BOARDED."

1338 Kamiseya responded to last *Pueblo* transmission "QSL (roger) YOUR LAST AND PASSING ALL INFO." No other transmissions this period, except a call by Kamiseya for *Pueblo* to transmit.

Kamiseya readdressed PINNACLE 2 as a special procedure message at 1338. At 1340 Kamiseya re-addressed PINNACLE 1 as a special procedure message.

1345– At 1345 *Pueblo* advised, "WE ARE
1409 BEING ESCORTED INTO PROB WONSON REPEAT WONSON. WE ARE BEING ESCORTED INTO PROB WONSON REPEAT WONSON." Kamiseya acknowledged this transmission and the following exchange took place for the remainder of the period:

1. At 1346 CNFJ initiated a second special procedure message based on *Pueblo* chatter about boarding.

Pueblo—"ARE YOU SENDING ASSISTANCE" (four times).

2. Subsequently, a total of 15 "follow-ups" special procedure were originated by CNFJ and Kamiseya, based on "chatter" from *Pueblo*.

Kamiseya—"WORD HAS GONE TO ALL AUTHORITIES. WORD HAS GONE TO ALL AUTHORITIES. COMNAVFOR-JAPAN IS REQUESTING ASSIT. WHAT KEY LIST DO YOU HAVE LEFT?"

"LAST WE GOT FROM YOU WAS 'ARE YOU SENDING ASSIT.' PLEASE ADVISE WHAT KEY LIST YOU HAVE LEFT AND IF IT APPEARS THAT YOUR COMM SPACES WILL BE ENTERED?"

3. Throughout the period CNFJ made several telephone calls to Commander, 5th AF with respect to AF assistance. At 1350 5th AF HQ advised no aircraft on alert.

Pueblo—"HAVE O KEYLIST AND THIS ONLY ONE HAVE, HAVE BEEN REQUESTED TO FOLLOW INTO WONSON, HAVE THREE WOUNDED AND ONE MAN WITH LEG BLOWN OFF, HAVE NOT USED ANY WEAPONS OR UNCOVERED 50-CAL. MAC. DESTROYING ALL KEYLISTS AND AS MUCH ELE EQUIPT AS POSSIBLE. HOW ABOUT SOME HELP, THESE GUYS MEAN BUSINESS. HAVE SUSTAINED SMALL WOUND IN RECTUM, DO NOT INTEND TO OFFER ANY RESISTANCE. INTERROGATIVE QSL.° INTERROGATIVE QSL. DO NOT KNOW HOW LONG WILL BE ABLE TO HOLD UP CIRCUIT AND DO NOT KNOW IF COMM SPACES WILL BE ENTERED."

Kamiseya—"ROGER, ROGER. WE DOING ALL WE CAN. CAPT HERE AND CNFJ ON HOTLINE. LAST I GOT WAS AIR FORCE GOING HELP YOU WITH SOME AIRCRAFT BUT CAN'T REALLY SAY AS CNFJ COORDINATING WITH I PRESUME KOREA FOR SOME F-105. THIS UNOFFICIAL BUT I THINK THAT WHAT WILL HAPPEN."

Pueblo—"ROGER YOUR LAST. ROGER YOUR LAST."

1410 Kamiseya sent, "STILL READ YOU QRK FIVER FIVER. GO AHEAD. KEEP KW-7 ON THE AIR LONG AS YOU CAN. WE STAYING RIGHT WITH YOU."

1411 *Pueblo* sent, "ROGER, ROGER, WILL KEEP THIS UP UNTIL LAST MINUTE WILL STAY UP UNTIL THE LAST MINUTE AND SURE COULD USE SOME HELP NOW."

1412 Kamiseya sent, "ROGER, ROGER. WE STILL WITH YOU AND DOING ALL WE CAN. EVERYONE REALLY TURNING TO AND FIGURE BY NOW AIR FORCE GOT SOME BIRDS WINGING YOUR WAY."

At 1412, Kamiseya commenced passing chatter to Com7THFLT via torn-tape relay at HAVCOMMSTA PHIL.

1413 *Pueblo* sent, "ROGER, ROGER, SURE HOPE SO. WE PRETTY BUSY WITH DESTRUCTION RIGHT NOW. CAN'T SEE FOR THE SMOKE."

1414 Kamiseya sent, "ROGER, ROGER, WISH I COULD HELP MORE. ALL INFO YOU PASS BEING SENT TO AREA COMMANDER AND THEY IN TURN CO-ORDINATING FOR WHATEVER ACTION GOT TO BE TAKEN. SURE PROCESS ALREADY BEING INITIATED FOR SOME IMMEDIATE RELIEF. COMSEVENTH-FLT, CNFJ, AND NSA GROUP PAC ALL GOT INFO RIGHT AWAY."

1415 *Pueblo* sent, "ROGER YOUR LAST AND SURE HOPE SOMEONE DOES SOMETHING. WE ARE HELPLESS AT THIS TIME. CANNOT DO ANYTHING BUT WAIT."

1417 Kamiseya sent, "WHO I GOT THAT END OF CIRCUIT. WHAT STATUS OF CLASSIFIED MATERIAL LEFT TO DESTROY?"

1418 *Pueblo* sent, "WE HAVE THE KW-7 AND SOME CARDS IN THE 37 AND 14 (crypto equipments KWR-37 and KG-14) TO SMASH. I THINK THAT JUST ABOUT IT."

1419 Kamiseya sent, "RIGHT. CONTINUE TO HANG TO P & I BUTTON. WE BE RIGHT THERE. YOUR SIGNAL MIGHTY GOOD AND HOPE STAYS THAT WAY. YOU GOT ANY FURTHER INFO THAT MIGHT HELP EVALUATE SITUATION?" *Pueblo* sent, "ROGER YOUR LAST. WILL STAY WITH AS LONG AS I CAN. WILL PUT (garble) ON AND LEAVE THEM UNTIL I NEED YOU."

1420 Kamiseya sent, "CNFJ ADVISED FIFTH AIR FORCE ALERTED REPEAT CNFJ ADVISED FIFTH AIR FORCE ALERTED."

At 1420 CNFJ notifies CINCPACFLT of incident by secure phone.

1421– *Pueblo* made transmission that was
1427 completely garbled and unreadable. Kamiseya made several requests for a repeat.

1428 Kamiseya sent twice, "IF OPERATIONS PERMIT, CAN YOU PROVIDE CURRENT SITREP INCLUDING INTENTIONS KORCOMS IF POSSIBLE, DAMAGE, AND INJURIES SUSTAINED."

1430 *Pueblo* sent, "ROGER AND DESTRUCTION OF PUBS HAVE BEEN INEFFECTIVE. SUSPECT SEVERAL WILL BE COMPROMISED." Kamiseya sent twice, "CAN YOU GIVE ME A LIST OF WHAT YOU HAVEN'T DESTROYED?"

1432 *Pueblo* sent, "HAVE BEEN DIRECTED TO COME TO ALL STOP AND BEING BOARDED AT THIS TIME. BEING BOARDED AT THIS TIME." Kamiseya sent, "ROGER YOUR LAST. IT ON WAY TO CNFJ." *Pueblo* sent, "FOUR MEN INJURED AND ONE CRITICALLY AND GOING OFF THE AIR NOW AND DESTROYING THIS GEAR." (last transmission) Kamiseya sent, "ROGER, GO AHEAD. CAN YOU TRANSMIT IN THE CLEAR?" Kamiseya repeated calls for the *Pueblo* to transmit in the clear for several hours.

3. *Analysis*—What actions were possible?
   Time to act before dark. 231330 to 231806 = 4^h36^m
   Time to act before seizure. 231330 to 231435 = 1^h5^m

Time to act until *Pueblo* abeam Ung Do island.

   231330 to 231645 = 3^h15^m

Time to act until *Pueblo* moored at the pier.

   231330 to 232030 = 7^h

APPENDIX 2

CREWLIST

Every published list of the *Pueblo* crew is different, leaving the impression no one was sure exactly who was on the vessel. Names are spelled differently. There is great discrepancy among the reported ranks of crewmen.

The following is Bucher's list with the addition of two men, Higgins and Hill, whom he omitted for some reason. All ranks are at the time of capture, as are their hometowns. Most are doubtlessly out of date now. I report the names here so that these men might be honored at this late date. In my opinion they should be given a medal and, if possible, a ticker tape parade.

Cmdr. Lloyd M. Bucher, Lincoln, Nebraska
Lt. Stephen R. Harris, Melrose, Massachusetts
Lt. Edward R. Murphy, San Diego, California
Lt. (jg) F. Carl Schumacher, St. Louis, Missouri
Ensign Timothy L. Harris, Jacksonville, Florida
CWO Gene H. Lacy, Seattle, Washington
Steward's Mate Rogelio P. Abelon, Ambabaay, The Philippines
CT2 Michael W. Alexander, Richland, Washington
Steward's Mate Rizalino L. Aluague, Subic City, The Philippines
CT2 Wayne D. Anderson, Waycross, Georgia
Fireman Richard E. Arnold, Santa Rosa, California
CT3 Charles W. Ayling, Staunton, Virginia
CT1 Don E. Bailey, Portland, Indiana
Hospital Corpsman 1 Herman P. Baldridge, Carthage, Missouri
Fireman Richard I. Bame, Maybee, Michigan
Fireman Peter M. Bandera, Carson City, Nevada
CT1 Michael T. Barrett, Kalamazoo, Michigan
Boatswain's Mate 2 Ronald L. Berens, Russell, Kansas
Fireman Howard E. Bland, Leggett, California
Engineman Rushel J. Blansett, Orange, California
Senior Chief CT Ralph D. Bouden, Nampa, Idaho
CT3 Paul D. Brusnahan, Trenton, New Jersey

Boatswain's Mate 3 Willie C. Bussell, Hopkinsville, Kentucky
Yeoman 1 Armando M. Canales, Fresno, California
Marine Sgt. Robert J. Chicca, Hyattsville, Maryland
Radioman 3 Charles H. Crandall, El Reno, California
CT3 Bradley R. Crowe, Island Pond, Vermont
CT3 Rodney H. Duke, Fayette, Mississippi
Seaman Stephen P. Ellis, Louisiana
Communications Specialist Victor D. Escamilla, Amarillo, Texas
Storekeeper 1 Policarpo P. Garcia, Point Mugu, California
CT1 Francis J. Ginther, Pottsville, Pennsylvania
Chief Engineman Monroe O. Goldman, Lakewood, California
CT3 John W. Grant, Jay, Maine
Electrician's Mate 1 Gerald Hagenson, Bremerton, Washington
Marine Sgt. Robert J. Hammond, Claremont, New Hampshire
Radioman 2 Lee R. Hayes, Columbus, Ohio
Engineman 3 John C. Higgins, St. Joseph, Missouri
Boatswain's Mate 3 Robert W. Hill, Jr., Ellwood City, Tennessee
Fireman Duane Hodges, Creswell, Oregon
CT3 Jerry Karnes, Havana, Arkansas
Chief CT James F. Kell, Culver City, California
CT3 Earl M. Kisler, St. Louis, Missouri
Boatswain's Mate 1 Norbert J. Klepac, San Diego, California
CT3 Anthony A. Lamantia, Toronto, Ohio
CT3 Peter M. Langenbert, Clayton, Missouri
Quartermaster 1 Charles B. Law, Chehalis, Washington
CT1 James D. Layton, Binghamton, New York
Signalman 2 Wendell G. Leach, Houston, Texas
Commissaryman 2 Harry Lewis, Springfield Gardens, New York
Photographer's Mate 1 Lawrence W. Mack, San Diego, California
Seaman Roy J. Maggard, Olivehurst, California
Seaman Larry J. Marshall, Austin, Indiana
Fireman Thomas W. Massie, Roscoe, Illinois
CT2 Donald R. McClarren, Johnstown, Pennsylvania
CT3 Ralph McClintock, Milton, Massachusetts
Fireman John A. Mitchell, Dixon, California
Electronic Technician 2 Clifford C. Nolte, Menlo, Iowa
Fireman Michael A. O'Bannon, Beaverton, Oregon
CT1 Donald R. Peppard, Phoenix, Arizona
Seaman Earl R. Phares, Ontario, California
Quartermaster 3 Alvin H. Plucker, Trenton, Nebraska

Commissaryman 3 Ralph E. Reed, Perdix, Pennsylvania
Seaman Dale E. Rigby, Ogden, Utah
CT1 David L. Ritter, Union City, California
CT3 Steven J. Robin, Silver Spring, Maryland
Seaman Richard J. Rogala, Niles, Illinois
Seaman Ramon Rosales, El Paso, Texas
Seaman Edward S. Russell, Glendale, California
Engineman 1 William W. Scarborough, Anderson, South Carolina
CT1 James A. Shephard, Williamstown, Massachusetts
CT3 John A. Shilling, Mantua, Ohio
Seaman John R. Shingleton, Atoka, Oklahoma
Fireman Norman W. Spear, Portland, Maine
CT2 Charles R. Sterling, Omaha, Nebraska
CT3 Angelo S. Strano, Hartford, Connecticut
Fireman Larry E. Strickland, Grand Rapids, Michigan
Gunners Mate 2 Kenneth R. Wadley, Beaverton, Oregon
Fireman Steven E. Woelk, Alta Vista, Kansas
CT2 Elton A. Wood, Spokane, Washington
Engineman Darrel E. Wright, Alma, West Virginia
Civilian Harry Iredale III, Holmes, Pennsylvania
Civilian Donnie Tuck, Richmond, Virginia

APPENDIX 3

QUOTED SOURCES

I am indebted to the authors of the following books which I quote or refer to in the text:

Armbrister, Trevor. *A Matter of Accountability.* New York: Coward-McCann, Inc., 1970. 408 pages.

Bamford, James. *The Puzzle Palace.* Boston: Houghton Mifflin Co., 1982. 465 pages.

Brandt, Ed. *The Last Voyage of the USS Pueblo.* New York: W. W. Norton & Co., 1969. 248 pages.

Bucher, Commander Lloyd M. with Mark Rascovich. *Bucher: My Story.* Garden City, N.Y.: Doubleday & Co., 1970. 447 pages.

Crawford, Don. *Pueblo Intrigue.* Wheaton, Ill.: Tyndale House Publishers, 1969. 125 pages.

Gallery, Rear Admiral (Ret.) Daniel V. *The Pueblo Incident.* Garden City, N.Y.: Doubleday & Co., 1970. 174 pages.

Harris, Lieutenant Commander Stephen R., as told to James C. Hefley. *My Anchor Held.* Old Tappan, N.J.: Fleming H. Revell Co., 1970. 160 pages.

Johnson, President Lyndon B. *The Vantage Point.* New York: Holt, Rinehart and Winston, 1971. 636 pages.

Kahn, David. *The Codebreakers.* London: Widenfeld and Nicolson, 1967. 1164 pages.

Murphy, Former Lieutenant Edward R., Jr., with Curt Gentry. *Second in Command.* New York: Holt, Rinehart and Winston, 1971. 452 pages.

Shumacher, F. Carl, Jr., and George C. Wilson. *Bridge of No Return.* New York: Harcourt Brace Jovanovich, Inc., 1971. 242 pages.

INDEX